THE INTIMATE LIFE

OF

ALEXANDER HAMILTON

THE INTIMATE LIFE

OF

ALEXANDER HAMILTON

BASED CHIEFLY UPON ORIGINAL FAMILY LETTERS
AND OTHER DOCUMENTS, MANY OF WHICH
HAVE NEVER BEEN PUBLISHED

BY

ALLAN McLANE HAMILTON

WITH ILLUSTRATIONS AND FACSIMILES

FOREWORD BY WILLARD STERNE RANDALL

Racehorse Publishing

First published in 1910 by Charles Scribner's Sons

First Racehorse Publishing Edition 2016

All rights to any and all materials in copyright owned by the publisher are strictly reserved by the publisher.

Foreword © 2016 Willard Sterne Randall

Racehorse Publishing books may be purchased in bulk at special discounts for sales promotion, corporate gifts, fund-raising, or educational purposes. Special editions can also be created to specifications. For details, contact the Special Sales Department, Skyhorse Publishing, 307 West 36th Street, 11th Floor, New York, NY 10018 or info@skyhorsepublishing.com.

Racehorse Publishing™ is a pending trademark of Skyhorse Publishing, Inc.®, a Delaware corporation.

Visit our website at www.skyhorsepublishing.com.

10 9 8 7 6 5 4 3 2 1

Library of Congress Cataloging-in-Publication Data is available on file.

Print ISBN: 978-1-944686-39-0
Ebook ISBN: 978-1-944686-41-3

Printed in the United States of America

CONTENTS

ILLUSTRATIONS

FOREWORD

THE LEAD BALL that ended Alexander Hamilton's life very nearly obliterated his place in the American pantheon as the brilliant founder of the American financial system. But even before the July dawn in 1804 when he faced Aaron Burr in a duel, the flamboyant first US secretary of the treasury had forged and shattered crucial collaborations with nearly every other Founding Father.

Chief aide-de-camp and legal adviser to Revolutionary War commander in chief George Washington, architect of the Constitution with James Madison and his coauthor in the Federalist Papers, it was Hamilton and his Cabinet colleague, Thomas Jefferson, who had struck the compromise that selected Washington, DC, as the site of the nation's capital. After his bitter rivalry with Jefferson induced a reluctant President Washington to accept a second term, Hamilton sided with John Adams in the bitter political struggle with Jefferson and Madison that produced the two-party system, something not envisioned in the nation's foundation documents. Then, when Hamilton undercut Adams's chances for reelection to a second term, the Boston Brahmin branded him "the bastard brat of a Scots pedlar," a damning double curse in Puritan—and commercial—New England. But it was Hamilton's dinner table description of Vice President Burr, once his fellow law student and cofounder of Tammany Hall, as "untrustworthy" that triggered the fatal face-off on the narrow bluff at Weehawken.

As his nineteenth-century historian Henry Cabot Lodge phrased it, "Hamilton's great contemporary reputation suffered after his death an almost complete eclipse." The success of the expansionist course chosen by Jefferson and Madison, his chief opponents, in purchasing the vast Louisiana Territory and waging the War of 1812—coupled with the utter failure of Hamilton's party to resist them—that caused Hamilton's Federalist Party to sink and his fame along with it.

Even scholars ceased to study his contributions in the first half of the nineteenth century. Only his highly partisan son, John Church Hamilton, attempted to cobble his father's papers into a biography that not only failed to preserve Hamilton's reputation but introduced a plethora of errors into the historical record.

Lodge, recipient of the first PhD in history from Harvard University, argued in 1886 in the preface to the twelve-volume *Works of Alexander Hamilton* that the great ordeal by fire of the Civil War awakened Americans, especially Northerners. They began to "realize the greatness" of Hamilton's work and "the meaning and power of the nation" Hamilton had helped to build. Symbolizing if not encouraging this rebirth was Hamilton's appearance on the $2 bill as the first Greenbacks replaced scarce hard money in 1862. After the Civil War, schools, universities, and the newly minted graduate schools began to teach American history "as never before," exploring every "nook and corner of our history."

No one profited more, Lodge asserted, than Hamilton. The first edition of five hundred copies of Lodge's *Works* sold out quickly. By the time he published a second edition eighteen years later on the centenary of Hamilton's death, a host of novels had romanticized his life and death. Hamilton continued to "loom ever larger." By the turn of the twentieth century, "more and more events" had "justified Hamilton's conception" of American government, the "soundness of his finance silently accepted."

Yet Lodge's multi-tome compendium, while illustrating Hamilton's fluency, remained lifeless. Resulting gaps and errata prompted Hamilton's grandson, Allan McLane Hamilton, to blow the dust off bales of family papers and produce this volume, *The Intimate Life of Alexander Hamilton,* its pages embellished for the first time with photographs. And what photographs! The counting house in Saint Croix where teenage Hamilton learned how to keep ledgers, wash down slaves newly arrived from Africa for auctioning off, and give orders to ships' captains when he was only seventeen. The dueling pistols borrowed from the husband of Hamilton's lover, his sister-in-law Angelica, lie in their case near the portrait of Hamilton's own eldest son, killed in a duel while clenching one of the hair-triggered weapons.

The 1910 *Intimate Life* depended on hundreds of family letters and accounts, documenting Hamilton's prodigious labors and explaining not only his accomplishments but also his failures. But the book opens with a flaw that runs like a fault line all the way through it. As later research would reveal, it did not correct Lodge's earlier error: Alexander Hamilton was born on January 11, 1755, not 1757, a not-insignificant fact. So long admired for his supposed precocity, Hamilton often had suffered resentment for the same reason.

Hamilton was born in the British colony of Nevis, in the Caribbean. His mother, Rachel Fawcett, daughter of a Huguenot refugee, was married at sixteen to Johann Levine, a much older German Jewish merchant-planter. He thought she had money; her mother thought he did. As he ran through her dowry and went ever deeper into debt, Levine abused Rachel. After they had a child, Peter, Levine had Rachel imprisoned for refusing his connubial rights. She fled to her family on the nearby Danish island of Saint Croix. Three years later, Rachel began a common-law relationship with James Hamilton, impecunious fourth son of a wealthy Scottish laird. Under the English law of primogeniture and entail, only the firstborn son inherited. James was apprenticed to a Glasgow linen trading firm. He sailed for the Caribbean just as the linen market collapsed.

Drifting from island to island, the Hamiltons, as they signed themselves in Anglican church records, had two sons. Alexander, the elder, was nine when his parents learned that, after a twelve-year separation, Levine, intending to remarry, had divorced her on grounds of adultery and desertion. Under Danish law, he could divorce her; under English law, she could not divorce. Under Danish law, he could remarry; under Danish law, she could not. To spare Rachel a charge of bigamy, James Hamilton sailed away. From that day on, Alexander Hamilton was considered a bastard. He never saw his father again.

Opening a dry goods business in Saint Croix, Rachel put Alexander to work after days in a school run by a Jewish mistress; illegitimate, he was barred from the island's Lutheran schools. In school, he learned a little Hebrew; from Rachel he learned fluent French. When he was thirteen, Rachel died of yellow fever. Levine seized her estate, Alexander's meager inheritance going to Peter Levine, the half-brother Alexander never met. Left a penniless orphan, Alexander was apprenticed to clerk in a New York trading firm trading in Saint Croix. He learned so quickly that when his boss had to go home on sick leave, he put seventeen-year-old Alexander in charge. Alexander gave orders to ships' captains, mapped out their voyages, rejected shoddy goods, learned all about cargo, foreign exchange, and smuggling, gleaning knowledge he turned on its head when he became the first US collector of the port of New York after the Revolution and then, as secretary of the treasury, when he founded the Customs Service and the Coast Guard.

Rewarded with a scholarship to study in mainland British America, Hamilton attended Elizabethtown Academy in New Jersey before matriculating for accelerated study at King's College (now Columbia University) in New York. He read international law and the classics, writing the unsigned Revolutionary pamphlets by candlelight at night. The future secretary of the treasury, poor at math, flunked it and failed premed.

When the Revolution began, Hamilton stole twenty-one cannons from the battery at Fort George while under fire from the man-of-war *Asia,* forming the first artillery company of the US Army. Assigned to build a fort at Canal Street in today's Greenwich Village, Hamilton, twenty-one and a

Continental Army captain, watched the American rout at Brooklyn Heights through a spyglass, sending Washington the escape plan that saved his army. Hamilton himself barely escaped, rescued by Captain Aaron Burr. With only two cannons, Hamilton held off British attacks as Washington fled across New Jersey. Washington personally witnessed Hamilton's valor at Trenton and promoted him to lieutenant colonel and made him his aide-de-camp.

Given charge of prisoner-of-war exchanges and espionage, Hamilton funneled information from 220 operatives behind British lines. With Baron von Steuben, he retrained the army at Valley Forge, writing the infantry training manual of arms, which remained in use until 1814. He uncovered the Conway Cabal, a plot to displace Washington as commander in chief. Washington eventually rewarded him by giving him his own light infantry battalion. Hamilton personally led the last crucial charge of the Revolution at Yorktown.

Marrying into the land-rich Schuyler clan, Hamilton read law in Albany and was appointed federal tax collector for the state of New York. While studying law, he could find no proper manual of legal procedures, so he wrote the first handbook for the use of practicing lawyers ever written in America. Hamilton quickly rose to the top rank of New York lawyers (there were only thirty-five at the time). A delegate to the Continental Congress, Hamilton for the first time argued the principle of judicial review, maintaining that international treaties must be considered the law of the United States. Between 1784 and 1791, Hamilton defended sixty-four Loyalists prosecuted under New York law, making New York the first state to reestablish the civil rights of Loyalists. Hamilton emerged, in Congress and in court, as New York's preeminent marine lawyer, becoming the advocate of commercial interests.

Hamilton's career as a public official has long been well known. A delegate to the Constitutional Convention of 1787, in his only speech, he lectured the Founders for six hours on the need for a strong national government under a president kept in check only by powers divided under three branches, executive, legislative, and judicial. Except for presidential tenure, his plan closely resembled the final Constitution. To influence ratification in New York, he wrote fifty-six of the eighty-five Federalist Papers, then led the fight for ratification in the New York Assembly.

On September 11, 1789, President Washington appointed Hamilton the first secretary of the treasury, giving him 120 days to come up with a plan to eliminate the staggering Revolutionary War debts. In a series of four "Reports" to Congress, Hamilton proposed creating a national debt that would assume all war debts and pay them at par. To facilitate this, he urged establishing a national bank, the first American corporation, a mint to mill a decimal currency, and a sinking fund to retire the debts with revenues from customs duties and the sale of government bonds. Attracting foreign investors, Hamilton's "blessing" immediately succeeded.

Yet Hamilton came into conflict with Secretary of State Jefferson and with Madison, author of the Bill of Rights. Hamilton never understood Jefferson's enmity, which stemmed from the Virginian's belief that Hamilton was scheming to erect an American version of the British system. Their rift created two political parties, an eventuality not foreseen in the Constitution. The result was that Hamilton emerged as the leader of the Federalist Party, forerunner of today's Republican Party, and Jefferson as leader of the

Democratic-Republicans, which became the Democratic Party.

Father of seven, Hamilton, constantly in debt, officially retired from public life in 1795 to work long hours as one of New York's two leading lawyers; Aaron Burr, the other, became his rival for control of New York state politics. Hamilton emerged on the national stage once more during the quasi-war with France when Washington would only agree to resume his duties as commander in chief if Hamilton were his second-in-command. Hamilton assumed the rank of major general and acted as inspector general of the Army, building up America's defenses.

Hamilton was forty-nine in July 1804 when he died in a duel with Burr over an insult. He is buried in Trinity churchyard, a few blocks south of the World Trade Center, so much a symbol of the financial new order that he, more than any other Founding Father, created.

His fame has continued to grow, in part because of a controversy over the proposed removal of his image from the $10 bill. The phenomenal success of the Broadway musical *Hamilton* not only averted that alteration to the nation's symbolism but has rekindled interest in the actual lives and roles of the highly competitive Founders.

—Willard Sterne Randall

PREFACE

THE purpose of the writer is to utilize a large number of original letters and documents, written by Alexander Hamilton and various members of his family as well as his contemporaries, and which in some measure throw light upon his private life and career as a soldier, lawyer, and statesman. Most of these have never been published, and were left to me by my father, the late Philip Hamilton, who was his youngest son. I have no more ambitious purpose than to produce a simple narrative, for there are several important works that fully and formally describe his public services. The latest of these is Oliver's excellent book, which is a noble monument to the memory of Hamilton. If I have gone into detail very minutely it is because of the belief that the familiar side of his life will be of interest to a great many people who have hitherto been furnished only with unauthentic generalities.

A few of the letters already published by the late John C. Hamilton and Senator Lodge, or which appear in the Life of James McHenry, have been used, and some of these are little known.

It is a pleasure to express my obligation to Delos McCurdy, Esq., and H. D. Estabrook, Esq., of the New York Bar; to Worthington C. Ford, Esq., Librarian of the

Massachusetts Historical Society; Wilberforce Eames, Esq., Librarian of the Lenox Library; Edward T. Holden, Esq., Librarian of the United States Military Academy; William H. Winters, Librarian of the New York Law Institute; to Richard Church, Esq., of Rochester, New York, and R. K. Bixby, Esq., of St. Louis, Missouri, as well as others, for kindly and valuable help.

ALLAN McLANE HAMILTON.

NEW YORK, *June* 1, 1910.

THE INTIMATE LIFE
OF
ALEXANDER HAMILTON

THE INTIMATE LIFE OF
ALEXANDER HAMILTON

CHAPTER I

ORIGIN AND PARENTAGE

ALEXANDER HAMILTON came into the world on January 11, 1757, his birthplace being Nevis, a mountainous island of the picturesque Antilles, 18° and 18' longitude and 62° 37' latitude. Nevis has an area of about sixty square miles, and was colonized by the British in 1728. It is quite near St. Christopher, or "St. Kitts," and both islands were in 1757, and are to-day, under the same local government. Within a comparatively short distance is St. Croix, which became a Danish possession early in the eighteenth century.[1] These three islands are the centre of the greatest interest so far as the early history of Hamilton is concerned.

Much unnecessary speculation has arisen regarding Hamilton's antecedents, but why there should have been so much mystery is a matter of wonder, considering that many of his own letters, referring to his family, have for a long time been in existence and are easy of access, so that there is little doubt as to his paternity or early history.

Gouverneur Morris, Bancroft, Lodge, and others, have from time to time hinted at vague stories regarding his

[1] 1733.

illegitimacy, and he has been described as the son of various persons, among them a Danish governor of one of the islands; and as a half-brother of his friend and playmate, Edward Stevens, whom he is said to have closely resembled, and who was afterward sent to the United States, to be educated by the Rev. Mr. Knox, with Hamilton. This early friendship was continued through life, although there does not appear to be anything in their subsequent intercourse to show that they were more than friends. Timothy Pickering left among his memoirs a statement which has been resurrected by Cabot Lodge, and, although alluded to by him as "mere gossip," was brought forward and published in his volume of the "Statesmen's Series." In this Mr. Pickering relates an interview which he had with a Mr. James Yard in Philadelphia, who was a brother-in-law of Mr. Stevens, both of them having married the daughters of a Danish governor of the West Indies named Walterstorff. Yard told Pickering that Hamilton was the son of a Scotch gentleman named Hamilton; that Hamilton and Stevens went to school together; that after the death of Hamilton, an aunt came to New York and spent some time in Hamilton's house, from which fact Yard concluded that Mrs. Hamilton must have received full information as to her husband's parentage, there being a vague inference that Hamilton and Stevens had the same father.

From documents in my possession, it does not appear that this lady, who was Mrs. Ann Mitchell, ever visited Mrs. Hamilton during Hamilton's lifetime, although she came to America before his death. She lived at Burlington, New Jersey, and was befriended by Elisha Boudinot, a brother of Elias, and, after the death of Alexander Hamilton, by Mrs. Hamilton, who provided for her. Although Hamilton seems to have been very fond of her—for he referred to her even in his last letter to his wife as his best friend—it is not at all certain that she was his aunt; in fact, in his expense account-book the following entry appears: "July 11, 1796: Donation to my Cozen[1] Mrs. Mitchell; draft upon me $100."

Lodge's speculations regarding the early history of Hamilton first appeared in 1882, and were based in part on the unsatisfactory and inexact statements made by his son, John C. Hamilton, who in his works made the mistake of not publishing the letters of his father in their entirety, for what reason it does not appear. It has been clearly shown that Hamilton's father lived until June 3, 1799, and his mother only until February 16, 1768, when the son was but eleven years old and she thirty-two.

These matters are settled by the church records of the island of St. Vincent, where the father lived for many years until his death,[2] and by those of St. Kitts, where the mother was buried, under the name of Rachel Levine, so that the confused story referred to by Pickering was not only wrong in regard to the statement that Hamilton's mother lived to a good old age, but probably erroneous as to his other information. That Hamilton knew of his origin is well attested by various letters that have been preserved, some of which are here reproduced. His father and younger brother, James, frequently wrote to him, or sent drafts which were honored; and in the expense book above referred to, in the years 1796–7, 8, and 9, this sum amounted to several thousand dollars, which was a great deal for him to pay, considering the crippled condition of his finances, and the

---

[1] Obsolete way of spelling cousin.

[2] Doctor Edward Stevens wrote to Alexander Hamilton August 12, 1803, saying that he had been to St. Croix and had asked Governor Walterstorff regarding the existence of a will left by Hamilton's father. This he traced to Doctor Knox, one of the executors, but it could not be found among the papers of the latter.

many other demands upon his slender purse. There is absolutely no proof, as has been stated, that his father was married twice, or that James was a half-brother.

That he was aware of the existence of his half-brother, Peter Levine, is shown by a letter to General Nathaniel Greene; in 1782 he also wrote to his wife as follows:

Alexander Hamilton to Elizebeth Hamilton[1]

Engrossed by our own immediate concerns, I omitted telling you of a disagreeable piece of intelligence I have received from a gentleman of Georgia. He tells me of the death of my brother Levine. You know the circumstances that abate my distress, yet my heart acknowledges the rights of a brother. He dies rich, but has disposed of the bulk of his fortune to strangers. I am told he has left me a legacy. I did not inquire how much. When you have occasion for money you can draw upon Messrs. Stewart & [illegible], Philadelphia. They owe me upwards of an hundred pounds.

That he really was the son of James Hamilton, and was aware of the fact, is also shown by letters written to his bethrothed as early as 1780, and later by those to others, among them Robert Troup.

Alexander Hamilton to Robert Troup, July 25, 1795

I hesitated whether I would not also secure a preference to the Drafts of my father, but these, as far as I am concerned, being a voluntary engagement, I doubted the justice of the measure, and I have done nothing. I repeat it lest they should return upon him and increase his distress. Though as I am informed, a man of respectable connections in Scotland, he became, as a merchant, bankrupt at an early

[1] Probably 1782.

THE HOUSE WHERE HAMILTON BEGAN HIS CAREER, WEST END, ST. CROIX

day in the West Indies and is now in indigence. I have pressed him to come to us, but his age and infirmity have deterred him from the change of climate.

James Hamilton to his son Alexander Hamilton[1]

ST. VINCENT, June 12, 1793.

DEAR ALEXANDER: I wrote you a letter, inclosed in one to Mr. Donald, of Virginia, since which I have had no further accounts from you. My bad state of health has prevented my going to sea at this time—being afflicted with a complication of disorders.

The war which has lately broken out between France and England makes it very dangerous going to sea at this time. However, we daily expect news of a peace, and when that takes place, provided it is not too late in the season, I will embark in the first vessel that sails for Philadelphia.

I have now settled all my business in this part of the world, with the assistance of my good friend, Mr. Donald, who has been of every service to me that lay in his power, in contributing to make my life easy at this advanced period of life. The bearer of this, Captain Sheriff, of the brig *Dispatch*, sails direct for Philadelphia, and has promised to deliver you this letter with his own hands; and as he returns to this island from Philadelphia, I beg you will drop me a few lines, letting me know how you and your family keep your health, as I am uneasy at not having heard from you for some time past. I beg my respectful compliments to Mrs. Hamilton and your children, and wishing you health and happiness, I remain, with esteem, dear Alexander,

Your very affectionate father,

JAMES HAMILTON.

---

[1] The Works of Alexander Hamilton, comprising his correspondence and his political and official writings, etc., edited by John C. Hamilton. Vol. V, p. 567. New York: John F. Trow, 1850.

Alexander Hamilton to his brother James Hamilton, Jr.[1]

NEW YORK, *June 23,* 1783.

MY DEAR BROTHER: I have received your letter of the 31st of May last, which, and one other, are the only letters I have received from you in many years. I am a little surprised you did not receive one which I wrote to you about six months ago. The situation you describe yourself to be in gives me much pain, and nothing will make me happier than, as far as may be in my power, to contribute to your relief.

I will cheerfully pay your draft upon me for fifty pounds sterling, whenever it shall appear. I wish it was in my power to desire you to enlarge the sum; but though my future prospects are of the most flattering kind, my present engagements would render it inconvenient for me to advance you a larger sum.

My affection for you, however, will not permit me to be inattentive to your welfare, and I hope time will prove to you that I feel all the sentiments of a brother. Let me only request of you to exert your industry for a year or two more where you are, and at the end of that time I promise myself to be able to invite you to a more comfortable settlement in this country. Allow me only to give you one caution, which is, to avoid if possible, getting into debt. Are you married or single? If the latter, it is my wish, for many reasons, that you may continue in that state.

But what has become of our dear father? It is an age since I have heard from him, or of him though I have written him several letters. Perhaps, alas! he is no more, and I shall not have the pleasing opportunity of contributing to render the close of his life more happy than the progress of it. My heart bleeds at the recollection of his misfort-

---

[1] "Reminiscences of James A. Hamilton or Men and Events at Home and Abroad During Three-Quarters of a Century," p. 2. New York: Charles Scribner & Co., 1869. (This letter is also published in its entirety in "A Few of Hamilton's Letters," by Gertrude Atherton. New York: 1903, p. 136.)

unes and embarrassments. Sometimes I flatter myself his brothers have extended their support to him, and that now he is enjoying tranquillity and ease; at other times I fear he is suffering in indigence. I entreat you, if you can, to relieve me from my doubts, and let me know how or where he is, if alive; if dead, how and where he died. Should he be alive inform him of my inquiries, beg him to write to me, and tell him how ready I shall be to devote myself and all I have to his accommodation and happiness.

I do not advise your coming to this country at present, for the war has also put things out of order here, and people in your business find a subsistence difficult enough. My object will be, by and by, to get you settled on a farm.

Believe me, always your affectionate friend and brother,
ALEX. HAMILTON.

Alexander Hamilton to Elizabeth Schuyler
(written prior to 1780)

I wrote you, my dear, in one of my letters that I had written to our father, but had not heard of him since, that the operations in the islands hitherto cannot affect him, that I had pressed him to come to America after the peace. A gentleman going to the island where he is, will in a few days afford me a safe opportunity to write again. I shall again present him with his black-eyed daughter, and tell him how much her attention deserves his affection and will make the blessing of his gray hairs. . . .

The general ignorance that exists regarding Hamilton's origin and intimate life has prompted me to publish fully all I know about him, and in doing this I must express my indebtedness to Gertrude Atherton, who has made a conscientious hunt for material, with remarkable success. The conclusions are that Alexander Hamilton was the son of James Hamilton, who was the fourth son of Alexander

Hamilton, Laird of the Grange, in the Parish of Stevenston, Ayrshire, Scotland, and his wife, Elizabeth (eldest daughter of Sir Robert Pollock), who were married in the year 1730.[1] The Hamiltons of Grange belonged to the Cambuskeith branch of the house of Hamilton, and the founder of this branch, in the fourteenth century, was Walter de Hamilton, who was the common ancestor of the Dukes of Hamilton, the Dukes of Abercorn, Earls of Haddington, Viscounts Boyne, Barons Belhaven, several extinct peerages, and of all the Scotch and Irish Hamilton families. He was fifth in descent from Robert, Earl of Mellent, created by Henry I of France and His Queen, who was a daughter of Jeroslaus, Czar of Russia.[2]

His mother, Rachel Fawcett,[3] was born in the island of Nevis, and when a girl of barely sixteen was forced into marriage with a rich Danish Jew, one John Michael Levine (or Lawein), who treated her cruelly. The marriage was evidently one of very great unhappiness from the beginning, so that she was forced to leave him and return to her mother's roof.

This was in 1755 or 1756. Her mother, from all accounts, although a woman of great loveliness and charm, was ambitious and masterful, and had very decided ideas of her own regarding her daughter's future.[4] She herself had had matrimonial troubles, and had separated from her husband

---

[1] Appendix A.

[2] "Historical and Genealogical Memoirs of the House of Hamilton, with Genealogical Memoirs of the Several Branches of the Family," by John Anderson, Surgeon, Licentiate of the Royal College of Surgeons, Edinburgh. Edinburgh, 1825. Simpkins & Marshall, London.

[3] Daughter of Dr. John Fawcett, a Huguenot exiled after the Revocation of the Edict of Nantes, and Mary, his wife.

[4] In 1768 a Mr. Hallwood, of St. Croix, a cousin of Alexander Hamilton, left him one-fourth of his estate. He was a grandson of James Lytton, who was probably a brother of Hamilton's maternal grandmother. See letter in Lodge's "Works of Alexander Hamilton," Constitutional Edition, vol. IX, p. 415.

late in life, after having had several children, but the mother
of Hamilton came a long time after the others, and was
brought up in unrestful surroundings, later witnessing the
family quarrels. Doubtless the influence of much of this,
coupled with the persuasion of her mother, led to the alliance
with a man much older than herself, who finally made life
insupportable. She appears to have been a brilliant and
clever girl, who had been given every educational advantage
and accomplishment, and had profited by her opportunities.
By Levine she had had one son, who was taken from her by
his father, and for a time lived with him, first at St. Croix,
and afterward in Denmark, and it was not until several years
afterward that she met James Hamilton, an attractive
Scotchman, of much charm of manner, in the West Indies,
with whom she quickly fell in love. Although, as has been
said, her mother had parted from her own husband, it was
impossible, owing to the disorderly condition of legal affairs
in the provinces, for the daughter to formally get her freedom
from the person who had so ruined her life, and although
every attempt was apparently made, both by Hamilton
and herself, they seemed unable to obtain any relief from
the local courts, and lived together until her death, which
occurred February 25, 1768, when she was thirty-two years
old. It is quite true that the courts of St. Croix were available, but this was a Danish island, and Levine was a Dane,
and a man of great local influence, which was used against
them, so that their efforts were thwarted.

The social life of England and the colonies during the
eighteenth century was, to say the least, unsettled, and this
is especially true so far as the morals of the better class were
concerned. According to Lodge, "divorce was extremely
rare in any of the colonies, and even in England, and in the
crown provinces it involved long, difficult, and expensive

proceedings of the greatest publicity."[1]   In fact, if we may be
guided by the existing reports, annulment was resorted to
much more often than divorce, and it is impossible to find
any account of the existence of divorce laws on the islands
of St. Kitts or Nevis; according to well-informed persons,
there was even no act providing for separate maintenance.

Marriage rites were informal and elopements common,
both in Great Britain and her dependencies; in fact, it was
not until the passage of Lord Hardwick's marriage bill, and
the energetic labors of Wilberforce, that the solemn nature of
the marriage rite was established.   Even then Hardwick's
bill was opposed by Henry Fox, who had married a daughter
of the Duke of Richmond, and with the subsequent ascendancy of the gay Walpoles and Pelhams there was more
tolerance with irregular marriages than ever.

Lecky[2] and, later, Sir George Russell,[3] referred to the
casual nature of the marriage customs, and the easy manner
in which unions were made and broken, and at this time the
pilgrimages to Gretna Green of those who were impatient of
the law's delays or the objections of discriminating parents,
were frequent.

In referring to the easily solemnized marriages which did
not endure, Swift said: "The art of making nets is very different from the art of making cages," and very little, if any,
odium was attached to those who took matters into their own

---

[1] Harold Hargrove, Esq., a member of the English bar, informs me that prior to
1857 the divorce proceedings known as *a vinculo matrimonii* (equivalent to our
modern nullity of marriage decree), which enabled the parties to marry again, could
only be obtained for some canonical disability, existing at the time of the marriage,
such as that the parties were within the prohibited degrees of consanguinity, or
one of them was not consenting, or not of sound mind, or unable to perform the
duties of matrimony, etc.   *It was not granted for adultery or cruelty* in any court of
law, and the only way to obtain it was by a private act of Parliament.   Divorce
a mensa et thoro (equivalent to our modern separation) could be obtained for
adultery or cruelty prior to 1857, but neither of the parties could marry again.

[2] "England in the Eighteenth Century," vol. I, p. 531.

[3] "Collections and Recollections," p. 87.

hands. In this country elopement was so common as to be a popular proceeding among the higher classes, and many of our forefathers chose this romantic and unconventional, but in those times perfectly innocent manner of mating. Four of General Philip Schuyler's daughters "arranged and took charge of their own marriages,[1] that of his daughter who married Hamilton being an exception. Her beautiful sister, Angelica Church, ran off with an Englishman who came to the colonies, it is said, after a duel, and who changed his name to Carter, but subsequently resumed his own cognomen of John Barker Church, and was afterward the Commissary for Rochambeau.

Many other young women did the same thing, among them a daughter of Henry Cruger, who eloped with Peter van Schaak, and "Peggy" White, who ran away with Peter Jay. Other young women of romantic inclinations were Susannah Reid and Harriet Van Rensselaer.

Hamilton's father and mother had much in extenuation of the bold step they took, and their subsequent mode of life does not appear to have been followed by any loss of caste; possibly because of the local sympathy, and the knowledge of the true facts of their unconventional relationship; and again, because there was no doubt of the sincerity and depth of their love for each other. From perfectly reliable sources it appears, and may be believed, that his mother's first husband was a coarse man of repulsive personality, many years older than herself. After Rachel left her mother's house and went to James Hamilton, Alexander Hamilton was born a year later. Levine then divorced her. In the records of the Ember Court of St. Croix it appears that "John Michael Levine (Lawein) was granted a divorce for

[1] "Catherine Schuyler," by Mary Gay Humphreys, p. 189. New York, 1891. Scribner.

abandonment, and Levine was permitted to marry again ; but she, being the defendant, was not."

It is said that Levine was not above depriving his wife's children by her union with Hamilton of the inheritance from their mother. At her death in 1768 she possessed several slaves which she left to her sons, Alexander and James Hamilton. John Michael Levine subsequently made application for these in "behalf of her lawfully begotten heir, Peter Levine."[1] It is here distinctly stated that the grounds for divorce were that she had "absented herself." Mrs. Atherton who, in her collection of letters, refers to these facts, has made painstaking and careful examination of the records of the courts, not only in the West Indies but in Copenhagen, and states positively that there was no evidence that she deserted her husband to live with Hamilton, but was living with her mother in St. Kitts in 1756, when the latter appeared upon the scene. In a letter written by Alexander Hamilton the fact of his mother's unhappy marriage, which was brought about by her mother, is mentioned, and there seems to be no reason to doubt its truth. Whether Levine's failure to apply for a divorce on more serious grounds was due to a belief in his wife's innocence, or to the realization that he had driven her, by his cruelty, to the arms of another man whom she truly loved, or whether the local court refused to take a severe view of her action because of its own knowledge of Levine, and the marriage itself, is a matter of speculation. Possibly he may have felt some of the magnanimity which, in more recent years, actuated Ruskin and Wagner. Certainly the best proof that no prejudice existed in after life in regard to Hamilton because of his birth are the facts, not only that General Washington invited him to become a member of his military

[1] The half-brother previously referred to.

family, but that General Schuyler heartily approved of the marriage with his daughter.

Hamilton's father does not appear to have been successful in any pursuit, but in many ways was a great deal of a dreamer, and something of a student, whose chief happiness seemed to be in the society of his beautiful and talented wife, who was in every way intellectually his superior. After her death he apparently lost all incentive he had before to continue any mercantile occupation, and left the island, going to St. Vincent, where he lived until a time shortly before his son's death.

It is not evident that Hamilton knew much of his Scotch relatives until after the War of the Revolution, although in a letter to his brother in 1783 he casually alludes to his uncles. In 1797 he wrote a long letter to Alexander Hamilton, the Laird of the Grange at the time, which tells very simply the story of his career in America and may be here used in an introductory way to what is to follow.

Alexander Hamilton from Alexander Hamilton.[1]

ALBANY, STATE OF NEW YORK, *May the 2d,* 1797.

MY DEAR SIR: Some days since I received with great pleasure your letter of the 10th of March. The mark it affords of your kind attention, and the particular account it gives me of so many relations in Scotland, are extremely gratifying to me. You no doubt have understood that my father's affairs at a very early day went to wreck; so as to have rendered his situation during the greatest part of his life far from eligible. This state of things occasioned a separation between him and me, when I was very young, and threw me upon the bounty of my mother's relatives, some of whom were then wealthy, though by vicissitudes to which human affairs are so liable, they have been since much re-

---

[1] "Hamilton's Works" (J. C. H.), vol. VI, p. 243.

duced and broken up.   Myself at about sixteen came to this
country.   Having always had a strong propensity to literary
pursuits, by a course of steady and laborious exertion I was
able, by the age of nineteen, to qualify myself for the degree
of Bachelor of Arts in the College of New-York, and to lay
the foundation for preparatory study for the future profession of the law.

The American Revolution supervened.   My principles
led me to take part in it;   at nineteen I entered into the
American army as Captain of Artillery.   Shortly after I
became, by invitation, aid-de-camp to General Washington,
in which station I served till the commencement of that campaign which ended with the siege of York in Virginia, and the
capture of Cornwallis's army.   The campaign I made at the
head of a corps of light infantry, with which I was present
at the siege of York, and engaged in some interesting operations.

At the period of the peace of Great Britain, I found myself
a member of Congress by appointment of the Legislature of
this State.

After the peace, I settled in the city of New-York, in the
practice of the law;   and was in a very lucrative course of
practice, when the derangement of our public affairs, by the
feebleness of the general confederation, drew me again reluctantly into public life.   I became a member of the Convention which framed the present Constitution of the United
States;   and having taken part in this measure, I conceived
myself to be under an obligation to lend my aid towards
putting the machine in some regular motion.   Hence I did
not hesitate to accept the offer of President Washington to
undertake the office of Secretary of the Treasury.

In that office I met with many intrinsic difficulties, and
many artificial ones proceding from passions, not very
worthy, common to human nature, and which act with peculiar force in republics.   The object, however, was effected
of establishing public credit, and introducing order in the
finances.

Public office in this country has few attractions.   The

pecuniary emolument is so inconsiderable, as to amount to a sacrifice to any man who can employ his time to advantage in any liberal profession. The opportunity of doing good, from the jealousy of power and the spirit of faction, is too small in any station, to warrant a long continuance of private sacrifices. The enterprises of party had so far succeeded, as materially to weaken the necessary influence and energy of the Executive authority, and so far diminish the power of doing good in that department, as greatly to take away the motives which a virtuous man might have for making sacrifices. The prospect was even bad for gratifying in future the love of fame, if that passion was to be the spring of action.

The union of these motives, with the reflections of prudence in relation to a growing family, determined me as soon as my plan had reached a certain maturity, to withdraw from office. This I did by a resignation about two years since, when I resumed the profession of the law in the city of New York under every advantage I could desire.

It is a pleasant reflection to me, that since the commencement of my connection with General Washington to the present time, I have possessed a flattering share of his confidence and friendship.

Having given you a brief sketch of my political career, I proceed to some further family details.

In the year 1780 I married the second daughter of General Schuyler, a gentleman of one of the best families of this country, of large fortune, and no less personal and political consequence. It is impossible to be happier than I am in a wife; and I have five children, four sons and a daughter, the eldest a son somewhat past fifteen, who all promise as well as their years permit, and yield me much satisfaction. Though I have been too much in public life to be wealthy, my situation is extremely comfortable, and leaves me nothing to wish but a continuance of health. With this blessing, the profits of my profession and other prospects authorize an expectation of such addition to my resources as will render the eve of life easy and agreeable, so far as may depend on this consideration.

It is now several months since I have heard from my father, who continued at the island of St. Vincent. My anxiety at this silence would be greater than it is, were it not for the considerable interruption and precariousness of intercourse which is produced by the war.

I have strongly pressed the old gentleman to come and reside with me, which would afford him every enjoyment of which his advanced age is capable; but he has declined it on the ground that the advice of his physicians leads him to fear that the change of climate would be fatal to him. The next thing for me is, in proportion to my means, to endeavor to increase his comforts where he is.

It will give me the greatest pleasure to receive your son Robert at my house in New York, and still more to be of use to him; to which end, my recommendation and interest will not be wanting, and I hope not unavailing. It is my intention to embrace the opening which your letter affords me to extend my intercourse with my relations in your country, which will be a new source of satisfaction to me.

From that time on he and his Ayrshire relatives not only kept up a correspondence but he was able to do much in this country for his young cousins, one of whom entered the American Navy. He, however, never had the chance to visit the home of his ancestors, though he came very near so doing. On this occasion, when he was urged to go abroad as a Commissioner to obtain a loan from France, he resigned in favor of his devoted friend John Laurens, who was anxious to go to England to seek the release of his father, who was then imprisoned in the Tower of London.[1] To a friend Hamilton wrote in 1794:

[1] Henry Laurens sailed for Holland in 1780 as a Commissioner to effect a commercial treaty between the United States and that country, in the *Mercury*, but was captured by the English frigate *Vesta*. Although he attempted to destroy his papers they were recovered, and he was taken to London and imprisoned in the Tower, charged with high treason, but was subsequently liberated through the influence of Lord Shelburne. His papers contained several which indicated the friendliness

My own hope of making a short excursion to Europe the ensuing Spring increases. Believe me I am heartily tired of my situation, and wait only the opportunity of quitting it with honor, and without decisive prejudice to public affairs. This winter, I trust, will wind up my plans so as to secure my reputation.

The present appearance is that the depending elections will prove favorable to the good cause, and obviate anxiety for its future. In this event my present determination is to resign my political family and set seriously about the care of my private family. Previous to this I will visit Europe. There I shall have the happiness of meeting you once more. But will not a few minutes afterwards give me a pang of final separation ? [1]

This plan like the other came to naught, and it does not appear that he ever after made even another attempt to cross the Atlantic, for his health became undermined by hard work and malarial infection incurred in military service. In a letter to Washington in November, 1795, he speaks of this, and a year later to the same person he wrote: "I seem now to have regularly a period of ill health every summer." In 1793 he was seriously ill, having been stricken with yellow fever, and his condition thoroughly alarmed his friends, among them Mrs. Washington, who showed the deepest solicitude, and in many ways attested her friendly interest in one who had been a member of the military family.

Martha Washington to Elizabeth Hamilton

I am truly glad my Dear Madam to hear Colo. Hamilton is better to day. You have my prayers and warmest wishes for his recovery. I hope you take care of yourself as you know

of the Dutch Government with the United States, and because of these and the later refusal of Holland to repudiate the acts of its agent in America, war was declared by Great Britain against the Dutch Republic.

[1] *"History of the Republic,"* by John C. Hamilton.

it is necessary for your family.—We were luckey to have these bottles of the old wine that was carried to the East Indies which is sent with three of another kind which is very good, and we have a plenty to supply you as often as you please to send for it of the latter.

The President joins me in devoutly wishing Colo. Hamilton's recovery—we expect to leave this to morrow—and beg you will send to Mrs. Emerson for anything that we have that you may want.

I am my dear madam your

Very affectionate Friend

M. WASHINGTON.

His sister-in-law also wrote from England:

Angelica Church to Elizabeth Hamilton

LONDON, *January 25th,* 1794.

When my Dear Eliza, when am I to receive a letter from you? When am I to hear that you are in perfect health, and that you are no longer in fear for the life of your dear Hamilton?

For my part, now that the fever is gone, I am all alive to the apprehensions of the war. One sorrow succeeds another. It has been whispered to me that my friend Alexander means to quit his employment of Secretary. The country will lose one of her best friends, and you, my Dear Eliza, will be the only person to whom this change can be either necessary or agreeable. I am inclined to believe that it is your influence induces him to withdraw from public life. That so good a wife, so tender a mother, should be so bad a patriot is wonderful.[1]

The ruined castle of the Cambuskeith Hamiltons was known as Kerilaw Castle, and in 1836 when visited by James A. Hamilton,[2] the second son of Alexander Hamilton,

---

[1] Hamilton resigned as Secretary of the Treasury in 1795.
[2] Hamilton, " Reminiscences," etc., p. 302.

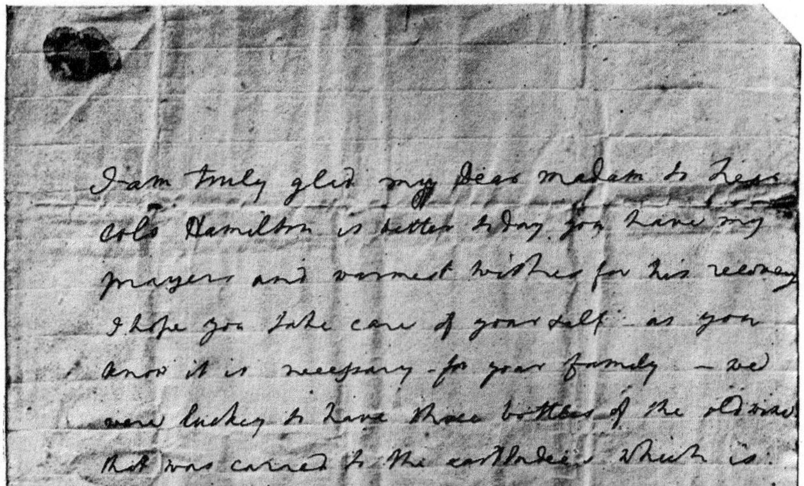

FACSIMILE LETTER OF MARTHA WASHINGTON

was near a comfortable modern home, then occupied by the last Laird of the Grange, who died a year later, and who sat in the sunshine feeding his pigeons, and entertained his visitor with quaint stories in the manner of Stevenson or Crockett, while in the evening he and his family very formally brewed their toddy, and ate oatmeal biscuit, while the "simple and agreeable tipple occupied the party for an hour or so in lively chat."[1]

Hamilton's early life has been so often referred to by historians that there is little to add, except that from the first he displayed all the precocity which led to his subsequent early advancement, and this was undoubtedly stimulated by his helpless condition, and the necessity for doing something. As is known, when but fourteen he conducted the affairs of Nicholas Cruger in his absence, writing important business letters which, in themselves, showed a mature knowledge and ripeness of judgment.

Alexander Hamilton to Henry Cruger

St. Croix, *February 24th*, 1772.

Henry Cruger, Esq.

Sir: The 9th ultimo Capt. Robert Gibb handed me your favour dated December 19th, 1771, covering Invoice and Bill of Lading for sundreys—which are landed in good order agreeable thereto. I sold all your lumber off Immediately at £16 luckily enough, the price of that article being now reduced to £12, as great quantitys have been lately imported from different parts of this Continent.—Indeed, there must be a vast Consumption this Crop—which makes it probable that the price will again rise—unless the Crops at windward should fall short—as is said to be the case,—whereby we shall fair to be Overstocked—the Oats and Cheese I have also sold, the former at 6 sh. per Bushell, and the latter at 9 sh. pr. Your mahogany is of the very worst kind or I could

[1] Appendix B.

readily have obtained 6 sh. pr foot for it, but at present tis blown upon, tis fit only for end work.

I enclose you a price Current & refer you thereto for other matters.

Capt. Gibbs was ready to sail seven days after his arrival but was detained two days longer by strong Contrary winds which made it impossible to get out of the Harbour.

Believe me Sir Nothing was neglected on my part to give him the utmost Dispatch, & considering that his Cargo was stowed very Hicheldy-picheldy—the proceeding part of it rather uppermost. I think he was dispatched as soon as could be expected.—Inclosed you have Invoice of Rum and Sugar shipt in the sloop agreeable to your Orders. I could not by any means get your Casks filled by any of the planters but shall dispose of the HHDS out of which the Rum was started for your account, from which however will proceed a small loss—Also have account of sloops Port Charges, of which I hope and Doubt not youll find right.—

Youll be a little surprised when I tell you Capt. Gibbs was obliged to leave his freight money behind; the reason is this; Mr. B—— would by no means raise his part—tis true he might have been compelled by Law, but that would have been altogether imprudent—for to have inforced pay- ment & to have converted that payment into Joes[1]—which were extremely scarce—would have been attended with de- tention of at least ten or twelve days, and the other freights were very triffling so that the whole now rests with me, and God knows when I shall be able to receive Mr. B—— part. who is long winded enough. Mr. B begs to present his re- spects, which concludes Sir.

Your very Humble St.

for N—C
A—H

When fifteen years old, having shown his cleverness in many ways, he was sent to the United States, and landed in Boston; subsequently reaching New York, where he met

---

[1] The joe was a Portuguese gold coin of the period.

Elias Boudinot, who helped him in the matter of obtaining his education.

At an early age Hamilton developed a facility in expression that widened with succeeding years, and he accumulated a remarkably extended vocabulary which is apparent in everything that he wrote and said, and if the power of thought is measured, as is generally admitted, by the extent and accumulation of symbols and ideas, he certainly possessed a rich store of both. This seems strange, for it does not appear that he had access to many books, or received more than the childish education at the knee of his mother to the time of her death, when he was but eleven years old, although it has been stated that in his earliest infancy he was able to read the Hebrew Decalogue.[1] It is certain that he understood French as well as English, and his early literary productions, among them the famous account of the tornado, show much precocity and fertility of composition. He certainly was able, not only to express himself well, but to make a selection of terse terms and vigorous English.

When Hamilton reached America in 1772 he brought letters which he delivered to the Rev. Hugh Knox and to William Livingston, afterward governor of New Jersey, and stayed with the latter at his house, which was known as "Liberty Hall," while he attended the school of which Dr. Barber was the head master, at Elizabethtown. In the

[1] This is evidently a misstatement upon the part of an enthusiastic biographer. In none of his writings is there anything to indicate his familiarity with Hebrew. It does appear, however, that he studied Semitic history, and in a fugitive scrap of writing, which is evidently a part of an essay, says: ". . . progress of the Jews and their [illegible] from the earliest history to the present time has been and is entirely out of the ordinary course of human affairs. Is it not then, a fair conclusion that the cause also is an extraordinary one—in other words, that it is the effect of some great providential plan? The man who will draw this conclusion will look for the solution in the Bible—He who will not draw it ought to give in another fair solution."

winter of 1773-4 he was ready for college and would have
entered Princeton, but he went to President Witherspoon
with a proposition that he should be allowed to pass from
one class to another when so qualified, instead of following
the usual routine of the university. This proposal was not
acceded to, so he turned his steps to King's College in New
York, which was then situated between the streets that are
now Church, Greenwich, Barclay, and Murray. The
president was the Rev. Dr. Myles Cooper, a stanch loyal
Englishman, who had succeeded Samuel Johnson, the first
president of the college, and with him were associated Dr.
Samuel Clossey, who taught medicine, and Dr. Peter Middleton. Dr. Clossey was a clever Irish surgeon and a
graduate of Trinity College, Dublin, and came to America
in 1764, when he was forty-nine years old. He left an
active medical practice to emigrate, and a year after his
arrival was appointed to King's College as Professor of
Natural Philosophy, but subsequently was selected for the
Chair of Anatomy, which he filled until 1774. He was a
loyalist and did not at all sympathize with the colonists, so
finding the atmosphere of New York uncongenial, returned to
England, resigning his professorial position, and giving up
his American practice. Dr. Peter Middleton lectured upon
Chemistry.[1]

[1] Hamilton subsequently, many years later, appeared to uphold the will of his old
teacher, Dr. Peter Middleton, and was opposed by Aaron Burr. This instrument,
made by Middleton in 1780, amongst other bequests, leaves to his old friends Doctors
Bard, Mallet, Michalis, and Bayley, all distinguished physicians of the period, who
took care of him during his last illness, each a mourning ring; and to his daughter
Susan, "my old wench Kaid, and also my negro lad Fortune, upon the express condition that my said daughter give over to John B. Middleton, above mentioned, all
her right and title to the negro child James, but should the said wench Kaid or lad
Fortune be inattentive to my said daughter or not promoting her interest and happiness as much as is in their power, as long as my said daughter is under age or unmarried; or, if they refuse going with her wherever her fortune or inclination may
induce her to go, I then direct my executors after-named to sell said wench Kaid or
lad Fortune to the highest bidder."

The Iliad of Homer

Book 12th

Lines

FAC-SIMILE OF EARLY GREEK EXERCISES

You will probably ere this reaches you have heard of the late incursion made into this city by a number of horsemen from New England under the command of Capt. Sears, who took away M[r]. Rivington's types and a Couteau or two. —Though I am fully sensible how dangerous and pernicuous Rivington's press has been, and how detestable the character of the man is in every respect, yet I cannot help disapproving and condemning this step.

In times of such commotion as the present, while the passions of men are worked up to an uncommon pitch there is great danger of fatal extremes. The same state of the passions which fits the multitude, who have not a sufficient stock of reason and knowledge to guide them, for opposition to tyranny and oppression, very naturally leads them to a contempt and disregard of all authority. The due medium is hardly to be found among the more intelligent, it is almost possible among the unthinking populace. When the minds of these are loosened from their attachment to ancient establishments and courses, they seem to grow giddy and are apt more or less to run into anarchy. These principles, too true in themselves, and confirmed to me both by reading and my own experience, deserve extremely the attention of those, who have the direction of public affairs. In such tempestuous times, it requires the greatest skill in the political pilots to keep men steady and within proper bounds, on which account I am always more or less alarmed at every thing which is done of mere will and pleasure without any proper authority. Irregularities I know are to be expected, but they are nevertheless dangerous and ought to be checked, by every prudent and moderate mean.——From these general maxims, I disapprove of the irruption in question, as serving to cherish a spirit of disorder at a season when men are too prone to it of themselves.——

Moreover, New England is very populous and powerful. It is not safe to trust to the virtue of any people. Such proceedings will serve to produce and encourage a spirit of encroachment and arrogance in them. I like not to see potent neighbours indulged in the practice of making inroads at pleasure into this or any other province.————

You well know too, Sir, that antipathies and prejudices have long subsisted between this province and New England. To this may be attributed a principal part of the disaffection now prevalent among us. Measures of the present nature, however they may serve to intimidate, will secretly revive and increase those ancient animosities, which though smothered for a while will break out when there is a favorable opportunity.

Besides this, men coming from a neighbouring province to chastise the notorious friends of the ministry here, will hold up an idea to our enemies not very advantageous to our affairs. They will imagine that the New Yorkers are totally, or a majority of them disaffected to the American cause which makes the interposal of their neighbours necessary: or that such violences will breed differences and effect that which they have been so eagerly wishing, a division and quarreling among ourselves. Everything of such an aspect must encourage their hopes.

Upon the whole the measure is condemned, by all the cautious and prudent among the whigs, and will evidently be productive of secret jealousy and ill blood if a stop is not put to things of this kind for the future.————

All the good purposes that could be expected from such a step will be answered; and many ill consequences will be prevented if your body gently interposes a check for the future. Rivington will be intimidated & the tories will be convinced that the other colonies will not tamely see the general cause betrayed by the Yorkers.—A favourable idea will be impressed of your justice & impartiality in discouraging the encroachments of any one province on another; and the apprehensions of prudent men respecting the ill-effects of an ungoverned spirit in the people of New England will be quieted—Believe me Sir it is a matter of consequence and deserves serious attention.

The tories it is objected by some are growing insolent and

clamorous: It is necessary to repress and overawe them.—
There is truth in this; but the present remedy is a bad one.
Let your body station in different parts of the province most
tainted, with the ministerial infection, a few regiments of
troops, raised in Philadelphia the Jerseys or any other province except New England.   These will suffice to strengthen
and support the Whigs who are still I flatter myself a large
majority and to suppress the efforts of the tories.   The pre-
tense for this would be plausible.   There is no knowing how ·
soon the Ministry may make an attempt upon New York:
There is reason to believe they will not be long before they
turn their attention to it—In this there will be some order &
regularity, and no grounds of alarm to our friends.—

     I am Sir with very great Esteem
                    Your most hum Servant
                                        A. HAMILTON.

     Jay subsequently wrote to Nathaniel Woodhull, President
of the Provincial Congress of New York, communicating
Hamilton's views:

     The New England exploit is much talked of and conjec-
tures are numerous as to the part the Convention will take
relative to it.   Some consider it as an ill compliment to the
Government of the Province, and prophesy that you have
too much Christian meekness to take any notice of it.   For
my own part I do not approve of the feat, & think it neither
argues much wisdom nor much bravery; at any rate, if it was
to have been done, I wish our own people, and not strangers,
had taken the liberty of doing it.   I confess I am not a little
jealous of the honour of the Province, and am persuaded
that its reputation cannot be maintained without some little
spirit being mingled with its prudence.

     Hamilton appears, even when the chance for a system-
atic education was denied him, to have gone on with his

studies, and to have worked constantly to the end of his life, acquiring a vast amount of learning of all kinds, which is manifest in everything he wrote, especially in his briefs, which always contained copious Latin and Greek quotations and every evidence of profound cultivation.

CHAPTER II

PERSONAL CHARACTERISTICS

MUCH misapprehension exists as to the appearance of
Hamilton, some of which is due to the idea that because his
birthplace was the West Indies, he presented the physical
characteristics of those born under a tropical sun.

He is referred to by various authors as a "Creole," or a
"swarthy young West Indian," and most of his biographers
picture him as being dark in color, and "having black hair
and piercing black eyes." One enthusiastic negro preacher,
extolling his virtues as champion of that race during the
Revolutionary War, when he favored the enlistment of black
soldiers, recently went so far as to suggest, at a public meeting
in the city of New York, that Hamilton's veins surely contained African blood. In reality he was fair and had
reddish-brown hair, and a specimen before me proves this
to have been the case. It has a certain glint which was probably more marked at an earlier period; but even now there
is no difficulty in finding that it belonged to a person of the
semi-blonde type.[1] His eyes were a deep blue—almost
violet—and he undoubtedly presented the physical appearance of his Scotch father rather than his French mother:[2]

[1] This lock of hair was given to his wife some time before December, 1780.
[2] George Shea ("Life and Epoch of Alexander Hamilton," Houghton, Osgood
& Co., Boston, 1879) confirms this and thus describes Hamilton's appearance: "A
bright, ruddy complexion; light-colored hair; a mouth infinite in expression, its sweet
smile being most observable and most spoken of; eyes lustrous with deep meaning
and reflection, or glancing with quick, canny pleasantry, and the whole countenance
decidedly Scottish in form and expression. . . . His political enemies frankly spoke
of his manner and conversation, and regretted its irresistible charm."

His eyes were deep set, his nose long, and of the Roman type, and he had a good chin, the jaw being strong; the mouth firm and moderately large.   He is variously referred to by his biographers as "The Little Lion," and "The Little Giant," but although short of stature, he was not notably so, being about five feet seven inches in height.

Sullivan described him as "under middle size, thin in person, but remarkably erect and dignified in his deportment.   His hair was turned back from his forehead, powdered and collected in a club behind.   His complexion was exceedingly fair, and varying from this only by the almost feminine rosiness of his cheeks.   His might be considered, as to figure and color, an uncommonly handsome face.   When at rest it had rather a severe, thoughtful expression, but when engaged in conversation it easily assumed an attractive smile.   When he entered a room it was apparent, from the respectful attention of the company, that he was a distinguished person."[1]

From the available portraits, which are numerous but are not artistically remarkable, and most of them evidently unreliable, very little impression is to be gained of his figure or how he actually looked, in repose or when animated.   Even such a fruitful painter as Trumbull rarely produced the same results in his different pictures; although his portraits are all powerful, yet they have a dramatic quality which is somewhat artificial.[2]   One of the most notable gives Hamilton bow-legs, while another in the Governor's Room in the New York City Hall portrays him as a well-shaped and graceful man, of more than medium height.   This artist

---

[1] "The Public Men of the Revolution," by W. Sullivan, Philadelphia, 1847, p. 260.

[2] There is now said to be in the family of Oliver Wolcott a pastel, copied in 1832 from an original painted in 1792, and referred to in Trumbull's book. ("Reminiscences of His Own Times" (1756–1811), by Col. J. Trumbull, Wiley & Putnam, 1841.)

seemed to have had special facility for studying his subject, for he was always an intimate and devoted friend, and after his death left a large number of personal relics of Hamilton, among them a fowling-piece and other belongings of his early friend, which he had evidently carefully treasured until the end of his life.[1]

At the end of the eighteenth century, itinerant portraits being in vogue, we find all kinds of daubs, and all grades of depicted ugliness in the canvases that have been preserved. Those of Peale are often decidedly unflattering, for he does not seem to have known how to paint the eyes of his subjects, and he has made sad work with Hamilton. There are numerous other portraits, but many of them are said to be those of other persons.[2]

The history of the Hamilton pictures is interesting, but it is often difficult to trace their wanderings.[3] That of Trumbull was painted at the request of Gulian Verplanck and others, who, in the year 1791, requested that it should "typify some act of his public career," but Hamilton deprecated any such advertising in the following words: "I shall cheerfully obey their wish as far as respects the taking of my portrait, but I ask that they will permit it to appear unconnected with any incident of my political life. The simple

[1] Hamilton paid for this fowling-piece and "old Peggy" (probably a dog) on May 2, 1798, the sum of $20.

[2] See a list of pictures and statuary enumerated in the "A. L. A. Portrait Index," p. 644, Washington, D. C., 1906.

[3] Charles Henry Hart, an indefatigable and usually well-informed collector, has written much regarding the history of the Hamilton and other portraits. He alludes to four only for which Hamilton sat, and to the curious fact that Trumbull's later pictures were made from Ceracci's bust. The four portraits were the Sharpless belonging to the author, the Trumbull in the N. Y. Chamber of Commerce, a wretched picture alleged to have been given to John C. Hamilton by Dr. Stevens, and one by Charles Wilson Peale painted in 1788. He also refers to the work of Archibald and Walter Robertson, no specimens of which can be found, although one is reported in Irving's "Washington" and the "National Portraits of Distinguished Americans." He also speaks of a youthful portrait which he seeks to identify, but I do not think it is of Hamilton.

representation of their fellow-citizen and friend will best accord with my feelings." This is the picture that hangs in the New York Chamber of Commerce, and of which there are several replicas. The best likenesses, however, were evidently those of Sharpless, an English artist who came to Philadelphia about 1796, and made various pictures of prominent people, after the Revolution, many of which are to-day in existence. Most of his portraits were small, but all were very carefully finished, and one of them is the frontispiece of this book. The most notable is the so-called Talleyrand miniature, by reason of the fact that this devoted friend and wily old diplomat was supposed to have purloined the picture while visiting in Philadelphia and taken it to France, later returning a copy in 1805. The picture he took was really a pastel by Sharpless, and upon the 6th of December, 1805, Mrs. Hamilton wrote, asking that it be returned to her, to which she received a reply from Théophile Cazenove, who for many years had been president of the Holland Company and a friend of Talleyrand, with this· letter:

Théophile Cazenove to Elizabeth Hamilton

PARIS, 10*th September*, 1805.

MY DEAR AND HIGHLY ESTEEMED LADY: Your letter of the 6th of December last did not reach me until July, and owing to the absence of M. Talleyrand it was sometime before I received an answer in reply to your request for the picture of the friend we have all lost. Notwithstanding the great value M. Talleyrand sets upon the image of the friend of whom we speak almost daily, your request and the circumstances are of a nature requiring self-sacrifice. The picture being executed in pastel, time and crossing the sea have impaired it, yet the likeness still remains, and on seeing it I fear your tender and afflicted heart will bleed, but tears will assuage these pangs, and my tears will flow with yours. May it bring comfort to the wife of the man whose genius and firmness have probably created the greatest part of the United States, and whose amiable qualities, great good sense, and instruction have been a pleasure to his own friends. Good God—must such a man fall in such a manner! . . . In fear the original picture should not reach you with my present letter, I have ordered a copy of it in oil-painting, which I send by another opportunity, and which I request you will give to my godson[1] in case the original shall reach you; if not to dispose of the copy in the manner you shall wish. . . . M. Talleyrand desires me to tell you of his respect and friendship and the part he has taken in your affliction.

Your obedient servant and friend,
THEOPHILE CAZENOVE.

The sculptor's chisel has also been busy, but with little result in the way of serious artistic production, if we may except the Ceracci bust, the Ball statue which was destroyed by fire, and the excellent modern work of Ordway Partridge, one of whose striking statues stands in front of a Hamilton Club in Brooklyn, and the other at the entrance of Hamilton Hall, a building of Columbia University. Ceracci's bust, which is very strong in its classical character, suggests a head of one of the Cæsars, and is more familiar than any other, although Houdin about the same time made a bust, when he executed that of Washington, which is also well known. Many other stiff and conventional statues exist, among them that in Central Park. The majority, however, are unworthy of serious consideration because they are commonplace or inartistic. Giuseppe Ceracci came here during the French Revolution, but returned to France and was guillotined after being concerned in a conspiracy against the life of Napoleon. A rather amusing entry in Hamilton's

---

[1] James A. Hamilton.

expense-book is the following: "$620.00 on March 3rd, 1796. For this sum through *delicacy* paid upon Ceracci's draft for making my bust on his own importunity, & 'as a favour to me.'"

Ceracci seems to have been a person with rather grandiose ideas, for he wrote to Hamilton from Amsterdam in July, 1797, suggesting that he should be employed by the United States Government to execute "a colossal, monumental group to commemorate National Triumph, and to celebrate the Epoch of Glory, to perpetuate the heroes of the Revolution. . . . To give an idea of the grandeur of the subject it is necessary to imagine a group in sculpture sixty feet high, and having a base three hundred feet in circumference. It is to be composed of sixteen statues fifteen feet high, of Colonels, and other characters in marble, an Eagle, and other objects; the whole to be surmounted by a figure of Hero in bronze. The blocks of marble for each statue would measure 16 x 6 perches." The cost was to be $50,000, an enormous sum in those days, and it was to be paid in ten portions.

There is little contemporary information regarding Hamilton's actual physical appearance, but two interesting Frenchmen who saw much of him and his family have written delightfully of the social life in New York during the latter half of the eighteenth century, giving us a quaint idea of the city as it then was. One of these was J. P. Brissot de Warville,[1] who, during the French Revolution was a Girondist and bitterly opposed to both Danton and Robespierre, and took a radical and active part in the affairs of the ever-troubled and unstable republic. As editor of the *Moniteur* and the *Patriot Francais* and other newspapers at the time

[1] "New Travels in the United States of America," including the "Commerce of America with Europe," etc., 2 vols., by the late J. P. Brissot de Warville, assisted by Etienne Clavière, 1797.

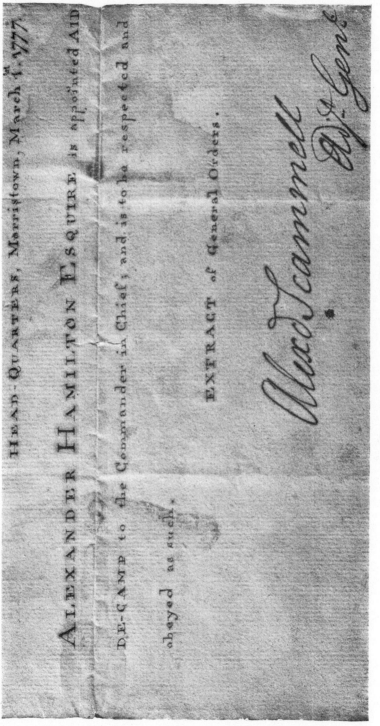

FAC-SIMILE OF APPOINTMENT AS AIDE-DE-CAMP

of the finest men in America, at least of those I have seen. He has breadth of mind, and even genuine clearness in his ideas, facility in their expression, information on all points, cheerfulness, excellence of character, and much amiability. I believe that even this eulogy is not adequate to his merit."

Alexander Hamilton to Angelica Church

PHILADELPHIA, *Dec.* 8, 1794.

Liancourt has arrived, and has delivered your letter. I pay him all the attention due to his misfortunes and his merits. I wish I was a Crœsus; I might then afford solid consolation to these children of adversity, and how delightful it would be to do so. *But now*, sympathy, kind words, and *occasionally a* dinner are all I can contribute.[1]

Hamilton's personality appears from all sources of information to indicate a mixture of aggressive force and infinite tenderness and amiability. The former led him always to speak his mind freely—perhaps too freely for his own comfort when he knew he was right, and when he had a wrong to master or disclose, or an end to accomplish.

This he did with an unselfishness and absolute fixity of purpose, and he often wondered why others did not think and act as he did, the righteous necessities of the case seemingly being so apparent. The energy of his nature is often shown in his letters, some of which are full of resentful impatience. In writing to Rufus King in regard to repudiation of the national debt, he says:

---

[1] This was written at about the time when he was obliged to give up his portfolio as Secretary of the Treasury and take up the practice of law to support his rapidly increasing family. The reader is referred to his letter to Robert Troup (Lodge's "Hamilton," vol. X, p. 107), regarding his financial embarrassment, and the provisions that were to be made in the event of his death.

Alexander Hamilton to Rufus King[1]

KINGSTON, *Feb.* 21, 1795.

MY DEAR KING: The unnecessary and capricious and abominable assassination of the national honor by the rejection of the propositions respecting the unsubscribed debt in the House of Representatives haunts me every step I take, and afflicts me more than I can express. To see the character of the government and the country so sported with—exposed to so indelible a blot—puts my heart to the torture. Am I, then, more of an American than those who drew their first breath on American ground? Or what is it that thus torments me at a circumstance so calmly viewed by almost everybody else? Am I a fool—a romantic Quixote—or is there a constitutional defect in the American mind? Were it not for yourself and a few others, I could adopt the reveries of De Paux as substantial truths, and could say with him that there is something in our climate which belittles every animal, human or brute.[2]

I conjure you, my friend, make a vigorous stand for the honor of your country! Rouse all the energies of your mind, and measure swords in the Senate with the great slayer of public faith—the hackneyed veteran in the violation of public engagements. Prevent him if possible from triumphing a second time over the prostrate credit and injured interests of his country. Unmask his false and horrid hypotheses. Display the immense difference between an able statesman and the man of subtleties. Root out the distempered and noisome weed which is attempted to be planted in our political garden, to choke and wither in its infancy the fair plant of public credit.

I disclose to you without reserve the state of my mind. It is discontented and gloomy in the extreme. I consider the cause of good government as having been put to an issue and the verdict rendered against it.

[1] " Hamilton's Works " (J. C. H.), vol. V, p. 624.
[2] " Récherches philosophiques sur les Américains, ou mémoirs intéressants pour Servir a l'Histoire de l'espèce humaine, Par M. De P. . . . ." A Berlin, 1768.

Introduce, I pray you, into the Senate, when the bill comes up, the clause which has been rejected, freed from embarrassment by the bills of credit, bearing interest on the nominal value. Press its adoption in this, the most unexceptionable shape, and let the yeas and nays witness the result.

Among the other reasons for this is my wish that the true friends of public credit may be distinguished from its enemies. The question is too great a one to undergo a thorough examination before the community. It would pain me not to be able to distinguish. Adieu. God bless you!

P. S.—Do me the favor to revise carefully the course of the bill respecting the unsubscribed debt and let me know the particulars. I wish to be able to judge more particularly of the under-plot I suspect.

He never hesitated to assail the corrupt wherever they were to be found, to quickly ferret out abuses and to publicly expose them. For this reason he made numerous bitter enemies, who did not hesitate on repeated occasions to try to ruin him. In a way he was at times tactless, but it cannot be denied that he rarely erred in judgment.[1] The passing of years undoubtedly has increased the number of his admirers, and has diminished the force of such faults as he had during his lifetime. As to his influence with men, reference may be made to the words of Oliver,[2] who says:

"No man whose object is personal glory will sacrifice his popularity to his opinions, and this was Hamilton's constant habit. At no great crisis of his life do we ever find him

---

[1] "He had a good heart," said Bancroft, "but with it the pride and the natural arrogance of youth, combined with an almost overwhelming consciousness of his powers, so that he was ready to find fault with the administration of others, and to believe that things might have gone better if the direction had rested with himself. Bold in the avowal of his opinions, he was fearless to provoke and prompt to combat opposition. It was not his habit to repine over lost opportunities. His nature inclined him rather to prevent what seemed to him coming evils by timely actions."

[2] "Alexander Hamilton: An Essay on American Union," by Frederick Scott Oliver, p. 395. London: Constable & Company, 1906.

engaged in considering whether a certain course of action will or will not conduce to his personal aggrandizement. He belonged to the class of men with whom the accomplishment of their objects is their most powerful motive. In the pursuit of renown he hardly rose above the average of public characters, but his desire for achievement was a passion."

John Adams disliked him in his way no less than Jefferson or Burr, and eventually quarrelled with nearly all the Federalists who were friendly to Hamilton. Some years before the powerful Livingstons in his own State had deserted the Federal cause, being ambitious of more power than was accorded them by Hamilton and Schuyler, and resented the election of Rufus King to the Senate, so that at the end but a few adherents remained, among them the doughty Timothy Pickering, who upon every occasion assailed not only Adams but Jefferson, and even after Hamilton's death worked valiantly to defend his memory against the assaults of unscrupulous political adversaries.[1]

During Hamilton's official career his vigorous methods kept him constantly in hot water, but he always emerged from each particular trouble, after the discomfiture of his enemies, quite ready for a new experience. While it is not possible in the limited space here available to go into these various plots, two or three well-known examples may be referred to that throw light upon his character and evidence his preparedness, for he was not found napping, and the accounts of his office were in such good condition and so well systematized that he never had any trouble whatever in producing documents and briefs to vindicate his good name in all attacks. In 1783, after he had won the test case of Rut-

---

[1] See "A Review of the Correspondence between the Honorable John Adams, etc., and the Late William Cunningham, 1803–1812," p. 109, *et seq.*

gers *vs.* Waddington which was the death of the unfair trespass act, he was most unpopular.

After Jay's treaty with Great Britain he was violently assailed in print, and as was the custom in those days replied in a forceful series of letters signed *Phocion*, to those of one Ledyard who was known as *Mentor*. The repudiation policy which had been favored by Governor Clinton at one time, and which was obnoxious to Hamilton and conflicted with his ideas of justice, was attacked by him with a force and convincing directness which enraged Ledyard's adherents. The result was that the members of a club of amiable gentlemen, of which the latter was the head, determined that Hamilton was best dead and out of the way, and without the knowledge of their president gravely proposed that they should challenge him in turn to fight until some one was so successful as to remove him. They, however, were quickly taken to account by Ledyard, who angrily repudiated this absurd plan, and taunted his associates because their act, if carried out, would be an admission that they were unable to refute Hamilton's charges. Upon two other occasions he was charged with financial irregularities by discharged treasury clerks who found the ears of his political enemies (see p. 54); in fact, it would appear that during his entire tenure of office much of his time was given to meeting assaults upon his integrity.

The admixture of Scotch and French blood which flowed in his veins was responsible for many of his striking traits and for many of his inconsistencies. If it be a fault, his great obstinacy in pursuing objects which were to be attained only at great risk and effort may be instanced and he sometimes persisted in disregard of the caution that ordinarily belongs to the Scot. This often implied that he did not resort to the smaller methods where conciliation would have

been much better than coercion.   He was not always a diplomat, and did not possess the qualities of Burr or other
more astute politicians ; in fact, he was above chicanery.

Upon an early occasion his dislike for Governor Clinton,
which was an outgrowth of the behavior of the latter at the
Poughkeepsie Convention and his imperious methods, led
to the alienation of members of his own party and subsequent
defeat, and undoubtedly the election of Burr and Jefferson
was largely brought about by his insistence, and failure to
provide for lesser politicians who surrounded him.

It is not extraordinary that a person whose mind was so
constantly engaged to the point of profound absorption—for
what he did was with the exercise of all his powers—should
have his periods of absent-mindedness.   We are told by
Trevelyan that "the New York Company of Artillery was a
model of discipline; its captain a mere boy with small, delicate, and slender frame who, with cocked hat pulled down
on his eyes, and apparently lost in thought, marched behind
his cannon, patting it every now and then as if it were a
favorite horse or pet plaything."   Possibly this was the same
kind of abstraction that was later shown and described in a
letter written by General Schuyler to his daughter.

Philip Schuyler to Elizabeth Hamilton

ALBANY, *October* 6, 1789.

MY BELOVED ELIZA: The following anecdote which I
learned from Judge Benson[1] may amuse.   A gentleman
travelling from New York to this place stopped at Kinder-
hook and made several turns in the street passing to and
fro before the store of a Mr. Rodgers.   Apparently in deep
contemplation, and his lips moving as rapidly as if he was in
conversation with some person—he entered the store, ten-

---

[1] Judge Egbert Benson.

dered a fifty-dollar bill to be exchanged. Rodgers refused to change it, the gentleman retired. A person in the store asked Rodgers if the bill was counterfeited. He replied in the negative. Why then did you not oblige the Gentleman by exchanging It,—because said Rodgers the poor Gentleman has lost his reason; but said the other, he appeared perfectly natural. That may be said Rodgers, he probably has his lucid intervals, but I have seen him walk before my door for half an hour, sometimes stopping, but always talking to himself, and If I had changed the money and he had lost It I might have received blame.—Pray ask my Hamilton if he can't guess who the Gentleman was. My Love to him, in which you participate. Adieu my Beloved Child.

Ever yours,   PH. SCHUYLER.

It would appear, from Hamilton's written productions, that what he did was always so thorough and systematic, and he was so given to detail that the activity of his cerebration must have been intense and his power of attention and application quite out of the ordinary. He undoubtedly possessed that form of nervous instability common to many active public men and characterized by varying moods, which was sometimes expressed by alternating depression on the one hand and gayety on the other. His perception was quick, and, despite the criticism of Mr. Lodge, he possessed a lively imagination, and was also deeply sensitive, as is shown in many little ways in his family life. In his letters to his wife his emotional changes are most evident, and his varying playfulness and gayety are at times dominant.

He wrote to her from Philadelphia, November, 1798:

"I am always very happy my dear Eliza, when I can steal a few moments to sit down and write to you. You are my good genius; of that kind which the ancient philosophers called a *familiar;* and you know very well that I am glad to be in every way as familiar as possible with you. I have

formed a sweet project, of which I will make you my con-
fidant when I come to New York, and in which I rely that
you will cooperate with me cheerfully.

> You may guess and guess and guess again
> Your guessing will be still in vain.

But you will not be the less pleased when you come to understand and realize the scheme.

> Adieu best of wives and best of mothers
> Heaven ever bless you & me in you.

A. H.

And again:

"After I had sent my letter to you to the Post Office I
received yours of the instant. My beloved chides me for not
having written on my first arrival here. I hope my letter by
Col. Burr will have removed her uneasiness as it informed
her that ill health and fatigue had been the cause of my
omission. Indeed, my Betsey, you need never fear a want
of anxious attention to you, for you are now dearer than ever
to me. Your happiness is the first and sweetest object of
my wishes and cares. How can it be otherwise? You are
all that is charming in my estimation and the more I see of
your sex the more I become convinced of the judiciousness
of my choice.

I hear your Heart ready to ask me, why instead of writing
this I do not come myself to tell it you—Your father's
pressing desire must be my excuse for reasons I shall explain
when we meet. But my departure will not be postponed
beyond Friday, that is, the day after tomorrow. I go in your
father's shay to Poughkeepsie and thence with Benson in his
shay to New York.

Monday at furthest I embrace my angel.

That Heaven may heap its blessings upon her and the dear
pledges of our affection is the constant prayer of her

A. HAMILTON.

Wednesday afternoon.

To MRS. ELIZABETH HAMILTON,
　　No. 57 Wall Street.

And still another letter, illustrating his tender solicitude is this :

I was made very happy, my beloved Betsey, by the receipt of your letter, informing me that one of mine had at length got to hand and that your spirits were recovered. I had suffered not a little at the idea that I must have appeared to you negligent, nor am I able to imagine what can have become of my other letters. There is certainly some very foul and abominable practice, which it will not be my fault, if I do not detect.

You said that you would not stay longer at Albany than twenty days which would bring it to the first of September. How delighted shall I be to receive you again to my bosom and to embrace with you my precious children! And yet, much as I long for this happy moment, my extreme anxiety for the restoration of your health will reconcile me to your staying longer where you are upon condition that you really receive benefit from it, and that your own mind is at rest. But I do not believe that I shall permit you to be so long absent from me another time.

Be cheerful, be happy my beloved, and if possible return to your husband with that sweet bloom on your looks which can never fail to delight him.

You must inform me beforehand when you set out. My intention is to meet you at Elizabeth Town. For I am unwilling to go through the bustle of another visit to New York so soon after my last.

Think of me—dream of me—and love me my Betsey as I do you.

Yrs. for ever,   A. HAMILTON.

Aug. 21,
MRS. HAMILTON.

There was at all times not a little sadness and sober sentiment mixed with concern as to her welfare.

The lightheartedness, which at times he manifested until the very end of his life appeared all the more striking when the stress and strain under which he labored are taken into consideration, and we bear in mind that he was constantly engaged with important public matters, some of the utmost seriousness. Most men would have been crushed by the malignant assaults of enemies who never ceased to lay traps and pitfalls, but these he easily avoided and laughed at because of his absolute consciousness of rectitude and his easy conscience.

There was something almost feminine in Hamilton's gentleness and concern for the comfort and happiness of other people. It is a matter of tradition that he endeared the soldiers of his own company to him by sharing their hardships, and providing them with necessities out of his own almost empty pocket. With his own children he was ever tender, entering into their sports, and forgetting all his serious cares for the moment. When New York and Philadelphia were crowded with refugees he would hunt up the poorest, and direct his wife to send food and little delicacies for the women and children. It had been his habit to travel upon the Circuit, as was the custom in those days with the different judges. One of these was Chancellor Kent, who told a story illustrating Hamilton's consideration and thoughtfulness.[1] After a disagreeable, wintry ride of many miles they reached a comfortless inn. Kent had gone to bed early after a jolly evening which broke up prematurely as Kent was out of sorts. The night was cold, and the kindly nature of Hamilton was evidently disturbed by the indisposition of his friend. On his retiring he entered Judge Kent's room bearing an extra blanket, which he insisted on tucking carefully about the recumbent figure saying, "Sleep warm, little Judge, and get well. What should we do if anything should happen to you?"

[1] "Memoirs and Letters of James Kent, LL.D., etc.," by Wm. Kent, his great-grandson, p. 33, N. Y., 1898.

JAMES KENT
By permission of Little, Brown & Co.

He had a love of the fine arts and was something of a print collector and an amateur painter, for it appears he advised Mrs. Washington in regard to the paintings she bought; but his purse was evidently too small to gratify his own tastes in this direction. Not only does his expense book contain items showing the occasional modest purchase of a print,[1] but he left behind numerous wood and copper line engravings and etchings, that to-day would be very valuable. I distinctly remember a set of Mantegna's superb chiaroscuro of the "Triumph of Cæsar," and a particularly fine Dürer which were in my father's possession; but the others have been scattered and can no longer be identified.

He had a rich voice, and rendered the songs of the day, among which was "The Drum," which he last sung at a meeting of the Cincinnati, a few days before the duel with Burr, which ran:

'Twas in the merry month of May
   When bees from flower to flower did hum,
Soldiers through the town marched gay,
   The village flew to the sound of the drum.

The clergyman sat in his study within
Devising new ways to battle with sin:
A knock was heard at the parsonage door,
And the Sergeant's sword clanged on the floor.

"We're going to war, and when we die
We'll want a man of God near by,
So bring your Bible and follow the drum.

His daughter Angelica often accompanied him upon the piano or harp, and appears to have been given all the advantages of a musical education.[2]

---

[1] February 12, 1799, for prints $28.

[2] August 28, 1795—"This sum paid duties on forte piano, 5 guineas the sum paid. Mr. Seton for cost and freight, £67.13.

    April 19, 1794—Paid to M. Young for music No. 5 and 6, $2.

    January 30, 1798—Subscription to Haydn Society, $5.

It has been said that Hamilton was vain. Gouverneur Morris,[1] whose cynicism and disposition to patronize his contemporaries was notorious, and who was said to be a friend of Hamilton's, and helped others to disentangle his affairs after his death seems to have been the only person to think him vain. At least no other available reference can be found where this criticism has been made, although in a vituperative age he undoubtedly came in for his share of abuse. Morris in his Diary thus soliloquizes after he had been asked by Mr. Hammond to deliver the funeral oration of his friend: "The first point of his biography is that he was a stranger of illegitimate birth; some plan must be contrived to pass over this handsomely. He was indiscreet, vain, and opinionated," and so he continues, making mental reservations, and damning the dead man with faint praise; yet on the 14th of July he delivered a fulsome funeral oration, seeming to have gotten over the struggle with himself as to what was "safe" to say and what to omit. Disregarding the humiliating confession Hamilton had made in the Reynolds case, to save his honor when accused of peculation, Morris said, "I must not either dwell on his domestic life: he has long since foolishly published the avowal of conjugal infidelity." After his return from the funeral he adds: "I find that what I have said does not answer the general expectation."

While it is true that Hamilton had very decided opinions of his own, and undoubtedly was self-reliant and enthusiastically assertive, there is not a letter or published paper of his that indicates the existence of the least vanity or boastfulness—in fact, he never indulged in self-exploitation, but as a rule submerged himself. As an evidence of his modesty may be instanced the anonymous letter he wrote to Robert Morris, then a member of Congress in 1780, recom-

[1] "Diary and Letters of Gouverneur Morris," vol. II, p. 456, *et seq.* New York: Chas. Scribner's Sons.

mending a financial scheme that undoubtedly led to his being made Secretary of the Treasury. If Morris wished to know more of the views of his unknown correspondent, he was to address "James Montague, Esq.—a lodger in the post office of Morristown," which would be a safe channel for all communications. It must be admitted that, although he prepared a large number of public papers and wrote many of Washington's letters in the field, and had a great deal to do with the preparation of the Farewell Address of the latter, he, upon no occasion, attempted to profit by what he did, or to glorify himself in any way, and it appears beyond question that he always assumed the position of one who toiled with others for the production of a common result, without thinking of reward, either in the nature of approbation or material return. At a time when the lawlessness of the French Republic had extended to the United States, Hamilton was called an aristocrat; and even before this he had been sneered at by his opponents at the Poughkeepsie Convention, Melancthon Smith having "thanked his God that *he* was a plebeian." A great deal of the dislike of decency, and contempt for blood and brains existed, and found vent in socialistic and even anarchistic conflicts with good order. Possibly some of this abuse was due to Hamilton's advocacy of our obligation to another foreign power, and his uphill work in making a large number of people live up to their treaty with Great Britain.[1] To some minds this meant respect for an aristocratic country, and he was spoken of as a "British sympathizer"; upon one occasion an out-

[1] There is something very ludicrous and indecent, as well as stupid and illogical in this statement of Jefferson, who ought to have known better. Upon one occasion he said ("Writings," vol. IV, p. 451): "Hamilton was indeed a singular character, of acute understanding, disinterested, honest, and honorable in all private transactions, amiable in society, and duly valuing virtue in private life—yet so bewitched and perverted by the British example as to be under thorough conviction that corruption was essential to the government of a nation."

rageous story was spread by a lawyer named Purdy, with the evident connivance of Governor George Clinton, to the effect that Hamilton and Adams and the King of England had, in 1798, entered into negotiations to introduce a monarchy into America, and that Canada was to be ceded to the United States, and that Prince Frederick, the Duke of York, and titular Bishop of Osnaburg was to be the ruler. After Hamilton's angry remonstrance Clinton, in a letter written in March, 1804, disclaimed any part in the ridiculous charge, and Hamilton replied as follows:[1]

Alexander Hamilton to George Clinton.

ALBANY, *March* 9, 1804.

SIR: I had the honor of receiving yesterday your Excellency's letter of the 6th inst. It is agreeable to me to find in it a confirmation of the inference that you have given no countenance to the supposition of my agency or co-operation in the project to which the story of Judge Purdy relates; and it only remains for me to regret that it is not in your power to furnish the additional clue, of which I was desirous, to aid me in tracing the fabrication to its source.

I shall not only rely on the assurance which you give me as to the future communication of the copy of the letter in question, should it hereafter come to your hands, but I will take the liberty to add a request, that you will be pleased to make known to me any other circumstances, if any should reach you, which may serve to throw light upon the affair. I feel an anxiety that it should be thoroughly sifted, not merely on my own account, but from a conviction that the pretended existence of such a project, long travelling about in whispers, has had no inconsiderable influence in exciting false alarms, and unjust suspicions to the prejudice of a number of individuals, every way worthy of public confidence, who have always faithfully supported the existing institutions of the country, and who would disdain to be concerned in an in-

---

[1] "Hamilton's Works" (J. C. H.), vol. VI, p. 565.

trigue with any foreign power, or its agents, either for introducing monarchy, or for promoting or upholding any other scheme of government within the United States.

Even his friend, Gouverneur Morris, ignoring the existence of *The Federalist* and everything else that Hamilton had written and done in regard to the construction of the Constitution, could not forbear condemning him, and quite unjustly.[1] "Speaking of General Hamilton," he said, "he had little share in forming the Constitution. He disliked it, believing a Republican Government to be radically defective, the British Constitution which I consider as an Aristocracy in fact, though a Monarchy in name. General Hamilton hated Republican Government because he confounded it with Democratic government, and he detested the latter because he believed it must end in despotism and be, in the meantime, destructive of public morals."

Morris's criticism, which was and is in accord with the views of those who prefer to misunderstand, or who are unable to appreciate Hamilton's consistent and persistent efforts to build up a republic in the true sense of the word, finds refutation in this letter to Timothy Pickering, in which he said:

This plan was in my conception conformable with the strict theory of a government purely republican; the essential criteria of which are, that the principal organs of the executive and legislative departments be elected by the people, and hold their offices by a *responsible* and temporary or *defeasible* tenure.

And again,

I may truly then say, that I never proposed either a president, or senator, for life; and that I neither recommended or meditated the annihilation of the state governments. . . .

[1] *Op. cit.*, vol. II, p. 523.

These were the genuine sentiments of my heart and upon them I acted.[1]

If Hamilton was called an aristocrat it was because he was intolerant of presumptuous ignorance, and possessed an intense contempt for anything that was low or coarse or harmful to the country as a whole. It was his warfare upon these things, and his blunt defiance of mob rule that earned for him this reputation.

If *aristocracy* be "the rule of the best in the land" his efforts were directed to that end, and the progress of history has certainly made us aware of the contrast between the staid and respectable forms of government, and the emotional and disreputable forms, and the triumph in the end of the stable kind of administration. It is true that for a long time Jefferson and Madison and their party flourished by the utilization of Hamilton's principles for their guidance long after his death, even though they pretended to despise them.

Hamilton certainly had respect for good blood and its belongings, and his friends were the well-bred and educated men of the world, many of whom came from France; yet in the true meaning of the word, he was intensely democratic, if we are to consider the simplicity of his daily life and his regard for the lowly and oppressed, and the readiness he always manifested to make friends with good men of all conditions and parties always furthering the protection of individual rights.

That Hamilton was ambitious is demonstrated by everything he did, yet it was not the ambition of selfish men nor the kind which led him to sacrifice others for his own advancement. A parallel, for instance, may be drawn between Napoleon, who was a contemporary, and himself, to the detriment of the former.

[1] Letter to Timothy Pickering, New York, September 16, 1803.

Estabrook,[1] an eloquent New York lawyer, in a rare appreciation says:

"To sum up Hamilton's temperament, therefore, I would say that he was nobly ambitious, but wisely cautious, sometimes most tentative when he was really most assured." When Washington wrote to Adams in his behalf he said: "By some he is considered as an ambitious man, and therefore a dangerous one; that he is ambitious.I shall readily grant, but it is of the laudable kind which prompts a man to excel in whatever he takes in hand. He is enterprising—quick in his perceptions—and his judgment intuitively great." The first few words have especial significance, when we consider that Hamilton's enemies had insinuated to Adams that the ambitious designs of the former would minimize his influence.

At an early age he longed to distinguish himself in the world, and his familiar letter to Edward Stevens, the friend of his childhood, may, in part, be reproduced to illustrate his early aspirations. This was written when he was a boy about twelve.

Alexander Hamilton to Edward Stevens.

St. Croix, *Nov.* 11, 1769.[2]

. . . As to what you say respecting your soon having the happiness of seeing us all, I wish for an accomplishment of your hopes, provided they are concomitant with your welfare, otherwise not: though I doubt whether I shall be present or not, for to confess my weakness, Ned, my ambition is prevalent, so that I contemn the grovelling condition of a clerk or the like, to which my fortune condemns me, and would willingly risk my life, though not my character, to exalt my station. I am confident, Ned, that my youth excludes me from any hopes of immediate preferment, nor do I desire

[1] "The Lawyer Hamilton," a paper read by Henry D. Estabrook before the American Bar Association, Aug. 22, 1901.
[2] "Hamilton's Works" (J. C. H.), vol I, p. 1.

it; but I mean to prepare the way for futurity. I'm no philosopher, you see, and may be justly said to build castles in the air; my folly makes me ashamed, and beg you'll conceal it: Yet, Neddy, we have seen such schemes successful when the projector is constant. I shall conclude by saying I wish there was a war.

Whatever his ambition may have been, in later years there does not appear to have been any indication that he expected political preferment or that he was engaged in any attempt to advance himself, and although he had been seriously considered as a successor to Washington, it is doubtful if he would have accepted the great office.[1] On the other hand, it seems to have been his constant and only desire to labor for the welfare of his country so long as he could do any good, and to retire as soon as possible to the quiet pursuit of a pastoral life.

Like all other public men, he had been approached by friends who did not think it amiss that he should give them information of impending public transactions that might be utilized for speculation. He undoubtedly had his temptations to help his friends, but he ever resolutely refused to disclose the operations of his own department. Even so circumspect a man as Henry Lee wrote a letter to him, which probably was sent without any dishonorable intentions whatever, but was ill advised.

"My dear Sir;" wrote Lee in 1789,[2] "Your undertaking is truly arduous, but I trust as you progress in the work, difficulties will vanish. From your situation you must be able to form with some certainty an opinion concerning the domestic debt; will it speedily rise? Will the interest accruing com-

[1] He was offered the nomination for Governor of the State of New York, and an appointment as Chief Justice of the Supreme Court of the United States, but declined both offices. (See "History of the Republic," by J. C. Hamilton.)

[2] "Hamilton's Reminiscences," p. 17.

mand specie, or anything nearly as valuable—what will become of the indents already issued? These queries are asked for my private information. Perhaps they may be improper. I do not think them so, or I would not propound them. Of this you will decide, and act accordingly—nothing can induce me to be instrumental in submitting my friends to an impropriety. . . .

"The anti-federal gentlemen in our own assembly do not relish the amendments proposed by Congress to the constitution. Yours always and affectionately,

"HENRY LEE.

"To Col. Alexander Hamilton."

Hamilton replied:[1]

MY DEAR FRIEND: I received your letter of the 16th of November. I am sure you are sincere when you say that you would not subject me to an impropriety, nor do I know there would be any in answering your queries; but you remember the saying with regard to Cæsar's wife. I think the spirit of it applicable to every man concerned in the administration of the finances of the country. With respect to the conduct of such men, *suspicion* is ever eagle-eyed, and the most innocent things may be misinterpreted. Be assured of the affection and friendship of yours.

A great deal of nonsense has been written about Hamilton's gallantry, and his name has been quite unjustifiably connected with that of Madame Jumel, the widow of a French wine-merchant, and before this the widow of a British officer with whom she eloped. Although her home at the upper part of Manhattan Island was a rendezvous for the gay young men of the day, it does not appear that either Washington or Hamilton, as has been alleged, knew her particularly well. Certainly it is absurd to say that Hamilton had an amour with her, as has been suggested, and this gossip may,

[1] "Hamilton's Reminiscences," p. 18.

with other contemporary scandal, be disregarded. She subsequently married Aaron Burr when he was an elderly man,
but the union did not last, for he misappropriated her funds
and otherwise behaved badly.

It is quite to be supposed that Hamilton with his attractive
equipment was like many others of his time so far as his
moral *lâches* was concerned, but his tender devotion to, and
kindly care of his wife were always evident in his letters that
have been preserved.

With Angelica Church he kept up a sprightly correspondence, which bristles with badinage, and to many suggests the existence of a more tender feeling than would appear to be conventional, but an inspection of his whole life
and hers disproves this.

Some of her letters, of which the following is an example,
are written in the flowery style of the day:

Angelica Church to Alexander Hamilton.

LONDON, *Oct.* 2, 1787.

You have every right, my dear brother, to believe that I
was very inattentive not to have answered your letter, but I
could not relinquish the hopes that you would be tempted to
ask the reason of my silence, which would be a certain means
of obtaining the second letter when perhaps had I answered
the first, I should have lost all the fine things contained in the
latter. I indeed my dear Sir, if my path was strewed with as
many roses as you have filled your letter with compliments, I
should not now lament my absence from *America*, but even
Hope is weary of doing anything for so assiduous a votary
as myself. I have so often prayed at her shrine that I am
now no longer heard. Church's head is full of Politics, he is
so desirous of making one in the British House of Commons,
and where I should be happy to see him if he possessed your
eloquence. All the graces you have been pleased to adorn
me with, fade before the generous and benevolent action of

my sister in taking the orphan Antil[1] under her protection. I do not write by this packet to either of my sisters, nor to my father. It is too melancholy an employment today, as Church is not here to be my consolation; he is gone to New Market. You will please to say to them for me everything you think that the most tender and affectionate attachment can dictate. Adieu, my dear brother! be persuaded that these sentiments are not weakened when applied to you and that I am very sincerely your friend,

A. C.

After the appearance of his report upon the finances which was presented to Congress, January 7, 1790, she wrote:

Many thanks to my dear Brother for having written to his friend at a moment when he had the affairs of America on his mind; I am impatient to hear in what manner your Budget has been received and extremely anxious for your success.

I sometimes think you have now forgot me and that having seen me is like a dream which you can scarcely believe.— adieu I will not write this idea of being lost in the tumult of business and ambition does not enliven my spirits—*adieu soyez heureux au dessus de tout le monde.*

At a time when he thought it possible that he might be sent to Europe to facilitate the acceptance of Jay's treaty, she wrote on August 15, 1793:

Are you too happy to think of us? Ah *petit Fripon* you do not believe it:—no I am not too happy, can I be so on this side of the Atlantic? ask your heart, and read my answer there.

My silence is caused by dispair; for do not years, days and moments pass and still find me separated from those I love! yet were I in America, would ambition give an hour to *Betsey* and to me. Can a mind engaged by Glory taste of peace and ease?

---

[1] The orphan daughter of one of Montgomery's aides adopted by Mrs. Hamilton.

You and Betsey in England. I have no ideas for such happiness, but when will you come and receive the tears of joy and affection?

Your devoted ANGELICA.

August 15th, 1793.

When Hamilton became Secretary of the Treasury his sister-in-law wrote about him: "All the members of Congress have made the first visit to the General, it is very rare to find a person in political or private life so respected and beloved—shall I say by both sexes?

"We dine tomorrow with Mrs. Bingham[1] and Viscomte *Importance.*[2] Madame de Tilley[3] is quite a la francaise, rouge and short petticoats—poor young creature she has been the victim to a negligent education. I have seen enough of Philadelphia."

The real and only authenticated mistake, which would have been the ruin of a weaker man, was the affair with the notorious Mrs. Reynolds, which was brought to light by the mean traps laid for him, principally by Monroe.

For a long time, as has been said, persistent attempts had been made when Hamilton was Secretary of the Treasury to find him guilty of peculation and misuse of the government funds, but each time Hamilton vindicated himself and put the combination to rout. Finally, Monroe, Muhlenberg, and Venables waited upon him with supposed damning proof that Hamilton had supplied one Reynolds and a confederate, Clingman, then in jail, with money to speculate in the public funds upon information supplied by Hamilton, who was supposed to make use of the knowledge of national affairs he

---

[1] Wife of William Bingham the banker. Bingham was a delegate to the old Congress in 1787–88, and later U. S. senator (1795–1801).

[2] Vicomte de Noailles.

[3] Comtesse de Tilly, formerly Elizabeth Berkeley, widow of Lord Craven. She was married to the Comte de Tilly in 1792.

possessed. The precious pair were in prison, but one of them subsequently escaped. These confident confederates, armed with ammunition supplied by the rascals who had already been turned out of their positions and arrested at the instance of the Secretary of the Treasury, were finally delighted with the idea that the daring Federalist might be shorn of his power and disgraced; but when he quietly made his innocence absolutely clear, two of them, Muhlenberg and Venables, were convinced and manfully made amends in apology, but Monroe for a long time held out and preferred to take his original view that Hamilton was guilty. This led to a virulent correspondence and demands from Hamilton that Monroe should retract, which, after much delay, he reluctantly did. Even then the question of a duel was raised. The copy of a challenge written by Monroe, but never sent, has been preserved.

It was necessary at this time for Hamilton to make, perhaps, the greatest sacrifice that can be imagined to save his honor, and this he did. He had given money to Reynolds, but it was in payment of blackmail imposed by that person and his wife, the former having been a *mari complaisant* for a long period. Oliver says:[1]

"Hamilton elected to tell the whole story; to publish every document in his possession, and to expound the situation, the motives of the parties, and the dangers to the community and to public life arising out of such methods, in that vehement and copious manner which he was famed for pursuing at the bar. . . .

"He exhausted the case. When he had made an end there was nothing more to be said. The statement is without a reservation, and yet it is never familiar. He shirks nothing, nor seeks for any shelter against the opinion of the world. His sole aim is to set his honesty in discharge of his public

[1] *Op. cit.*, p. 309.

duty beyond attack. A single departure from the strictest rule of simplicity, a single disingenuous excuse or sentimental quaver, would have made the statement odious. Temptations to an eternal loss of dignity lay on every side, but he had only one concern; to clear his honour. No one has yet been bold enough to challenge the completeness of his vindication."

The wonder is, how a man of Hamilton's refinement and critical sense should ever have been led into an amour with a coarse and illiterate woman, apparently of a very low class, and this is quite inconceivable to most people. The letters and notes of Mrs. Reynolds to him are monuments of vulgarity and bad spelling, and it is to be wondered what he found to admire in such a person that would lead him to run the risk he did.[1] There certainly could not have been anything but rather indifferent physical attractions. Such an entanglement can only be understood by those who are familiar with the sporadic lapses upon the part of other great men who have been tempted to give way to some such impulse, and for a time degrade themselves, often to their lasting ruin. To the psychiatrist the matter is simple, for it is a well-known fact that those possessing the highest order of intelligence; professional men, great statesmen, and others; even those teaching morals, manifest at times what can be only looked upon as a species of irresponsibility that accompanies the highest genius, and impulsively plunge into the underworld in obedience to some strange prompting of their lower nature.

[1] "Observations upon Certain Documents Contained in Nos. V & VI of the History of the United States from the Year 1796, in which the Charge of Speculation Against Alexander Hamilton, Late Secretary of the Treasury, is fully refuted. Written by Himself." Philadelphia: Printed for John Fenno, by John Bioren, 1797.—See Appendix K.

CHAPTER III

HAMILTON AS A WRITER AND ORATOR

HAMILTON'S literary activity suffered no interruption from the time he wrote his well-known account of the hurricane in his West Indian home until his death. Not only was it his keen pleasure to write, but his pen was always at the service of others who appealed to him, the result being the production of an enormous amount of general correspondence, political and other essays, and even occasional verse. Laurens,[1] in December, 1776, regarding General Lee's "Infamous Publication," and the fitness of Hamilton's answer, playfully wrote to the latter: "The ancient Secretary is the *Recueil* of modern history and anecdotes, and will give them to us with candour, elegance and perspicacity. The pen of Junius is in your hand and I think you will, without difficulty, expose in his defence letters and last productions, such a tissue of falsehood and inconsistency as will satisfy the world, and put him forever to silence." The part he played throughout the Revolution, as the secretary and aide-de-camp of Washington, was one requiring a great amount of literary work, his duties being ever of an onerous kind, and his writings of the most diversified nature. The collection of military papers that remain and are now at the Congressional Library show that most of Washington's orders in the field were largely Hamilton's work, and it is to be presumed from their nature that he had most to do with their preparation.

[1] "Hamilton's Works" (J. C. H.), vol. I, p. 68.

All of them are singularly free from correction, and are legibly and carefully written. This power of prolific creation seems to have increased until his death, and while his correspondence was not as voluminous as that of Jefferson, who is said to have written twenty-five thousand letters, Hamilton's facility for expressing himself on paper led him to write upon every occasion, and the newspapers of the day are a veritable repository of articles upon every conceivable political subject. Worthington C. Ford, in a personal letter, says in this connection: "Think of the man who writes himself hundreds of letters required of him when organizing the provisional army in 1798! It makes the modern General of Industry seem insignificant with his small following of typewriters and a highly organized system of red tape." In the twelve volumes that constitute Lodge's works, most of Hamilton's important reports, speeches, pamphlets, and letters are reproduced, and the list is by no means complete. His communications upon Foreign Relations were thirty-three in number, on Finance and the National Bank thirty-nine, on Commercial Relations twenty-seven, and on Manufacturing and the Whiskey Rebellion seventeen each. His published military letters number seventy-six, his other papers on Coinage, the Mint, Taxation, and the Fisheries seven; and there are no less than thirty-two speeches presented in this work alone. Other miscellaneous papers, relating to the Jefferson and the Adams controversy and the Reynolds affair, numbered seventeen. Of the eighty-five articles in *The Federalist* it is believed that he wrote sixty-three unaided, and three in collaboration with Madison.[1]

In this collection we, therefore, find over three hundred and twenty-eight important productions brought forth in a

[1] This is the enumeration in a copy of *The Federalist* belonging to his nephew Philip Church, and presented to him by Hamilton himself.

period of less than thirty years. If we are to include the various other papers and letters contained in Hamilton's works, edited by his son, or reproduced elsewhere, the number would be very great.[1] From time to time, as in the life and correspondence of McHenry, valuable and hitherto unpublished letters have been unearthed in the last few years. The writer's collection contains many papers relating to both public and legal matters, and that at Washington is still, to some degree, untouched by the historian.

As was the custom of the eighteenth century, Hamilton wrote under various pseudonyms, and these include the well-known *James Montague, Phocion, Continentalist, Pericles, An American Citizen, A Plain Honest Man, Pacificus, Tully, No Jacobin, Americanus, Horatius, Civis, Titus Manlius, Observer, Anti-Defamer Cato* and *Publius*, the last having been made use of in the production of *The Federalist*. With Rufus King he adopted *Camillus* in writing in defence of Jay's treaty with Great Britain and many other matters. King is said to have written eight of this series. The first important communication of Hamilton was the well-known letter to Robert Morris in regard to the establishment of a national bank, which his modesty forbade him signing. This was in 1780,[2] at the time he was attached to Washington's staff, and but twenty-three years of age, and probably marked the first exhibition of his pent-up desires to identify himself with national affairs. The history of the subsequent action of Morris, who availed himself of Hamilton's suggestions, is too well known to need more than passing reference, but he promptly suggested the latter for the Treasury. Previous to this, as early as 1774, he wrote his remarkable

---

[1] Lodge has omitted nearly three hundred letters, papers, and various reports and opinions published in the J. C. Hamilton "Works."

[2] Sumner says there was some doubt as to this date—the year possibly being 1779.

pamphlet entitled "The Full Vindication," which was an answer to the "Westchester Farmer." The writer of the latter, who was believed to be Bishop Samuel Seabury, had indulged in offensive criticism of the Continental Congress. Upon the title-page of Hamilton's paper, which was printed by James Rivington, the printer and bookseller, who in later years became one of his clients, appears the motto, "Veritas magna est et prevalebit," and the sub-title "Sophistry is Exposed, his Cavils confuted, his Artifice detected, and his Wit is ridiculed," is appended. A reply to Hamilton appeared later, and the second answer prepared by him and entitled, "The Farmer Refuted," was still more drastic and convincing.[1] As Lodge says: "These two productions in patriotic interest excited much attention were widely read, and were attributed by Dr. Myles Cooper, the President of King's College, to Jay. Few suspected that they would prove to be the work of a college boy, and all were amazed when the true author was known. These two pamphlets are the first important efforts of Hamilton's pen. They are, however, little short of wonderful when we remember they are the work of a boy not yet eighteen years old."[2] He was ever a contributor to the newspapers and periodicals, among them the *United States Gazette*, edited by his friend John Fenno, who had come from Boston. Even before this he had written an article for *Holt's Gazette* in defence of the destruction of tea in 1774. According to Hudson, the *United States Gazette* was started in New York, its original name being *The Gazette of the United States*, and it was first issued in New York, which was then the seat of the National Government, but afterward was transferred to Philadelphia when it became the capital, in 1790. It was always the organ of the Federalists and never lost an occa-

[1] Appendix C.   [2] Lodge, vol I, p. 3.

sion to attack the Jacobins, as the Democratic sympathizers
with the French Revolutionists were called. For this reason
it was opposed to the *Aurora* and the *Daily Advertiser*, edited
by William Duane and Philip Freneau, which were the
organs of Jefferson and his friends. Fenno died of yellow
fever in 1798, and his son George Ward Fenno succeeded him,
conducting the paper until it ceased to exist in 1820.[1] These
papers conveyed to the Jays, Kings, Churches, and other
Americans abroad the only information regarding the progress of events in their native country. Not only was such
news delayed many months, on account of the slow progress of packets, but all manner of interruptions, which are
strangely in contrast to the newsgathering in the twentieth
century, are evident in the New York newspapers of the day.
The presses were even often stopped to publish fresh material
that had come by stage-coach two days later than that printed
by their contemporaries.

Angelica Church wrote to her sister from London, June
the 4th, 1793:

MY DEAR ELIZA: I am returned from our ambassadors
very much edifyed by reading Fenno's paper, for it speaks
of my Brother, as he deserves, and as I and all who *dare* to
know him think.

We are going to our country house. Mrs. Pinckney[2]
passes the week with me, and whilst we admire the taste and
elegance of Great Britain, we shall still more regret the
society, the pleasures, and friendships of America. Ah my
dear Sister after all, nothing repays us for a separation from
those we have been long attached to. Mr. and Mrs. Bache[3]
are to be at Mr. Morris's Villa, which is not far from Down
Place. I shall visit her to see it; but request of her to tell

---

[1] His daughter Mary married Gulian C. Ver Planck in 1811. See Frederick
Hudson's "Journalism in the United States from 1690–1872," pp. 181–182.

[2] Wife of Thomas Pinckney, Minister to Great Britain, 1792–94.

[3] This Mr. Bache was the son-in-law of Benjamin Franklin.

you what she has seen, but as she does not like chit chat it will be difficult to prevail on her.   They are soon to return to America.   Why am I not to be of the party!   It is an age since we arrived, and if I had not seen Mr. Fenno's paper my impatience would have been extreme.

Adieu my dear Betsy.

And again on June 5, 1793.

My dear: The packet is arrived, and you are well, this is however not all I wish to know; but it is a great pleasure yet relief to get a letter from you; my love to Alexander the good, and the amiable.   Shall I tell you a secret?   I have more and better hopes within these days than ever of crossing the Atlantic.

Philip Freneau was an exceedingly cultivated man, and an early American poet of some ability, and the *Daily Advertiser*, which he edited, had a long and apparently prosperous career.   Freneau was born in 1752, and was graduated from Princeton in 1771.   It is said that he lost his life in 1832 from exposure, having gone astray in a bog-meadow on returning home from Freehold, New Jersey.   His attacks upon the Federalists were mild in comparison with those that he subsequently published in the *National Gazette*.   This journal was established October 31, 1791, and was bitter in its abuse of and opposition to Hamilton and the others.   Freneau was clever and witty, and did so much to please Jefferson that the latter made him a salaried interpreter in the State Department, which led to much scandal at the time.   The new sheet contained numerous scurrilous articles, some of them attacking Hamilton who was then Secretary of the Treasury, and in Fenno's paper, over the signature of "The American," the latter charged Jefferson with the part he had played in providing Freneau with the sinews of war, and extending to him his patronage.[1] Jefferson's explanation was extremely lame. He acknowledged that "he had heard with pleasure of the publication which promised to administer an antidote to the aristocratical and monarchical doses lately given by the unknown writer of the 'Discourses on Davila' and which also would probably reproduce, at his request, certain extracts from the *Leyden Gazette*, concerning French politics. Subscriptions he admitted to have solicited from a charitable desire to aid his clerk, whom he thought to be a man of good parts. He protested in the presence of heaven that he had made no effort to control the conduct or sentiments of the paper."[2]

In Philadelphia, journalistic controversies were most disorderly, especially when a certain amount of public sympathy was extended to the representatives of the French Republic. It is quite conceivable how Hamilton must have raged internally against the blackguardly abuse of the *Aurora* and the daily attacks of Bache; but although public opinion of the right kind was finally aroused, Hamilton appears to have, meanwhile, kept silent. So inexcusable were the attacks of the anti-Federalistic journals that the editors were constantly in trouble with the authorities. Even when Washington retired to Mount Vernon the abuse was so disgraceful that a company of veterans known as the Spring Garden Butchers, who had fought directly under the latter in the war, went to the office of the *Aurora* and looted and de-

---

[1] Jefferson's bitterness against this editor found vent in a letter to a friend in Paris, written probably in 1793: "The Tory paper, Fenno's, rarely admits anything which defends the present form of government in opposition to his desire of supporting it, to make money for a king, lords, or commons. There are high names here in favor of this doctrine. Adams, Jay, Hamilton, and Knox and many of the Cincinnati. The second says nothing, the third is open. Both are dangerous. They pant after union with England as the power which is to support their projects, and are most determined anti-Gallicians."

[2] "Life of Alexander Hamilton," J. T. Morse, vol. II, p. 5.

molished the premises. On the 9th of May, 1798, the intolerance of the sane public made itself especially manifest
in a demonstration of violence.   This day had been appointed
as one of fasting and prayer, and the attitude of those who
openly fraternized with the French representatives, and who
were obsessed with the unhealthy doctrines of the republic,
could no longer be tolerated. Declarations were made
against the "Jacobins, philosophers, freemasons, and the
illuminati," and a political riot marked the limit of patriot
endurance. The office of the *Aurora* was again attacked,
where Bache had intrenched himself with a number of friends,
who were armed to the teeth.   After doing what damage they
could, the rioters—many among them being Federalists—
broke the windows and plastered the statue of Franklin,
who was Bache's uncle, with mud. After Bache's death,
from yellow fever, the paper was edited by William Duane, a
still more vehement partisan of the Jacobins. In November, 1799, Hamilton was the plaintiff in a libel case against
a New York newspaper called the *Argus*. In its issue of
October 6 appears the following excerpt from the Philadelphia publication:

An effort has been recently made to suppress the *Aurora*,
and Alexander Hamilton was at the bottom of it. Mrs.
Bache was offered $6,000 down in presence of several persons
in part payment, the valuation to be left to two impartial
persons, and the remainder paid immediately on giving up
the paper, but she pointedly refused it, and declared she
would never dishonour her husband's memory, nor her
children's future fame by such baseness; when she parted
with her paper it should be to Republicans only.'

On November 21 David Frothingham, the foreman of the
office, was indicted on complaint of General Hamilton.   The
case was brought to trial before Judge Harrison, the recorder,

and the mayor of the city of New York. Cadwallader Colden and Alexander Hamilton were sworn. The former, who was assistant attorney, testified that Frothingham had been called upon and said he supposed he was liable, but saw no criminality as the letter was copied from another paper. Hamilton then testified that he was innocent of the conduct imputed to him. This testimony was objected to by Brockholst Livingston, the defendant's counsel, and the objection was sustained. Hamilton was then asked to explain certain innuendoes in the indictment respecting speculations, etc. This having been done he was interrogated as to what was generally understood by secret service money. He replied it meant money appropriated by a government generally for corrupt purposes, and in support of the government which gave it. On being asked if he considered the *Aurora* as hostile to the United States, he replied in the affirmative. In defence Livingston tried to prove that Frothingham was not responsible, and that the editor should have been arrested instead. Ogden Hoffman, who appeared for Hamilton, replied that even every journeyman was liable to prosecution, and Frothingham, as foreman, was especially so. The jury rendered a verdict of guilty with a recommendation to mercy, and the defendant was fined one hundred dollars, and given four months in Bridewell.[1]

Later we find Hamilton constantly writing for the many journals that appeared from time to time in the interest of the Federalist cause. There is no doubt that he worked in conjunction with William Cobbett, whose caustic pen made every one uncomfortable. Cobbett was an English subject who, though he lived among those who had just gained their independence, was ever loyal to the English king. He had

---

[1] A full account of this case, of which the above is an abstract, is given in Hudson's "Journalism in the United States from 1690–1872," p. 216.

been a private soldier in New Brunswick, and when he came
to Philadelphia, supported himself by giving English lessons
to the French *émigrés* who flocked from Santo Domingo, and
by these he earned from four to five hundred pounds per
annum.   He first took a shop in Philadelphia, publishing a
number of clever but stinging pamphlets, one being an attack
upon Dr. Priestley, who was driven out of England in
June, 1794,[1] and another entitled "A Bone to Gnaw for the
Democrats."   He also wrote "A Little Plain English and a
New Year's Gift to the Democrats."

Urged by Hamilton he, from 1794 to 1801, published a
paper called the *Weekly Political Register*, which remained
in existence from 1794 to 1800, when he returned to England
by way of New York, and died there in 1835.   Under the
pseudonym of *Peter Porcupine*, he bitterly attacked the
French and their American sympathizers, and warmly defended Washington, Hamilton, and others of the Federal
party.   His stay in Philadelphia was not entirely free from
turmoil and embarrassment, for upon several occasions he
narrowly escaped personal violence from those he had attacked.   During the yellow fever outbreak he severely criti-
cized Dr. Benjamin Rush, who was a popular idol, sneering
at his treatment of the plague by large doses of mercury
and bleeding.   He went further, and called Rush a *San-
grado*, for which offence suit was brought for libel, and
after two years judgment was recorded against Cobbett for
five thousand dollars.   This was too much for the journal,
which succumbed, and its editor transferred his activities to
a new field.

William Duane vied with Callender and Freneau in bitterness of invective, which was directed against the administrations of Washington and Adams, Hamilton always com-

[1] See chap. x, pp. 346 and 347.

ing in for his share. Duane's libels were so virulent that he was prosecuted under the Sedition Act, but the suit was allowed to drop.[1]

In November, 1801, several prominent Federalists, among them Hamilton, Troup, Richard Varick, Archibald Gracie, Samuel Boyd, and William Woolsey, established the *New York Evening Post*, which has remained in existence ever since. They were fortunate enough to command the services of William Coleman, a Bostonian and a clever and successful lawyer, who, for a short time, was a partner of Aaron Burr. So close was Hamilton's connection with the *Post* that pretty much everything in it relating to politics was ascribed to him, for it mercilessly attacked the Jeffersonians. Its columns were filled, not only with signed letters, but unsigned editorials and communications covering every political situation, and Coleman and Hamilton were ever on the outlook for the tricks of the other side. As illustrating the deliberation of their methods Hudson in his valuable work refers to the delay between the receipt of Thomas Jefferson's annual message in December, 1801, and its critical discussion five days later. After it had been digested it was gravely and forcibly torn to pieces in a letter signed *Lucius Crassus*, which was probably written by Hamilton.

Coleman was a pugnacious and witty adversary, and more than a match for Duane or Cheetham, both of whom were journalistic rivals, and upon one occasion expressed himself in the manner of the day as follows:

> "Lie on, Duane, lie for pay.
>   And Cheetham lie thou too,
> More against truth you cannot say
>   Than truth can say 'gainst you."

[1] See Appendix D.

This, or some other galling squib, led to the serious consequence of a challenge by Cheetham, the actual duel, however, being averted, as both antagonists were arrested by
order of Judge Brockholst Livingston, but allowed to go
free upon their promise to abandon the encounter.   However, within a few days, a Captain Thompson accused Coleman of cowardice in the Cheetham matter, was challenged
by the latter, and a duel was fought in Love Lane, which
is now Twenty-first Street, with the result that Thompson
was mortally wounded, and his antagonist returned to the
Evening Post office "and got out the paper in good style,
although half an hour late."

Coleman frankly admitted the influence of Hamilton in
the conduct of the *Post*.   Hilliard says "Jeremiah Mason
asked him (Coleman) who wrote or aided in the preparation
of certain articles; Coleman replied that he made no secret of
the fact that his paper was set up under the auspices of General Hamilton.   I then asked him, 'Does he write in your
paper?' 'Never a word.' 'How, then, does he assist?'
His answer was, 'Whenever anything occurs on which I
feel the want of information I state matter to him, sometimes in a note; he appoints a time when I may see him,
usually a late hour of the evening. He always keeps himself minutely informed on all political matters. As soon as
I see him he begins in a deliberate manner to dictate and
I to note down in shorthand; when he stops, my article is
completed.'"[1]

The bitterness of invective indulged in by the rival journals of both parties has never been approached since. From
May, 1803, to shortly before the duel with Burr the papers
were filled with venomous attacks upon every one, including
Hamilton and Burr.   In an issue of the *Portfolio*, a Federal-

[1] Hilliard's "Life of Jeremiah Mason," pp. 32, 33.

ist sheet, June 5, 1804, appears the following: "Wanted, for the *Aurora* service, three fellows without ears, two with backs flagrant from the beadle, one traitor, and a couple of Deists, none need apply but who can come well recommended from Newgate, or their last place.   N. B. Any young imp of sedition who would make a tolerable devil may have everything found him except his washing."

Angelica Church's continued unvarying interest in Hamilton's work is again shown in a letter written to her sister.

Angelica Church to Elizabeth Hamilton.

LONDON, *April 25,* 1788.

At last my dear Eliza I have the best grounded hopes that we shall pass the remainder of our lives in the same city, how many happy evenings have I already past! from dwelling on my future happiness!

Colonel Beckwith[1] tells me that our dear Hamilton writes too much and takes no exercise, and grows too fat.   I hate both the word and the thing, and I desire you will take care of his health and his good looks, why I shall find him on my return a dull, heavy fellow!

He will be unable to Flirt as Robert Morris; pray, Betsey, make him walk, and ride, and be amused.   You will see by some of Church's letters which have caused me to shed the most delicious tears of joy and gratitude, that it will not be long before we return to America.

Embrace poor dear Hamilton for me, it is impossible to know him, and not to wish him health and pleasure, and then I am really so proud of his merit and abilities, that even you, Eliza, might *envy my feelings.*

Adieu my dear friends, be happy.

And again later:

I am my dear Sister, extremely delighted with the hopes of seeing America happy, if the new constitution is acceded to

---

[1] Sir George Beckwith, from 1787 to 1791, when there was no British minister in the United States, acted in a diplomatic capacity.

we will enjoy it. I shall then have the prospect that my children will at least be happily settled in a country it has cost me so much to give up. Will you send me the newspapers regularly instead of sending me fruit, for it is generally spoiled, and the trouble getting it thro the custom house is immense, but the papers must be those that contain your husband's writings. Adieu my dear, embrace your *master* for me, and tell him that I envy you the fame of so clever a husband, one who writes so well; God bless him, and may he long continue to be the friend and the brother of your affectionate ANGELICA.

Hamilton was an omnivorous reader, for everywhere among his papers long lists of books of reference are to be found of the most varied nature, ranging from the classics to the novels of the day, and it is certain that they all played a part in much that he did and wrote. In the library left by him are to be found these books, amongst others: Hume's "Essays," "The Letters of Pliny," "Œuvres Posthumes de Frédéric, Roi de Prusse," "Traité Générale du Commerce," "Œuvres de Moliére," "Histoire de Turenne," "Gil Blas," "De la Felicité Publique," Diderot and D'Alemberts "Encyclopédie Méthodique," La Rochefoucauld-Liancourt's "Travels," *Journal des Etats Généraux*, "Plutarch's Lives," Hampton's "Polybius," Lord Chesterfield's "Letters," Voltaire, Winn's "History of America," Cicero's "Morals," Bacon's "Essays," Ralt's "Dictionary of Trade and Commerce," Montaigne's "Essays," Cudworth's "Intellectual System," "The Orations of Demosthenes," Hobbes's "Dialogues," Robertson's "Charles V," and Enticle's "History of the Late War", "The Works of Laurence Sterne," "The Works of Edward Gibbon," "The Connoisseur," Walpole's "Anecdotes," "Works of Sir Thomas Browne," Goldsmith's "Essays," "Hudibras," "The Works of St. Anselmo," "The Letters of Socrates," and Ruther-furd's "Institutes."

His studious tastes and habits drew forth the famous com-ment of Talleyrand, who one night passed Hamilton's win-dow and found him at work, and later wrote, "I have," he said, "seen a man who made the fortune of a nation, labor-ing all night to support his family."

He managed to devote a great deal of time to the study of the languages. Even as late as 1794 he further perfected himself in French with the aid of a Mr. Dornat, a Phil-adelphia teacher, although this seems a superfluity, for he always used this tongue in his talks with Volney, de Noailles, and the many other clever men who were driven from France, and who contributed to the charm of Philadelphia society. He subscribed for, and assiduously read, *La Chron-ique Mensuelle, Le Trône Mensuel*, and the *Journal Etoile*.[1]

The Churches, who were in England, were ever on the lookout for literature that might be of use to him, and Mrs. Church, in writing to her sister from London, February 4, 1790, says: "I shall send by the first ships every well-written book that I can procure on the subject of finance. I can-not help being diverted at the avidity I express to whatever relates to this subject." She sent him Adam Smith's "Wealth of Nations," and it is somewhat curious to find Sumner[2] saying, that Hamilton did not seem to have been guided by the works of Adam Smith, although the "best-known book of this writer" was in his library, nor does he seem to have read Hume's economic writings, nor the finan-cial essayists of the French. Though "he refers contemptu-

---

[1] Many of the French books in Hamilton's library were bequeathed to him by his friend and client William Constable. There were three hundred and forty in number and were collected in Paris during the French Revolution for Mr. Constable by the then American Consul Joseph Picarine.

[2] *Op. cit.*, p. 9.

ously to Turgot and Condorcet," who committed suicide by poison rather than go to the guillotine, he actually was influenced, according to one of his biographers, by John Law, who was an able but unscrupulous financier, the originator of the Mississippi Bubble, and responsible for much of the ruin of France during the reign of Louis XIV. When he wrote of John Law he was only twenty-two years old, but he recognized him then in a letter to James Duane as a person of "more penetration than integrity." Had he seen the Dutch caricatures of the Rue Quimquempoix or read Saint Simon's memoirs, it is doubtful if he would have taken John Law seriously.

Even Callender, one of his bitterest antagonists, admitted that "as a political writer Alexander Hamilton holds the same rank in America that Burke enjoys in England.[1]" Apart from the intrinsic merit of what he wrote his literary style was perfect, and did not partake of the florid and grandiloquent character of the productions of the latter part of the eighteenth century, and in many respects was quite his own. It was free from redundant verbiage, exceedingly direct, and he never was at a loss for words to clothe his new ideas. Sumner, whose praise is sometimes faint and often patronizing, says: "Hamilton was industrious. He wrote in a clear style although prolix." In reference to his work while at head-quarters during the Revolution he says that "he was capable of taking the General's orders and composing a letter, to publish them which would rank as of very high literary merit among the writings of those days."

Oliver,[2] whose insight into Hamilton's character is unusual for a foreigner, but is also valuable from the intelligence and knowledge of men displayed, says: "There is in all Hamil-

[1] "The History of the United States for 1796." Phila.: Snowden & McCorcle, 1797. [2] *Op. cit.*, p. 429.

ton's work—writings and speeches—the intense seriousness of youth. The qualities that made him a great statesman and a terrible combatant were force, lucidity, and conviction. His confidence in himself and in his ideas is amazing, amounting almost to fanaticism. If we seek for a complete presentment of the man in what he wrote and spoke we shall not find it. He treats his public ceremoniously and with reserve. An excessive gravity is the rule. Anger is the only passion which is permitted to appear; not a beam of humor, or a flash of wit. The whole procedure is stately and tense. This, also, is in accordance with the nature of youth." While to some extent this is true, and possibly Oliver has never had access to Hamilton's intimate correspondence, there are a few letters in existence that show the lighter vein in which he indulged. Among them are the breezy epistles to his wife, to her sister, and to the two or three French officers with whom he was on intimate terms. No better illustration of the occasional exercise of his graceful wit can be found than a letter to Miss Kitty Livingston, who seems to have been a rather light-headed and casual person. On one occasion, when she sought to secure his aid to enable certain friends to pass through the lines when the army was at Morristown, he replied:

Alexander Hamilton to Kitty Livingston.

HEADQUARTERS, *March* 18, 1779.[1]

I can hardly forgive an application to my humanity to induce me to exert my influence in an affair in which ladies are concerned, and especially when you are of the party. Had you appealed to my friendship or to my gallantry, it would have been irresistible. I should have thought myself bound to have set prudence and policy at defiance, and even to have attacked wind-mills in your ladyship's service. I

[1] Sedgwick's "Life of William Livingston," J. J. Harper, New York, 1833, p. 320.

am not sure but my imagination would have gone so far as to have fancied New York an enchanted castle—the three ladies so many fair damsels ravished from their friends and held in captivity by the spells of some wicked magician—General Clinton, a huge giant, placed as keeper of the gates—and myself, a valorous knight, destined to be their champion and deliverer.

But when, instead of availing yourself of so much better titles, you appealed to the cold, general principle of humanity, I confess I felt myself mortified, and determined, by way of revenge, to mortify you in turn. I resolved to show you that all the eloquence of your fine pen could not tempt our Fabius to do wrong; and, avoiding any representation of my own, I put your letter into his hands and let it speak for itself. I knew, indeed, this would expose his resolution to a severer trial than it could experience in any other way, and I was not without my fears for the event, but if it should decide against you, I anticipated the triumph of letting you see your influence had failed. I congratulated myself on the success of my scheme; for, though there was a harder struggle upon the occasion between inclination and duty, than it would be for his honor to tell; yet he at last had the courage to determine that, as he could not indulge the ladies with consistency and propriety, he would not run the risk of being charged with a breach of both. This he desired me to tell you, though, to be sure, it was done in a different manner, interlaced with many assurances of his great desire to oblige you, and of his regret that he could not do it in the present case, with a deal of stuff of the same kind, which I have too good an opinion of your understanding to repeat. I shall, therefore, only tell you that whether the Governor and the General are more honest or more perverse than other people, they have a very odd knack of thinking alike; and it happens in the present case that they both equally disapprove the intercourse you mention, and have taken pains to discourage it. I shall leave you to make your own reflections upon this, with only one more observation, which is that the ladies for whom you apply would have every claim to be gratified, were it not that it would operate as a bad precedent. But, before I conclude, it will be necessary to explain one point. This refusal supposes that the ladies mean only to make a visit and return to New York. If it should be their intention to remain with us, the case will be altered. There will be no rule against their coming out, and they will be an acquisition. But this is subject to two provisos—1st that they are not found guilty of treason or any misdemeanor punishable by the laws of the State, in which case the General[1] can have no power to protect them; and 2dly, that the ladies on our side do not apprehend any inconvenience from increasing their number. Trifling apart, there is nothing could give me greater pleasure than to have been able to serve Miss Livingston and her friends on this occasion, but circumstances really did not permit it. I am persuaded she has too just an opinion of the General's politeness not to be convinced that he would be happy to do anything which his public character would justify in an affair so interesting to the tender feelings of so many ladies. The delicacy of her own ideas will easily comprehend the delicacy of his situation;— she knows the esteem of her friend.

A. HAMILTON.

The General and Mrs. Washington present their compliments.

Hamilton was a busy letter writer, and many of the products of his pen remain as examples of the lost art of correspondence. His chirography was artistic, graceful, and quite characteristic of the man, while his pithy and well-turned phrases remind one of the perfect English of Addison. Hawthorne thus commented upon one of his letters in his analysis of a book of autographs:[2]

We turn another leaf, and find a memorial of Hamilton. It is but a letter of introduction, addressed to Governor Jay

---

[1] General George Washington, the Commander-in-Chief.
[2] "A Book of Autographs, Hawthorne's Writings", Old Manse Edition, vol. XVII, p. 346.

in favor of Mr. Davies, of Kentucky; but it gives an impression of high breeding and courtesy, as little to be mistaken as if we could see the writer's manner and hear his cultivated accents, while personally making one gentleman known to another. There is likewise a rare vigor of expression and pregnancy of meaning, such as only a man of habitual energy of thought could have conveyed into so commonplace a thing as an introductory letter.

His autograph is a graceful one, with an easy and picturesque flourish beneath the signature, symbolical of a courteous bow at the conclusion of the social ceremony so admirably performed.

Hamilton might well be the leader and idol of the Federalists; for he was pre-eminent in all the high qualities that characterized the great men of that party, and which should make even a Democrat feel proud that his country had produced such a noble old band of aristocrats; and he shared all the distrust of the people, which so inevitably and so righteously brought about their ruin.

It is almost superfluous to say that Hamilton's greatest literary work was done in writing the major part of *The Federalist*, and as years have rolled by the full credit has been accorded him. "It has," says one of his biographers, "long since been acknowledged to be the ablest treatise on our Constitution which has ever been or is ever likely to be written; and no person interested in such topics fails to become familiar with it or admire it." Hamilton's contributions were made at a trying time, when he was giving himself body and soul to the formation for, and adoption of, a Constitution by discontented patriots. Incidentally he went hither and thither to try his cases. These productions were composed under the most uncomfortable circumstances—in the cabin of a small Hudson River sloop; by the light of a dim candle in a country inn; in fact, they were regarded by their author only as essays for suggestive and contempo-

rary use. That there existed with Hamilton and his associates Madison and Jay some degree of uncertainty as to how
far they should go is shown by the introduction.

It is said that Hamilton, with Jay and others, at this very
time suppressed the Doctor's Mob, which took place on
April 13, 1787, on the occasion of the exposure of a part of
a human body in one of the windows of the New York Hos-
pital by young medical students who were engaged in dissection, and this riot was the culmination of great popular
indignation that had been caused by body snatching. It is
related by Lossing[1] that Hamilton had already been engaged
on *The Federalist*, and had written the fifth essay, but was
so badly injured by the rioters that he was laid up for a long
period. Though some of the Madison papers which he
contributed to *The Federalist* were published in the *New
York Packet and Daily Advertiser*, the bulk of them appeared,
eventually, in the *Independent Journal* and afterward in the
other papers.[2]

The *Independent Journal* was published by J. and A.
McLean of Hanover Square who, in 1788, collected the
essays and printed the book as a whole.

The original edition was in two volumes, sometimes bound
together, but there is nothing in it to indicate the authorship
of the many essays.

Despite the evident importance of the work it did not at
first have a large sale, although published at the moderate
price of six shillings; yet since its appearance it has gone
through many editions, has been translated into many languages, and a copy of the original first edition within a year
or two has brought at auction the sum of one hundred and
twenty dollars.

In this connection the following letter from the printers,

---

[1] "Pictorial Field Book of the Revolution," vol. I, p. 384.   [2] Appendix E.

who, apparently, found the venture anything but profitable, may be reproduced:

From Arch. McLean to Robert Troup

NEW YORK, *Oct.* 11*th*, 1788.

SIR: The inclosed Account is my charge for printing and binding *The Federalist.* When Coll. Hamilton, or the Gentlemen of the Committee examine the Work, they will find the charge exceeding low, considering the bulk of it.

When I engaged to do the work, it was to consist of twenty Numbers, or at the utmost twenty-five, which I agreed to print for thirty pounds, five hundred copies. I made my calculations accordingly and issued proposals, each Subscriber to pay six shillings.

The Work increased from 25 numbers to 85, so that instead of giving the subscribers one Vollume containing 200 pages for six shillings, I was obliged to give them two vollumes containing upwards of 600 pages.

The money expended for Printing, Paper, Journeyman's Wages and Binding was upwards of two hundred and twenty Pounds; of which sum I have charged Coll. Hamilton with 144 pounds, which is not three shillings per Vol; I have several hundred copies remaining on hand, and even allowing they were all sold at the low price I am obliged to sell them at, I would not clear five pounds on the whole impression. However I must abide by the consequances, nor could I expect the Gentlemen would make up a loss, which was sustained, in a great measure, by my own voluntary aid.

The many obligations, Sir, I lay under to you and Coll. Hamilton will ever be remembered, and I hope the amount will meet with the approbation of that Honorable Gentlemen.

I am, Sir, with the utmost respect your obliged, humble servant

ARCH. MCLEAN.

Robert Troup.

There is no doubt that its influence in the affairs of other nations and our own has been far-reaching and of the greatest

importance. The Baron Kaneko, one of the most learned
and advanced Japanese, who has had much to do with the
renaissance of his native land, told me that when the Japanese Constitution was framed, reference was frequently
made to *The Federalist,* which was considered by them to be
the greatest authority upon constitutional subjects extant.
It was of the greatest use to those who recently brought
about the unification of the South African Colonies, and I
am in receipt of a letter from Sir Walter Hely-Hutchinson,
who had always had so much to do with the reconciliation
of Boor and Britain.[1] Certainly with us to-day, especially
in the United States Courts, it is of valuable assistance to
many jurists. The opinions of competent critics are all in
accord, and Oliver speaks of this book as "one of the
most remarkable of human documents. . . . The crowning
merit of these papers, which were produced under great pressure—often while the printer's boy was waiting in the office—
is that they succeeded in accomplishing what they set out to
accomplish. They were the greatest forces that worked on
men's minds to make them consent to the adoption of the
Constitution."

Despite the assertion that Hamilton was lukewarm in regard to this instrument, Oliver[2] very properly says: "When
he signed it he became its champion, and afterward labored
to perfect it and make it possible, and to teach his fellow
citizens what he really meant."

Much controversial discussion has arisen as to the authorship of the different articles in this great work, and this
has often been acrimonious.[3]

---

[1] See Appendix F.   [2] *Op. cit.,* p. 167.

[3] In 1864 this fight became heated, for in that year Dawson's edition, to which Cabot Lodge gave his unqualified approval, because it contained many new features,
including a biographical introduction, synoptical table of contents, and various
notes, was published. Its appearance was immediately followed by a bitter attack

Henry B. Dawson, one of the greatest and most exact students of American history, in his edition of *The Federalist* has presented the different tables of contents, using the data in Hamilton's own handwriting given to Egbert Benson, that given to Chancellor Kent by Hamilton, the entries in the copies of the book left by Madison, which is now in the Congressional Library, and strangely enough bears the autograph of Mrs. Hamilton as well as that of Madison, and a list by Rush. He also had access to Kent's manuscript notes and Mr. Jay's "Recollections." There seems to be no dispute about the authorship of the first sixteen articles, but as to the others, there is some difference of opinion. As to these, the eighteenth, nineteenth, and twentieth are claimed by Madison to be entirely his own, while joint authorship was asserted on all occasions by Hamilton, and this claim was held by Ames, who knew much about the preparation of the book. All agree that the articles from twenty to thirty-seven, and from fifty-four to eighty-five inclusive, were from Hamilton's pen. Much unnecessary speculation has been indulged in as to what part Hamilton took in the preparation of Washington's Farewell Address,[1] and as to the qualifications of the two men. Some of the many who have discussed the matter have declared that it was wholly Hamilton's work, while others, among them John Jay, who were equally positive, have insisted that no other hand than that of the first President could have composed it. Jay, in writing to Judge

upon the part of John Jay, the grandson of one of the original contributors. It had been Dawson's object to use the original text and to utilize the manuscripts of Madison, Jefferson, Chancellor Kent, and Rush. Jay's rejoinder to Dawson's prospectus was so offensive that it was withdrawn and destroyed.

[1] Timothy Pickering wrote to one of Hamilton's sons in 1829 in reference to an interview he had with Chief Justice Marshall, February 10, 1811: "In conversation this day with Chief Justice Marshall, he said that he had read the whole of General Washington's *private* correspondence; and expressed his astonishment at the vast portion of it from General Hamilton—that he could, in addition to his official labors, write so much that was not official."

Richard Peters early in 1811, takes this position. Richard Peters wrote to Jay in February, 1811, stating that a copy of the Farewell Address in Hamilton's handwriting had been found among the latter's papers, and that another copy had been found in the possession of "a certain gentleman" in the same handwriting. To this Jay replied, that "this intelligence is unpleasant and unexpected," and went on to say that it may be presumed from these facts that General Hamilton was the real and the President only the reputed author. This he doubts, for the reason that Washington was "a character not blown up into transient splendour by his great and memorable deeds, but stands, and will forever stand, a glorious monument of human excellence." He then proceeds to argue further that "it was impossible for the President, because of his very greatness and the excellence of all his virtues and his familiarity with all the public affairs, to be anything else than the author of the document. But his ability to write well need not be proved by the application of maxims (which he quotes); it is established by facts. We are told to judge a tree by its fruit; let us, in like manner, judge of his pen by its performance." After this he proceeds to give the history as it was known to him, to wit: Some time before the address appeared Colonel Hamilton told Jay he had received a letter from Washington, with a draft of a farewell address which the latter had prepared, and on which was required an opinion. An appointment was made and kept, and Hamilton told Jay that he had read the address, and the "easiest and best" way was to leave the draft untouched and in its fair state, and to write the whole over with such amendments, alterations, and corrections as he thought were advisable, and that he had done so. It was read over and agreed to by both and met with "mutual approbation." There was one provision that did not meet with Jay's approval, and he hints at it in a letter to the President.[1]   Binney[2] has reviewed the whole matter of the authorship, and Ford[3] has published nearly all the correspondence.   James A. Hamilton has produced copies of letters from Washington to Hamilton, and *vice versa*, which certainly prove that the major part of the final adopted address was the work of Hamilton.   Oliver[4] who, it must be admitted, is a capable, historical scholar, goes so far as to say, "In September, 1796, Washington issued his Farewell Address, one of the most famous documents in American history, and this also was from Hamilton's pen."   Binney says Washington was undoubtedly the original designer of the Farewell Address.   The fundamental thought and principles were his, but he was not the composer or writer of the paper.

It will be seen that many of these conclusions were not based upon facts but impressions, and the actual conversation between Hamilton and Washington certainly favors the assumption that Hamilton's part was the chief one, even if documentary evidence of another kind is lacking.   After his father's death, James A. Hamilton diligently sought confirmation from those who had known him, and were conversant with the circumstances.

George Cabot, of Boston, wrote to the latter: "When that address was published, it was understood among your father's friends that it was written by him.   It was, however, considered important that it should have the influence of Washington's name and character, and I must advise that until

---

[1] "The Life of John Jay, with Selections from His Correspondence," etc., by his son, William Jay, New York, 1833, vol. II, p. 336.   Also "Inquiry into the Formation of Washington's Farewell Address," September, 1859.

[2] "The Life of Horace Binney," by C. C. Binney, p. 287, 1903, Philadelphia.

[3] "The Writings of George Washington," by W. C. Ford.   Putnam's, New York, vol. XIII, pp. 190, 193, 194, 221, 264, 269.

[4] *Op. cit.*, p. 351.

it has ceased to do its work, the question of the authorship should not be discussed."

William Coleman, the editor of the *New York Evening Post*, in a letter to the same person written October 21, 1824, says:

"Colonel Troup told me that on entering your father's office one morning he found him earnestly engaged in preparing a composition which he told me was the Farewell Address; that it was nearly finished; that he actually *read the MSS. or heard* it read, and that it was the original of what afterward appeared in print under the name of 'Washington's Farewell Address.'"

Some extracts from letters that passed between Washington and Hamilton, and collected by James A. Hamilton, may be reproduced. These, after Hamilton's death, remained in possession of Rufus King, and came into my uncle's hands only after the threat of a lawsuit. Why they should have been withheld can only be accounted for by the supposition that it had been determined by a coterie of friends to give Washington the full credit for the address. They certainly show that there was collaboration at least, and probably that much of the original material, and many of the suggestions, originated with Hamilton.[1]

Hamilton to Washington, July 30, 1796 [2]

I have the pleasure to send you a certain draft which I have made as perfect as my time and engagement would permit. It has been my object to render this act importantly and lastingly useful, and avoiding all cause of present exception to embrace such reflections and sentiments as will

---

[1] Appendix G.

[2] These letters appeared in the "Reminiscences of James A. Hamilton," a book that had so limited a circulation that I may be pardoned for reproducing them. Some of them also appear in Ford's Washington's letters.

wear well, progress in approbation with time, and redound to future reputation. How far I have succeeded you will judge. If you should intend to take the draft now sent, and after perusing, and noting anything you wish changed, send it to me, I will with pleasure shape it as you desire. This may also put it in my power to improve the expression, and perhaps in some instances condemn.

Washington to Hamilton, August 10, 1796

The principal design of this letter, is to inform you that your favor of the 30th ult, with its enclosure, came safely to hand by the last post, and that the latter shall have the most attentive consideration I am able to give it. A cursory reading it has had, and the sentiments therein contained are exceedingly just and such as ought to be inculcated.

Washington to Hamilton, August 26, 1796

I have given the paper herein enclosed, several serious and attentive readings, and prefer it greatly to the other drafts, [his own included] being more copious on material points, more dignified on the whole, and with less egotism; of course less exposed to criticism, and better calculated to meet the eye of discerning readers, and foreigners particularly, whose curiosity I have no doubt will lead them to inspect it attentively, and to pronounce their opinions on the performance.

Washington to Hamilton, September 1, 1796

About the middle of last week I wrote to you, and that it might escape the eye of the inquisitive, (for some of my letters have lately been pried into), I took the liberty of putting it under cover to Mr. Jay. Since then revolving over the paper that was enclosed therein on the various matters it contained, and on the just expression of the advice or recommendation which was given in it, I have regretted that another subject, (which in my estimation is of interesting concern to the well being of the country) was not touched upon also.   I mean *Education* generally as one of the surest means of enlightening and giving just ways of thinking to our citizens; but particularly the establishment of a University.

Hamilton's Reply

The idea of the University is one of those which I think will be most properly reserved for your speech at the opening of the session.

Washington to Hamilton, September 6, 1796

If you think the idea of a University had better be reserved for a speech at the opening of the session, I am content to defer the communication of it until that period, but even in *that case I could pray you as soon as convenient* to make a draft for the occasion.

Washington to Hamilton

The draft now sent comprehends the most if not all these matters, is better expressed, and I am persuaded goes as far as it ought with respect to any personal mention of myself.

I should have seen no occasion myself for its undergoing a revision, but as your letter of the 30th ult., which accompanied it, intimates a wish to do this, and knowing that it can be more correctly done after a writing has been out of sight for some time than while it is in the hands of its author, I send it in conformity thereto. . . . If change or alteration takes place in the draft let them be so clearly interlined, erased, or referred to in the margin, that no mistake may be made in copying it for the press.

To what editor in *this* city do you think it had best be sent for publication ?   Will it be proper to accompany it with a note to him expressing . . . or if you think the first not eligible let me ask you to sketch such a note as you may judge applicable to the occasion.[1]

[1] Also see Hamilton's draft of the Farewell Address in Ford's "Writings of George Washington," vol. XIII, p. 277 and the completed MS. Address in the New York Public Library purchased from the printer by the late James Lenox.

It is to be regretted that Hamilton made a great mistake when he wrote his letter censuring John Adams. Not only was the act a foolish one, but it can hardly be realized how a man possessing, ordinarily, such good judgment could make what was almost a hysterical attack upon another public character, no matter how great the provocation. The pamphlet appeared in 1800, and created great excitement among his brother Federalists who, upon its appearance, quickly advised him to suppress it. This he tried to do, but Burr, securing a copy, immediately flooded the market with others bearing upon the title-page "Re-printed Pro-Bono-Public." It was an abusive attack upon Adams, which was tactless in the extreme, and gave his enemies an opportunity to unmercifully gore him. The inconsistency of abusing Adams, and then, in a half-hearted way, advising the Federalists to vote for him, was a glaring political error, and can only be explained by a state of mind largely induced by his own private sorrows, and the growing desperation which was the outgrowth, not only of the dissensions in his own party, but a gain in the strength of the anti-Federalists, whose arrows were, anew, dipped in venom. The most irritating of his critics were Callendar and Cheetham. In an "answer" from the latter it is suggested to Hamilton that his dislike of Adams arose from the fact that he had not been appointed Commander-in-Chief. "Have you dreamt," said Callendar, "that you possessed the martial qualities of a Frederick and a Marlborough, a Turenne and a martial Saxe? Let the hour of vigilance inform you, that your imagination must have been intoxicated by the most delirious vanity." This was especially unjust and untruthful, as Washington's only insistence in reorganizing the army was that Hamilton should be senior of the three major-generals, though Adams objected. Hamilton never aspired to be Commander-in-

Chief, and there is nothing on record to even support this claim. Even after Hamilton's death the attacks upon him did not cease, and within three months after the fateful eleventh of July some doggerel verse called the "Hamiltoniad" was published, which viciously ridiculed him as well as his friends.

The tendency to versification so general in the eighteenth century was shared by Hamilton, a few of whose fragmentary productions remain. One of these possesses a certain interest from the fact that he was but fifteen years old when the verses were written. It appears that he sat up with the young child of his friend and adviser, Elias Boudinot, during its fatal illness, and after its death prepared the following for the sorrowing mother. Only as an example of a precocious effusion are they presented.

> For the sweet babe, my doating heart
> Did all a Mother's fondness feel;
> Carefull to act each tender part
> And guard from every threatening ill.
>
> But what a loss availed my care?
> The unrelenting hand of death,
> Regardless of a parent's prayr
> Has stopped my lovely Infant's breath.
>
> With rapture number o'er thy charms
> While on thy harmless sports intent
> [*Illegible*]
> Or pratling in my happy arms.
>
> No more thyself Important tale
> Some embryo meaning shall convey
> Whilst, should th' imperfect accents fail
> Thy speaking looks would still d'play.

Thou'rt gone, forever gone—yet where;
Oh! pleasing thought; to endless bliss.
Then why Indulge the rising tear
Cans't thou, fond heart, lament for this?

Little babe thou enteredst the world weeping while
all around you smiled; continue so to live, that
you may depart in smiles while all around you
weep.

His interest in educational institutions is well known, and
in 1792, with others, he founded an Indian school at Oneida,
and his name headed the list of trustees. This has since
become Hamilton College. His public services were appreciated by many universities which have since become
famous. As early as 1788 Columbia College, empowered
by act of Legislature, made him a Doctor of Law, while the
same honor was conferred by Dartmouth in 1790. In the
archives of this college is an autograph letter written from
Philadelphia and dated January 18, 1791, sending thanks
to Dr. Wheelock, then the president, for this compliment.
In 1791 the College of New Jersey, now Princeton, gave him
this degree, and in 1792 both Harvard and Brown Universities followed the example of the other institutions. In reply
to the president, the Reverend Joseph Willard, of Harvard,
Hamilton wrote from Philadelphia, September 6, 1792: "The
honour which has been done me by the Overseers of the
antient and justly celebrated institution, over which you preside, is appreciated by me, as it merits, and receives my most
cordial acknowledgement. Among the many painful circumstances, that surround a station like mine—this flattering
mark of the esteem of a body—so respectable—is a source
both of satisfaction and consolation." At a meeting of the
American Philosophical Society, the oldest scientific body in

America, held January 21, 1791, "The U. S. Secretary & Treasurer, Alexander Hamilton, was elected a member of this Society." At the same meeting Attorney-General Randolph, Alexander Addison, Albert Gallatin, and others became members.

At a meeting held April 4, 1800, the Rev. Dr. Collier made a statement of the sums received by him to aid Michaux's projected expedition. That he had received April 13, 1793, a donation of $12.50 from Alexander Hamilton, George Washington $25, Robert Morris $20, Thomas Jefferson $12.50, etc."

As a public speaker Hamilton was regarded by all his contemporaries in the same way—and no praise seems to have been too great.

A person who was very familiar with Hamilton's methods in this respect was Chancellor James Kent. Though he was Hamilton's junior by seven years, they were always close and intimate friends. "Hamilton," said Kent, "generally spoke with great earnestness and energy, and with considerable and sometimes vehement gesture. His language was clear, nervous and classical. He went to the foundation and reason of every doctrine which he examined, and he brought to the debate a mind richly adorned with all the learning that was applicable."

Lodge writes:[1] "There was certainly no one who was in active public life during the same period, unless it be John Adams, or Fisher Ames on one memorable occasion, who could compare with him as an orator"; and again: "It is very plain, too, that Hamilton's success in this direction was by no means wholly due to what he said or to his power of reasoning and of lucid and forcible statement. The man was impressive."

[1] *Op. cit.*, p. 273.

There is little information as to how Hamilton actually
looked and spoke, if we may except what James Kent has
said.   It is certain from such knowledge as we possess that
he was eminently fair in his arguments, and always fully
presented both sides of the question—his trial notes show
this.   He was always explanatory, and did not cloud the
issue by a flow of turgid or high-flown rhetoric.   It would
appear that his appeals and his statement of any case had the
effect of a great narration, and then after drawing his conclusion there was often an impassioned burst of eloquence.
As Morse says, "When he closed he left upon his hearers the
impression, generally correct, that they had been over the
whole ground—not over selected parts."   Though slight and
of comparatively small stature, he was forceful and impressive, and had the full powers of suggestion and fascination.
In fact he made his hearers believe as he did.

CHAPTER IV

ELIZABETH HAMILTON

VERY little is known about the early life of Elizabeth Hamilton, and we are dependent for information chiefly upon the writings of those Frenchmen who were entertained at General Schuyler's house at Albany, and the diary of Tench Tilghman. She was the second daughter of Philip Schuyler, and was born August 9, 1757, within a year of her husband. Her mother was Catherine van Rensselaer, daughter of Colonel John R. van Rensselaer, who was the son of Hendrik, the grandson of Kiliaen, the first Patroon, and Engeltke (Angelica) Livingston.

Tench Tilghman thus gives his impressions of the girl, who then must have been sixteen or eighteen years of age: "In the afternoon, having taken leave of my host, I called at the General Schuyler's to pay my compliments to the General, his Lady and Daughters. I found none of them at home except Miss Betsey Schuyler, the General's second daughter, to whom I was introduced by Mr. Commissary Livingston, who accompanied me. I was prepossessed in favor of this young lady the moment I saw her. A Brunette with the most good natured, dark, lovely eyes that I ever saw, which threw a beam of good temper and benevolence over her Entire Countenance. Mr. Livingston informed me that I was not mistaken in my Conjecture for she was the finest tempered Girl in the World."[1] Unlike her eldest sister, An-

[1] "Memoirs of Lieut.-Col. Tench Tilghman," etc., pp. 89 *et seq.* Albany, N. Y.: J. Munsell, 1876.

gelica, who had gone to New Rochelle to the best school available at the time, Elizabeth had but few educational advantages and all her later correspondence shows deficiency of early training, though it was nothing unusual to find misspelling in most of the letters of the young women of the period, even those of Martha Washington being conspicuous in this respect, and perhaps worse than many of the others. Though lacking the superficial grace and accomplishments of many of her more sprightly and dashing friends, she must have possessed a quiet charm of her own. From all accounts she was gentle and retiring, yet full of gayety and courage, fond of domestic affairs, and probably her mother's chief assistant in the management of the house and slaves. From early childhood she should have been accustomed to the sight of weapons, and have early learned the necessity for prompt alertness, for the Indians, at times, terrorized the district, and a sleepy existence was unknown. One of her sisters, Mrs. Cochran, made the thrilling rescue of a younger child when the Schuyler place was raided by the savages, and even to-day the banister rail of the old house bears the scar of the tomahawk hurled at her as she dashed up the stairs, with her baby sister in her arms. Her father's military career undoubtedly brought stirring accounts of heroic duties, of long-suffering, and privation into the busy home, and to these vivid, childish impressions may have been due the unquenchable spirit she afterward exhibited under agonizing tests. As is well known, the Schuyler home, at Albany, was practically an open house during the Revolution, and the younger daughters must have been incessantly occupied, supervising the arrangements for their many military guests, and providing gayety immeasurable in those days of haste and stress. English, French, and Americans alike seem to have carried away pleasant impressions of Betsey's intelli-

ELIZABETH HAMILTON: AGE 28

From a painting by Ralph Earle in 1787

be immediately removed from our neighborhood, or that some other nymph qualified to maintain an equal sway come into it. By dividing her empire it will be weakened and she will be much less dangerous when she has a rival equal in charms to dispute the prize with her. I solicit your aid.

The girl friends of Elizabeth Schuyler, among others, included Kitty Livingston, the youngest daughter of Governor William Livingston of New Jersey, and Gertrude, the daughter of Robert R. Livingston. The latter married General Morgan Lewis, who afterward became a distinguished jurist. The letters that passed between these friends in some measure indicate the relations that existed between them at a time when letter writing was more in vogue than it is to-day. The first two were probably written when Elizabeth Schuyler was at her father's head-quarters at Morristown in 1780.

Kitty Livingston to Elizabeth Schuyler

MY DEAR GIRL: I wrote you a long thoughtless letter some days since; did you receive it? My happy Brother was this day, eight days, the Father of a little Cherib, who bears every appearance of Health and good humor. Apropos Cushion, Dash, and Bear, are in the possession of Mrs. Duncan of Philadelphia. I will be much obliged to you to buy me thread of such sorts as are most useful to yourself. As you have not yet answered my last, I presume you will embrace this opportunity of writing; one thing more and I will excuse you; Will you if you have any conveyance to Mr. Lott's, send my Compliments to Mrs. Lott and let her know the above important intelligence?

Fare Well dear Bess, believe me most affectionately
your
Friend KITTY LIVINGSTON.
Valley of Lebanon, 13th of May, 1779.
Present my love to Mrs. and Dr. Cochran.[1]

---

[1] Dr. John Cochran, who married Gertrude Schuyler.

*Kitty Livingston to Elizabeth Hamilton, then at Head-quarters
at New Windsor*

RHINEBECK, *February* 7, 1781.

MY DEAR BETSY: Willing to avail myself of an opportunity
I this moment heard of, I take my pen with pleasure to assure
my dear Girl, no one can be more sincere than her Friend
Kitty, in every Kind and tender wish for her felicity. I
should not have thus long delayed answering your agreeable
Favor, had a safe conveyance been in my power, tho' if I were
inclined to plead a bad example, or an excuse yours would
naturally occur.

I have just returned from a most delightful ride, the
weather was divine, the season seems to have lost its usual
vigor, and Winter wears no frowns. I believe in my heart,
the world, tiring of revolving the same course since the
Creation, and seeing all things changing but itself, has by
some extraordinary effort taken a leap nearer the Sun, and
we are now where Maryland should be, Lady Kitty[1] declares
she has not yet got thoroughly cooled, since August last, and
one would from motives of benevolence wish to prepare her
to endure the heats of Summer, which appears to be fast approaching. She and Miss Brown are at Clermont whither
I repair tomorrow.

Present my compliments to Colonel Hamilton and assure
him of my best wishes, though I feel myself much hurt at an
assertion he made some time since at Mr. D.——'s—that I
was soon to be connected to Mr. C.——

I have lately received (tho' the date was not a very early
one) a long letter from my friend Angelica,[2] and she continues
to love, and to tell me so in terms so tender, so well adapted
to the constancy and purity of her affection, that I do not at
all fear absence will lessen our Friendship, or time render it
less interesting and sincere. She is in short the most amiable
of women, and when I cease to think her so, my nature or hers
must change.

---

[1] Lady Kitty Stirling.   [2] Angelica Church.

I have purchased your apron and will if possible send it on by the person who takes this. I enclose my measures for a pair of shoes. Putman makes them at Phi——a as well as *Boston*. If I did not know an apology made a bad thing worse, I would endeavor to say something in behalf of this poor letter, pray do not let Colonel Hamilton see it. His forte is writing I too well know, to submit anything I can say tonight to his inspection—from your Friendship I know I have nothing to dread—

Farewell, my dear Eliza
believe your affectionate
Friend
CATH. LIVINGSTON.

Disappointed in the conveyance mentioned I send this per post and with Miss Brown's love to you, and Family will present my most respectful compliments to Mrs. & Gen'l W.— My love to Mrs. Cochran—Pray do you talk of a Jaunt to New York? I have heard such a rumor, if you do say everything from me to Ann that you Know I would myself repeat,— How is Col. Tilghman? Miss Brown says very ill. I hope he is recovering—Farewell once more, I wish I could tell you so in person

Ever yours
KITTY LIVINGSTON.

Clermont, February 11th.

Miss Kitty appears to have been a belle, and something of a coquette. She certainly was not as sedate as her sister Susan who married John Jay, and it may be inferred from her father's letters and that sent to Hamilton and printed elsewhere, that she was somewhat spoiled and generally, if possible, had her own way. During a visit to Philadelphia in August, 1779, her father wrote:[1] "I know there are a number of flirts in Philadelphia equally famed for their want of modesty as want of patriotism who will

[1] *Op. cit.*, p. 338.

triumph in our complaisance to the red-coat prisoners lately arrived in that Metropolis. I hope none of my connexions will imitate them either in the dress of their heads or the still more tory feelings of their hearts."

Mrs. Morgan Lewis to Elizabeth Hamilton

MY DEAR FRIEND: It is not my intention by writing this to engage you in a settled Correspondence with a person so useless to you, and in a situation so eventless as I am here tho' such a commerce would be highly agreeable to me, I am not so selfish as to make the request, yet I Flatter myself that notwithstanding these disadvantages this testimony of my love and regard will not be received with indifference by you for whom I feel the warmest sentiments that the most perfect esteem and Friendship can inspire.

Tho' I have long loved you My Dear Eliza yet I think you was never so Dear to me as now that we are about to be separated without a prospect of meeting soon. Sure I owe it to some Evil Genius that I am thus deprived of the pleasure of being more with one to whose Company and conversation I owe many of the happiest hours of my life. I know of nothing that will make up the loss of your Society to me but as I have a Mind naturally disposed to be Cheerful I will turn my thoughts to that which will give me most Comfort, and will cherish the hope that you will sometimes think of your absent Friend with affection forgetting her faults and remembering her Chief merit which is that she Knows how to love and value you. I have also a peculiar pleasure in reflecting that our Friendship has been Constant, uninterrupted by suspicion or envy, tho I am very conscious that you excel me in all that has any claim to applause yet I take a pride in hearing you commended for Virtues I imitate very imperfectly.

I had some faint hope of seeing you at N. Y. but was disappointed by Mr. Lewis[1] being obliged to attend the Court at Albany this I regret very much tho tis a sad Consolation to

---

[1] Morgan Lewis, afterward presiding judge in the Croswell case.

take leave. I did not hear you was at Albany till I heard you was about to leave it or I should have endeavored to have seen you there. Mr. Lewis has this Day set out for that place and has left my little Peggy and me alone, she is now asleep and I with neither Talents nor Topics to entertain you cannot quit scribbling because it cheers my solitude as I seem to be talking to you And forget that you are perhaps two hundred miles from me but wherever you are my Heart is with you I wish it was in my power to serve you that I might shew you how much my actions would exceed my profession.

Have the goodness to commend me to Col. Hamilton and the Dear Children in whose Welfare I take a lively interest tell the Renowned Philip[1] I have been told that he has outstript all his Competitors in the race of Knowledge and that he dayly gains new Victorys by Surpassing himself but that with all his acquirements he can not *decline* his lesson. Excuse this Folly.

With your usual Friendship and goodnature excuse what is wrong in this letter, I never could write.

Farewel to you whom I love for all that can create affection and esteem accept of every good wish that an Heart alive to the tenderest sensation can breathe from

October 17, 1800.   Yours G. Lewis.

The surroundings and circumstances of Elizabeth Schuyler's life had all tended to prepare her for her future as Hamilton's wife. Had she been any other than what she was, despite all his genius and force of character, Hamilton could never have attained the place he did. His letters show deference to her judgment and opinion, so we may conclude that he confided all his thoughts and plans, and made her a party to much that he did, yet his tender concern for her must have spared her many worries, and the knowledge of much that was harrassing in his career. There is a general solicitude in

---

[1] The first son of Alexander and Elizabeth Hamilton.

his letters and especially in the last two he ever wrote, which are the saddest of all. From many short letters and notes that remain it is evident that he apprised her of all his movements both in the field and afterward, and the conditions of his affairs.

She was remarkable for her piety, benevolence, and sympathy for every form of distress. She and Hamilton seem to have been agreed on that point all through their married life. When Philadelphia was filled with French *émigrés*, they both were among the first to give, and many widows and orphans were assisted with money and clothing. I have found an old subscription paper of this kind containing many interesting names of prominent persons connected with the early history of America, which is worthy of introduction and is in Hamilton's handwriting. The "Mary Morris" who heads the list was the wife of Robert Morris, the financier:

List of French Distressed Persons

1. Madame le Grand with two Children lives near the little Market at the house of Mr. Peter French, Hatter, in the greatest Indigence.
2. Madame Demarie blind with a daughter who is a widow, and a little Child, No. 19 Cedar Street in dreadful distress.
3. Madame Noel 7 Children and an orphan of whom she takes charge, Mulbery Street No 223—has not yet experienced so great extremity as the former, but is at present without money and owes 26 Dollars.
4. Madame Robard with 4 Children.
5. Madame Benoit with two both in the greatest indigence. Their residence at present unknown—

Subscriptions for the Relief of the foregoing persons————————————(viz)

Mary Morris	10 dollars
Eliza Hamilton	20 dollars
M. Cazenove	Ten dollars

Susan Kean . . . .   5 dollars
Cash . . . .   10 Dollars
Dr. Huger[1] 5 Dollars.50
Ann H. Livingston . . . .   3 Dollars
O. Stewart . . . .   Five dollars
paid L. Knox . . . .   Ten Dollars
pd. D. M. Smith . . . . - . . . .   five Dollars
pd. Dalton . . . .   five Dollars
pd. I. Williams . . . .   five Dollars
pd Cash . . . .   5 Dollars
pd. H. Breck . . . .   ten Dollars
pd. R. Izard . . . .   Five Dollars.50
pd. E. Lageremme . . . .   Five Dollars
pd. Y. Z. . . . . Fifteen Dollars
Paid—Capt. . . . .   5 Dollars
paid—Eliz[h] Powel   10 Dollars
paid—T. L. . . . .   8 dollars
paid—Eliz[h] Cabot . . . .   5 Dollars.
                                              R. K. 46.
R. King—   5 Dollars paid R. K.
O. Ellsworth . . . . 5 Dollars paid R. K.
P. Butler . . . . 5 Dollars paid R. K.
M. Coxe   . . . . 3 Dollars paid.
Nohitosidos   . . . . 5 Drs.
John Guest gives   10 Doll.

As one who knew Elizabeth Hamilton said: "Hers was
a strong character with its depth and warmth, whether
of feeling or temper controlled, but glowing underneath,
bursting through at times in some emphatic expression.
Hers was a stern ordeal; within a few years she experienced
the shock of two violent deaths by duels—those of her
eldest son and husband, the death of her sister and mother
and father; her eldest daughter's insanity, and with this,
little or no means with which to support and educate her
family of seven children, five growing sons, her invalid
daughter and a younger daughter.   No wonder the light of

[1] Who helped Lafayette to escape from the prison of Olmutz.

youth had vanished from her face when the widow's cap replaced the Marie Antoinette coiffure." From the rapidity with which her children came she must have had little or no time for social pleasures, although much of her early married life was spent in Philadelphia and New York, where her husband was either taking part in the affairs of the government or practising law. Her sister writes to the former place from London: "Do you live as pleasantly at Philadelphia as you did at New York? or are you obliged to bear the formalities of female circles, and their trifling chit chat? To you who have at home the most agreeable Society in the World, how you must smile at their manner of losing [their?] time—"

She was, undoubtedly, most energetic, and possessed a great deal of the Dutch tenacity, for she lived to the great age of ninety-seven with apparently no diminution of intelligence, still continuing to take interest in public affairs and the careers of her children, and writing letters even after her ninetieth year, which, despite a little tremulousness, were all they should be so far as intelligent expression was concerned. It cannot be denied that Hamilton made money easily, and that he had very grand ideas which it took a long purse to materialize. That he was something of a spendthrift is shown in his purchase of much real estate, and the preparation of a somewhat magnificent scheme for his country place in the upper part of Manhattan. It was probably his wife who made him more conservative than he would have been without such a check. McHenry, in a letter to Hamilton, said of her: "She has as much merit as your Treasurer as you have as Treasurer of the wealth of the United States."[1] Still, when Hamilton was prosperous after he had become fairly

[1] "Life and Letters of James McHenry," etc., by B. C. Steiner. Cleveland: Burrows Bros. & Co., 1907.

launched in the practice of law they lived comfortably but evidently quite up to their income, which, in those days, was large.

Angelica Church, in writing from Putney, October 5, 1796, to her sister says: "Colonel Nobel is returned very much pleased by his reception in New York, and has assured me that you republican Ladys live with as much splendour and expense as her slaves. I do not mean this for you dear Eliza who have a better taste."

Other letters of Mrs. Church indicate the affectionate relations of the two sisters.

Angelica Church to Elizabeth Hamilton.

PARIS, *Jan.* 27, 1784.

DEAR SISTER: I have written to you twice since I have been at Paris but have not received a line from you or Col. Hamilton. I intended to have called my little girl Eliza after Mr. Church's mother, but she thinks Angelica a much prettier name. Mr. Church is also of that opinion, but I promise that the next girl I make shall be called Betsey.

I should like Paris exceedingly if it was nearer to America, for I have a very agreeable sett of acquaintance, particularly a Madame de Ture who is a great admirer of our dear papa. She says he is the most amiable man in the Continent. Mr. Franklin[1] has the gravel, and he desires to return to America; they talk of Papa or Col. Hamilton as his successor, how would you like to cross the Atlantic, is your lord a Knight of Cincinnati. It has made a most wonderful noise here, but it is remarked that the order will probably exist in France when it will be neglected in America.

Adieu, my dear Betsy, I embrace you with all my heart, give my Compliments to Col. & Mrs. Lewis[2] and Mrs. Montgomery, and do me the favor to write to me very often.

[1] Benjamin Franklin.
[2] Col. Morgan Lewis. Mrs. Lewis was a sister of Mrs. Montgomery, the widow of General Richard Montgomery, killed before Quebec.

Mrs. Jay[1] lives in a small house very clean and neat about half a mile from Paris. The Americans have the pleasure to drink tea with her once a week. Tell Colonel Hamilton if he does not write to me that I shall be very angry.   A. C.

Ten years later she wrote:

Angelica Church to Elizabeth Hamilton

LONDON, *December* 11, 1794.

I received my dear Eliza, a short but very kind letter from my brother, dated Bedford. During his absence, my love, I know that you have been very unhappy and I have often thought of you with more than common tenderness.

Do you believe there is hope of your going to New York to live for life. If you remain at Philadelphia, I must be there. My inclinations lead me to prefer New York, my affections where you reside, but altogether for my love to You Eliza, my dear, Hamilton has his share in this determination, you see that I make no plans without your advice.

It is an age since I have had a letter from Mrs. Craig, pray tell her so, I am informed it is much more expensive living in Philadelphia than in cities of the same size in England. I wish you would employ some idle man of your acquaintance to send me a list of prices of articles in daily use, I receive so many applications for information, and I am ashamed to be so very ignorant as I am on this subject, it would be very amiable, my dear, to write me *long* letters and to think how much they console me in your absence.

I send you a letter which you will oblige me by having carefully delivered. I never heard of Mrs. Cochran.[2] If she is alive, pray tell her that I inquired after her. Catherine[3]

[1] Mrs. John Jay.

[2] Evidently a satirical reference to her sister Gertrude.

[3] Her daughter. Angelica Church later wrote (Putney, Dec. 6, 1796): "Catherine is proud of Alexander's commendation and with reason, for he is the arbiter of wit and elegance, it is not a female mind not to believe herself deserving; his praises have made a powerful impression: I have, when much older, been very vain of them."

has a cold and slight fever, or she meant to have written you. Why did you not let Mr. Trumbull[1] draw your picture for me? He has Mrs. Washington's which is wonderfully like her. I looked at it with a sentiment of gratitude for her many acts of kindness when I was in America with you. My dear, if you think proper present my respects to her and the general. A long letter, my dear sister, will be the best New Year's gift that I can receive.

When you see Messrs. Baumetz and Talleyrand tell them that they are indeed American citizens, I know it from their having forgot to write to their absent friends, their friend Madam Adele is still in Switzerland and there likely to continue from the difficulties of traveling. I am very sorry to trouble you with my confessions, you have spoiled me Eliza.

Pray let Angelica[2] learn French. A person who speaks the language well might teach her giving her a lesson an hour every day. Adieu, my dear, embrace your children for me, I long to have that pleasure myself. My family join in love with you and adieu,

Your affectionate sister,

A. C.

Has Peggy[3] been to Philadelphia or must she always be within the sound of the Dutch bell?[4]

After her husband's death Mrs. Hamilton's life seems to have been devoted not only to her numerous charities, but to the ceaseless and vigilant efforts, to the end that her husband should receive full justice, that his memory should be vindicated, and that his manuscripts should be published; so we find her making repeated appeals to the government, and journeying from one part of the country to the other to interest public men in this work. As many succeeding

---

[1] John Trumbull, the artist, born June, 1756, died November, 1843.
[2] The eldest daughter of Alexander Hamilton.
[3] Margaret Schuyler, who married Stephen van Rensselaer.
[4] At Albany?

administrations were opposed to Hamilton and his political faith, she did not meet with the encouragement that she deserved, and there seems to have been a reluctance even upon the part of some of Hamilton's closest friends—Rufus King, for example—to give her certain letters and papers which they wrongly thought it might be impolitic to publish. Among these were documents relating to Washington's Farewell Address, which disclosed the part taken by Hamilton in its preparation. She always maintained that her husband was its author, and insisted that this fact should be known. She and her son James were constantly at work to effect this end. James was then a grown man and a lawyer, and at his instance a suit in Chancery was brought to obtain certain parts of the correspondence that had passed between Washington and Hamilton, which was successful, and they were used by the younger Hamilton in his "Reminiscences." The discussion of how much Hamilton had to do with this memorable address has been ever active, and even bitter, as has been shown elsewhere, and is by no means now fully settled. The venerable widow, when she was eighty-two, reiterated her belief in her husband's responsibility for most of it, and the following paper was executed, probably at a time when she was more disturbed than usual, by the insistent claims of those who sought to belittle him, and gives her impressions of Hamilton's share of the work:

Elizabeth Hamilton's Statement as to Washington's Farewell Address

Desirous that my children should be fully acquainted with the services rendered by their Father to our country, and the assistance given by him to General Washington during his administration, for the one great object, the Independence and Stability of the Government of the United States, there is one thing in addition to the numerous proofs which I leave them and which I feel myself in duty bound to State; which is: that a short time previous to General Washington's retiring from the Presidency in the year 1796 General Hamilton suggested to him the idea of delivering a farewell address to the people on his withdrawal from public life, with which idea General Washington was well pleased, and in his answer to General Hamilton's suggestion gave him the heads of the subjects on which he would wish to remark, with a request that Mr. Hamilton would prepare an address for him; Mr. Hamilton did so, and the address was written, principally at such times as his office was seldom frequented by his clients and visitors, and during the absence of his students to avoid interruption; at which times he was in the habit of calling me to sit with him, that he might read to me as he wrote, in order, as he said, to discover how it sounded upon the ear, and making the remark, "My dear Eliza, you must be to me what Molière's old nurse was to him."

The whole or nearly all the "Address" was read to me by him as he wrote it and a greater part if not all was written by him in my presence. The original was forwarded to Gen. Washington who approved of it with the exception of one paragraph, of, I think, about four or five lines, which if I mistake not was on the Subject of public schools, which was stricken out. It was afterwards returned to Mr. Hamilton who made the desired Alteration, and was afterwards delivered by General Washington, and published in that form, and has ever since been Known as "General Washington's Farewell Address." Shortly after the publication of the address, my husband and myself were walking in Broadway, when an old soldier accosted him, with a request of him to purchase General Washington's Farewell address, which he did and turning to me Said "That man does not know he has asked me to purchase my own work."

The whole circumstances are at this moment, so perfectly in my remembrance, that I can call to mind his bringing General Washington's letter to me[1] which returned the

---

[1] In the hall of the house where we then resided in Liberty Street, near Broadway.

"address," and remarking on the only alteration which he (General Washington) had requested to be made.

New York, Aug. 7th, 1840.

ELIZ[TH] HAMILTON.[1]

Witness
         as
J. A. Washington ⎱
J. A. Macdonald. ⎰

General Schuyler left a large amount of property and, some years after his death, his other sons and daughters generously deeded much of their shares to their widowed sister, because of Hamilton's impoverishment.   Some of this was in Saratoga County, some near Utica, some near Owego, and small portions were in the cities of New York and Albany.   It was Mrs. Hamilton's custom, when interested in any particular charity, to sell piece by piece, and devote the proceeds to the particular object, so that when she died she was in straitened circumstances, and had, for some time, been entirely dependent upon her children and the back pay awarded Hamilton by the government.   "Her grief over the two children she had lost," said a contemporary writer, "took the form of protection of those who were poor and unfriended, as well as orphaned.   To Mrs. Hamilton is directly owing the first orphan asylum of New York.   On its fiftieth anniversary a memorial service was held in the Church of the Epiphany (in Washington, where she then was for the winter), and the work and its greatly extended good were gone over.   The seed had become a tree with mighty branches. Mrs. Hamilton was feeble and could not sit through the whole service, but came only for a part; always to the communion service.   This Sunday she came in toward the

---

[1] Then eighty-four years old.

close. Our minds and hearts were filled with the good work of this gentle lady when she entered—a very small, upright little figure in deep black, never altered from the time her dark hair was framed in by the widow's cap, until now the hair was as white as the cap.

"As she moved slowly forward, supported by her daughter, Mrs. Holly, one common feeling made the congregation rise and remain standing until she was seated in her pew at the front."[1]

Her great effort seems to have been to the end that the letters left by her husband should be published, and his life written by some competent person. Unfortunately, one of her clergymen was chosen to do the latter, and as it was not a judicious selection, the result was unsuccessful. She first wrote to Bushrod Washington, a nephew of the President, whose reply is appended, but nothing seems to have come of all this. It was not until many years later that her son John C. Hamilton wrote a life of his father collecting and publishing many of his letters in a series of seven volumes.

Bushrod Washington[2] to Elizabeth Hamilton

MT. VERNON, *Dec.* 14, 1819.

MY DEAR MADAM: Your favor of the 5th of Nov[r] was received by Mr. Herbert, whilst I was in Philadelphia and was not placed in the bundle of letters which he delivered me upon my return. He had accidently put it by itself, and found it a day or two ago, when he delivered it to me. This must be my apology for the delay of this answer.

It affords me great pleasure to know Mr. Hopkinson[3]

---

[1] "Souvenirs of my Time," Mrs. Frémont.

[2] A nephew of George Washington. Associate justice of the United States Supreme Court.

[3] Probably Joseph Hopkinson, son of Francis, the Signer. He was leading counsel in Dr. Rush's suit against Cobbett, and later justice of the U. S. Circuit Court in Pennsylvania. He was the author of "Hail Columbia."

has undertaken to write the life of Genl. Hamilton, not only because his fine talents will enable him to do justice to the work, but because he admired, in common with every American patriot, the virtues, and the distinguished talents of that Great man.

The Contract which I made with Mr. Wayne, the publisher of the life of Gen'l Washington was, to assign the copyrights of the work to him, and to receive from him one dollar per volume, for every volume subscribed for, or sold during the period of the copyright. This dollar per volume was equally divided between C. Justice Marshall,[1] *the author*, & myself. There were 7000 copies subscribed for, and Mr. Marshall and myself received from Mr. Wayne the amount calculating it at a dollar each volume. I think that, as to all sales that were made over that number, we made a compromise with Mr. Wayne & received from him $4000. I should expect that a contract of this nature would be as favorable to you as you could expect to make.

I do not know whether I have ever yet acknowledged my obligation to you for the seeds you were so good as to send me; if I have not, permit me now to do it, and to assure you that my silence did not proceed from unthankfulness for the favor. The corn met my approbation so fully that I shall plant the whole of my crop, at one farm, next year, of that kind—It comes very early, & the ear is of good size.

Present my best regards & wishes to my favourite Eliza[2] and believe me, good friend, that nothing could afford me a higher gratification than to pass a day or two with you and her at the Grange—I have not heard of or from William[3] since he went into the wilderness.

The family of my niece and Mr. Woodlawn are all well,— Frances not yet married, but all in good time. She is a charming girl, as is her sister Agnes, now nearly grown up. Mrs. Washington's health is much the same as when you

---

[1] Chief Justice John Marshall. Besides his well-known "Life of Washington," he wrote a "History of the Colonies Planted by the British in North America."

[2] Her youngest daughter Mrs. Holly.

[3] Her son William Stephen.

were here; she yet continues to retire from company at home and abroad.

I am with sentiments of esteem, respect and regard,

My dear Madam,

Yr. friend and faithful humb. serv.

BUSHROD WASHINGTON.

In 1849 the Hamilton MSS. were purchased by the government. From the time of her husband's death almost to her own in 1854 Mrs. Hamilton was constantly engaged in writing to the leading Federalists all over the country and making inquiries to enable her to ascertain all the facts she could. Besides corresponding she made long journeys to carry out her quest with more or less success. She wrote to her daughter Mrs. Holly, in Philadelphia, in 1832:

"I have my fears I shall not obtain my object. Most of the contemporaries of your father have also passed away. I have since you left this, seen Mr. S. Kane, he is doing all he can, as is Mr. Clymer."

Shortly before her death a friend wrote as follows: "The widow of Alexander Hamilton has reached the great age of ninety-five and retains in an astonishing degree her faculties and converses with much of that ease and brilliancy which lent so peculiar a charm to her younger days. And then, after passing the compliments and congratulations of the day, insists upon her visitors taking a merry glass from General Washington's punch bowl, which, with other portions of his table set, remains in her possession." At this time she showed a great deal of physical vigor, walking from her own house in H Street to visit her old friend, Judge Cranch, three miles away, on Capitol Hill, in the city of Washington. Her last illness was a comparatively short one, and until a few days before her death her mind was perfectly clear.

Mrs. Hamilton could never forget the behavior of Monroe when he, with Muhlenberg and Venables, accused Hamilton of financial irregularities at the time of the Reynolds incident. Many years afterward, when they were both aged people, Monroe visited her and an interview occurred which was witnessed by a nephew, who was then a lad of fifteen. "I had," he says, "been sent to call upon my Aunt Hamilton one afternoon. I found her in her garden and was there with her talking, when her maid servant came from the house with a card. It was the card of James Monroe. She read the name, and stood holding the card, much perturbed. Her voice sank, and she spoke very low, as she always did when she was angry. 'What has that man come to see me for?' escaped from her. 'Why, Aunt Hamilton,' said I, 'don't you know, it's Mr. Monroe, and he's been President, and he is visiting here now in the neighborhood, and has been very much made of, and invited everywhere, and so—I suppose he has come to call and pay his respects to you.' After a moment's hesitation, 'I will see him,' she said.

"The maid went back to the house, my aunt followed, walking rapidly, I after her. As she entered the parlor Monroe rose. She stood in the middle of the room facing him. She did not ask him to sit down. He bowed, and addressing her formally, made her rather a set speech—that it was many years since they had met, that the lapse of time brought its softening influences, that they both were nearing the grave, when past differences could be forgiven and forgotten—in short, from his point of view, a very nice, conciliatory, well-turned little speech. She answered, still standing, and looking at him, 'Mr. Monroe, if you have come to tell me that you repent, that you are sorry, *very* sorry, for the misrepresentations and the slanders, and the stories you circulated against my dear husband, if you have come to say this, I understand it.   But, otherwise, no lapse of time, no nearness to the grave, makes any difference.'   She stopped speaking, Monroe turned, took up his hat and left the room."

In this connection it may be said that the oft-repeated story of the meeting of Mrs. Hamilton and Aaron Burr, many years later on an Albany steamboat, is a fiction, but it was probably suggested by the Monroe incident.

CHAPTER V

COURTSHIP AND MARRIAGE

THE years from 1779 to 1783 included a most interesting
period of American history, and in this brief space a number
of events occurred which not only directly concerned Hamilton, but also his father-in-law. In the late spring of 1780
Sir Henry Clinton had captured Charleston and returned to
New York, leaving Cornwallis in command, who reorganized the British forces and defeated Gates at Camden in September of that year, putting the latter to inglorious flight.
Even Greene, who was considered the best general of the
American army, and who had been sent to succeed Gates,
was twice defeated, once at Guilford Courthouse and again
at Hobkirk Courthouse, in South Carolina. Later Cornwallis proceeded northward, making a junction with Arnold,
who had espoused the British cause and escaped to the man-
of-war *Vulture* after eluding Hamilton who was sent to capture him near West Point. Arnold, however, was sent to
New York to join Clinton who had become alarmed. Washington, whose good generalship was always evident, with the
aid of Rochambeau, made a pretended assault upon that
city, with the result that Clinton was so embarrassed that he
hastily sent to Cornwallis, begging for additional help. The
next step was the advance of the American army into Virginia where, with the co-operation of the French fleet under
DeGrasse and the French allies under Rochambeau, the
attack was made upon Cornwallis who had intrenched him-

self at Yorktown. It is hardly necessary to refer to the surrender of the brave English leader, or the details of the siege or battle; suffice it to say that Hamilton's conduct had much to do with the success of the American forces, and gained for him a great deal of his military reputation.

Clinton was yet in New York, but the Patriot army, still further reduced by its late experience, preferred to play a waiting game, and no attack was made. Meanwhile General Schuyler had been active in the north, but through a conspiracy and the action of an incompetent and prejudiced Congress, he was suspended and deprived of his command by Gates.

Profiting by Schuyler's partially accomplished work, Gates forced the surrender of Burgoyne; he, however, ultimately met with reverses and his own triumph was short-lived. When puffed up with ambition he later attempted not only to undermine and supplant Washington with the help of the notorious Conway Cabal, but essayed a military rôle which was a failure, and was subsequently ignominiously defeated by Cornwallis. In this connection a letter written by General Schuyler to Hamilton throws much light upon the disordered state of affairs in the upper part of the State of New York.

Philip Schuyler to Alexander Hamilton

Saratoga, *November* 12, 178&.

My DEAR SIR: Both your favors of the 17th and 22d I had the pleasure to receive about the latter end of the month, since which this place has been a scene of Confusion and distress, the Inhabitants flying for shelter to the Interior part of the state, and the Militia moving up with a tardiness which has given me more real Concern than the Enemy's depredations have done, as It evinces either disaffection in too

many, or that they are heartily tired of the Contests. I
fear there is too much of both.

I hope General Green will reach Virginia in time to Collect a body of troops and bring matters into proportion before the troops you suspect to be destined from N York for
Virginia arrive there, as by the affair of the 16th of August
Gen. Gates has lost the command in that quarter, I Consider
rather favorable to us, for certain I am that his want of
abilities would have proved extremely prejudicial to us, I
sincerely wish he may never command, at any Important
post.—

The disaster which the British have experienced in the
Spanish dominions on this continent will I hope rid Spain
of her fears and Induce unanimity in the Court of Madrid.[1]
A peace at this Juncture between Spain and Britain would
very Materialy Injure our cause.

I am exceedingly sorry to find that a certain expedition
was not agreeable to Count De Rochambeau and the more
so as I know how Impracticable It is to prosecute one without the immediate aid of the French troops. I believe the
Gallic commander has private Instructions to the Contrary,
otherwise I think he would not forego a command in which
he would reap many laurels with little trouble, for as to success It appears to me that would have been beyond a doubt.
—The reduction of Canada since the Indians are generally
become hostile is a matter certainly of the first Importance,
as we shall have no alternative left in the ensuing Campaign
but that of abandoning the present frontiers from Virginia
to New Hampshire Inclusive, or keeping a body of troops for
their protection equal to the Conquest of Canada.

I was on the point of commencing my Journey to Hartford
when the british on Lake Champlain a second time reached
this quarter, that and their manœuvre on the Grants prevented me from prosecuting It, and It is now too late. Mr.
Benson[2] paid me a visit a few days before he set out for
Hartford. The conversation we had together I hope will

---

[1] The reverses in the West Indies and elsewhere.
[2] Egbert Benson.

tend to public utility. He is strongly Impressed with the necessity of Immediately and permanently compleating the army, and of another matter which I formerly mentioned to you. Both appear to me so necessary that I form no great expectations from the first without the latter.

I have advised the Governor to call the Assembly at any early day. I think It of great importance that a final surrender should be made with the people on the Grants. They are capable of strengthening the army and aiding In the defense of the pontoons, and I do not despair of rendering them useful in both ways, If I can bring the legislature to adopt my Ideas.

Be assured that we shall be happy to see the Gentlemen you mention, and such others as you may bring with you.

Mrs. Schuyler joins me in the most affectionate wishes. Adieu. I am Dear Sir Most Sincerely,

Your serv. etc.

PH. SCHUYLER.

Colo. Hamilton.

The "grants" here referred to were those allotted to the settlers by Governor Wentworth, the territory being that which now forms the States of New Hampshire and Vermont, but at that early time was a disputed region not comprised in the lands deeded to New York by Massachusetts and Connecticut, and lying above the division line.

Hamilton's duties were most engrossing, and the available correspondence that passed between him and his superiors and friends makes us wonder that he found time for any social distractions whatever. It appears that he was sent to meet Rochambeau, and again was despatched to West Point to capture Benedict Arnold, while his connection with the trial of Major André at about the same time shows that his billets were numerous and important. However, he found sufficient opportunity to fall in love with Miss Elizabeth Schuyler, who was the second of the General's daughters, a girl of about his own age, she having been born in 1757.

In the winter of 1779–80 Washington was for the second time encamped at Morristown, under very much better conditions than when he was there previously, and, thanks to the provisions made by Robert Morris and General Schuyler and the help afforded by France, the troops were better clad and housed, although there was still great destitution and, later, great discontent. This, in measure, was due to the fact that they had not, for a long time, been paid, and a mutinous spirit was engendered which had been taken advantage of—without any success, however—by British emissaries.

In spite of all this, as well as the proximity of the British, who came over from Staten Island to Elizabethtown, there may be said to have been a breathing spell for the little American army.

Washington and his officers, despite their discomfort and sufferings, managed to extract a considerable amount of pleasure from life, and there appears to have been a great deal of gayety, which was participated in by a merry collection of young people, among whom were the Frenchmen attached to head-quarters.

Governor William Livingston, who had befriended Hamilton upon his arrival in America in 1772, occupied his large, comfortable house known as Liberty Hall at Elizabethtown, which was built in 1776. With him were his pretty daughters, one of whom, Sarah, married John Jay, and the youngest, Kitty, who was an attached friend of Elizabeth Schuyler. These charming young women with their neighbors, Lady Kitty Stirling and her sister, and Susan Boudinot, vied with each other in making the routine life of the young army officers more bearable.

In the neighborhood were the quarters of Generals Greene, Knox, Philip Schuyler, and Surgeon-General Cochran.

Routs and balls were common, and the letters of the time detail in the quaint style of the period much of the camp gossip. The military family, as it was called, of Washington planned many entertainments, and the chief spirits were Hamilton, Tilghman, and McHenry.

On March 18, 1780, McHenry wrote to Hamilton, who had been sent off to exchange prisoners:

The family since your departure have given hourly proofs of a growing weakness. Example I verily believe is infectious. For such a predominance is beauty establishing over their hearts, that should things continue to wear as sweet an aspect as they are now beheld in, I shall be the only person left, of the whole household, to support the dignity of human nature. But in good earnest God bless both you, and your weakness, and preserve me your sincere friend.

The Vicomte de Chastellux,[1] afterward marquis, was one of the many French noblemen who risked their lives in the War of Independence, and have left us unique impressions of the men, manners, and customs of that period, and especially of the Morristown encampment.

During the winter of 1780 he took advantage of the lull in operations to go on a journey from his post in Rhode Island to visit General Washington at his head-quarters in Morristown, then to visit General Schuyler at Albany, and to inspect the various scenes of the struggles in which he himself had not participated.

Bad weather, still worse roads, the intense cold, and difficulties in obtaining shelter for man and beast could not dampen his spirits, or lessen his interest in all he heard and

[1] " Voyage de M. le Marquis de Chastellux dans l'Amérique Septentrionale," Paris, 1788, p. 113, vol. I.

saw, and it may be the contrast with the forlorn outer world that prompted him to give so vivid a picture of the home comforts and pleasant intimacy that he found at Morristown.

Amongst other delightful comments upon his arrival and welcome he describes the first dinner and says: "I adapt myself very well to the English *toast;* one has very small glasses—one pours for oneself the quantity of wine desired without being urged to take more, and the *toast* is but a kind of refrain to the conversation"; and again: "I observed that at dinner the toasts were more ceremonious: some were for etiquette, others were suggested by the General and named by whichever aide-de-camp was doing the honors; for every day one of them sits at the end of the table beside the General in order to help all the dishes and dole out the bottles; now, that night the toasts were called by Colonel Hamilton and he gave them just as they occurred to him, haphazard and informally.

"At the end of supper the guests are always asked to give a *sentiment*, that is, any woman to whom they may be attached by some sentiment, either love, friendship, or simple preference. This supper or conversation lasts from nine to eleven at night, always easy and agreeable."

Notwithstanding Chastellux's stories of the prodigality of Washington's table, and the apparent luxurious mode of life during his visit, it may be stated on the authority of Trevelyan that the entire cost of maintaining the Head-quarters' Staff, and the obligatory hospitality to outsiders during four and one-half months, and of a hungry army for the same time, was less than £500.

Washington's head-quarters were in the old Jacob Ford place. According to Lossing[1] the General and his family

---

[1] " The Pictorial Field Book of the Revolution," vol. I, pp. 306–315. N. Y.: Harper Bros., 1859.

H★MILTON

AT THIS PERFORMANCE

Alexander Hamilton	JAVIER MUÑOZ
Eliza Hamilton	LEXI LAWSON
Aaron Burr	BRANDON VICTOR DIXON
Angelica Schuyler	MANDY GONZALEZ
George Washington	NICHOLAS CHRISTOPHER
Marquis de Lafayette/Thomas Jefferson	ANDREW CHAPPELLE
Hercules Mulligan/James Madison	OKIERIETE ONAODOWAN
John Laurens/Philip Hamilton	JORDAN FISHER
Peggy Schuyler/Maria Reynolds	ALYSHA DESLORIEUX
King George	RORY O'MALLEY
Philip Schuyler/James Reynolds/Doctor	DONALD WEBBER, JR.
Samuel Seabury	THAYNE JASPERSON
Charles Lee	NEIL HASKELL
George Eacker	RICKEY TRIPP
Ensemble	HOPE EASTERBROOK, NEIL HASKELL,

SASHA HOLLINGER, THAYNE JASPERSON, ELIZABETH JUDD,
RICKEY TRIPP, KAMILLE UPSHAW, TANAIRI SADE VAZQUEZ,
NIK WALKER, DONALD WEBBER, JR., ZELIG WILLIAMS

occupied the whole of the house except two rooms on the eastern side which were reserved for Mrs. Ford and her family. Two log additions made to the house were used as a kitchen, and as an office for Washington, Tilghman, and Hamilton, while near the head-quarters were huts erected for the life guard, then commanded by General William Colfax, who had succeeded Caleb Gibbs.

Hamilton's love-making was evidently pursued with the same activity as everything else he did, and his addresses, as was the fashion of the day, necessitated a vast expenditure of paper, ink, and blotting sand; and some of his characteristic letters are presented. His attentions to Miss Schuyler met with the hearty approval of her father, who wrote to him as follows:

You cannot my dear Sir, be more happy at the connection you have made with my family than I am. Until the child of a parent has made a judicious choice his heart is in continual anxiety; but this anxiety was removed the moment I discovered on whom she had placed her affections. I am pleased with every instance of delicacy in those who are dear to me, and I think I read your soul on that occasion you mention. I shall therefore only entreat you to consider me as one who wishes in every way to promote your happiness, and I shall.

Shortly after this he wrote to his future mother-in-law the following:

Alexander Hamilton to Mrs. Philip Schuyler

MADAM: The inclosed letter came to hand two days ago, and I take the earliest opportunity of forwarding it. I cannot forbear indulging my feelings, by entreating you to accept the assurances of my gratitude for your kind compliance with my wishes to be united to your amiable daughter. . . . I leave it to my conduct rather than expressions to testify the sincerity of my affection for her—the respect I have for her parents—the desire I shall always feel to justify their confidence and merit their friendship. May I hope Madam, you will not consider it as mere profession, when I add, that though I have not the happiness of a personal acquaintance with you, I am no stranger to the qualities which distinguish your character—and these make the relation in which I shall stand to you, not one of the least pleasing circumstances of my union with your daughter. My heart anticipates the sentiment of that relation and wishes to give you proof of the respectful and affectionate attachment with which I have the honor to be

Madam
Yours

ALEXANDER HAMILTON.

Hd. qr. April 14. 80.

But few letters remain which enable us to mark the advance of Hamilton's wooing, but a little verse is in my possession which was found in a tiny bag hanging from his wife's neck after her death, and which she had evidently always worn, and it was quite probably given to her when they were together this winter.[1] What is apparently a sonnet was written upon a piece of torn and yellow paper, fragments of which had been sewn together with ordinary thread.

ANSWER TO THE INQUIRY WHY I SIGHED

Before no mortal ever knew
A love like mine so tender—true—
Completely wretched—you away—
And but half blessed e'en while you stay.

If present love [illegible] face
Deny you to my fond embrace
No joy unmixed my bosom warms
But when my angel's in my arms."

[1] 1779-80.

The letters written to his sweetheart varied much in their nature—some were ardent and full of the extravagant language of the time, others were of greater interest to the historical student of to-day, because in narrative form they gave a graphic idea of the happenings at this important period. It is impossible to separate them, and, as the dates are sometimes omitted, identification is difficult. It is hoped, however, that their presentation will at least afford some idea of what Hamilton felt and did during the time he was paying his addresses to Elizabeth Schuyler.

Alexander Hamilton to Elizabeth Schuyler

MORRISTOWN, *July* 2, 1780.

I have been waiting, my love, for an opportunity of writing to you but none has offered. I sit down to have a line ready for a sudden call which will be enclosed to Col. Hay. The enclosed was sent to you at Morristown, but missed you, as it contains ideas that often occur to me I send it now. Last evening Dr. Cochran delivered me the dear lines you wrote me from Nicholsons. I shall impatiently long to hear of your arrival at Albany and the state of your health. I am perfectly well proof against anything that can assail mine. We have no change in our affairs since you left us. I should regret the time already lost in inactivity if it did not bring us nearer to that sweet reunion for which we so ardently wish. I never look forward to that period without sensations I cannot describe.

I love you more and more every hour. The sweet softness and delicacy of your mind and manners, the elevation of your sentiments, the real goodness of your heart—its tenderness to me—the beauties of your face and person—your unpretending good sense and that innocent symplicity and frankness which pervade your actions, all these appear to me with increasing amiableness, and place you in my estimation above all the rest of your sex.

I entreat you, my charmer, not to neglect the charges I gave you, particularly that of taking care of yourself and that of employing all your leisure in reading. Nature has been very kind to you, do not neglect to cultivate her gifts and to enable yourself to make the distinguished figure in all respects to which you are entitled to aspire. You excel most of your sex in all the amiable qualities, endeavor to excel them equally in the splendid ones. You can do it if you please, and I shall take pride in it,—It will be a fund too to diversify our enjoyment and amusements and fill all our moments to advantage.

I have received a letter from Major Laurens soliciting an interview, on the Pennsylvania Boundary. The General had half consented to its taking place. I hope to be permitted to meet him, if so I will go to Philadelphia and then you may depend, I shall not forget the picture you requested.

Yours, my angel, with inviolable fidelity—

ALEX. HAMILTON.

July 4.

It is now the fourth and no opportunity has offered. I open my letter just to tell you your Papa has been unwell with a touch of the Quinsy, but is now almost perfectly recovered. He hoped to be at Head Quarters today. He is eight miles off. I saw him last evening and heard from him this morning. I mention this least you should hear of his indisposition through an exaggerated channel and be unnecessarily alarmed.

Affectionately present me to your Mamma.

Adieu my love.

The engagement of Elizabeth Schuyler certainly created a stir among her young friends, and Kitty Livingston, a boon companion, in a letter written from Lebanon, June 20, 1780, says: "If you should see the Col. present my compliments and tell him I hope to see him on the Banks of Hudson near Claremont where Flora shall mix his Laurels with Flowers and Pomona heap him with fruit."

Hamilton and Elizabeth Schuyler were engaged some time during 1779, but were separated for a great part of the time, and the courtship was interrupted by long journeys undertaken by him, and by the occurrence of important conferences, or of dramatic events of the most thrilling character.[1] .He had been sent to Perth Amboy to exchange prisoners, and undoubtedly the social courtesies for the time prevailed. Doubtless many of the English officers who toasted Elizabeth Schuyler and her sister had, at an earlier period, accepted General Schuyler's hospitality at Albany or Saratoga.

Alexander Hamilton to Elizabeth Hamilton

AMBOY, *Mar.* 17, 1780.
Thursday afternoon.

MY DEAREST GIRL: I wrote you a hasty letter two days ago, since which I have had the happiness of hearing you were well by Colonel Webb,[2] and did not forget me when he was coming away. Every moment of my stay here becomes more and more irksome, but I hope two or three days will put an end to it. Colonel Webb tells me you have sent for a carriage to go to Philadelphia. If you should go out before I return, have the goodness to leave a line informing me how long you expect to be there. I beg, too, you will not suffer any considerations respecting me to prevent your going, for though it will be a tax upon my love to part with you so long, I wish you to see that city before you return. It will afford you pleasure and whatever does that will always be most agreeable to me, only let me entreat you to endeavor not to stay there longer than the amusements of the place interest you in complaisance to friends, for you must always remember your best friend is where I am. If possible, and

---

[1] In May, 1780, he wrote: "The day after to-morrow I set out with the General for Hartford to an interview with the French General and Admiral, and we may possibly go farther eastward. Colonel Hay will forward your letters to me."
[2] General Samuel Blatchley Webb.

you give me your consent, I shall try to make a short visit to the city while you are there, but it is very uncertain whether I shall be able to do it.   If I were not afraid of making you vain, I would tell you that Mrs. Carter,[1] Peggy[2] and yourself are the daily toast at our table, and for this *honor* you are chiefly indebted to the British gentlemen; though, as I am always thinking of you, this naturally brings Peggy to my mind, who is generally my toast.   Captain Beebe[3] is here and talks of her sometimes, but I will not give my consent to his being her favorite.   I do not think him clever enough for her.   He sings well and that is all.   Your little Delancey[4] is not of the party.   I am told he is a pretty fellow.   I have learned a secret by coming down here.   Our interview is attended with a good deal of sociability and good humor, but I begin, notwithstanding, to be tired of our British friends.   They do their best to be agreeable and are particularly civil to me, but, after all, they are a compound of grimace and jargon and, out of a certain fashionable routine, are as dull and empty as any gentlemen need to be. One of their principal excellencies consists in swallowing a large quantity of wine every day, and in this I am so unfortunate that I shall make no sort of figure with them.   You must not think me prejudiced, for the picture is a true one.[5]

Alexander Hamilton to Elizabeth Schuyler[6]

September 6, 1780.

Most people here are groaning under a very disagreeable piece of intelligence just come from the southward, that Gates has had a total defeat near Camden, in South Carolina.

Cornwallis and he met in the night of the fifteenth, by accident, marching to the same point.   The advanced guards skirmished, and the two armies halted and formed till morn-

[1] Angelica Church (then Carter).
[2] Margaret Schuyler.   [3] Captain Bezabel Beebe.
[4] Possibly Oliver Delancey, a Tory and British officer.
[5] This letter evidently crossed that written by James McHenry, March 18, see p.123.
[6] " Hamilton's Works " (J. C. H.), vol. I, p. 169.

ing. In the morning, a battle ensued, in which the militia, and Gates with them, immediately ran away, and left the Continental troops to contend with the enemy's whole force.

They did it obstinately, and probably are most of them cut off. Gates, however, who writes to Congress, seems to know very little what has become of his army. He showed that age and the long labors and fatigues of a military life had not in the least impaired his activity, for in the three days and a half he reached Hilleborough, one hundred and eighty miles from the scene of action, leaving all his troops to take care of themselves, and get out of the scrape as well as they could.

He has confirmed, in this instance, the opinion I always had of him. This event will have very serious consequences to the southward. People's imaginations have already given up North Carolina and Virginia; but I do not believe either of them will fall. I am certain Virginia cannot. This misfortune affects me less than others, because it is not in my temper to repine at evils that are past, but to endeavor to draw good out of them, and because I think our safety depends on a total change of system, and this change of system will only be produced by misfortune.

A. Hamilton.

Benedict Arnold, who had married a daughter of Edward Shippen, had become involved in debt and led an extravagant life, in consequence of which he was accused of questionable financial operations and "disorderly official conduct." Having been taken to task for this, an aggrieved animosity was engendered which led him to revenge himself by plotting treason with the enemy, and every one is too familiar with his scheme for the betrayal of West Point, his utilization of Major André, and with the pitiful end of that brave and gallant young officer.

No better account of these happenings can be found than in the two following letters written by Hamilton, which may be reproduced as examples of the sensible correspondence in which Hamilton and Miss Schuyler indulged, and showing, as well, that she was quite in sympathy with all he did, and quite familiar with his military duties.

Alexander Hamilton to Elizabeth Schuyler[1]

September 25, 1780.

Arnold, hearing of the plot being detected, immediately fled to the enemy. I went in pursuit of him, but was much too late; and could hardly regret the disappointment, when, on my return, I saw an amiable woman, frantic with distress for the loss of a husband she tenderly loved; a traitor to his Country and to his fame; a disgrace to his connexions; it was the most affecting scene I ever was witness to. She, for a considerable time, entirely lost herself. The General went up to see her, and she upbraided him with being in a plot to murder her child. One moment she raved, another she melted into tears. Sometimes she pressed her infant to her bosom, and lamented its fate, occasioned by the imprudence of its father, in a manner that would have pierced insensibility itself. All the sweetness of beauty, all the loveliness of innocence, all the tenderness of a wife, and all the fondness of a mother, showed themselves in her appearance and conduct. We have every reason to believe, that she was entirely unacquainted with the plan, and that the first knowledge of it, was when Arnold went to tell her he must banish himself from his country and from her forever. She instantly fell into a convulsion, and he left her in that situation.

This morning she is more composed. I paid her a visit, and endeavoured to soothe her by every method in my power; though you may imagine she is not easily to be consoled; added to her other distresses, she is very apprehensive the resentment of her country will fall upon her (who is only unfortunate) for the guilt of her husband.

I have tried to persuade her that her fears are ill-founded; but she will not be convinced. She received us in bed,

[1] " Hamilton's Works" (J. C. H.), vol. I, p. 186.

with every circumstance that would interest our sympathy, and her sufferings were so eloquent, that I wished myself her brother, to have a right to become her defender. As it is, I have entreated her to enable me to give her proofs of my friendship. Could I forgive Arnold for sacrificing his honour, reputation, and duty, I could not forgive him for acting a part that must have forfeited the esteem of so fine a woman. At present she almost forgets his crime in his misfortunes; and her horror at the guilt of the traitor is lost in her love of the man. But a virtuous mind cannot long esteem a base one; and time will make her despise if it cannot make her hate.

A. HAMILTON.

Hamilton was probably at New Windsor when the following letter was written, which, at the time, was occupied by the American Army:

Alexander Hamilton to Elizabeth Schuyler

(Written probably in *October*, 1780.)

I have told you and I told you truly that I love you too much. You engross my thoughts too entirely to allow me to think anything else. You not only employ my mind all day, but you intrude on my sleep. I meet you in every dream and when I wake I cannot close my eyes again for ruminating on your sweetness. 'Tis a pretty story indeed that I am to be thus monopolized by a little *nut brown maid* like you and from a soldier metamorphosed into a puny lover. I believe in my soul you are an enchantress; but I have tried in vain, if not to break, at least to weaken the charm and you maintain your empire in spite of all my efforts and after every new one I make to draw myself from my allegiance, my partial heart still returns and clings to you with increased attachment. To drop figures my lovely girl, you become dearer to me every moment. I am more and more unhappy and impatient under the hard necessity that keeps me from you, and yet the prospect lengthens as I advance.

Harrison has just received an account of the death of his Father and will be obliged to go to Virginia. Meade's affairs (as well as his love) compel him to go there also in a little time. There will then remain too few in the family to make it possible for me to leave it till Harrison's return, but I have told him *I will not be delayed beyond November.*

Oct. 5th.

P. S. I promised you a particular account of Andre. I am writing one of the whole affair of which I will send you a copy.

Indeed, my dear Betsey, you do not write me often enough. I ought at least to hear from you by every post, and your last letter is as old as the middle of September. I have written you twice since my return from Hartford.[1] You will laugh at me for consulting you about such a trifle, but I want to know whether you would prefer my receiving the nuptial benediction in my uniform or in a different habit. It will be just as you please, so consult your whim and what you think most consistent with propriety. . . . Tell my Peggy I will shortly open a correspondence with her. I am composing a piece, of which, from the opinion I have of her qualifications, I shall endeavor to prevail upon her to act the principal character. The title is "The way to get him, for the benefit of all single ladies who desire to be married." You will ask her if she has any objections to taking part in the piece and tell her that if I am not much mistaken in her, I am sure she will have none. For your own part, your business is now to study the way to keep him, which is said to be much the most difficult task of the two, though in your case I thoroughly believe it will be an easy one and that to succeed effectually you will only have to wish it sincerely. May I only be as successful in pleasing you, and may you be as happy as I shall ever wish to make you.

[1] Where he had gone to meet Rochambeau on September 21, 1780.

MAJOR ANDRÉ

Alexander Hamilton to Elizabeth Schuyler[1]

TAPPAN, *Oct. 2d,* 1780.

Poor Andre suffers today. Everything that is amiable in virtue, in fortitude, in delicate sentiment, and accomplished manners, pleads for him; but hard-hearted policy calls for a sacrifice. He must die.—I send you my account of Arnold's affair; and to justify myself to your sentiments, I must inform you, that I urged a compliance with Andre's request to be shot; and I do not think it would have had an ill-effect; but some people are only sensible to motives of policy, and sometimes, from a narrow disposition, mistake it.

When Andre's tale comes to be told, and present resentment is over; the refusing him the privilege of choosing the manner of his death will be branded with too much obstinacy.

It was proposed to me to suggest to him the idea of an exchange for Arnold; but I knew I should have forfeited his esteem by doing it, and therefore declined it. As a man of honour he could not but reject it; and I would not for the world have proposed to him a thing which must have placed me on the unamiable light of supposing him capable of meanness, or of not feeling myself the impropriety of the measure. I confess to you, I had the weakness to value the esteem of a dying man, because I reverenced his merit.

A. HAMILTON.

There is some doubt about the date of the marriage, the general opinion being that it occurred in December, 1780.

No better place could have been chosen for this happy event than the grand old house of General Schuyler, built in 1765, which has been so well pictured by Chastellux and which has been the scene of so many interesting episodes, among them the famous attempt to kidnap its

[1] " Hamilton's Works" (J. C. H.), vol. I, p. 187.

owner by Waltermeyer—and the dramatic escape of his daughter Margaret from the savages, to which reference has already been made. It was during the Revolution, and before, visited by many distinguished people, among them Benjamin Franklin, Charles Carroll, de Noailles, General St. Clair, Baron Riedesel, and even Burgoyne, who enthusiastically described the generous hospitality of its owner.

But little remains of its former elegance for, like many old places, it has suffered through the ravages of time, or been encroached upon by a growing city, or has been so altered as to lose its characteristic charm of former days. There is little to carry one back to the joyous happenings that took place within its walls during the American Revolution; it is at present occupied by Sisters of Charity, orphans, and the poor children of the neighborhood.

The house, which is now occupied as a Catholic school, and surrounded by a squalid tenement settlement, retains much of its original attractiveness. . . . It is built of yellow brick. On each side of the hexagonal vestibule are three windows; above these are seven windows, measuring the unusual breadth of the house.

Within is a spacious hall sixty feet long, to which the windows on each side of the door give light. It is a noble room, wainscotted in white. Doors lead on one side into the sitting-room, on the other into the drawing-room, splendidly lighted, with deep window-seats and broad mantels handsomely carved. . . .

The main hall is divided from the back hall, which is divided by a fine old colonial door, with fan and side lights enriched by delicate tracery, and making an attractive feature of the larger hall. The back hall receives the staircase, not more remarkable for its historic incidents than for the beautiful sweep of its lines, and the fine carving of its splendid balustrade.

GENERAL PHILIP SCHUYLER'S HOMESTEAD AT ALBANY

Behind the sitting-room is the dining-room, the scene of forty years of generous hospitality. On the other side the drawing-room leads into a private hall and a room, . . . that was used as a nursery. Behind this was the library. Here there is the story of a bricked-up enclosure which formerly led to a subterranean passage in connection with the river, to be used in case of surprise. The staircase leads to the upper hall. . . . This was used as a ballroom, and on either side are the chambers, in which cluster so many historic reminiscences.[1]

McHenry, then a member of Washington's staff, went to Albany for Hamilton's wedding and wrote these verses, which he subsequently sent to his friend, Otho Williams, on the morning after :[2]

'Tis told, my friend, in poets lore.
The muse has an exhaustless store
From which she draws with wond'rous skill
Of choicest fancies what she will.
With these she decks the heroes' hearse.
Or forms with these immortal verse.
Last night I sought her dear retreat
And laid me at the fair one's feet.
She knew my errand, sway'd her wand,
Then pointed to a rising stand,
From whence the fairy world was seen
And you embosomed with your Queen.
(As thus ye lay the happiest pair
A rosy scent enriched the air
While to a music softly sounding
Breathing, panting, slow, rebounding)
Love arose with pow'rful spell,
Hence, he cried, to dismal dell
Imps who haunt the gloomy breast
Ever jealous—never blest;

[1] " Women of Colonial and Revolutionary Times," p. 66, by Mary Gay Humphreys.   [2] Op. cit., p. 29.

This is ground for holy feet
Here the sports and pleasure meet.
Then in whispers caught the ear
What the gifted only hear.
"Chains of Priests or modes of art
"Weakly hold the human heart,
"Hence my Eloisa said
"Give me those that love has made."
Now his fluttering wings outspread
Three times he bless'd the bridal bed,
While o'er it Faith her mantle threw
And said small care would keep it new.
Last Prudence came, in sober guise.
With Pilgrim's pace, and wisdom's eyes;
Forth from his stole a tablet took
Which you received with thankful look.
Genius had deeply mark'd the ground,
And Plutus finely edg'd it round,
This done, he bade you long improve
In all the sweets of mutual love.
And now would friendship's voice prevail
To point the moral of the tale.
Know then, dear *Ham*, a truth confest
Soon beauty fades, and love's a guest.
Love has not settled place on earth;
A very wan'rer from his birth;
And yet who happiness would prove,
Like you must build his hopes on love,
When love his choicest gifts has giv'n
He flies to make another heav'n;
But as he wheels his rapid flight
Calm joys succeed and pure delight.
Faith adds to all; for works we're told
Is Love's alloy, and faith the gold.

Now genius plays the lover's part;
Now wakes to many a throb the heart;
With ev'ry sun brings something new,
And gaily varies every view;

Whilst Prudence all his succour lends
To mark the point where pleasure ends.
For, borne beyond a certain goal,
The sweetest joys disgust the soul.
He too instructs us how to use,
What's more a blessing than the muse (wealth):
For well he knows, deprived of this
That toil and care is human bliss.

All these attendants *Ham* are thine,
Be't yours to treat them as divine;
To cherish what keeps love alive;
What makes us young at sixty-five.
What lends the eye its earliest fires;
What rightly managed still inspires.

To which Hamilton answered:

I thank you Dear Mac for your poetry and your confidence. The piece is a good one—your best. It has wit, which you know is a rare thing. I see by perseverence all ladies may be won. The Muses begin to be civil to you, in spite of Apollo and my prognosis.

You know I have often told you, you wrote prose well but had no genius for poetry. I retract. Adieu.

A. HAMILTON.

Sep. 12.[1] (1780)

Hamilton certainly benefited by his marriage and by his connection with a powerful family with far-reaching influence, and one having so much to do with the early history of the country. As Oliver intimates, Hamilton was too proud and independent in regard to money matters to accept any aid from his father-in-law, and it does not appear that any financial assistance was ever offered him.

[1] This date is probably an error in the transcription of the original letter, for Hamilton's letters and available and satisfactory data fix the day as December 20, 1780.

Even after his death and when his poverty became known Mrs. Hamilton, who was sensitive to a degree, indignantly denied a story that she was in possession of six thousand dollars, given to her by her father some time before, and wrote to one of her brothers:

"Let me assure you it is an untruth. It has given me some pain that I should be held up to the public in so unfavorable a point of view as on the one hand to request you to make provision for me, by some arrangement, and on the other, (as it is said) to be so amply provided for by my father. What but ill intent toward me could have been the motive to have given such an idea to the world and to my sisters and brothers? But this world is a world of evil passions, and I thank my God He strengthens my mind to look on them as steps to an entire resignation to His will, which I pray may fast approach me, and in that fullness of grace which may be pleasing in His sight. Oh! my brother, may my sighing and sorrowing be seen by Him who tempers the wind to the shorn lamb—shorn, indeed, to the quick." She continues: "My friend here has taken the necessary steps towards bending the public mind from this ill impression and he is very much gratified by your correct, liberal and affectionate conduct to me."

It is true that General Schuyler at all times sent to the young pair prodigal gifts and supplies from the Albany homestead, and when the Grange was built some years later, supplied Hamilton with most of the lumber. Like most patriots Schuyler was not really well-to-do, although he owned a great deal of land which, in those days, was not worth much, and some of it was rented by small farmers for trifling sums. His contributions to the cause of independence were very large, however, and at one time, at the request of Robert Morris, he sent to the destitute army a thousand barrels of flour, with little or no assurance that he would be repaid.

Through the peculiar position of his property and the fact that it appeared to be open to the attacks of marauding forces, he suffered immense losses during the early part of the war. Not only did the cannon of Burgoyne wreck and set on fire his great house at Saratoga, but to prevent their crops from falling into the hands of the enemy his wife, Catherine Schuyler, applied the torch to the ripening grain. There was, however, not only enough left to shower hospitality upon the many distinguished strangers who were always welcome, but in material ways to add to the comfort of his many children.

Hamilton's honeymoon was a short one, and during the early months of 1781 he was not only busy with military affairs, but prepared his second memorandum upon the establishment of a national bank, which was sent to Robert Morris. He was then but twenty-four. In May, with Washington and others, he again met Rochambeau at Hartford, and with de Ternay, the commandant of the French fleet, made arrangements for a joint campaign. De Grasse, in command of the squadron then in the West Indies, was to proceed toward the north, which he later did.

Hamilton during the summer had gone South to crown his military career, taking part in the investment of Yorktown, and the attack which led to the surrender of Cornwallis.

His letters to his wife, at this time, detail his plans and the operations of the army.

Alexander Hamilton to Elizabeth Hamilton[1]

August, 1781.

In my last letter I informed you that there was a greater prospect of activity now, than there had been heretofore. I did this to prepare your mind for an event which, I am sure, will give you pain. I begged your father, at the same time, to intimate to you, by degrees, the probability of its taking place.

A part of the army, my dear girl, is going to Virginia, and I must, of necessity, be separated at a much greater distance from my beloved wife. I cannot announce the fatal necessity, without feeling everything that a fond husband can feel. I am unhappy. I am unhappy beyond expression. I am unhappy, because I am to be so remote from you; because I am to hear from you less frequently than I am accustomed to do. I am miserable, because I know you will be so; I am wretched at the idea of flying so far from you, without a single hour's interview, to tell you all my pains and all my love. But I cannot ask permission to visit you. It might be thought improper to leave my corps at such a time, and upon such an occasion. I must go without seeing you—I must go without embracing you;—alas! I must go. But let no idea, other than of the distance we shall be asunder disquiet you. Though I said the prospects of activity will be greater, I said it to give your expectations a different turn, and prepare you for something disagreeable. It is ten to one that our views will be disappointed, by Cornwallis retiring to South Carolina by land. At all events, our operations will be over by the latter end of October, and I will fly to my home. Don't mention I am going to Virginia.

[1] " Hamilton's Works " (J. C. H.), vol. I, p. 268.

Alexander Hamilton to Elizabeth Hamilton[1]

HEAD OF ELK, *September* 6, 1781.

Yesterday, my lovely wife, I wrote to you, inclosing you a letter in one to your father, to the care of Mr. Morris. Tomorrow the post sets out, and tomorrow we embark for Yorktown. I cannot refuse myself the pleasure of writing you a few lines. Constantly uppermost in my thoughts and affections, I am happy only when my moments are devoted to some office that respects you. I would give the world to be able to tell you all I feel and all I wish, but consult your own heart and you will know mine. What a world will soon be between us! To support the idea, all my fortitude is insufficient. What must be the case with you, who have the most female of female hearts? I sink at the perspective of your distress, and I look to heaven to be your guardian and supporter.

Circumstances that have just come to my knowledge, assure me that our operations will be expeditious, as well as our success certain. Early in November, as I promised you, we shall certainly meet. Cheer yourself with this idea, and with the assurance of never more being separated.

Every day confirms me in the intention of renouncing public life, and devoting myself wholly to you. Let others waste their time and their tranquillity in a vain pursuit of power and glory; be it my object to be happy in a quiet retreat with my better angel.

A. HAMILTON.

Shortly before the end of the war he wrote this letter:

Alexander Hamilton to Elizabeth Hamilton[2]

PHILADELPHIA, *July* 22, 1783.

I wrote you, my beloved Eliza, by the last post, which I hope will not meet with the fate that many others of my letters must have met with. I count upon setting out to

---

[1] " Hamilton's Works " (J. C. H.), vol. I, p. 269.
[2] *Ibid.*, vol. I, p. 396.

see you in four days; but I have been so frequently disappointed by unforeseen events, that I shall not be without apprehensions of being detained, till I have begun my
journey.

The members of Congress are very pressing with me not
to go away at this time, as the House is thin, and as the
definitive treaty is momently expected.

Tell your father that Mr. Rivington, in a letter to the
South Carolina delegates, had given information, coming
to him from Admiral Arbuthnot that the *Mercury* frigate
is arrived at New York with the definitive treaty, and that
the city was to be evacuated yesterday, by the treaty. I
am strongly urged to stay a few days for the ratification of
the treaty; at all events, however, I will not be long absent.

I give you joy of the happy conclusion of this important
work in which your country has been engaged. Now, in
a very short time, I hope we shall be happily settled in
New York. My love to your father.

Kiss my boy a thousand times.

A. HAMILTON.

Before this Hamilton had left the army and had gone to
Albany to study law—and on August 11 his friend, McHenry,
wrote:

James McHenry to Alexander Hamilton[1]

If you are not in the humor to read a long letter, do,
prithee, give this to the child to play with and go on with
your amusement of rocking the cradle.[2] To be serious,
my dear Hamilton, I have been thinking of late upon my
own situation and this led me as often to think of yours.
Some men, I observe, are so born & tempered, that it is
not till after long bustling & battling it in the world (and
some scarcely then) that they come to learn a little prudence.
Much I begin to suspect that you & I want a great deal of
this quality to bring us on a level with our neighbors and
to carry us cheerfully through life. Have we not both of

[1] *Op. cit.*, p. 43.
[2] See Hamilton's Letter to Lafayette, Nov. 3, 1782.

DR. JAMES McHENRY

From an engraved portrait by St. Memin
By permission of Burrows Bros. & Co.

us continued long enough in the service of the public? Should not I exercise my profession or some profitable business & should not you, putting off the politician, exert yourself *only* to acquire a profession? I find that to be dependent on a father is irksome, because I feel that it is in my power to be independent by my own endeavours. I see that the good things of this world are all to be purchased with money and that the man who has money may be whatever he pleases.

Hamilton, there are two lawyers in this Town, one of which has served the public in the General Assembly for three years with reputation, and to the neglect of his practice. The other has done nothing but attend to his profession, by which he has acquired a handsome competency. Now the people have taken it into their heads to displace the lawyer which has served them till he is become poor, in order to put in his stead the lawyer who has served himself & become rich. Let me add to this anecdote a bon mot of our friend Fleury's. Talking to me the other day. "You are a senator," said he, "pray what is your salary." I told him it might perhaps defray about two thirds of our expenses while attending the Senate, and that we were only paid during our attendance, provided one was unmarried & lived frugally. "Then," said he, "I pity Maryland, for her Senate must be composed chiefly of rich fools." What is the moral of all this, my dear friend, but that it is high time for you and I to set about in good earnest, doing something for ourselves.

I hear you are chosen a delegate to Congress. Will you forgive me for saying that I would rather have heard that you had not been chosen. If you accept of the office, there is a stop to any further study of the law, which I am desirous you should finish, because a few years practice at the bar would make you independent, and do you more substantial good than all the fugitive honors of Congress. This would put it in your power to obtain them and to hold them with more certainty, should you still be inclined to risque in a troubled sea. The moment you cease to be a candidate for public places, the people will lament your loss and wait with impatience till they can persuade a man of your abilities to serve them. In the mean time, you will be doing justice to your family. Besides, you know that there is nothing at present to be had worthy your acceptance. The negotiators for peace have been long since appointed. The great departments of Government are all filled up. Our foreign ministers sit firm in their seats. It is not to be expected that any new ministers will be created before a peace. And when this comes, be assured, long residence and large possessions in this country will prelude superior merits.

I wish, therefore, my dear friend that I could prevail upon you to avoid a disappointment & a loss which I think I foresee. For, should you go to Congress, you will lose another year of time that is become more precious than ever and retire, perhaps in disgust, to renew your studies and to those domestic endearments which you will regret to have forsaken. How would it vex me to learn that you had exclaimed in the stile of an English cardinal—If I had best served my family as faithfully as I have the public, my affairs would have been today in a very different order.

It appears to me, Hamilton, to be no longer either necessary or a duty, for you and I to go on to sacrifice the small remnant of time that is left us. We have already immolated largely on the altar of liberty. At present, our country neither wants our services in the field or the cabinet, so that it is incumbent upon us to be useful in another line. By pushing your studies to a conclusion, you at once perfect your happiness. But, I wonder, nor recollect, whilst my own life runs on in idleness and small follies that I stand in most need of the advice which I am presuming to offer. You have a wife and an increasing offspring to urge you forward, but I am without either—without your incitements to begin a reform or your perseverance to succeed. Write me, then, what you are doing—What you have done and what you intend to do, that I may endeavor to follow your example. And be full, for I really intend to be wise and you shall be my Apollo.

I have been a second time on the point of gaining immortality by a fever. It seized me a little after the arrival of the French troops here and has only permitted me to come abroad a few days since Mrs. Carter[1] & Miss Peggy[2] are with us and of course you will think I have been often with them. But I must tell you something of your relations. Mr. Carter is the mere man of business and I am informed has riches enough, with common management, to make the longest life very comfortable. Mrs. Carter is a fine woman. She charms in all companies. No one has seen her, of either sex, who has not been pleased with her, and she pleased every one, chiefly, by means of those qualities which made you the husband of her sister. Peggy, though perhaps a finer woman, is not generally thought so. Her own sex are apprehensive that she considered them poor things, as Swift's Vanessa did, and they, in return, do not scruple to be displeased. In short, Peggy, to be admired as she ought, has only to please the men less and the ladies more. Tell her so. I am sure her good sence will soon place her in her proper station.

My dear Hamilton, adieu. Remember a man who lives in this world, without being satisfied with it. Who strives to seem happy among a people who cannot inspire happiness, but who thinks it unbecoming the dignity of man to leave his part, merely because it does not please him. I am melancholly you perceive. This plaguy fever has torn me to pieces and my mind yet shares in the weakness of my body. But I will recover spirits, as I recover strength. In the meanwhile do not fail to write me. Again my friend and philosopher adieu.

JAMES McHENRY.

It is somewhat interesting to note, despite McHenry's warning, that Hamilton not only entered public life, but at the same time made a success at the bar.

[1]Mrs. "Carter" was Mrs. John Barker Church, born Angelica Schuyler and sister of Mrs. Alexander Hamilton. During the Revolution her husband was known as Carter.

[2] Margaret Schuyler, married Stephen van Rensselaer.

CHAPTER VI

HAMILTON, THE LAWYER

HAMILTON's choice of a profession was made even before the end of the war, for in his well-known letter to General Schuyler, written February 18, 1781, in which he recounted his quarrel with Washington and his future prospects, he said: "If a handsome command in the campaign in the light infantry should offer itself, I shall balance between this and the artillery. My situation in the latter would be more solid and permanent, but as I hope the war will not last long enough to make it progressive, this consideration has less force. A command for the campaign would leave me the winter to prosecute my studies relative to my future career in life." Although it has been stated that after he went to Albany to prepare himself, in 1782, he was admitted to the bar after less than five months' study, there are those who believe that he had, for many years, been accumulating a knowledge of the law, for he could not have accomplished what he did in so short a space of time. Certainly the early literary work in which he engaged, which was called forth by Seabury's Tory pamphlets, indicated a trained and logical mind. Estabrook, who has written an exceedingly interesting paper, said that Hamilton not only argued like a lawyer, but displayed the knowledge and habits of a lawyer, even as far back as 1774; and his two papers to which reference has been made, namely, "A Full Vindication," and "The Farmer Refuted," bore intrinsic evidences of a familiarity with the law and the authorities of the time, and a capacity for logical deduction quite beyond his years.

While his genius was everywhere apparent, the trend of his mind was always analytical, and his systematic habits of thought and argument served him in good stead, not only in his chosen calling, but later in the conduct of public affairs. Certainly the observations of De Tocqueville as to the value of legal training as the requirement of a states-man had, in this case, ample proof and illustration. He entered into his new calling with enthusiasm, and although it did not receive his undivided attention, for he was, at the same time, devoting his energies to the construction of the American Constitution, he no doubt had enough lucra-tive work to do when he left Albany and opened his office at No. 57 Wall Street.

About this time he wrote to Lafayette:

ALBANY, *November* 3, 1782.[1]

I have been employed for the last ten months in rocking the cradle and studying the art of *fleecing* my neighbors. I am now a grave counsellor-at-law, and shall soon be a grave member of Congress. The Legislature, at their last session, took it into their heads to name me, pretty unani-mously, as one of their delegates.

I am going to throw away a few months more in public life, and then retire a simple citizen and good *paterfamilias*. I set out for Philadelphia in a few days. You see the dis-position I am in. You are condemned to run the race of ambition all your life. I am already tired of the career, and dare to leave it.

With his partner, Balthazar De Heart, his services were now everywhere in demand. Naturally, many of his cases were connected with the claims of those people who had suf-

[1] " Hamilton's Works" (J. C. H.), vol. I, p. 320.

fered by the war, and whose property had been taken from
them by order of Governor Tryon and other Tories. Among
these were claims for damages arising from the seizure of cattle on Long Island, and actions growing out of the trespass
law. Again we find that he appeared as counsel in the will
cases of Dr. Peter Middleton, Philip Livingston, and Henry
Beekman.

Suits for reprisal and claims for damages engaged his
attention, and the papers he left, throw much light upon
matters connected with the American Revolution, and the
unsettled period at its conclusion. It would appear that
in those days petty political officers were not above recourse to extortion and graft, which at times since, has
distinguished the municipal affairs of the city of New
York. We find that during the early part of the Revolution, when the statue of George III was torn down and
demolished, and the types of Printer Rivington distributed
and condemned for the purpose of making bullets, there
was a general levy upon the citizens of New York for the
lead in the window-sashes throughout the city for the same
purpose, and that subsequently, when restitution was demanded for this form of contribution, it was the custom
for the representative of the auditor to mulct the com-
plainant nine shillings for a certificate showing the validity
of the claim. One Peter R. Fell employed Hamilton as
his counsel to prepare a memorial to the Assembly of the
State of New York, in which he urged his grievances. In
this he stated that he was one of those from whose windows
leads were taken by order of the Convention at the commencement of the late war; that soon after the last sitting
of the legislature it was learned that one Daniel Dunscomb
was ordered to render an account to the auditor of the leads
so taken; that Fell requested Dunscomb to give a certificate

to this effect, but the latter exacted nine shillings therefor
from the messenger, although he, Dunscomb, had been
allowed twenty pounds by the auditor as full compensation for his services. He naturally complained that "as
leads were taken from one thousand houses in the city,
the exaction of nine shillings is a species of petty extortion, highly censurable, and unbecoming the publick confidence."

The members of the rich Livingston family, whose holdings of land were enormous, were much in the courts, and
when Robert, the first proprietor of the lordship or manor,
died, his sons Robert, Philip, and Gilbert indulged in
acrimonious litigation which was carried on for a few years.
An action brought by Philip against his neighbor Robert,
the Chancellor, was one of the most important, and John
Morin Scott was the attorney of record, and Hamilton was
retained as counsel. This was on April 24, 1783, and concerned the establishment of a grist-mill on the stream known
as Roeloff Jansen Kill, which emptied into the Hudson
River. Another case was that of Livingston *vs.* Hoffman,
for trespass, in which Hamilton appeared for the defence.
These cases in the early days were usually ill-founded,
and as a rule advantage was taken of the fact that the party
of one side or the other had taken sides with the enemy and
forfeited his rights.

The feeling against the Tories who had taken possession
of the houses of the patriots who were obliged to flee during
the occupation of New York by the British, was so intense
as to lead to the passage of the celebrated trespass law,
which was framed in the interests of the patriots, but was
in direct conflict with the provisions of the treaty made
with Great Britain, which expressly provided for the rights
of Tories after the declaration of peace. Although a wave

of intolerance swept over the State, and the persecution
of those who had not taken active sides with the rebellious
colonists was general, Hamilton, in 1783, appeared in behalf
of a Tory tenant named Waddington, who had been sued by
a Mrs. Elizabeth Rutgers, thereby making himself exceedingly unpopular. Considerable sympathy was felt for the
plaintiff in this case, who was supposed to be a poor and
helpless widow, but an inspection of the papers would go to
show that she could drive a sharp bargain, and the sympathy
extended to her was certainly misplaced.

In 1778 the premises, which consisted of a brewery and
malt-house in Maiden Lane, were rented to Benjamin Waddington & Co., who found them in very bad order, "and
stripped of everything of any value except an old Copper,
two old Pumps and a leaden Cistern full of holes." Before
the new tenant could begin to brew £700 were spent in
repairs. From the 1st of May, 1780, to the 1st of May,
1783, the Waddingtons had paid a rent of £150 per annum for the same to John Smyth, Esq., a Tory, in consequence of an order from General Robertson, the British
commander.

On the 20th of June, 1783, after the return of the American forces they received an order from General Birch, the
commandant of the city, to pay the rent from the 1st of
May preceding to the son of Mrs. Rutgers. After this
the troubles of the Waddingtons began. They were quite
ready to pay her, but her representative demanded back
rent, and would not adjust matters in any other way, or
take into account the improvements made by the tenants.
The demands of Mrs. Rutgers finally became so exorbitant
that Waddington & Co. refused to pay at all, and to add to
their difficulties the brew-house was, about this time, burned
to the ground, entailing upon them a loss of £4,000. At

the time of the fire they were not in possession of the premises, having surrendered the key to the owner. It was then that the Widow Rutgers found many friends and sympathizers who urged her to avail herself of the new law, and she brought a suit, engaging John Laurance as her lawyer, and an action was brought in the mayor's court.

I am in possession of Hamilton's original argument in this proceeding, which comprises nineteen pages of closely written foolscap, and in which we find everywhere evidenced much labor and thought.[1] Although this brief has been elsewhere quoted, reference may be made to his contention that this was a national and not a local issue, and that the recent law then passed by the State of New York could have no force against the law of the nation, which was common law; in other words, the State of New York had no common law of nations. In fact, it was the strongest plea for Federalism that came from him in the whole course of his career, for he insisted that the law of each State must adopt the laws of Congress, and that though in relation to its own citizens local laws might govern, yet in relation, to foreigners those of the United States must prevail. "It must be conceded that the legislature of one State cannot repeal the law of the United States—all must be construed to stand together."

It was only after a vigorous fight, in the face of general opposition and disorderly expressions of public sympathy, that Hamilton convinced the judges by his incontrovertible demonstration of the law itself, that he was in the right, when they rendered a judgment in his favor.

Not only after this was he besieged by many clients with similar cases, but he appeared in behalf of patriot house-

[1] Appendix H.

holders who had been imposed upon by tenants who had improperly taken advantage of the trespass law.

One of these cases was that of Alexander McDougall vs. Catharine Leonard, the husband of the latter being a notorious Tory who had taken up arms with the British and had gone to Newburg, where he stayed nutil the end of the war. McDougall, it will be remembered, was, with Isaac Sears, John Morin Scott, and others, one of the original "Sons of Liberty," who precipitated the Revolution in New York City by the destruction of British property and resistance to the tax law. McDougall afterward became a brigadier-general in the American forces.

Mrs. Leonard appears to have been remiss in the payment of her rent for the premises 75 Beekman Street, even after the conclusion of the Revolution, and in a letter to her McDougall says: "I do not wish to have any dispute with a woman, or I should not have had the Forbearance to you which I have exercised, nor taken the trouble of writing this.—I now expect to have the Ballance from you by Thursday, two o'Clocke, or I shall be under the disagreeable Necessity of Sending for it by Another."

In the early part of Hamilton's career his associates at the bar were his intimate friends, and these included Brockholst Livingston, the son of the Governor of New Jersey and an early schoolmate at the academy at Elizabethtown, Richard Harrison, Robert Troup, Colonel Varick, Burr, and Laurance. An inspection of the many musty law papers that have come into the writer's possession suggests the great variety of the forms of action in which he was engaged, as in those days there was no specialization, and Hamilton appeared as often in the mayor's court as in the higher ones of the State, and did both civil and criminal work. He even

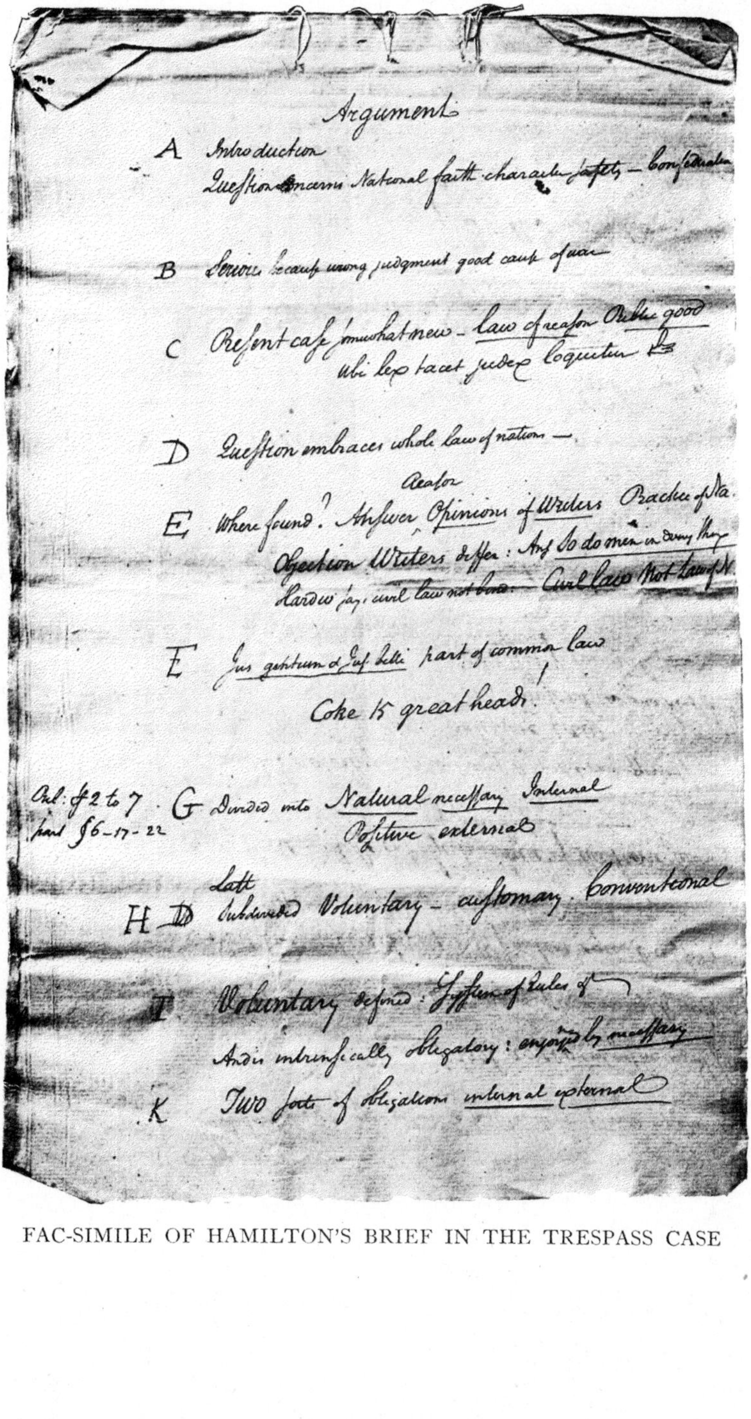

Argument

A Introduction
Question concerns National faith character safety — Confederation

B Serious because wrong judgment good cause of war

C Present case somewhat new — law of reason Public good
ubi lex tacet judex loquitur

D Question embraces whole law of nations —

E Where found? Answer, Reason Opinions of Writers Practice of Na
Objection Writers differ: Ans So do men in every thing
Hardw says civil law not bind: Civil law Not Law of N

F Jus gentium & Jus belli part of common law
Coke 15 great heads

Vol: §2 to 7
prel §6-17-22
G Divided into Natural necessary Internal
Positive external

H Latt Subdivided Voluntary — customary. Conventional

I Voluntary defined: System of Rules of
And is intrinsically obligatory: enjoined by necessary

K Two sorts of obligations internal external

FAC-SIMILE OF HAMILTON'S BRIEF IN THE TRESPASS CASE

tried a rape case,[1] as well as others for assault and murder, but his fondness was, evidently, for civil proceedings.

His clients were not always reasonable or patient, although the unreasonable ones were in the minority. One of the latter appears to have been Stephen Delancey, the son of James, who, in the language of the day, was a Tory and so "attainted" that his property was seized by the Americans. Stephen owned a large tract of land in Westchester County, and had many tenants who gave him a great deal of trouble, among them the "Delivans," and "Baileys," for whom he engaged Hamilton to issue writs. Impatient at the latter's alleged neglect of his affairs and supposed inaction he wrote from Scarsdale, New York, September 12, 1785: "I could wait no longer in New York at an expence to see you as you was gone to Court on Thursday morning and when to see you I knew not, if I had stay'd I have to lay out about 30^s/ on this Journey and I find money so scarce to be had, that I must insist on ye moneys being Refunded to me. I beg you to Inform me what method I am to pursue with my wicked tenants in Distraining for Rent of them."

Another gentleman, who had repeatedly urged Hamilton to collect a certain indebtedness for him, remarked that "Mr. W——has certainly received money, but what sum, is in the womb of Time to Discover."

Others were more considerate and appreciative of Hamilton's busy life, and the limited amount of time at his disposal.

J. Campbell wrote (1786): "May I hope forgiveness for

---

[1] This case was that of Russell *vs*. Murphy, and Hamilton represented Murphy, who was accused, on the fourth day of December, 1785, of having in the East Ward of the city of New York, "with force and Arms to wit with Sword and Stones and Knives made an Assault on her, the said Margaret Russell, with intent her the said Margaret, an infant as aforesaid to Ravish and Deflour, and her the said Margaret then and there beat, wounded and evilly treated so that her life was greatly despaired of and other enormities."

encroaching on your goodness. It is that Goodness which is the Source of all the trouble I have given you, and extended to me the flatering hopes of Acess to your future Advice and Assistance, uppon that I plead for the honour of seeing you in the Course of this day."

A consideration of the various appeals to him shows how greatly his opinion was respected. Some of them are very naïve and simple, but all attest the confidence of the writers who desired his professional help at the time.[1]

Nathaniel Ruggles wrote, in 1795: "I would Inform you that I have Business of Consequence Likely to Commence & Wish you to engage for Me as my Attorney in A Case of Fraud which is much Approbated in my Favour by the Principle gentlemen of this Place. I Have not Any Fee at Present to Advance Though I have Property. Sir, I Humbly Request You would not take A Fee Against me." George Pollock sought to retain him in January, 1795, in another case. Hamilton's endorsement on the paper is as follows: "I am not sure that I could with propriety. Will decide in June. Will not be concerned against him." Richard Platt, in April 26, 1796, wrote to him about an impending case and said: "The amount of the Debt is too triffling to ask any interposition of you as Counsel on the Defendant's side, but the Consequences of its possible result may involve a Question of the first magnitude to all persons in future subject to prosecution for Debt when and where the hearts of Creditors (as is well known to be too frequently the case) are instigated by the Devil. Thus situated and well knowing there is a susceptibility for the Verdict of

---

"[1] He gave time and money with a lavish hand to all who sought his aid," says Lodge. This is borne out by his books which are full of loans, but the credit side of the ledger is usually empty. The only return in a good many entries of sums of money lent, is a barrel of hams that were intended to discharge an indebtedness of six pounds.

Renown, it is, that I wish your Union with Troup & Brockholst to-morrow. They will possess you with the necessary
documents on application and I have no doubt but Judge-
ment of the Bench will be of that sort which Lord Mansfield would not blush to own."

Some of his clients languished in the debtors' prison.
One, Henry A. Williams, wrote from there, March 31,
1798, to Hamilton: "I am again necessitated to write you
from this gloomy place (viz.—the gaol) where a trifling sum
compared to the amount of Schenck's mortgage holds me."
When it was possible quickly to apprehend a delinquent
debtor, many important people found their way to the
Bridewell prison. William Duer, whose financial irregularities were of a gigantic nature, was there held for some time;
and Earle, the artist, who was also imprisoned for debt,
painted Mrs. Hamilton's portrait,[1] and in this way earned
enough to obtain his freedom.

Arrest and imprisonment for debt were general, and
some of his clients kept him fully informed of their debtors who were at large, in more or less pressing and vindictive communications. One gentleman, whose chance
presence here was awaited with interest and anxiety, was
Pierpont Edwards of New Haven, who studiously kept out
of the State.

The delicacy of Hamilton's professional relations must have
been, at times, great indeed, for upon one occasion he appeared for Mrs. Phœbe Ward, who, in petitioning Governor
Clinton and the General Assembly, sought to gain her point
by calling attention to the shortcomings of her husband, who
was evidently a Tory. She presented her case in the following language: "Whereas I, Phœbe Ward, wife of Edward
Ward, do Humbly beg Leave to Address your Honours

[1] In 1787.

with this my Petition, Humbly beging Leave to Acquaint
your Honours with the true Situation of Matters.   My
Husband, Edward Ward, it was not supos'd he Altogether
Condescended into Political Sentiments with the Country
in General, therefore I hope your Honours will now Consider that a Wife cannot alter Principles or Dictate a Husband so far as to change his present conduct in Matters of
so great Moment and of so great Importance as this present
or past Revolution."

   The Rev. Jacob F. Hardenbergh was one of the striking
figures of the Revolution and known as an energetic patriot, and by many was called the "fighting parson."   At a
time when so much unsettlement existed regarding the
boundary lines of property, actions for trespass, as has been
said, were much more common than they have ever been
since.   The son of Mr. Hardenbergh wrote to "Col. Hamilton, Col. Troup, and Col. Harison," from Raritan, July
14, 1785:

   By order of my Father I wrote to you a few Days ago,
beging of you, and the other Gentlemen imployed for
him, not to be detained against him in any Suit, at least
until he may have had an opportunity of Consulting upon
the Subject with them.   Since that he has wanted me to
write to his Attorney on the Subject of the late Verdict
against him.   That Verdict Creates him uneasiness.   He
suspects undue Influence upon, at least, one or another
of the leading Persons among the Jury.   Also some abominable fraud in that Marked Stone in a certain line, &c.
The night before I came away, he was informed that a certain man should have said, If he had not been Subpœnaed
on the other side, he could have evidenced when the letters
were put on that Stone, and who did it, &c.   He also heard
that Mr. Gale should have been Invited and dined with
one of the Principle Inhabitants of the Town, That he was

to take a ride out of Town. He had not yet had an opportunity to examin into the ground of these Reports when
I left home. This carresing of the Jury by the plaintifes
should have been after the commencement of the court.
The old gentleman seemed Determined, to try further,
if there is any Prospect of obtaining what he believes to be
his just right. I therefore wish the Gentlemen who have
faithfully served him in this cause would let him know
their candid opinion about that Matter, they are now acquainted with the Matters pro & con. If they judge his
cause not supportable by proper evidence, to dissuade him
from any farther prosecution. If the contrary, to send
him their opinion about the matter of farther prosecution.
He seems inclined to attempt setting aside this Verdict,
and risk a new tryal.

When Hamilton came to New York he was immediately
the recipient of many offers of help; and there were as well,
although he had just entered upon the practice of his profession, many applications from fathers and others who
wished him to receive their sons into his office as pupils.
On June 29, 1784, William Hull[1] wrote from Newton, Mass.,
proposing that he should take Charles Jackson for instruction, and give him employment. Charles was the son of
General Michael Jackson, and was "himself an Official at
the Close of the War, and as soon as Peace took place,
applied himself to study. Last year he graduated at Harvard College, since which as I before observed he has read
law with me."

In Hamilton's books it is stated that Pierre V. Van Cortlandt became a clerk in February, 1784, and $150 was paid
for his tuition. In May of the same year, Jacob A. LeRoy
commenced his clerkship, and his father paid $150. The

---

[1] Hull commanded the North-western army, and was an uncle of Commodore
Isaac Hull who commanded the *Constitution* in her fight with the *Guerrière*.

following note is appended in Hamilton's handwriting: "Mr. LeRoy did not continue his Clerkship, so the money was refunded." In February Dirk Ten Broeck also commenced his "clerkship" and Hamilton received $150 from him.

1786   Oct. 1 (Samuel Broome)   To this sum due for
           fee with your son a clerk $150.

  "   Oct 1   This day Mr. S. Broome, Junior entered
            the office as Clerk and this 1st of May absented himself to return 1789.

On July 20, 1789, John Adams paid $20 for his son, who became a clerk. This was "remitted." Many men were recommended as partners, among them a Mr. Griffiths who was suggested by Elisha Boudinot, but it would seem that his only real associate was Balthazar De Heart, who appears to have been what is now known as a managing clerk.

Hamilton tried many cases with his attached friend Troup, and others with Aaron Burr, although, later in his career, these occasions became more and more infrequent. Again, they were on opposite sides. Burr's temptations to indulge in discreditable operations were not always resisted. He was a notorious speculator, and not overscrupulous in money affairs, as appears from his relation with the Holland Company and the affairs of the Pulteney Estate. Lord Ashburton, who was Baring, the celebrated English banker, was especially incensed because of Burr's trickery, and wrote a scathing letter to Hamilton who represented him, alluding to the duplicity of the former. A case in which he appeared illustrating Burr's methods, and his desire to escape, if possible, the responsibility of his actions, was that of Lewis vs. Burr, in which Hamilton appeared for the plaintiff, and which has unusual interest for other reasons. It was an action to hold Burr liable as an endorser on a note for $3,500.[1]

On June the first, one Roger Enos made his promissory note payable to the order of Aaron Burr, thirty days after date. Burr endorsed the note to Francis Lewis, the plaintiff in the action, and the note was not paid. By its terms it fell due on the 4th of July, days of grace included. The 4th of July was a national holiday, being the anniversary of the Declaration of Independence, and on that day business, according to the custom then obtaining in the city of New York, was suspended. It was claimed that the three days of grace, which would have expired on the 4th of July, were, by reason of that day being a holiday, abridged, and that the note fell due on the 3d of July. Efforts were made to demand payment of the maker on the 3d, but he could not be found and, therefore, an excuse for making a demand was presented. The jurors being in doubt as to the law of the case returned a special verdict as to the facts, and submitted for the determination of the court this question of law, as to whether the note fell due on the 3d or 4th of July.

If the effort to make the demand on the 3d was sufficient to put the maker of the note in default and was not premature, then Burr was liable to the plaintiff upon his promise to pay as endorser; but if the demand was not properly sought to be made on the 3d, then Burr was not liable. The whole question was one of law as to whether the note was due on the 3d or 4th of July, and the special verdict was for the purpose of presenting all the facts to the court so that it might determine this simple question. That was in accordance with the practice which prevailed at the

[1] This case is reported in "2 Caine's Cases," p. 194.

time the action was pending, and the court would direct judgment on the verdict in accordance with its decision. The case was carried up to the Supreme Court in bank, and was argued there in 1796, and the court held that the 4th of July was a public holiday, and that the note fell due July 3d, and judgment was rendered against Burr. I was informed by the late Justice Edward Patterson that this decision was the precedent for all subsequent rulings of the Courts.

When Hamilton came to New York the second time his friends, without exception, welcomed him most hospitably, and none more kindly than his former associates in the directorate of the Bank of New York. One of them, Comfort Sands, provided an office for him and wrote: "As soon as your furniture arrives, I will take care of it and put it in my store. If it is possible I will engage a room for you for an office. It will be difficult to get one. I hope to be able to get my house done so that I may remove at the time I promised. I hardly doubt that I shall." After a time numerous young men again made application to enter his office as students or clerks, and William Laight addressed to him the following letter regarding his own son who was an applicant:

Had there not been frequent Instances in many respectable offices in this City where Events of a similar kind have been effected, which I am now solicitous of obtaining, I should deem it presumptuous to address you on the subject: Let this, in addition to the solicitude of a Parent for the Establishment of a Son in the line of his Profession, be my Apology:—

Edward W. Laight, after his matriculation at Columbia College, was instructed in the Rudiments and Principles of Law by Cole: Burr, & finished the usual Course of his

Studies with Mr. Munroe—He has been admitted to the Bar as an Attorney.—Of his qualifications Professional Men are better Judges than myself.—The Object I aim at is, to have him patronized by a Person of Merit & Celebrity, more for the purpose of improvement than for present Emolument.—To obtain this End, there is no pecuniary Compensation, within my reach, which I would not readily advance, & as my Aim is to his future, not immediate, Interest, He would be advised to accept such a proportion of Income as his Principal might hereafter deem adequate to his exertions of usefulness.—

The wish of my heart is, that Cole: Hamilton should be such a Patron.—If, therefore, it is not incompatible with Cole: Hamilton's Views to receive as an Attorney in his office a Young Man, of, at least decent Manners & educated as above mentioned, I should be made happy by his giving me an opportunity of acceding to such Terms as he himself would prescribe.

Respectfully &c

WM. LAIGHT.

Cole: Hamilton—14 March 1797.

It was with great regret that Hamilton resigned from the Treasury, but the demands of a growing family were such that he could not live upon a salary of but $3,000 per annum. Of course, many of his bitter enemies, those who had never ceased to accuse him of overweening ambition, or even of actual dishonesty, were not slow to make many fresh insinuations, but these were all unjust, and his return to work was a necessity. A paper making Robert Troup his executor, found after his death, disclosed his comparative poverty on leaving office. In commenting upon this Lodge says: "It furnished a striking commentary on the charges of corruption made against Hamilton by Jefferson and his tools, and on Madison's cold sneer that Hamilton retired from office alleging poverty as a cause." No one under-

stood better than General Schuyler the desperate straits of
his son-in-law, and in a letter from Poughkeepsie, January 5,
1794, he wrote to Hamilton: "As soon as I found that
Fairly[1] and others of his complexion assigned as one of the
motives for your resignation a wish to be Governor of this
State, that person also assigned another, to wit, that the
affairs of your department were so deranged, that it was not
possible for you to extricate It from the confusion In which
It was Involved. Doubting If I was at liberty to name my
author who had heard Fairly make the assertions, I contented myself with an opportunity of declaring in his presence that the propagator of such a calumny was a liar and
a villain."

To his family his retirement from public office to again
take up law was a matter of great moment, but all believed
in his success, and gave hearty encouragement. Mrs.
Church wrote to her sister from London in 1795: "I see
by the American papers that our dear Hamilton has been
received with joy by the inhabitants of New York. I partake in every event that is agreeable to him, and often with
a warmth which would lead one to imagine I was his own
sister as well as his attached friend," and again later: "Mr.
Gore[2] tells me that Colonel Hamilton's popularity is very
great, and that he had a warm welcome at New York; those
that are swayed by his opinions will always pursue their
country's welfare; but my dear Eliza when you and I are
with him he shall not talk politics to us. A little of his
agreeable nonsense will do us more good."

He carried from Philadelphia the best wishes of most of
his official associates, and those with whom he had labored so

---

[1] Fairlie was the clerk of the N. Y. Supreme Court, and an unscrupulous politician.
[2] Christopher Gore, Commissioner in London to enter American spoliation
claims under Jay's treaty.

devotedly. His attached and distinguished friend, Richard Peters, at one time a justice of the United States Circuit Court in Pennsylvania, wrote from Philadelphia, February 15, 1795, asking him to do him a professional favor. "This use I make of you will be some but a very insignificant Antidote against the Regret I feel at parting with you—But it is well to make the most of Misfortunes. Wherever you go, you carry with you my best Wishes for your Happiness, for as to Money & you will pick that up fast, owing to the Enmities & not the Friendships of your Fellow-Cits. God bless you and believe me," etc. And again in March: "I hope your *otium cum Dignitate* agrees with you. I was afraid of your being too idle and have on this account put a teazing employment upon you," and he asked him to proceed against Wm. Coghlan, for land bought twenty years before. His friend's wishes evidently were realized, for Hamilton's practice began to flourish, and nearly all the merchants came to him with profitable cases. Among these were Le Guen, with the most important of all, McEvers and Bayard, and a host of others; in fact, his "agenda" contained a list of nearly every one of wealth and influence in New York, who was obliged to seek the help of the courts.

Much of Hamilton's time was now taken up with Admiralty practice, and as the relations with France and Great Britain were so unsettled during the end of the eighteenth century, the depredations upon commerce were frequent and annoying. Hamilton, a few years before, while Secretary of the Treasury, had, with Washington, fought the impudent Genet, who actually fitted out privateers in our very ports. One of the most flagrant of the insults to which we had been subjected was the defiant attitude of this person regarding the privateer *Little Sarah* or *Petit Democrat*, and Hamilton's drastic rebuke administered to

Genet was everywhere appreciated and applauded by the
owners of American ships. Hamilton appeared in no less
than thirty or forty cases, either for the United Insurance
Company or for various aggrieved ship-owners. Nearly all
of these were of the greatest interest, and the depositions and
briefs that he left among his papers read more like extracts
from Cooper, Marryat, or Stevenson, than dry legal papers.
Many of them are quaint accounts of captures at sea, hand-
to-hand fights, and hair-breadth escapes, the case of the
Fair American being one in point, and the deposition of her
owner is before me as I write:

The Brig *fair American* Robert Forest Master of Philadelphia and bound there, was Captured and taken possession
of on the 16th November by the French Privateer *Jealous*,
Ruff Master, who took out the Mate and three men, put in
a Prize master & eight men and ordered her for Gaudaloup
on the 19th Inst. (I believe) at abot eleven or twelve o'Clock
at night was recaptured by the American armed Ships, *Montezuma*, *Norfolk & Retaliation* who took out the Frenchmen
(Prizemaster excepted) and put in an Officer and 3 men and
directed us to follow them. On the next morning we were
again Captured by the French Frigates, the *Insurgent* &
Volante and a French lugger who sent on board a Prizemaster & 5 men and ordered us for Gaudaloup without
taking any person out of the Brig.

In the Afternoon Captain Forest, the SuperCargo, and
Mr. Griswold began to form a plan for recapturing the Vessel (which originated with Captain Forest) and was immediately agreed to, abot eight o'Clock in the Evening the
Frenchmen being on the Quarter Deck Capt. F. seized the
Cutlass from the French officer on Deck, took possession
of the Helm and Mr. Griswold & Shoemaker run up
out of the Cabin, one armed with a Brace of Pistols and one
with a Sword both belonging to Mr. G. which with the Cutlass of the French officer was all the Arms on board, all the

men assisted to drive the Frenchmen below who made but little resistance. Mr. G. & S. then took Charge of them and watched all night, Capt. F. navigating the Brig and bore away for Antigua *were* we arrived next evening.

When we recaptured the Brig there were two Frigates abot 4 miles ahead which we believe were the French ones that Captured her.

This Statement is made by me at the request of Capt. Murray at the same time I reserve to myself the priviledge of making any further Statement or Explanation respecting the Business which I may conceive requisite or proper.

I further observe that I do not believe the Brig would have been recaptured had not Mr. Griswold his Sword & Pistols & 3 men from the *Montezuma* been on board.—

(Signed)   Jos. SHOEMAKER, JR.

Beside the cases of the *Diana, Harlequin, La Belle Créole, Reindeer, Neptune, Happy Return,* and many others when intricate legal questions arose by reason of capture or loss or insurance, we find that upon one occasion Hamilton appeared for the United Insurance Company in the case of the brig *Nancy.* This vessel, which was owned in Baltimore, subsequently met with a strange adventure on a voyage to Curaçoa, via Hayti, which began in July, 1799. When at sea her course was changed so that she brought up at the Dutch island of Aruba, where she disposed of her mixed cargo of dry goods and provisions, and took on another of arms and ammunition, which she intended to trade with the French at Hayti for coffee. On August 28 she was overhauled by the British war cutter *Sparrow,* belonging to the English flag-ship, and sent to Jamaica. Two days later a Lieutenant Fitton of H. M. S. *Ferret* caught a large shark near the coast of Hayti, and upon opening its belly a package of papers, which undoubtedly belonged to the *Nancy,* was found therein, and was delivered later to Lieutenant Wylie of the cutter that had captured the *Nancy*. Subsequently the vessel was condemned by the advocate-general as a lawful prize. Almost at the same time other papers were found concealed in the cabin of the *Nancy* which were a complement of the original, and together proved the unlawful conduct of the captain of the brig.

Not a little of his work was connected with the land companies that were formed in various parts of the United States. He was counsel for Théophile Cazenove, the president of the Holland Company, and acted for those who sought to put upon its feet the celebrated Georgia Company, which later went to pieces when the Assembly of that State repudiated its action in giving a charter. One of his most painful experiences was in connection with the extraordinary operations and speculations of Robert Morris. Not only did Hamilton himself lose heavily by Morris's conduct, but his brother-in-law, John B. Church, for whom he appeared, and who held a mortgage from Morris, was mulcted, previous to Morris's apprehension and imprisonment. This was undoubtedly a sad blow to Hamilton who, in the early part of his career, was helped by the great financier, who really suggested his name for the treasuryship, and to whom he owed so much. Morris's letters to him are pathetic, and in one, after speaking of his difficulty in raising money and referring to his intention of suing Greenleaf, who had deserted him in his land speculation, he said: "I will immediately turn my attention to another source of reimbursement for you. My promise to you on this point is sacred and shall be fulfilled. You will speedily hear from me in regard to it. I hope Mr. Church has too much spirit and too high a sense of honor to entertain a desire of posessing himself of my property at less than its value, and at its value I am willing to sell it to him. I trust to your assurance of serving me in this business."

As has been said, the most important commercial case with which Hamilton was connected was that of Le Guen *vs.* Gouverneur and Kemble[1]—both parties being shipping merchants, and the issue being alleged misrepresentation and substitution of a cargo of indigo, cotton, and other substances. Numerous side issues arose in which various Jewish merchants named Lopez, Gomez, and Lepine were also concerned. This great case, which was ultimately decided in the Court of Errors, led to much litigation. Le Guen, a Frenchman, was represented by Hamilton, Burr, and others, and the defendants by Gouverneur Morris and associates. The counsel were permitted by the court to speak repeatedly out of the ordinary course, so great was the interest and desire to get at all the facts. Morris was most offensive to Hamilton in court, and there was an interchange of retorts between the two, and the "commanding" figure, melodious voice, and authoritative manner of the former made a great impression. James A. Hamilton refers to this incident.[2] Morris, during his argument and after speaking in praise of what Hamilton had said, used these words: "Before I have done I am confident I shall make my learned friend cry out, 'Help me, Cassius' (pointing to Burr) 'or I sink.'" When Hamilton's turn came to reply, he

---

[1] Mr. Gouverneur had originally tried to retain Hamilton, but the latter declined, and wrote to Gouverneur: "Mr. B. last evening delivered me your letter enclosing a copy of your correspondence with Mr. Lewis. In one other respect I feel myself painfully situated, having received a favorable impression of your character. I am sorry to observe anything to have come from you which I am obliged to consider as exceptional. Your second letter to Mr. Lewis contains a general and, of course, an unjustifiable reflection on the profession to which I belong, and of a nature to put it out of my power to render you any service in the line of that profession. I really believe that you did not attend to the full force of the expression when you told Mr. Lewis, 'Attorneys like to make the most of their bills of cost;' but it contains in it other insinuations which cannot be pleasing to any man in the profession, and which must oblige anyone that has the proper delicacy to decline the business of a person who professedly entertains such an idea of the conduct of this profession."

[2] Hamilton's "Reminiscences," p. 12.

treated Morris with great courtesy, reviewed his arguments
without mercy, exposing all their weakness, and then alluded
to the boast of his friend in a strain of irony that turned the
laughter of the court and audience against him.

On the same day, after the court had closed, there was a
dinner given to the counsel, judges, and others, by Stephen
Van Rensselaer of Albany, the patroon.   Hamilton went
to his father-in-law's General Schuyler's, to dress for dinner.
Morris and the rest to the Patroon's.   When Hamilton arrived, Van Rensselaer met him at the door, and to put him
on his guard informed him that Morris was in a very bad
humor.

Hamilton went into the room, approached Morris most
amiably, and said: "My friend, you will rejoice, I hope,
that by Cassius's help I meet you here with our friends at
dinner!"

The case, like many others at the time, attracted great attention and the court-room was crowded.[1]   General Schuyler wrote to his daughter, February 13, 1800: "So much
has my dear General's time been engrossed by his law business that we have had but a small portion of that Company
which is always so pleasing and so instructive.   Mr. Morris
of Counsel for Mr. Gouverneur, showed much indiscretion by
observations injurious to my Dear General, but such a reply
was given as afforded General pleasure to the Court and
Audience, and which Mr. Morris felt so sensibly, that I hope
he will profit by It for I very sincerely wish him well."

My dear Eliza: We arrived here last evening well and
shall proceed immediately on our journey.

I forgot my brief in the cause of Le Guen against Gouverneur which is in a bundle of papers in my armed Chair in

---

[1] See "Johnson's Cases," vol. I, p. 437.

the office.   Request one of the Gentlemen to look for it and
send it up to me by the post of Tuesday.   Beg them not
to fail—Adieu my beloved.   Kiss all the Children for me.

yrs. A. H.

Peeks Kill April

16th 1797

When it was finally won by Hamilton it is said that he refused a generous fee proffered him by his grateful client,
alleging that it was too much.   Rufus King, in his memoirs,
refers to this incident, and compares Hamilton's modesty to
Burr's exaction of a disproportionate sum for his services.
Luckily I have found Le Guen's letter which states the fact.

Louis Le Guen to Alexander Hamilton

General Hamilton   NEW YORK, 1st *May*, 1800.

DEAR GENERAL: Still deeply moved by your generous proceedings, and full of gratitude, I find myself obliged to do what
you yesterday forbade me to, confining myself to remitting
you herewith the moderate sum of fifteen hundred dollars.
Kindly accept it and at the same time the assurance that no-
body in the world is more respectfully attached to you, or
more disposed than I am to seize every opportunity to shew
you all my gratitude.   Therefore, dear General, be so kind
as to make use of them, and also be well assured of the sincerity of my feelings, which will last as long as I live. . . .

I also enclose a little account of what I have paid to
Mr. Burr, including interest at seven per cent. upon divers
sums that I have advanced him amounting altogether to
$4,636.66.

I beg you to kindly settle this bill with him, so that he
will be satisfied; he has promised to settle up with me tomorrow for the sum of 13,200 dollars that he owes me, fallen
due the 15th of last month, the only business that keeps me
here.

April 1800.
To account of Mr. Burr for onorarium up-to-date . . $2900.
Several accounts upon his order to Mr. Green . . . 290.

BILL OF INTERESTS

Upon $11200 - - - - - that I advanced in three
separate sums at different times. From the month of
July to August 1798—to the 19th April 1799— For
8 months at the rate of 7% 522.66
Interest for one year—upon a bill of $13200 . . . 924.00

$4636.66

The affairs of the new or Park Theatre,[1] which was commenced in 1794, engaged Hamilton's attention, for, owing to
the vicissitudes incident to insufficient capitalization and bad
management, the prospect of building this important place
of amusement languished, but was finally carried out after
many people had lost a great deal of money. The land upon
which it was erected was owned by a Mrs. Ann White, and
the various subscribers to the building fund included the
names of pretty nearly every person of note in New York
at the time. Some of them were: Stephen Van Rensselaer,
James Watson, William Constable, Nicholas Cruger, William Bayard, Isaac Gouverneur, Elias Hicks, Gerret Ket-
tletas, Robert S. Kemble, Nicholas Low, Dominick Lynch,
Julian Ludlow, Stephen Tillinghast, Pascal N. Smith,
George Scriba, Julian Verplanck, Joshua Waddington,
Nathaniel Prime, Rufus King, Charles Wilkes, DeWitt
Clinton, Brockholst Livingston, Josiah Ogden Hoffman,
John Watts, Nathaniel Fish, Thomas Lispenard, and about
seventy others.

Finally, after much disappointment and trouble, the
matter was referred to Chancellor Livingston, and Hamilton was employed. Even later, when the theatre was act-

---

[1] It stood on the east side of the present City Hall Park, near Beekman Street.

ually opened, it had trouble in paying its taxes. It appears that a forcible attempt was made to attach ready money, or, in other words, what are now known as "the box-office receipts." This led to a suit in which William Henderson, Jacob Waltham, Morton Carlyle, and Pollock brought action against William Brown for trespass and for breaking and entering the plaintiffs' close, called the New Theatre, and taking and carrying away three hundred and twenty-five pieces of silver coin of the value of one dollar each. Hamilton defended Brown who, it appears, was duly appointed collector of direct taxes for the district in which the theatre was situated. "He had been also duly furnished with a list in which the *locus in quo* was designated as the dwelling house of one John Hoffman, and as such was taxed at three hundred and twenty-five dollars, and the tax being unpaid he entered and took the silver coin in question in the nature of a distress for the same. The Theatre and appurtenances upon which the tax was laid and levied was, in fact, not the dwelling house for any person whatever, but a Theatre for the exhibition of dramatic performances, but by mistake it was inserted in the list of dwelling houses by the assessor."

Hamilton was employed on the 12th of May, 1789, by Dr. P. J. More, of Charleston, to collect a bill against a Mr. John Tayleur, who formerly kept a jeweller's shop in Queen Street, near the Coffee House, New York. Hamilton's name had been suggested to the plaintiff by Mr. Pringle, and he was urged to make the absconding patient pay his bill, "and to have no indulgence for a Man so faithless."

Certainly the doctor was most liberal with his patient, for he had agreed to furnish all medicine, and that he should not be paid anything at all if he failed to cure Mr. Tayleur, and even if he did cure him he was to be paid only ten guineas at once, and ten guineas more six months after.

One of the doctor's chief grievances was that the patient owed "hard specie" and he had paid him a part of it. His fear was that he might take advantage of the circulation of paper money and discharge the rest of his obligation in depreciated currency.

The doctor informed Hamilton that Tayleur "had acknowledged himself that his disorder had already costed him about £200 sterling; I thought I had," he said, "to deal with an honest Man. I did not hurry him for the payment. It was only Eight days after his departure but I was informed that it was not the first French leave he had been guilty of. If I had known it sooner I would have dealt with him quite in another manner, but I took him to be an honest man and would never have mentioned the nature of his disorder if he had acted as such. After you received the payment, you'll be so Kind as to take your due; and send me the ballance. You will be so good as to Observe that in New York it is hard Specie and here paper medium."

One of Hamilton's official acts when Secretary of the Treasury was, in 1794, to propose a tax on carriages, which afterward became a law,[1] and its enforcement was opposed on the ground that it was a direct tax and, therefore, unconstitutional. Madison, who was then in the House, bitterly fought the proposed measure. Later Hylton, a Virginian, brought suit in the Supreme Court to determine its legality. Hamilton, who appeared with the Attorney-General and Charles Lee, warmly defended the constitutionality of the law, and after an eloquent speech was upheld by the Court, who decided that the carriage duty was an excise and not a direct tax. There seems to have been some friction in the Su-

---

[1] I am informed that among the archives of the Alexandria, Va., court-house there is a record of the indictment of General Washington for a failure to pay his carriage tax.

preme Court, for the Chief Justice and Justice Cushing did not sit in the case, and Justice Wilson gave no reasons for the opinion of the Court. William Bradford, the Attorney-General, subsequently wrote to his friend Hamilton as follows:

William Bradford to Alexander Hamilton

PHILADELPHIA, *Aug.* 4, 1795.

MY DEAR SIR: The record of the proceedings in the case relating to the Carriage Tax is not yet returned—but I expect it this week. I learn, however, that Taylor,[1] who has published his speech, has advised the defendant to make no further argument and to let the Supreme Court do as they please,—and that in consequence of this advice no counsel will appear in support of the writ of Error. I have desired that the District Attorney would take measures to counteract this manœuvre—which is of a piece with the rest of Taylor's conduct. Having succeeded in dividing the opinions of the Circuit Court, he wishes to prevent the effect which a decision of the Supreme Court *on full argument* would have and perhaps by the circulation of his pamphlet in the mean time to indispose the people of Virginia to paying the next annual Duty on their carriages.—If the Defendant persists in pursuing this advice, I presume your attendance will not be necessary; for in such case I would think it most advisable to submit the cause to the court upon the two arguments that have been already made. That of Mr. Wickham's has arrived in manuscript; that of Taylor we expect by the next post.—I will take care however to apprise you as soon as the record arrives what is to be expected.

In consequence of the situation of things and some new occurrences, it has been thought advisable to request the President to return to Philadel.—He is expected to be here next week.—

The crazy speech of Mr. Rutledge joined to certain information that he is daily sinking into debility of mind and body,

[1] Counsel for Hylton.

will probably prevent him to receiving the appointment I mentioned to you.   But should he come to Philad¹. for that purpose, as he has been invited to do—& especially if he should resign his present office—the embarrassment of the President will be extreme—but if he is disordered in mind in the manner that I am informed he is,—there can be but one course of procedure.¹—I write in great haste & can only add that I am with great regard
Your friend, &c
W_M. B.

¹ John Rutledge, after his nomination as Chief Justice of the United States Supreme Court, July 1, 1795, became insane, and his name was rejected when the Senate met in December.

CHAPTER VII

HAMILTON, THE LAWYER (Concluded)

THE case by which Hamilton is best known, because of its national importance, was that of the People *vs.* Croswell, which, to a great extent, established the present law of libel in the United States.

Croswell was the editor of a small newspaper called the *Wasp*, which he published at Hudson, New York. He subsequently edited the *Balance*, which was continued after Hamilton's death.

In the issue of September 9, 1802, he republished with comments an article, originally written by John Holt and published in the New York *Evening Post*, which reflected upon Thomas Jefferson. The objectionable matter was this: "Holt says the burden of the Federal Song is that Jefferson paid Callender for calling Washington a traitor, a robber, a perjurer; for calling Adams a hoary-headed incendiary and for most grossly slandering the private characters of men he well knew were virtuous. These charges not a democratic Editor has yet dared or ever will dare to meet in an open and manly discussion."

Callender, the person referred to, was the editor of *The Prospect Before Us*, published in Richmond, Virginia, and at the time he was constantly engaged in most intemperate abuse of the Federalists—and Washington, Hamilton, and others were the particular victims of his enmity; in fact he, like Freneau, was an instrument of Jefferson. and there is no doubt but that he was engaged by the latter, as has been fully proved, to libel Washington and Adams.

Croswell was arrested, arraigned, and tried at Claverack, New York, before Chief Justice Morgan Lewis, on July 11, 1802, and convicted in spite of the fact that he had announced his inability to proceed without the presence of Callender, who was a material witness, and he had expected to prove by the latter the truth of the charge as set forth in the indictment—to wit: that "Thomas Jefferson, Esq., President of the United States, well knowing the contents of the said publication, called *The Prospect Before Us*, paid or caused to be paid to the said James Thompson Callender the two several sums of fifty dollars, one of which it seems was paid prior to the publication of the said pamphlet for the purpose of aiding and assisting him, the said Thompson Callender for the publication thereof, and the other subsequently thereto as a reward, etc." [1]

Things looked very black for Croswell, as the judge on the bench and every one in power were Democrats and supporters of Jefferson, and prejudiced to the last degree. Even the sheriff and grand jury were of this political complexion, and were determined, not only to punish the prisoner, but, if possible, to silence the active and annoying portion of the Federal press that had done so much, up to that time, to make them uncomfortable. Judge Lewis held that the English law laid down by Lord Mansfield, to the effect that the "jury were judges only of the fact, and not of the truth or intent of the publication," this decision being in distinct opposition to the precedent fixed by the Zenger trial (the defendant also being an editor and being defended by another

---

[1] Chief Justice Lewis is reported to have said that even if a witness on the stand knew of the truth of the libel, he would not permit him to testify.

Hamilton[1]), left no other alternative but a conviction. In fact, no one could have been treated more unjustly than the unfortunate Croswell.

He had appealed to Hamilton to defend him, but the latter at first could not free himself from his other engagements to be present at the trial; subsequently, however, he argued a motion before the Court of Errors at Albany in a manner which Chancellor Kent said was the greatest effort Hamilton had ever made. "He had bestowed," said Kent, "unusual attention on the case, and he came prepared to discuss the points of law with a perfect mastery of the subject. There was an unusual solemnity and earnestness on his part in the discussion. He was, at times, highly impassioned and pathetic. His whole soul was enlisted in the cause. The aspect of the times was portentous, and he was persuaded that if he could overthrow the high-toned doctrine of the judge it would be a great gain to the liberties of this country. . . . The anxiety and tenderness of his feelings, and the gravity of his theme, rendered his reflections exceedingly impressive. He never before, in my hearing, made any effort in which he commanded higher reverence for his principles, nor equal admiration for the power and pathos of his eloquence." It is to be regretted that Hamilton's speech, which lasted six hours, has never been fully reported, although I am in possession of an incomplete report of the trial, which belonged to him, where but sixteen pages are devoted to his address.[2]

---

[1] Andrew Hamilton.

[2] In the N. Y. *Evening Post*, Caine is abused for his unsatisfactory report of the proceedings in the Croswell case which is all we have to-day; though Hamilton spoke six hours, his speech is condensed to six pages. "Should Mr. Caine think we have not given his book so favorable a reception as he thinks it is entitled to, why then we frankly declare that we can never have much patience with one who exhibits Harrison and Hamilton to the world as men speaking neither sense nor grammar."

The other lawyers who appeared were Mr. Van Ness, who afterward served as Burr's second in the duel, Ambrose Spencer, the Attorney-General, and Mr. Harrison. The latter was associated with Hamilton for the defence, as was Mr. Van Ness.

This trial attracted the most wide-spread attention, and the papers filled their columns with pungent criticism of the proceedings and of each other. The *Ulster County Gazette*, a Federal sheet, was especially active, and articles from the pen of Mr. Elmendorff were directed against General Armstrong, a radical Democrat, who wrote for a paper in the same town, called the *Plebeian*. Members of Hamilton's own party met at Claverack and afterward at Albany, and the issue was felt to be one of the first importance, involving, as it did, the liberty of the press, and the opportunity of the Federalists to fight in future for their cause which, by this time, was almost hopeless.

General Schuyler, who was ever at the elbow of his energetic son-in-law, wrote from Albany, June 23, 1803, to Mrs. Hamilton who was then in New York:

I have had about a dozen Federalists ask me, intreating me to write to Your General if possible to attend on the 7th of next month at Claverack, as Council to the Federal printer there who is to be tried on an Indictment for a libel against that Jefferson, who disgraces not only the place he fills but produces immorality by his pernicious examples—To those applicants I have answered with the citizens of N. York we extend to all the first week in July that I believed it would not be possible for him to be at Claverack—I shall, however, intreat you to mention it to him—If his business will permit, the aide would be of service and the results such as his real friends wish.

It has been alleged, that at the time Ambrose Spencer tried the case for the people he had just been elected a judge, and that he proceeded with more confidence because he thought that the respect for his position would entitle him to immunity from hot rejoinders of the lawyers, but this statement was, without doubt, a slander of the period. Later Spencer admitted all of Hamilton's great qualities.

Hamilton contended that "the greater the truth the greater the libel" was an outworn dictum, bad in morals and bad in law. After a long argument the court was divided; Kent and Thompson were against Lewis and Livingston and in favor of Hamilton, but the opinion of Chief Justice Lewis stood as law.

Hildreth states that "a declaration bill was later introduced into the assembly, but delayed for political reasons. At the next session an act allowing the truth to be given in evidence was proposed, but defeated by the Council of Revision, composed of the judges and chancellor. The act, with some modification however, became the law the next year, and is now in force throughout the United States.[1]"

Hamilton's notes in this great trial are before me, and may be reproduced in their entirety.

I. The liberty of the prefs confists in the right to publish with impunity Truth with good motives for justifiable ends though reflecting on Gov't, Magistracy or Individuals

II. That the allowance of this right is efsential to the preservation of free Governm't, the difallowance of it fatal.

III. That its abufe is to be guarded against by fubjecting the exercise of it to the animadversion and controul of the Tribunals of Justice; but that this controul cannot safely be entrusted to a permanent body of Magistracy and requires the effectual co-operation of Court and Jury.

IV. That to confine the Jury to the mere question of publication and the application of terms; without the right of inquiry into the intent or tendency referring to the Court

---

[1] "Hudson's History of Journalism," p. 742.

the exclufive right of pronouncing upon the construction tendency and intent of the alleged libel, is calculated to render negatory the function of the Jury; enabling the Court to make a libel of any writing whatsoever the moft innocent or commendable.

V.   That it is the general rule of criminal law that the intent conftitutes the crime and that it is equally a general rule, that the intent, mind or *quo animo* is an inference of fact to be drawn by the Jury.

VI.   That if there are exceptions to this rule they are confined to cafes on which not only the principal fact but its circumstances can be and are specifically defined by Statute or Judicial Precedents.

VII.   That in respect to libel there is no such specific and precise definition of facts and circumstances to be found; that consequently it is difficult if not impofsible to pronounce that any writing is per fe and exclusive of all circumstances libellous.   That is libellous character must depend on intent and tendency the one and the other being matter of fact.

VIII.   That the definitions or descriptions of libels to be found in the books predicate them upon some malicious or mischievous intent or tendency; to expose individuals to hatred or contempt or to occafion a disturbance or breach of the peace.

IX.   That in determining the character of a libel the Truth or falsehood if in the nature of things a material ingredient though the truth may not always be decifive but being abufed may still admit of a malicious and mifchievous intent which may constitute a libel.

X.   That in the Roman Law one fource of the doctrine of libel, the truth in cafes interesting to the public may be given in evidence.   That the antient Statutes probably declaratory of the common make the falsehood an ingredient of the Crime; that antient precedents in the Courts of Justice correspond and that the precedents to this day charge a malicious intent.

XI.   That the doctrine of excluding the truth as imma-

terial originated in a tyrannical and polluted fource, the
Court of Star Chamber and that though it prevailed a considerable length of time yet there are leading precedents
down to the Revolution and ever fince in which a contrary
practice prevailed.

XII.   That the doctrine being against reason and natural
justice and contrary to the original principles of the common
law enforced by Statutory provisions, precedents which support it deferve to be confidered in no better light than as
malus ufus which ought to be abolished.

XIII.   That in the general distribution of powers in our
System of Jurisprudence the cognizance of law belongs to
the Court, of fact to the Jury; that as often as they are not
blended the power of the Court is absolute and exclusive.
That in civil cafes it is always so and may rightfully be so
exerted.   That in criminal cafes the law and fact being always blended, the Jury for reasons of a political and peculiar
nature, for the security of life and liberty, is entrusted with
the power of deciding both law and fact.

XIV.   That this distinction results:

1. From the ancient forms of pleading in civil cafes none
but special pleas being allowed in matter of law, in criminal
none but the general ifsue.

2. From the liability of the Jury to attaint on civil cases
and the general power of the Court, as its substitute in granting new trials and from the exemption of the Jury from
attaint on criminal cafes and the defect of power to controul
their verdicts by new trials; the teft of every legal power
being its capacity to produce a definitive effect liable neither
to punishment nor controul.

XV.   That in criminal cases neverthelefs the Court are
the constitutional advisers of the Jury in matter of law;
who may compromit their consciences by lightly or rafhly
disregarding that advice; but may still more compromit
their consciences by following it, if exercising their judgments with discretion and honesty they have a clear conviction that the charge of the Court is wrong.[1]

[1] From the original trial notes.

A part of Hamilton's time was devoted to land operations and litigation arising therefrom. His voluminous correspondence refers, not only to the establishment of the Ohio Company, but to the settlement of his own State. Much litigation, in which his father-in-law was concerned, had to do with Cosby's Manor, and with the lands originally granted to Sir William Johnson, or deeded to Robert Morris by the Commonwealth of Massachusetts. Sir William Johnson, who was so closely identified with the French and Indian wars, and who was such a power with the Indian "Six Nations," married one Catharine Wisenburgh, the daughter of a German emigrant. This was in 1739. Some years later he took into his house a squaw named "Molly" Brant, sister of the celebrated Mohawk Chief, Joseph Brant, or Thayendanega, with whom he seems to have spent a contented and happy life. By her he had eight illegitimate children. Many years afterward Hamilton was called upon to give an opinion regarding Sir William's will, of which opinion this is a transcript:

I have examined that clause of the will of Sir William Johnson which contains a devise to his natural son, Peter Johnson, and also a subsequent clause which respects a devise over in case of the death of any of his eight natural children without issue, in connection with the fact stated to me that the said Peter died under age, unmarried and without issue, and thereupon I am of opinion that the survivors of the eight children were entitled to an estate of inheritance in the premises before devised to the said Peter.

ALEXANDER HAMILTON,
January 25, 1796.

Toward the latter part of the year 1799, the citizens of New York were greatly excited by the discovery of the body of a young girl named Guilielma Sands, which was found in one of the wells of the Manhattan Company at the corner of Barclay and Prince Streets. She was fully dressed, and her muff was suspended from her neck. Guilielma was the niece of Elias Ring and his wife, quiet and respectable Quakers who lived in the upper part of Greenwich Street, who had several male boarders, among them one Levi Weeks. It was known that she was engaged to Levi, who was the brother of a prosperous builder named Ezra Weeks, who constructed many important buildings in the city of New York, among them the present City Hall, and later, Hamilton's country house, known as The Grange.

Levi lived, at first, with his brother at the corner of Harrison and Greenwich Streets, and afterward boarded with the Rings. For some days after the murder, which took place between eight and nine o'clock on the night of December 22, 1799, no clew could be obtained as to the identity of the murderer, but finally Weeks was arrested and indicted. He was in every way an exemplary young man, and the girl's relatives were loath to believe him guilty; nevertheless, suspicion pointed very strongly, at least, to his knowledge of the fate of Guilielma, if he himself was not actually the murderer. It was known that she was last seen with him upon the night of her death, and their voices were heard in the hallway of the Ring house shortly before she left, never to return. He was almost distraught, but could give no explanation of what had occurred. The girl's body, when found, bore abrasions, but no indication of strangulation or other violence. After his arrest Weeks engaged Hamilton and Aaron Burr, who were associated with Brockholst Livingston in the trial, while the prosecution was represented by Assistant Attorney-General Cadwalader Colden. The case was tried at the old City Hall, formerly the Federal Hall, at the north-east corner of Wall and Nassau Streets, and the site of the present Sub-Treasury building, before Mr. Justice John Lansing, the then Mayor Richard Varick, and the Recorder Richard Harrison.

The trial was exceedingly sensational and, if anything, attracted more attention than any recent proceeding. It began Tuesday, March 31, 1800, and continued several days. Burr made the opening speech, and Hamilton interrogated most of the witnesses, and summed up. It would appear that from the first the presiding justice was not convinced of Weeks's guilt, and regarded the evidence as so flimsy that he virtually directed the jury to bring in a verdict of acquittal, which they did. This, however, was most distasteful to the excited public, who were quite sure of the prisoner's culpability, and wanted him punished. It appeared in evidence that though the deceased girl, who was very beautiful, had been very intimate with Weeks, her relations with others had been decidedly promiscuous and improper; it was likely, therefore, that some of them had made away with her. Mrs. Ring's anger and violence when the verdict was brought in were intense. Shaking her fist in Hamilton's face she said, "If thee dies a natural death I shall think there is no justice in heaven." In this connection it is a curious fact that both Chief Justice Lansing and Hamilton died as she had predicted. The former was not seen alive after he left his hotel one day, in 1829, to reach the Albany boat, and his body was never found.

An alleged sensational incident of the trial, which is, however, untrue, has been referred to by several of Hamilton's biographers. It is in effect, that one of the witnesses, a man of bad character named Croucher, who was suspected of being the real murderer, was made to betray himself by a dramatic expedient devised by Hamilton, who held two lighted candles close to his face while he was on the stand during the latter part of the day. Although this witness Croucher was a lodger in the Ring house, there was no proof that he had anything to do with the crime, but he sought to throw suspicion upon his rival Weeks. The report of the trial shows that a lighted candle was simply used for the identification of Croucher.

Parton, who was Burr's biographer, has made him the hero of the story, In this connection it may be stated that Hamilton had always believed in the innocence of his client, and that he would not have taken his case had he had any doubts of his position. In fact, some of his legal associates at the time, in giving their impressions of his methods, have stated that he never entered a case simply as an advocate, but that he first convinced himself of the suspected individual's innocence, and then went heart and soul into the defence.

The field of his professional labors was no restricted one, and he was often in Albany, or again in Kingston, or Poughkeepsie, or other places, taking long journeys by river sloops, or stage-coaches, or in the saddle in company with other lawyers who followed the circuit. Much of his intimacy with Chancellor Kent grew from this close contact. In his expense-book appears a charge of four hundred dollars for eight days' work at New Haven, at fifty dollars per day, he having been employed by the State of New York. From the same source we are informed that on May 10, 1796, he received a retainer of five hundred dollars from the "United States for attendance on Philadelphia for a fortnight's work in arguing the question of the Constitutionality of the Carriage Tax."

His letters to his wife were written under the most varying conditions. He wrote from Albany, October 7, 1796, to Mrs. Hamilton at 69 Stone Street: "This moment I came from Court and I fear I shall not be disengaged from it before Saturday.   Judge of my impatience by your own.   I am quite well.   Adieu my darling Eliza."   He later said, he hoped to "finish my business so as return on Thursday.   If vessel offers at the time and a fair wind, I may take that mode of conveyance."   He again informed her from Albany of his painful detention there by the slow progress of the court, and of his extreme anxiety to be with her, and tells her he has written to her "by water to the care of Capt. Boyed."   Being engaged in court in Poughkeepsie, he refers to the excessive heat and says: "I have resolved to moderate my movements which will unavoidably occasion delay. But my Betsy will prefer my staying somewhat longer to my seriously risking my health.   The Vessel passed West Point in the night so that I shall have to make that visit on my return.   Have patience, my Angel & love me always as you have done.   God bless you prays always yr aff. A. H."

From Hudson he writes: "I am chagrined at the prospect of being detained longer than I expected.   Our adversaries have made strong efforts to postpone the cause to another circuit, and though defeated in this they have obtained a delay till Wednesday next.   However disagreeable and inconvenient to me to stay, it is not possible for me in this situation to quit."   This was probably during the Le Guen trial.

What has been said of his modest idea of the value of his services which was shown in the Le Guen case may be again referred to.   Moreover it would appear that he would not consent to ally himself with any case that was at all suspicious, or in which his professional reputation might suffer. He evidently carried this very far if we may judge from the many endorsements to the applications that were made to him.

As an example of what is meant, the following incident may be related. One of his clients wrote to him in May, 1796:

DEAR SIR: Wishing to have the benefit of your much esteemed counsel as a lawyer in important cases, if unfortunately I should be hereafter involved in any, I have enclosed you my note for one thousand dollars, payable in five years at five per cent per annum, which I beg you to accept with interest.

This was endorsed by Hamilton: "Returned as being more than is proper. A. H."

Many of his papers are also endorsed with comments which show that he would not accept employment if the interests of other clients could, in the least way, be affected by his action. In fact, he was punctilious to a degree in the matter of professional ethics.

His ideas of compensation were certainly not extravagant, especially in the beginning of his career, although it is said his professional income was considerable before he accepted the Treasury portfolio. Legal compensation in those days was paltry compared with the charges of to-day, when the return from a single great case is likely to make the lawyer rich for the rest of his life; but it must be remarked that the labors of a lawyer then were more conservative than they now are, and the modern pursuit of promotion was almost undreamed of. Specialties, too, were unknown. The hardworking lawyer of the latter part of the eighteenth century was as much at home in the criminal court as in the trial of civil actions, and it was not considered *infra dig.* to lend one's talents and efforts to the defence of an accused person, no matter how poor. It is somewhat curious to find, notwithstanding the dignity and conservatism of the practitioner of

those days, that even Hamilton was not above a retaining or
conditional fee, as the following note will show:

> Johnathan Jackſon for Argument
> Barnett vs. Underwriters
> prepared and attending at Albany $100
> If succeſsful an additional hundred.

As a rule, his retaining fee in the many years of his practice, and even afterward, was one pound sterling, although
he received many yearly retainers, for his services as counsel
to several corporations with which he was connected, of two
hundred and fifty dollars and more. In 1782–5 his fees
were much smaller than those he received at a later date,
and in the years just before his death he made from twelve
thousand to fourteen thousand dollars per annum.

Some idea of his professional work and the sums received therefor may be derived from an inspection of a kind
of journal or cash book to which reference has already been
made.

Receipts from practice & disbursements.

1783	May 30. Isaac Sears, a retainer in a cauſe ex-	
	pected to be commenced by Soderstrom	
	against Sears & Smith, and advice thereon	
	at various times	£6. 0.0.
1784	May 1. Bank of New York To this ſum paid	
	Mr. Maxwell in part of a houſe purchaſed on	
	account of the bank	£150. 0.0.
1783	Sepr. 29. Manor of Renfelaerwick Drawing a	
	memorial to the Legiſlature	£3. 4.0.
1785	Robert Bowne drawing a petition & reſpecting	
	rents to perſons within the Britiſh line	£1.10.0.
"	Nov. 30. John Murray, Advice concerning the	
	propriety of ſuing a perſon in whoſe hands	
	goods were attached	£1.10.0.
"	Nov. 25. Isaac Moſes. Drawing a release of	
	Dower	£2. 0.0.

1785 Nov. Actually engrofing   0. 0.8.
"   Aug. 30. Stephen Delancey. To dead charge on the circuit in Weftchefter to try your caufe being a critical caufe, and having fucceeded   £20. 0.0.
"   Aaron Burr. To one half the Tavern expense of a reference between Dutcher & Vacher, paid summons   1.13.0.
"   Johannes Hardenberg. To 9 days abfence to try your caufe at £5 per day.   45. 0.0.
"   Retainers in fuits againft ten perfons at £1.10 each 15. 0.0.
"   Nov. 14. To this fum received by him of Truftees of Schenectady as a Retainer 5. 0.0.
1786 Mar. 22. The agents of the Proprietors of Way-wayanda. To account for advice & fervices rendered this day Attending at Chefter and divers attendance at New York   150. 0.0.
"   Nov. 1. The Minifter of Spain to amount paid gaol-keepers fees affumed by me.   29.14.0.
     To advice & fervices as Counsel   37. 6.8.
"   Apr. 1st. (Mofes Hazen) for drawing a fpecial indemnifying bond to fureties   1. 0.0.
1786 Henry & McClellan. Drawing memorial to Congrefs refpecting Canadian affairs.   £1.10.0.
"   Executors of Defbrofs for arguing fucefsfully a Question on citation act.   10. 0.0.
"   Aug. 10. Advice concerning Brandy left with you by Mr. Price   1.10.0.
1787 Nov. 5. John J. Van Renfflaer. To cafh paid your draft on me in favour of Mr. Stevenfon 80.
"   Aug. 30. Samuel Van Hyde. To council for attending circuit in your caufe with Mr. Willet on trying the caufe absent three days (traveling expenfes, &c.   10.
1788 Rafael N. Smith. Surviving partner of Sears & Smith. To opinion concerning the eftate of Ifaac Sears   1.10
"   Oct. 8. Minister of United Netherlands Opinion concerning certain public certificate affigned by Benjamin Esq., Inquiries at the Treafury &c   · 3.4.

1788   Oct. 10.   Cash paid A. Burr, Esquire in full of
              your part of J. Lloyd vs B. Snethen.——
"   Nov. 28.   To Pintard draft of Controverfy with
              Mr. Shedden   3. 4.0.
                      200
"   Draft in favor of B. Walker 100 Paid bank for a
              note endorfed by him   200.
1795   Apr. 29.   James Greenleaf opinion in divorce $10.
              "   "   " concerning " $10.
        Br. vefsel captured & recaptured by her crew $10.
        subsequent advice at different times   15.
                                          25.
        Opinion on Revenue laws   20.
"   Ph. Schuyler & Afsociates Dr. to Cash $1514.18
              for this sum paid Peter Goelet the $\frac{1}{4}$ part
              of a tract of 6761 acres sold by the Truftees
              of the American or Ringwood Iron Co.
              situate in Cosby's manor payable in 4
              quarters payments, 1 down, 2d 1st of April
              next 31 Octo'r next 4[h] 1st April 1797.
"   Aug. 14th.   Received from Fifher for opinion
              concerning conveyance of soldiers' rights $15.
              received from Van den Heuvel for opinion
              concerning abandonment   15.
1796   Jan.   Opinion for Mr. Keep regarding an opin-
              ion concerning a Gang Way   10.
"   Feb'y to Dr. Lenox for opinion concerning his
              marriage   10.
"   Mar. 17.   For this fum received of, for opinion
              on two policies, one refpecting right of aban-
              donment of vefsel after acquittal & appeal, $20.
        The other refpecting cafe of infurance blockaded
              & for this fum received of Quackenbufh &
              Ogilvie   20.
"   Letter to Th. Cazenove for opinion concerning
              act of Legiflature refpecting Land of Dutch
              Co.[1]   25.
"   July 2d & 20.   Th. Cazenove for opinion &
              confultation with Judge Benfon & Mr. Jones
              concerning a certain act of legiflature.

[1] Holland Company.

1796	July 11. Le Roy & Bayard for opinion refpecting conveyances from Robert Morris to Dutch Co. Guilder Mefser & Co.	5.
"	Aug. 26. For attendance & trial of two ejectments in Kings County. Thos. Ten Eyck for retainer Caracci who applied to me	$15.
"	Nov. 29. Le Roy & Bayard on act of Services relating to a sale of land to Aaron Burr.[1]	$56.
1797	Lunace Caufe	$15.
	Cazenove	$500.
"	Oct. 16. Difcounted with Aa. Burr by Oliver & Thompfon	50.
"	Oct. 24. Dutch Co. "for infpecting feveral papers refpecting power to James Wadfworth for a tract of land contracted for with A. Burr & Advice.	10
		15
"	Apr. 5. Henry Capt for defending him on two Indictments	50.
	Opinion in writing concerning money stipulated to Indians.	25.
	Bache for trying his cafe	50.
1798	July 5. LeRoy & Bayard & McEvers for opinion concerning Truft for Certain Indians	10.
	Examination of Titles to a lot to be mortgaged to the Bank of N. Y., inspection of deeds, &c	20.
	Received retainer for United Infurance Co. for retainer for 1798	$250.
"	May 2. Paid Col. Jay for part of fee in cafe of Infurance in Ship *Grand Turk*	125.
"	Trinity Church for opinion in conjunction with Mr. Harrifon	50.
"	Rec'd 1234.44 from Le Guen Paid Col. Burr	$290.
"	May 9. For opinion concerning the Acts of Britifh Courts with diftricts comprehending the Weftern posts subfequent to Treaty of peace	50.
"	June 30. Wm. Conftable for attending at his houfe to draw his will. & drawing it	$50.

[1] This purchase is referred to repeatedly in Aaron Burr's " Journal."

1798	Aug. 4. Edward Gould & fon for attendance twice on trials of the case of *Aftrea*	100.
"	July term. Bill for argument & sucefsully, for caufe againft Am. & Barn.	75.
"	July term. Arch. Gracie for arguing sucefsfuly the case of the *Hercules*	100.
"	Dec. 18. For opinion to Mr. Cazenove concerning the effect of an attachment of Mr. R. Morris' property upon that conveyed to the Dutch Comp. etc.	10.
"	Dec. 24. Consultation on 24 with Mr. Troup & opinion concerning the question whether *fpecie* is to be confidered as Merchandise	5.
1799	Louis Le Guen for attending to the arrangement of his Marriage Contract	20.
"	July 1. Alexander Macomb Dr. to Costs & fees, for opinion and advice refpecting forgeries of Arnold	20.
	Bank of N. Y. Retainer in cafe of Arnold	20.
"	United Ins. Co. retainer Trial & argument fee in the Cafe of the *Minerva*	$75.
	Hallet & Jenks (Brig *Nancy*)	
1800	May, for my services in their suit in Chancery refpecting lands of Sir William Johnson, various consultations arguing feveral collateral queftions arguing at final hearing & on appeal	$500.
	Ex. of Ph. Livingston for my fervices in their fuit with Jouet	500.

An inspection of a large number of trial notes and briefs shows that Hamilton prepared his cases with great care, in which work he was usually unaided. His artistic handwriting, as a rule, was fine, but often bold, attracting the eye in places by the underscoring of words. It varies but little in character. He was never careless, and the end of a brief was as legible as the beginning. He rarely, as has been pointed out, "crossed his t's," and never "dotted his i's," but was scrupulous in punctuation and arrangement, and

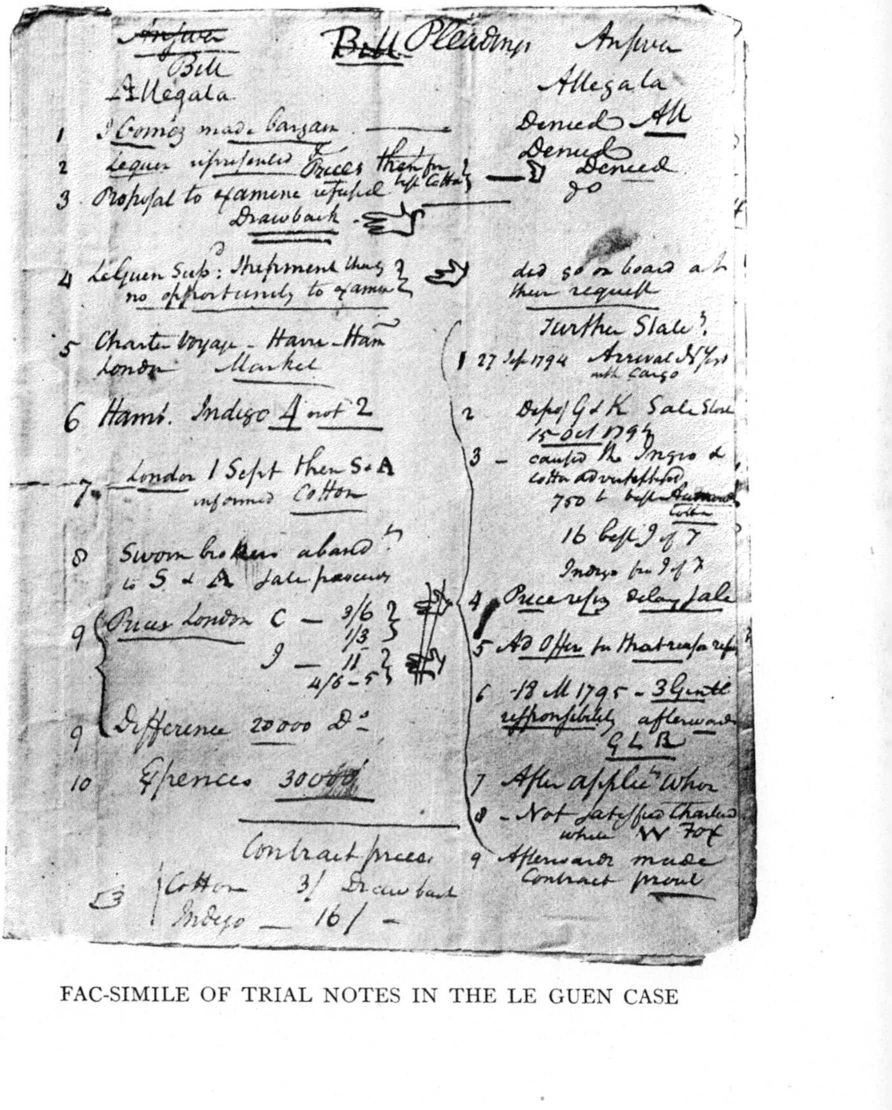

~~Answer~~ ~~Bill~~ Pleadings Answer

Bill — Allegata — Allegata

1 J. Gomez made bargain — Denied All

2 Le Guen represented Prices then for best Cotton — Denied — Denied

3 Proposal to examine refused — do

Drawback

4 Le Guen Sup: Shipment there no opportunity to examine — did so on board at their request

Further State.

5 Charter voyage — Havre — Ham London Market

1 27 Sep 1794 Arrival N York with Cargo

6 Ham. Indigo 4 not 2

2 Depos G & K Sale Store 15 Oct 1794

7 London 1 Sept then S & A informed Cotton

3 — caused the Indigo & Cotton advertised 750 b best Cotton 16 best 9 of 7 Indigo best 9 of 7

8 Sworn brokers aboard to S & A sale process

4 Price refused delay sale

9 Price London C — 3/6 1/3 I — 11 4/6-5

5 An offer for that reason refused

9 Difference 20000 Ds

6 18 M 1795 — 3 Gentl responsibility afterwards G & R

10 Expences 3000 Ds

7 After applicn Whor

8 — Not satisfied Charles W Fox

Contract prices

9 Afterwards made Contract proved

£3 Cotton 3/ Drawback Indigo — 16/ —

FAC-SIMILE OF TRIAL NOTES IN THE LE GUEN CASE

his use of English was perfect.   There is, in his briefs, great freedom from corrections, indicating that when he wrote anything it was well thought out and decided upon before-hand.   The trial notes intended for his own use are most interesting, containing as they do frequent apt and pungent suggestions to be used in court, and are all orderly and free from redundancies.   He never repeated himself, while his headings of subjects and lines of argument prepared to demolish his antagonist were progressive in their perti-nency and gained in force as he proceeded.   In the Le Guen trial, the little duodecimo booklet of manuscript fastened together at the back with a needle and thread contains many curious reflections, among which are the following:

"A man must have been a blockhead who would part with such a valuable lien knowingly," and again he says that it is "the clearest case he ever met with.   We could not expect that any judge would be unwilling to be wiser today than tomorrow."   He insists that he "will want no books [to convince the jury] but will appeal to principle written in the heart of man."   As a compliment to the judge, under the caption of "*Politesse*," he says, "This proves he did right to send it [the case] to a Jury," and again, "How necessary for those who sit in judgment, when life, fame, &c is concerned to preserve their minds cold and dis-passionate."   He observes satirically that there is much ex-tenuation.   "Immoral acts are not always *morally wrong.*" And that "persons habituated to deal where verbal contracts are not attended to, merit more loose in their conversation. They will hazard more with reason."   He refers to his an-tagonists as the "dupes of their own virtues."

He never went into court without a preparedness which is shown by the arsenal of authorities usually referred to in abbreviated titles, and enumerated on the left-hand side of the paper. Elsewhere we find long and very legible Latin quotations of which he might avail himself, as was the custom of the day.

In these times the progress of a trial is often interrupted by a recess granted for the purpose of sending out to the library for an authority. No such thing occurred in the early history of our courts, if we may judge from Hamilton's notes, and it is probable that all the lawyers of the time followed his example. The chief works referred to are Vatel, Blackstone, Fonblanque, Burrowes, Atkyns, Lord Raymond, Coke, Comyns, Grotius. Among Hamilton's own law books were the standard folios, many of which are printed in Latin. One of his English books was "Practice Commonplaced; or Rules and Cases of Practice in the Court Arranged, Etc.," by G. Crompton, which was published in London in 1783. A copy that recently found its way to an auction room bore his signature on each of ten pages, including the title-page and fly-leaf, with MS. notes on various other pages. This was one of his first books, bought by him in 1785 and used during his early years of practice.

One may almost grasp and appreciate the mental operations of Hamilton when he prepared his notes, for they to-day almost breathe his individuality. He freely uses the index mark, either singly or in multiple, to direct attention to points of varying importance which he is to emphasize; again, there is not only curious underscoring, but words or sentences are printed in large letters or bracketed. There are interesting comments upon the veracity of the witnesses, and his opinions of them and these are not always complimentary. In one place he makes the note to "Speak rather lightly of Doctor Baker," a witness who seems to have been guilty of concocting a plan to palm off a baby upon the defendant in a

breach of promise case, and, at the same time, evidently
posed as a medical expert. In another case the competency
of a man is considered who "was never conceived to be deranged, but at times he was a good deal in liquor." This
gentleman, however, was by another witness regarded as
"very rational and pretty sociable."

Possibly, with the exception of Aaron Burr, no professional associate of Hamilton in New York can be found
who withheld from him the praise which his work merited,
and the tributes to his genius have been most hearty
and sincere. It would almost seem as if time strengthened
the glory of his reputation, for with the lapse of years the
rancor of political rivalry has been forgotten, and jurists
everywhere to-day seem to be almost unanimous in admit-
ting his greatness as one of the foremost of American lawyers.[1]
As an example I may quote James Brown Scott, a recent
and most agreeable writer, who says,[2] "He [Hamilton] had
no past of his own; he settled in a country with none, and
dreamed and planned of a future for himself and country. . . .

"And for the practice of law Hamilton was admirably
fitted. In the matter of physical presence he was as favored
as Lord Erskine, and he possessed a power of speech hardly
inferior, it would seem, to the Scotchman. These are qualities not to be despised, but while they may make the verdict
getter they do not make the lawyer. A knowledge of the
history of the law added to the power of searching analysis
and philosophic grasp are essential to the lawyer in the

[1] It may be stated, however, that recently (1909) a congressman in the House, in
objecting to an appropriation for a statue, not only minimized his ability as a lawyer,
but declared his moral example to have been a very bad one for the youth of the
country.

[2] "Great American Lawyers," edited by William Draper Lewis. "Essay on
Alexander Hamilton," by James Brown Scott, pp. 359, 369–372.

scientific sense. In rounded completeness they make the jurist."

Justice Ambrose Spencer, who presided in the Anscoll case, said some years after the duel: "Alexander Hamilton was the greatest man this country ever produced. I knew him well. I was in situations often to observe and study him. I saw him at the bar and at home. He argued cases before me while I sat as judge on the Bench. Webster has done the same. In power of reasoning, Hamilton was the equal of Webster; and more than this can be said of no man. In creative power Hamilton was infinitely Webster's superior."

Chancellor James Kent, one of his dearest friends, wrote at one time: "He rose at once to the loftiest heights of professional eminence, by his profound penetration, his power of analysis, the comprehensive grasp and strength of his understanding, and the firmness, frankness, and integrity of his character. We may say of him, in reference to his associates, as was said of Papinian: 'Omnes longo post se intervallo reliquerit.'" And again: "I have been sensibly struck, in a thousand instances, with his habitual reverence for truth, his candor, his ardent attachment to civil liberty, his indignation at oppression of every kind, his abhorrence of every semblance of fraud, his reverence for justice, and his sound, legal principles drawn by a clear and logical deduction from the purest Christian ethics, and from the very foundations of all rational and practical jurisprudence. He was blessed with a very amiable, generous, tender, and charitable disposition, and he had the most artless simplicity of any man I ever knew. It was impossible not to love as well as respect and admire him. . . . He was perfectly disinterested. The selfish principle, that infirmity too often of great as well as of little minds, seemed never to have reached him. It was entirely incompatible with the purity of his taste and the grandeur of his ambition. Everything appeared to be at once extinguished, when it came in competition with his devotion to his country's welfare and glory. He was a most faithful friend to the cause of civil liberty throughout the world, but he was a still greater friend to truth and justice."

In Coleman's history of the duel and funeral, numerous newspaper articles from the press of those days of persons who had, during his lifetime, been both friends and foes are recorded. None of them is more touching than the tribute of Croswell, in whose behalf Hamilton had appeared, and to which reference has elsewhere been made. Croswell was then the editor of the *Balance*, and after the duel said: "From the editor of this paper something more is due to the departed Hamilton than common panegyric and general encomium. This, a whole nation is bound to bestow—this, not a citizen of America seems disposed to withhold. But to me he once rendered unequalled service, apart from that rendered to his country generally. In my defence, and in defence of the American press, he once exerted his unrivalled eloquence. In my cause, this greatest of men made his mightiest effort— an effort which might have palsied the uplifted hand of power; an effort which might have carried terror to the bosom of a tyrant. For this service, *voluntarily rendered*, I owed him a debt of gratitude which never could be cancelled—never diminished. But, by offering my feeble aid to the support of principles which he advocated, I hoped, at least, to show my sense of the obligation under which I was laid, by his disinterested exertions. Alas! he is gone—and I have only returned him the *professions* of my gratitude. But '*His fame is left*'—*dear as my blood; my life shall be devoted to its protection!*"

CHAPTER VIII

FAMILY LIFE

WHEN Hamilton left the army he diligently studied law, and in a few months felt himself able to take up a new and congenial profession. To one of his warmest friends he wrote:

Alexander Hamilton to Richard K. Meade[1]

ALBANY, *August 27, 1782.*

. . . As to myself, I shall sit down in New York when it opens; and this period, we are told, approaches. No man looks forward to a peace with more pleasure than I do, though no man would sacrifice less to it than myself, if I were not convinced the people sigh for peace.—I have been studying the law for some months, and have lately been licensed as an attorney. I wish to prepare myself by October for examination as a counsellor; but some public avocation may possibly prevent me. I had almost forgotten to tell you, that I have been pretty unanimously elected, by the Legislature of this State, a member of Congress, to begin to serve in November. I do not hope to reform this State, although I shall endeavor to do all the good I can.

God bless you,

A. HAMILTON.

Robert Morris had, however, been so impressed with Hamilton's mental qualities and great energy that in May, 1782, he appointed him receiver of the Continental taxes in

---

[1] "Hamilton's Works" (J. C. H.), vol. I, p. 298.

the State of New York, a position which proved to be a
thankless and uphill job. It would appear that he accepted the office only after continued urging, and remained
a congressman at the same time. So in debt was the country
then that it was spoken of as a "bankrupt Confederation."
His friend, Chancellor Livingston, smarting under his own
excessive taxation, thus wrote to Hamilton at a later time:

Robert R. Livingston to Alexander Hamilton

CLERMONT, 5th *March*, 1787.

I received your information relative to the law for dividing
the district. I am much obliged by your attention to that
object. While I condole with you on the loss of the im-
post, I congratulate you on the laurels you acquired in
fighting its battles. I see you are making some progress in
the new system of taxation, but I could hardly credit my
eyes when I saw Jones opposed to the clause for a tax on
houses, since if I am not extreamly deceived I heard him
commend to you your ideas on that subject at a law dinner.
Be very tender on the point of taxation. I am convinced no
direct tax of any importance can be raised. The minds of
the people in this part of the state are sore and irritable—
The Collectors are all disturbed upon not being able to collect the quota of the £50,000 tax. Indeed the improvi-
dent grants of money both in this and Dutchess County for
the building of Court Houses and the collection of arrears
all within six months have fallen extreamly heavy. You
will be astonished when I tell you that my tax in this past
year upon an estate which has never produced me £400 per
annum is upwards of £600 in certificate and £260 specie, including arrears of one year and one year's arrears when I
lived in Philadelphia and was not an inhabitant of this State.
I shall endeavor to make my stay here useful by effecting
some changes in the representation which I have good hopes
of accomplishing in Dutches County. When I have conversed with most of the leading people at this end of it who

agree with me in thinking a change necessary, the County will I think remove five of their old members.

I expect that this will produce some attack on me or my salary by those who know I am opposed to them. All I expect for my friends will be that they do not suffer such reductions to be made as will be dishonourable to [illegible]. A liberal and honourable appointment such as would enable me to live as I would wish constantly in New York I cannot expect it from the prevailing party.

Hamilton was elected to Congress in November, 1782, and held this office for a year, meanwhile studying and acting as Receiver of Taxes.   When he finally devoted himself to law, he did not entirely relinquish his other affairs, for his interest in the young government was incompatible with more selfish concerns, so that from 1786, when he took part in the Annapolis Convention, to May, 1787, when the new convention was called to meet in Philadelphia, his practice was of secondary moment.   In his own State he fairly lashed the obstructionists into line, the rout of Clinton and his followers taking place at the meeting in Poughkeepsie, and as a result he, with Yates and Lansing, were sent to Congress as delegates.

Hamilton lived in New York most of the time, and after his triumph in securing the adoption of the Constitution by his own State received the great ovation which his talents and labor had merited.   The Federalists at first were by no means in harmony, and Clinton and his faction were loath to accept a new plan of government which would interfere with the exercise of local power and the continuance of existing privileges.   Hamilton, almost alone, fought the majority, and by sheer endurance and obstinacy and unanswerable arguments won over many of his most stubborn adversaries.   He did what was necessary to stir up public opinion and to bring all disorderly and warring elements into unity, so that the Constitution was ratified and New York tardily came into line in favor of a National Government. The victory was nowhere more appreciated than in his own State, and a great Federal parade and celebration took place in New York City, a miniature full-rigged ship being carried through the streets, which was typical of the Federal party, and bore the name "Hamilton."

The depleted condition of the Treasury at this time, and the same causes that led the unruly troops to rebel at an earlier period, must have existed to some extent throughout Hamilton's early tenure of office. His cash-books certainly indicate that he was practically obliged to equip his company of artillery out of his own pocket, and it is probable that he was helped by others, for he had no money, or at least very little. When he first had time to keep accounts, we find this borne out by various entries, but usually on the credit side.

MILITARY ACCOUNT

Dr. State of New York.

1784	To this sum lost in 1776 by the desertion from the Company, by which stoppages became impossible as per Memorandum Book No. 3.	£65.10.
	To this sum paid Mr. Thompson Taylor by Mr. Chaloner on my acct. for making Cloathes for the said Company.	34.13.9.
1785 May 9,	To ballance of Alsop Hunt and James Hunt's account for leather Breeches supplied the Company per receipts.	6. 8.7.
1786 Sept. 26,	To account of my expenses to Baltimore as Commissioner	£76.18.*
June 7,	Advanced door-keeper of the Assembly forward	20.——
	To amount of expenses to and at Philadelphia —I believe paid. To amount of An^d. N. Y. Massachusetts	112.——
	To my wages as delegate from 21st February when I commenced with Gansevoort to 5th of May when he left the City. Deduct Omissions.	
	From May 26 when sworn in with Yates to 14 June when went to Convention.	
	From 30 July when returned to Congress to Oct. 2d when removed.	
	From Oct. 4th when attended at New House to 16th when closed for want of Congress.	

Contra

By ballance of account for Sundries furnished my company of Artillery which was to have been deducted out of their pay.		£76.18.

* Paid

On September 13, 1789, when called to the Treasury, he still lived in New York, but later went to Philadelphia in August, 1790, where he resided until 1795, when he came back to his own city. After his resignation on the 31st of January, 1795, he went to the house of his father-in-law, General Schuyler, at Albany, and in the fall of that year returned to New York and again took up the practice of his profession. From a document, signed by Richard Varick, then the mayor of New York, in the Congressional Library, it is stated that he was extended the freedom of the city, and welcomed with great cordiality by all classes. On February 27, 1795, a banquet was given by the Chamber of Commerce to manifest its respect for Alexander Hamilton, the late Secretary of the Treasury. An account of the affair is thus given in a contemporary paper:

A splendid Dinner was given at their Hall in the Tontine Coffee Houfe.

The Corporation on the feftive occafion was honored by the Company of the Chancellor of the State, the Judges, the Speakers of the Afsembly, the Recorder of the City, the Prefident of Columbia College and many others prefent of which a great number were merchants. The company confisted of two hundred guefts, the room not being large enough to accommodate more. Great decorum as well as conviviality marked the entertainment, and the Company exprefsed peculiar satiffaction in this opportunity of demonftrating their refpect for a man who by difcharging the duties of an important office, HAS DESERVED WELL OF HIS COUNTRY. A toast was drunk as follows:

1. Prefident of the United States . . . . . 3 cheers.
2. The Vice Prefident and Congrefs . . . . "
3. The Governor of the State . . . . . . "
4. Agriculture . . . . "

5. Commerce . . . . 3 cheers.
6. Induſtry and Improvement . . . . . .   "
7. Liberty and Law . . . .   "
8. Social order and social happineſs . . . .   "
9. The People of the United States Brothers of
   one Family . . . .   "
10. General Wayne and the Army . . . . .   "
11. National Credit . . . .   "
12. Integrity and Knowledge . . . .   "
13. Patriotiſm and Honeſt Favour . . . . .   "
14. The Eſteem of their Fellow Citizens an Ineſ-
   timable reward, to thoſe who have deſerved
   well of their country—3 times 3 cheers.

Volunteer Toasts.

1. By the chair.   The immortal memory of Baron Steuben.
2. By Mr. Hamilton.   The merchants of New York, may
   they never ceaſe to have Honour for their commander,
   Skill for their Pilot and Succeſs for their Port—9
   cheers.
3. By the Chancellor.   May Love and Honour be the
   Reward of Virtue.
4. By Judge Lanſing.   The Commerce of the City of New
   York.
5. By Judge Benſon.   The Honeſt Merchant.
          After Mr. Hamilton had withdrawn.
By the chair—ALEXANDER HAMILTON—9 cheers.

Hamilton, during the early years of his practice, lived at
57 Wall Street before his removal to Philadelphia with
the rest of the Cabinet.   On his return in 1795 he occupied a small house at 56 Pine Street, and later moved to
58 Partition Street[1] (now Fulton Street), then to Liberty

[1] 1797–99.

Street, near Broadway. From there he went to 26 Broadway,[1] where he lived until 1802, when he built and occupied his country seat, nine miles above the city, which he called "The Grange," after the Scotch home of his ancestors.

From his letters to his wife at various times we find that she visited, in his absence, at the house of Dr. Cochran, as well as that of G. L. Ogden, at 69 Stone Street, and various other places.

When he lived at 26 Broadway, the west side of that thoroughfare below Trinity Church was, with one exception, built up and occupied by well-to-do and prominent persons. This exception was a small gun-shop on the south-west corner of Morris Street. On the east side all were private dwellings except two, one a shoemaker's shop at 28, and the other a small wooden house below that of Governor Jay. According to my uncle, James A. Hamilton, this was owned and occupied by Slidell, a German candle maker, the grandfather of John Slidell, who figured in the Civil War. This little man was often seen in the afternoon sitting on his wooden stoop, in apron and cap, smoking his pipe, with drip candles hanging in the window.

New York, in 1786, was a city containing 24,000 white males, almost three times as many as there were in 1756; and in 1796, 50,000. The Dutch element preponderated up to the commencement of the eighteenth century, and this was especially the case during the early years of Hamilton's practice. Brissot de Warville made many pungent comments upon the manners of the community, and in 1794 said: "Colonel Lamb, who was at the head of the Custom matters, envelopes all his operations in the most profound mystery, it is the effect of the Dutch spirit which still governs

[1] The site of the present Standard Oil Building.

this City. The Dutchman conceals his gains and commerce; he lives but for himself." And again: "If there is a town on the American Continent where the English luxury displays its follies, it is New York. You will find there the English fashions. In the dress of the women you will see the most brilliant silks, gauzes, hats, and borrowed hair. Equipages are rare but they are elegant. The men have more simplicity in dress. They disdain gewgaws, but they take their revenge in the luxury of the table. Luxury forms already in this town a class very dangerous to society, I mean, bachelors. The expense of women causes matrimony to be dreaded by men."

Angelica Church wrote from London, March 4, in this connection, to her sister: "I would write you an account of fashion, but I hear American ladies are at the head of everything that is elegant; give my love to Alexander, and tell him that some day when I am in very gay and witty humour I will write to him."

When in Philadelphia Hamilton lived, for a part of the time, outside of the city at the Hills, where Robert Morris had his magnificent country estate, but before this at the south-west corner of Walnut and Third Streets. Although the Hamiltons did not stay very long at one place, the Schuyler homestead at Albany was always open to them, as well as to the various children of the General, and it seems to have been a refuge in time of trouble and illness. Chastellux described his meeting with Alexander Hamilton and the wife at the father-in-law's house, probably at the time when he was preparing himself for his profession. Among the other French travellers who visited the Schuylers during the Revolution, he thus speaks of the family: "It consisted of Mr. Schuyler, his second daughter, whose face is gentle

WALL STREET IN THE SEVENTEENTH CENTURY

and pleasing; a Miss Peggy Schuyler, whose features were
animated and interesting; and another charming daughter
only eight years old, and of three boys, the oldest of whom
is fifteen, and who are the finest children possible, and
then he is himself a man of about fifty, but already ailing
and subject to gout. He has a considerable fortune, which
will increase for he owns an immense extent of territory, but
his talents and acquirements gain him greater respect than
his wealth." General Schuyler always suffered from this disease, which seems to have been the curse of his adult life,
and there is scarcely one of the later letters written by him
that does not contain some allusion to his sufferings and in-
capacity. It seriously interfered with his various military
campaigns, and more than one of his malignant enemies[1]
had intimated that he made it an excuse for his reluctance
to meet the enemy! It certainly led to his being carried
upon the shoulders of men, or by more comfortable con-
veyances, to the scene of his active operations in the north-
eastern part of the State during the border operations. He
gloomily writes to his daughter, July 28, 1795: "I have
not drank any champaign since I experienced Its pernicious
effects upon me—and shall not venture on It again." He
also announces his intention of going to the Lebanon Springs
for a cure.

The children referred to by Chastellux and others grew
up and married and went their various ways, none of them,
however, achieving any great distinction. The daughters,
especially Angelica, as has been said, were witty and attractive. Between Elizabeth Schuyler, her husband, and her
brothers and sisters, there always existed a pleasant relation,
but none of them entered into the intimate life of the Ham-

---

[1] See "History of New York During the Revolutionary War," by Thomas Jones,
vol. II. New York Historical Society, 1879.

iltons except General Schuyler,[1] Angelica Church, his daughter, and Philip, son of John Bradstreet Schuyler, who spent most of his early life with them.

The children of Elizabeth and Alexander Hamilton were eight in number, the first Philip being born January 22, 1782, while a second Philip came June 2, 1802, and was named after his elder brother, who had been killed in a duel the year before. Between these two were,

Angelica,	born September 25, 1784.
Alexander,	" May 16, 1786.
James Alexander,	" April 14, 1788.
John Church,	" August 22, 1792.
William Stephen,	" August 4, 1797.
Eliza,	" November 20, 1799.

Philip, the first child, seems to have been the most beloved and the most written and spoken about of all, for he was evidently the flower of the family. In a letter to General Meade, from Philadelphia, dated March, 1782, when Hamilton had left the army and was preparing to take up his professional work, an amusing allusion is made to the birth of this child.

[1] PHILIP SCHUYLER MARRIED CATHERINE VAN RENSSELAER

Angelica, born February 22, 1756; married John Barker Church.
Elizabeth, born August 7, 1757; married Alexander Hamilton.
Margarita, born September 24, 1758; married Stephen van Rensselaer.
Cornelia, born August 1, 1761, died young.
John Bradstreet, born October 8, 1763, died young.
John Bradstreet, born July 23, 1765; married Elizabeth van Rensselaer.
Philip Jeremiah, born January 20, 1768; married, 1, Sarah Rutsen; married, 2, Mary A. Sawyer.
Rensselaer, born January 29, 1773; married Eliza Ten Broeck.
Cornelia, born December 22, 1776; married Washington Morton.
Cortlandt, born May 15, 1778, died young.
Catharine van Rensselaer, born February 20, 1781; married, 1, Samuel Malcolm; married, 2, James Cochran.

PHILIP HAMILTON (THE FIRST): AGE 20

Alexander Hamilton to Richard K. Meade[1]

PHILADELPHIA, *March*, 1782.

A half hour since brought me the pleasure of your letter of December 1st. It went to Albany, and came from thence to this place. I heartily felicitate you on the birth of your daughter, I can well conceive your happiness on that occasion, by that which I felt on a similar occasion. Indeed, the sensations of a tender father of the child of a beloved mother, can only be conceived by those who have experienced them.

Your heart, my Meade, is peculiarly formed for engagements of this Kind. You have every right to be a happy husband—a happy father. You have every prospect of being so. I hope your felicity may never be interrupted. You cannot imagine how entirely domestic I am growing. I lose all taste for the pursuits of ambition. I sigh for nothing but the Company of my wife and my baby. The ties of duty alone, or imagined duty, Keep me from renouncing public life altogether. It is, however, probable I may not any longer be engaged in it. . . .

Imagine, my dear Meade, what pleasure it *must* give Eliza and myself to Know that Mrs. Meade interests herself in us. Without a personal acquaintance, we have been long attached to her. My visit at Mr. Fitzhugh's confirmed my partiality.

Betsy is so fond of your family that she proposes to form a match between her boy and your girl, provided you will engage to make the latter as amiable as her mother.

Truly, my dear Meade, I often regret that fortune has cast our residence at Such a distance from each other. It would be a serious addition to my happiness if we lived where I Could see you every day; but fate has determined it otherwise.

I am a little hurried, and can only request, in addition, that you will present me most affectionately to Mrs. Meade, and believe me to be, With the warmest

And most unalterable friendship

Yours A. HAMILTON.

[1] "Hamilton's Works" (J. C. H.), vol. I, p. 298.

On many occasions we find in letters that passed between his father-in-law and himself, as well as others, frequent references to the career of this promising boy, who, at the time of his death, was, evidently, dearer to Hamilton than any of his other children, and this feeling seems to have been shared by the family. Many years after the Meade letter Angelica Church wrote from London:

"I have received with inexpressible pleasure your long letter, and thank my Eliza for the agreeable details respecting your children. Philip inherits his father's talents. What flattering prospects for a mother! You are, my dear sister, very happy with such a Husband and such promise in a son."

Philip, like his father, had attended Columbia College, where he graduated with high honors in 1800, and was intended for the bar, but in a discussion with one George I. Eacker regarding a political matter, a challenge passed between them, and the young man, who was less than twenty, fell November 23, 1801, at the same place where Hamilton himself met his death three years later. It would appear that, like his father, he too was forced into an encounter which was in conflict with all his principles.

Many accounts of the circumstances which led to the affair have been given, but none of these are capable of verification, although the most probable is the one which states that the quarrel grew out of a Fourth-of-July speech made by Eacker in praise of Burr, and in which he incidentally reflected upon Alexander Hamilton.

In the duel, which was fought at three o'clock in the afternoon, Philip received a mortal wound, but lingered on until the morning of the next day.

The event attracted a great deal of newspaper discussion, and as at that time the *American Citizen and General Advertiser* was bitterly inimical to Hamilton, it was its endeavor to

show that his son was to blame. The *Evening Post*, however, took the ground that the affair was due to the intolerable provocation of Eacker. It appears from this description
that Philip Hamilton and a young man named Price were at
the theatre in a box adjoining that of Eacker, and that they
indulged in satirical comments upon a Fourth-of-July oration.
Eacker, overhearing them, invited the young men to step
into the lobby, and called some one a d——d rascal. They
adjourned to a public house, where an explanation was demanded, and when asked whom the offensive expression was
meant for, he declared that it was intended for each. As
they parted Eacker said, "I shall expect to hear from you,"
when they replied, "You shall." A challenge followed.
Eacker met Price on the following Sunday, and four shots
were exchanged without harm to any one. The seconds interfered, and the parties left the field. On the next day
Hamilton met Eacker, and received a shot through the body
at the first discharge, and fell without firing.

Angelica Church wrote to her brother, who was in Albany:
"His [Hamilton's] conduct was extraordinary during this trial.
I cannot reach particulars now, my sister is a little composed,
and the corpse will be removed from my house within an
hour." About two weeks afterward General Schuyler
wrote:

Philip Schuyler to Elizabeth Hamilton

ALBANY, *Dec.* 6, 1801.

MY DEARLY BELOVED AND AMIABLE CHILD: I trust that
resignation to the Divine Will has so far tranquillized your
mind as to mitigate the severity of the anguish which has
been inflicted on you and all of us. It ought my beloved
child to afford us much consolation that our dear departed
child afforded such decided evidence of his aversion to shed-
ding of blood, that he pursued every measure which propri-

ety and prudence could dictate to avoid it, that thus he has left this life without seeking or even wishing to take away that of his intemperate adversary, and that we have reason to trust that by the unbounded mercy of his Creator, his Spirit is in the realms of Eternal bliss.

In a letter to my Dear Hamilton, I urged him to bring you with him to us, I must reiterate the request to you my Dear Child that I may have the consolation of embracing you, of mingling my tears with yours and with Hamilton, and then by comforting each to dry them.

I suggested measures for this Journey since which have reflected if there should be no sledging that It would be better to send my strong horses to your Brother's at Rynbeck with my Coachman to relieve your horses, but If there should be sledging, I will send my covered Sled and horses to your Brothers and then your Coaches may be left there—but I ought to be advised in time of the day on which you will probably leave New York.

Your Coach is sufficiently roomy to bring the nurse and the three younger children with you which will add greatly to our satisfaction.

Adieu my Dear Love—Your Mama and sister unite with all in love to you, your Hamilton and the dear Children and in prayers that every blessing of which mortality is susceptible of may be yours and theirs.

   I am my dearly beloved Child,
    Most tenderly & affectionately yours
        PH. SCHUYLER.

Hamilton never fully recovered from this loss, for the career of the young man had been his pride, and he had high hopes that he would, eventually, take up his own work. Letters from Talleyrand and many friends speak of this, and all condoled with him later.

But few of Philip Hamilton's letters to his father are preserved, and these show that a most affectionate sympathy existed between the two, for the father, despite his absorption in public affairs, and the demands upon his time which were constantly being made by others, conducted his boy's education, giving him frequent hints in regard to the selection of studies, and the manner in which he should live, and a set of rules for the guidance of the son after his graduation from Columbia, when he was preparing for his chosen profession. These were:

RULES FOR MR. PHILIP HAMILTON

From the first of April to the first of October he is to rise not later than six o'clock; the rest of the year not later than seven. If earlier, he will deserve commendation. Ten will be his hour of going to bed throughout the year.

From the time he is dressed in the morning till nine o'clock (the time for breakfast excepted), he is to read law. At nine he goes to the office, and continues there till dinner-time. He will be occupied partly in writing and partly in reading law.

After dinner he reads law at home till five o'clock. From this time till seven he disposes of his time as he pleases. From seven to ten he reads and studies whatever he pleases.

From twelve on Saturday he is at liberty to amuse himself.

On Sunday he will attend the morning church. The rest of the day may be applied to innocent recreations.

He must not depart from any of these rules without my permission.

Several years before he entered Columbia, when Philip was a small lad at school, the father wrote to him:

Alexander Hamilton to his son Philip[1]

PHILADELPHIA, *Dec.* 5, 1791.

I received with great pleasure, my dear Philip, the letter which you wrote me last week. Your mama and myself were very happy to learn that you are pleased with your situ-

---

[1] Hamilton's "Reminiscences," p. 4.

ation, and content to stay as long as shall be thought best for you. We hope and believe that nothing will happen to alter this disposition. Your teacher also informs me that you recited a lesson the first day you began very much to his satisfaction. I expect every letter from him will give me a fresh proof of your progress, for I know you can do a great deal if you please, and I am sure you have too much spirit not to exert yourself, that you may make us every day more and more proud of you. You remember that I engaged to send for you next Saturday, and I will do it, unless you request me to put it off, for a promise must never be broken, and I will never make you one which I will not fill as far as I am able, but it has occurred to me that the Christmas holidays are near at hand, and I suppose your school will then break up for a few days and give you an opportunity of coming to stay with us for a longer time than if you should come on Saturday. Will it not be best, therefore, to put off your journey till the holidays? But determine as you like best, and let me know what will be most pleasing to you. A good night to my darling son."

Six years later Philip wrote to the father, who was then at Albany, a letter which appears to have been sent from Columbia College, and it suggests that he possessed some of the mental traits of his father.

Philip Hamilton to Alexander Hamilton

April 21, 1797.

DEAR PAPA: I just now received the enclosed letter from Grandpa [Schuyler], in answer to a letter I wrote to him, in which he has enclosed to me three receipts for shares in the Tontine Tavern, amounting to £100. I have given the receipts to Mama. I delivered my speech to Dr. Johnson to examine. He has no objection to my speaking; but he has blotted out that sentence which appears to be the best and most animated in it; which is, you may recollect it—

"*Americans, you have fought the battles of mankind; you have enkindled that sacred fire of freedom which is now,*" and so forth.

Dear Papa, will you be so good as to give my thanks to Grandpapa for the present he made me, but above all for the good advice his letter contains—which I am very sensible of its being extremely necessary for me to pay particular attention to, in order to be a good man. I remain your most affectionate son.

P. S. You will oblige me very much by sending back the letter I have enclosed to you.

The careers of the other sons were, in a measure, commonplace. Little remains to show that they ever distinguished themselves. If an exception can be made, it is in the case of James Alexander Hamilton who, in his Reminiscences, referred to elsewhere, sketches the active part he took in the adjustment of various delicate diplomatic affairs during the administration of Andrew Jackson and Martin Van Buren.

Alexander, the second son, was graduated from Columbia in 1804, and he, too, became a lawyer, but went abroad and joined the Duke of Wellington's army, then in Portugal, where he acquired a military training and some of the strategical methods of the great English general. Previous to the war of 1812 he came home, became a captain of infantry, and served with his father's old friend, General Morgan Lewis. After the war he supported himself by his profession, and in 1822 became a United States district attorney of New York, as well as land commissioner. He finally became identified with the development of real estate in New York City.

James Alexander also graduated from Columbia in 1805, was an officer in the war of 1812, and was made Secretary of State *ad interim* by Andrew Jackson in 1829. He subsequently became United States district attorney for the southern district of New York, and was later engaged in important diplomatic work.

The fourth son, John Church, named after the husband of his Aunt Angelica, after his graduation at Columbia in 1809, also studied law and took part in the war of 1812, and it was he who prepared his father's papers for publication.

The fifth son, William Stephen, after entering West Point, served in the Black Hawk War, and afterward went to the Far West, where little is known of him except that he died in California.

Philip, the youngest, was but two years old at the time of the duel with Burr, and is often referred to as "little Phil." He studied law in New York, and for a time was assistant United States district attorney, under his brother James, and achieved considerable distinction by the able manner in which he tried and convicted the celebrated pirate Gibbs, who was hanged on Bedloe's Island.

The grandfather wrote to his daughter shortly before the birth of this last baby.

Philip Schuyler to Elizabeth Hamilton

ALBANY, *August 23*, 1802.

MY DEARLY BELOVED AND AMIABLE CHILD: How your endearing attentions rivet you continually to my heart. May the loss of one be compensated by another Philip. May his virtues emulate those which graced his brother, and may he be a comfort to parents so tender and who have endeared themselves to theirs.

A long absence has prevented my attention to my private affairs. I hope soon to arrange these, and propose a visit to you, but I believe it can not be until after the Supreme Court in this City. . . . I hope you keep Your Children as much as possible in the country, as the city at this season

PHILIP HAMILTON (THE SECOND), "LITTLE PHIL":
AGE 78

is generally injurious to the health of Children, especially as they can with so much facility indulge with fruit and frequently with that which is unripe.—Embrace them all for us. They all share with You and My Dear Hamilton in our Love.

Adieu My Dear Child. May those blessings which are the portion of the virtuous attend You all is the prayer of Your Affectionate parent

Mrs. Hamilton.   Ph. Schuyler.

There was a great difference between the ages of the daughters. Angelica, a very beautiful girl, was born shortly after her father's residence in New York City after the peace.

She was evidently a charming character and very much like the aunt after whom she was named, being clever and talented. She seems to have had good musical training, and this lady frequently speaks of her in her letters from London. "Adieu, my dear Eliza," wrote Angelica Church in 1796, "I shall bring with me a Governness who understands music pretty well, she will be able to instruct Angelica and Eliza."

Upon receipt of the news of her brother's death in the Eacker duel, she suffered so great a shock that her mind became permanently impaired, and although taken care of by her devoted mother for a long time there was no amelioration in her condition, and she was finally placed under the care of Dr. MacDonald of Flushing, and remained in his charge until her death at the age of seventy-three. During her latter life she constantly referred to the dear brother so nearly her own age as if alive. Her music, that her father used to oversee and encourage, stayed by her all these years. To the end she played the same old-fashioned songs and minuets upon the venerable piano that had been bought for her, many years before, in London, by Angelica Church, during her girlhood, and was sent to New York through a friend of her father. She survived her mother by two and a half years. The younger daughter, with whom the mother lived in her old age, and at whose house she died, in Washington, seems to have been a woman of a great deal of strength of mind.

Although all of Hamilton's sons marked out for themselves legal or military careers, it cannot be said that any one, in a conspicuous way, resembled his father.

William did not marry, but sought a frontier life, and occasionally returned to see his mother and brothers. He first went to that part of the Northwest which is now Wisconsin, and in 1837, when in her eightieth year, Mrs. Hamilton made the long journey to see him. She wrote, on her way to my father, as follows:

Mrs. Alexander Hamilton to Philip Hamilton

March 19, 1837.

MY DEAR SON: I wrote to your Brothers of my continued health. I am now on the Ohio quite well, at Pitsburgh I was visited by Mr. Ross[1] the friend of your Father. He laments the state of our country, and fears his efforts will not be of the duration that good minds wish.

The Director of the Bank, he informed me, saw your Brother's letter and immediately determined not to issue specie. As soon as the Bank opened they were required to make a payment in specie to a considerable amount by persons that had been travelling night and day.[2] Pittsburgh is a considerable town on the junction of three rivers, no beauty but good Buildings, gloomy from the use of coal. I shall write you from Cincinnati where I shall be today. Adieu! write to me and let me know how Angelica is.

Your Affectionate Mother,

E. HAMILTON.

[1] John Ross, United States Senator, 1794–97. Active in suppressing the Whiskey Insurrection.

[2] Probably a reference to the great panic of that year.

Later she wrote:

Mrs. Alexander Hamilton to Philip Hamilton

MISSISSIPPI, *May* 23, 1837.

MY DEAR SON: I have passed the Ohio, the river is very spacious, but very difficult of navigation, the shores beautiful and the vessel approaching the shore at the distance of one dozen feet; no wharf, the water is so mixed with clay that it is not drinkable without wine. This evening we shall be at St. Louis on the Mississippi. Our passage will be tedious as we go against the stream. Let me hear from you, particularly respecting Angelica and all the family.

Your affectionate mother

ELIZABETH HAMILTON.

And again:

Mrs. Alexander Hamilton to Philip Hamilton

I thank you My Dear Son for yours of the fifteenth. I hope you may have leisure and the opportunity to have the Speach of your beloved Father copied. Solicit it most anxiously, and if that won't do request it as a favour for me. Hire a person to copy it and let me be at the expense. How desirous must you be to see all given to the publisher that your father has done for our country.

I wish you to make inquiry where the location is to be made and when this is the last of your father's services of the grant of land.[1] I am quite recovered. I wish you may see some of General Washington's family and that you go to Mount Vernon. Adieu. Your Brothers are all well,

Every Blessing attend you prays

Your Affectionate Mother

ELIZABETH HAMILTON.

New York, February 21, 1839.

---

[1] A certificate for a section of land was awarded Hamilton by the United States for military service, but he never took advantage of this allotment.

Very few of the children presented any of the father's dominant attractions. William Stephen, however, must have been a winning character. He certainly possessed a great deal of his father's personal beauty, and much of his charm of manner, but it is said that he was unconventional and something of a wanderer.

The youngest son, Philip, also manifested much of his father's sweetness and happy disposition, and was always notably considerate of the feelings of others, and was punctilious to a fault in his obligations. In his old age he devoted much of his time to helping others in many quiet ways, and no one came to him in vain for advice or such material help as he could afford. Born at a time when his mother was in great poverty, he was denied those advantages accorded to his elder brothers, and had, in every sense, to make his own way. He had no college education, but studied law with one of his brothers; had a hard, up-hill professional life, and died comparatively poor. Much of his time was given up to unselfish acts, and the number of his poor clients, especially those who followed the sea, was very great.

James A. Hamilton described the family life in New York when he and his brothers and sisters were children.[1] "I distinctly recollect," he says, "the scene at breakfast in the front room of the house in Broadway. My dear mother seated, as was her wont, at the head of the table with a napkin in her lap, cutting slices of bread and spreading them with butter, while the younger boys, who, standing at her side, read in turn a chapter in the Bible or a portion of Goldsmith's 'Rome.' When the lessons were finished the father and the elder children were called to breakfast, after which the boys were packed off to school."

During the time that Hamilton was Secretary of the Treas-

[1] Hamilton's "Reminiscences," p. 3.

ury and when he lived in Philadelphia, his family worries
were increased by reason of the menace of yellow fever,
which seems to have been prevalent. As the result of the
absence of all needful sanitary precautions and ignorance of
the disease, we find that this scourge flourished in Philadelphia
to an alarming extent during the latter part of the eighteenth
century. It was sometimes given its familiar name, and
again spoken of as the "plague." Nothing could be more
pitiful than Robert Morris's description of its invasion of
the debtors' prison, where he was confined, which was known
as "Prune Street." Not only the corridors, but every available space was filled with coffined bodies, and the prisoners
were dying like sheep.[1] Hamilton and his family were
exposed, and it is said that some of them were stricken, but
all managed to recover. The alarming extent of the disease upon several occasions practically led to the abandonment of Philadelphia by those who could afford to go. After
leaving their house in that city, the Hamilton family first
went to the hills and then to Albany, but for a time were
quarantined outside of the limits of the latter place.

Previous to this time the Schuylers devised measures to
lessen the danger of contagion and to remove the children
to a healthier spot, and when the danger became alarming
this was done. Later they prevailed upon the Hamiltons to
join their children. In the following letter the "little one"
referred to is John Church Hamilton who was then more
than a year old.

---

[1] One writer whose book bears the title of "Occasional Writings on the Yellow
Fever. Addresses to Those Who have not Forgotten what has Happened Within
a Few Years Among their Friends and Fellow Citizens, by a Philadelphian," pre-
sents tables showing the enormous death-rate up to 1802. Upon the authority of
Benjamin Johnson, 13,394 persons were buried in "Potter's Field" in that city from
August 1 to November 9, 1793.

Philip Schuyler to Elizabeth Hamilton

ALBANY, Sundy 16, 1793.

MY DEARLY BELOVED CHILD: I feel that It will give you pain to be deprived for some time longer of the pleasure of embracing your Dear Children, but the reasons assigned in my letter to my Dear Hamilton are such as I trust your good sense will acquiesce in,—especially when you reflect what additional anxiety I should be exposed to If the Children were with you before It is fully ascertained that all danger from the dreadful disorder is at an end.—

The tenderness and affection which your Dear Children evince for us every moment of the day, their docility, the health they enjoy are so many sources of happiness to their parents and to us. The little one strives to articulate, he will soon succeed, he walks from one end of the hall to the other with ease,—eats well, and is the most lively of children.

Your Dear Mama and all the family join me in love,—I hope you are still at fair Hill, and that you will remain there at least until the result is known from the return of the inhabitants who had left the city during the prevalence of the calamity.

Adieu My beloved Child, the best blessings and warmest prayers of Your affectionate parents attend you.

Yours ever affectionately,

PH. SCHUYLER.

Mrs. Hamilton.

General Schuyler's solicitude for the comfort of his daughter and her children led him, at this time, to devise means for alleviating their distress, and to bring them to the family home in a Hudson River sloop where they would be safe. In those days the passage from New York to Albany was really in the nature of a voyage. In 1732 a certain *Dr.* Alexander Hamilton,[1] whose travels took him to Albany,

---

[1] "Hamilton's Itinerarium, being a Narrative of a Journey," etc., etc., by Dr. Alexander Hamilton. Edited by A. B. Hart, LL.D., printed for private distribution in 1907. Bixby Publications.

devoted a week to the journey and graphically pictures the discomforts of the sloop, which was the only method of conveyance, and this he does as one would nowadays refer to a transatlantic trip. Fifty years later Hamilton himself, in letters to his wife, speaks of the miserable and comfortless pilgrimages and the dirty and crowded little vessels, which were often obliged to lie to under the lea of the Highlands to await changes in the weather and tide.

The next autumn General Schuyler again wrote to Mrs. Hamilton, urging her to leave Philadelphia.

Philip Schuyler to Elizabeth Hamilton

N. YORK, Monday, *Sept.* 29, 1794.

MY DEARLY BELOVED CHILD: Reports confirm the former accounts that the Yellow fever prevails in Philadelphia. I must therefore and most earnestly repeat my request that You leave the city immediately, and as you may be exposed to inconveniences on your journey I wish you to go to some decent tavern on the road towards New York. At the Macleroys at Bristol if possible and as soon as you receive this to write me, and if You are determined to come away I will set out on Friday with a Stage Wagon which I shall especially engage to bring You, the Children and Servants over. If you have not two horses, to bring your Carriage, bring at least Your Chair as you will travel with more ease in that than in the Waggon.—Pray fail not to write immediately on receipt of this, and if the post should be already come away, send Your letter by some person coming in the Stage, and a copy of It by post—God bless You my Amiable and beloved Child. Embrace the Children for me.

Yours affectionately,

PH. SCHUYLER.

Mrs. Hamilton.

As we know, the fever made its appearance in New York as well in 1795, and Mrs. Hamilton's sister Angelica wrote to her:

November the 24, 95.

I implore you my dear Eliza to write to me, there are letters in town so late as the 10ʺ October from New York. I have not a line, and a dreadful fever rages there, and you and yours are there, if you knew what I suffer you would write to relieve a thousand apprehensions—Adieu my Dear Sister.
I embrace you with tendrest
affection. Yours   A. Church.

Hamilton, whose many-sided genius found expression in various ways, suggested the cold-water treatment,[1] which, in later years, has been again adopted not only for this disease, but for all toxemic conditions with high temperature. He thus wrote to his wife upon this subject:

Alexander Hamilton to Elizabeth Hamilton

Rye 30 Miles from New York,
Tuesday Even.

I am arrived here my Dear Eliza in good health, but very anxious about my Dear Child. I pray heaven to restore him and in every event to support you.—If his fever should appear likely to prove obstinate, urge the Physician to consider well the propriety of trying the cold bath—I expect it will, if it continues, assume a nervous type, and in this case I believe the cold bath will be the most efficacious remedy—but still do not attempt it without the approbation of the Physician. Alas my Betsy how much do I regret to be separated from you at such a juncture. When will the time come that I shall be exempt from the necessity of leaving my dear family. God bless my beloved and all my dear Children.   A. H.
Mrs. Hamilton.

[1] Neglected and forgotten in those days, although one of the oldest therapeutic agents known in medicine.

The Churches went twice to England, where their life was evidently most delightful, surrounded, as they seem to have been, by all the distinguished people of the day; but although John Church took an active part in public affairs, and became a member of Parliament, his wife was always most intensely patriotic, and yearned for America and her family. At a time when a return to America seemed impossible she wrote from Yarmouth, England, to Mrs. Hamilton: "You and my dear Hamilton will never cross the Atlantic, I shall never leave this Island and as to meeting in heaven—there will be no pleasure in that."

When in this country she wrote to Elizabeth Hamilton from Philadelphia at the time Congress was sitting, and when Hamilton was Secretary of the Treasury:

PHILADELPHIA, Tuesday Morning
[about 1793]

You will hear with pleasure, my dear Eliza that our Kitty is much better, she is going to a ball this evening, her dancing has been so much praised that I fear she will give more disappointment than pleasure. My brother [1] seemed very sad yesterday, and when I questioned him, I was sorry to find little William's health to be the cause of his dejection, his sensibility suffers from the least anxiety to you or your babes, is Miss Pretty *less firm in her manner* and does Angelica see her Cousin often?

During her absence in Europe in 1787 several of her girl friends were married, and in writing to her sister she said: "Amongst all the distresses that distract my poor country I am happy to hear that celibacy is not one of the number." Several years later her own daughter, Kitty, then a charming young woman who afterward became Mrs. Cruger, had a romance of her own, and met and evidently fascinated the

[1] Alexander Hamilton.

Chevalier de Colbert, who had inherited the great Georgia lands from Comte d'Estaing, who was one of Hamilton's early friends, and in pressing his suit he wrote Hamilton the following interesting letter, in which he asked the latter to intercede for him:

The Chevalier de Colbert to Alexander Hamilton

LONDON, this 7th *May*, 1800.

It is with great pleasure, Monsieur, that I learn from a letter from the Vicomte D'Orléans, that, confirming the choice already made by the public, the President has appointed you to fill the position of Commander-in-chief of the army, left vacant by the death of General Washington, so that what I told you a month ago is already partly realized, time will bring the rest, and I am very sure that in whatever post Fortune places you, you will justify the discrimination that put you there.[1]   The trumpet of war has once more sounded, the Austrians are boasting of great successes in Italy, and they certainly must have had some as they have taken Bocheta, which must entail the capture of Genoa, but the French declare they have had brilliant victories on the Rhine.

We must expect exaggeration on both sides; in one or two months at the earliest shall we be able to foretell upon which side Fortune will declare itself.

Condé's army, paid by England, is marching upon Italy, where it is to don the White Cockade and the old French uniforms; they have orders to make as many recruits as they can.

From what Monsieur le Comte d'Artois told me yesterday, Monseigneur le Duc D'Angoulême has left Mittau for Italy to join Monseigneur le Prince de Condé.

General Abercromby leaves here for the Mediterranean with 4,000 men; it seems that England intends to raise an army in order to attack the South of France, where mal-

---

[1] He probably referred to Hamilton's appointment as Senior Major-General; Hamilton resigned from the army July 2, 1800.

contents are numerous; it is said that the Russians who are
in Italy will join them, they also talk of a descent upon Nor-
mandy to cause a diversion; all that will I think, depend
upon the successes that the Austrians or the French will have
on the Rhine and in Italy. In the meantime all the *emigrès*
are returning to France, I am expecting letters that will decide my course; I know that the sale of my property in Nor-
mandy has been forbidden; three months hence I shall know
how I stand. You know why I long for wealth. Ah! my
dear General, do not be so much my enemy and hers as to
allow them—by taking advantage of her submission and respect for her father—to force her into contracting any bonds,
that, *if her heart be not entirely changed,* will make her
wretched, and drive me to despair, if, as I hope, I can soon
offer her the competence that would satisfy hers and my desires. I know too that Mr. Ch.[1] and you *think I am too old.* I
see very well that you do not know the French. The warmth
of their blood prolongs their youth. Away from her I love
her as much as all your Americans put together; near her I
love her, and *shall love her* as at twenty, and I could *love well.*

Moreover you are experienced enough, and she is reasonable enough to know that all the transports of love are
often only too shortlived with young men, and that similari-
ties of taste, friendship and confidence are the true foundations of happiness.

Such being the case, I have thirty—perhaps forty years
in which to try to contribute to hers, and you know whether
I desire it. You may remember that when I left you you
told me that time might bring happy changes; I replied that
I should have the perseverence and courage that sooner
or later overcome fate. I shall have them to the end, and I
assure you that before long I shall be able in uniting the little
she has *by right* to what I shall have—to offer her, if not so
brilliant a lot as I could wish, at least one that need give her
no anxiety for the future.

I have neither time nor inclination to reproach you for
your silence. Mme. Ch.[2] who so kindly led me to hope for
news of her, has also completely forgotten me. Some one

[1] John Barker Church.   [2] Angelica Church.

must have played me a very nasty, dirty trick to blacken me
in her eyes; it is a fine game to speak evil of the absent.
Assure her that that is not what we do here when I am with
the Princesse de Craon and *Bonnè*, a young woman who is
with her, and who is very fond of Mdlle Kitty; she has
begged me to send her two books of music, one of which is of
her own composition.   I am entrusting to some one who is
going to Philadelphia, I send it to you as well-meaning
people will not fail to think that this packet encloses something else.   You can reassure them, and may open the
Scroll before the whole assembled family. *Adieu, mon
général*, now that you have an army do not take advantage
of your superiority to ingloriously fight a Soldier who has
nothing but love on his Side, and who has everything to
struggle against.   With every respect and assurance of my
unchanging attachment,   Le Chev. de C.

Hamilton's ultimate resignation from the Treasuryship
caused a great deal of commotion in the family, and much
discussion on the part of General Schuyler, Mrs. Church, and
his friends at large.   As has been stated, he left public office
impoverished, and when he was thirty-seven, and but ten
years before his death.   It is apparent from his letters that
this step was a hard one to take, as his entire life and interests had been merged in the public trust he did so much to
organize, and which has altered so little in more than one
hundred years.   The following letters that passed between
himself and his sister-in-law, to whom he often turned,
graphically convey his motives and feelings:

Alexander Hamilton to Angelica Church

Philadelphia, *December 8, 1794.*

You say I am a politician, and good for nothing.   What
will you say when you learn that after January next, I shall
cease to be a politician at all?   So is the fact.   I have formally and definitely announced my intention to resign at

that period, and have ordered a house to be taken for me at New York. My dear Eliza has been lately very ill. Thank God, she is now quite recovered, except that she continues somewhat weak.

My absence on a certain expedition was the cause.[1]

You will see, notwithstanding your disparagement of me, I am still of consequence to her. Liancourt[2] has arrived, and has delivered your letter. I pay him the attention due to his misfortunes and his merits. I wish I was a Crœsus; I might then afford solid consolations to these children of adversity, and how delightful it would be to do so. *But now,* sympathy, kind words, and *occasionally a dinner, are all I can Contribute.* Don't let Mr. Church be alarmed at my retreat. All is well with the public. Our insurrection is most happily terminated. Government has gained by it reputation and strength, and our finances are in a most flourishing condition. *Having contributed to place those of the Nation on a good footing, I go to take a little care of my own; which need my care not a little.*

Love to Mr. Church. Betsey will add a line or two. Adieu.

And again later, after the actual resignation:

Alexander Hamilton to Angelica Church

ALBANY, *March* 6, 1795.

To indulge in my domestic happiness the more freely, was with me a principal motive for relinquishing an office in which 'tis said I have gained some glory, and the difficulties of which had just been subdued. Eliza and our children are with me here at your father's house, who is himself at New York attending the Legislature. We remain here till June, when we become stationary at New York, where I resume the practice of the law. For, my dear sister, I tell you without regret what I hope you antici-

---

[1] With the army to suppress the Whiskey Rebellion in Pennsylvania.
[2] The Duke de la Rochefoucauld-Liancourt.

pate, that *I am poorer than when I went into office.*[1]   I allot myself full four or six years of more work than will be pleasant, though much less than I have had for the last five years.

Angelica Church to Elizabeth Hamilton

LONDON, Feb. 24, 95.

I sincerely congratulate you my dear Eliza on the resignation of our dear Hamilton & on your return to New York where I hope to pass with you the remainder of my days, that is if you will be so obliging as to permit my *Brother* to give me his society, for you know how much I love & admire him.

I do not by this Ship write to my *amiable*,[2] but you will thank him for his letters.   I was very proud to have the American Ministers intreating me for information from America.   I did boast of very long letters & give myself some airs of importance.   Mr Jay[3] is very desirous of getting to his fireside, & Mrs. Pinckney[4] preparing for Spain.

The Churches eventually arrived in New York.   Hamilton secured a house and expended upon it large sums to fix it for the occupancy of his rather exacting sister-in-law, and these we find entered in his books—as well as records of how the family lived, and what they did for a number of years. Among other items charged to Mrs. Church, it appears that he paid "Cash for passages of yourself and servants on ———— Dolls. 370.66," and at an earlier date he "paid

---

[1] Hamilton, in a private letter dated June 26, 1792, wrote: "The Legislature might reasonably restrain its officers from future *buying* and *selling* of stock, but could not reasonably prevent them making a disposition of property which they had previously acquired according to the laws of their country.   All my property in the funds is about eight hundred dollars, three per cent.   These at a certain period I should have sold had I not been unwilling to give occasion to cavil."   This stock was sold by Mr. Wolcot to pay Hamilton's small debts when he left Philadelphia.

[2] Hamilton.

[3] John Jay.

[4] Mrs. Pinckney, wife of Thomas Pinckney, Minister to Spain, 1794-96.

acct. of your last landlady for rooms, & some damage done by your servants in removing, £23.9.3."

His own accounts are all neatly and carefully kept up to 1799, but show, after that time, some carelessness and brevity which is in contrast with earlier years. This was probably owing to his multifarious occupations, and possibly to his anxiety about the affairs of his own political party, which then was in the midst of its troubles. A list of excerpts is, I think, worthy of reproduction.

	G. Washington expense to Mess,[1] to Morton	$16.
1796.	Nov. 11. Contribution for erecting R. C. Church at Albany	5.
	July 11. For this sum paid to W. McDonald towards Presbyterian Church at Albany	15.
1795.	Oct. 25. Household expenses for this sum paid Henry Seaman for Mourning for Mrs. Hamilton.[2]	43.25
	Philip Schuyler paid for Mrs. Schuyler	22.42
		65.67
	Dec. 6. Account of Expences, for this sum paid tax on carriage	10.
	for this sum paid Mr. Beekman for half a years rent of stable	50.
	Dec. 21. George Washington, President for this sum paid for an express to Messrs. Troffer & Matin	16.
	May 6. For this sum paid in full for Tuition of my Children in the French language say dollars Eighteen five shillings & 4d (L. Maillet)	£18.6.5
	May 18. Household Furniture for a Dining Table & Bed Stead	Doll. 108.74
1793.	Ju. 10. Account of Donation for the sum given away	30.
	ditto July 4	1c.
	To Stock Account for price of Horse & Chaise Sold	250.
1796.	For this sum paid M. Ten Eyck ¼ house rent	218.75

[1] Messenger.

[2] For the funeral of John Bradstreet Schuyler, one of General Schuyler's sons.

1796.	Sept. 7. Account of Donation for this sum paid on account of rent for Isaac Sherman	37.50
	Sept. 12. For this sum deposited for payment of duties on a pipe of wine	60.
	Oct. 11. For this sum paid Archibald Drummond for stationery	21.20
	For Sundry books & account	50.
	Paid Doctors Bard & Hosack	
	1795 & 1796	110.
	1798	100.
	1802	246.50
	1804 pd. Dr. Hosack July 3	120.
	1797 Apothecaries bill	14.
	1795. Sum for Bendon's note given to Mrs. Hamilton to take out in groceries	£13. 5.
	for a guinea in addition paid for Mrs. Hamilton	£1.17.4
1795.	For two guineas given to a poor French	.9.33
	family given in private character	£1.
	Account of expenses. Dr. to Cash. for this sum paid Judy Perkins Negro woman for her wages several years ago, which she alleges was detained from her in consequence of a claim by Major Turner who demands her wages as his servant (p Rect on Receipt Book Dr.	12.50
1795.	for this sum paid for keeping of horses & Carriage	8.
1795.	Aug. 28. for this sum paid for Cabinet Wares	67.13
	Sept. 22. Account of donations Dr. in Cash for this sum paid to Henry King for Board of Mrs. De Grove a French refugee	19.
1796.	Oct. this sum del'd Mrs. Hamilton on going to Albany	100.
	this sum on my return November 1	20.
	my expences to and from Albany	40.
	Oct. 4. for Subscription to Dancing Assembly	20.
	Nov. 11. for this sum paid Hallet & Browne for 2 Chaldrons of Coal	30.
	for fruits	3.
	24. J. Lyon & Co. for 2½ Chaldrons of Coal	37.50
	Dec 6 this sum paid Doctor Jones for two firkins of butter	50.55
	(£20.4.6)	
	Dec. 23. paid Berry & Rogers for Books	10.

1796.	Dec. for this sum in Charity	17.
	"	5.
	"	5.
	"	5.
	Paid Sherrard his account	£13.7.6.
1797.	Feby 13. Library, paid J. Rivington for books	22.37
	Febr 24. paid Subscription to ball	5.
	Mar. 7. William Duer cash lent this day	30.
	Mar. 10. paid Mrs. Hamilton for subscription to a Bible	5.
	May 22. R. Troupe for parchment purchased of him 30 skins at 5/10	21.88
	May 29. John B. Church paid for a negro woman & child	225.
	Aug. 29. Tax on house & Stabel	43.40
	" " personal tax	9.30
	Oct. 16. paid Crier Albany in full	10.
	Nov. 24. paid Hair dresser's bill	20.
1798.	Feby 1. for my expenses to and from Albany	50.
	Subscription towards Reading Room	1.50
	Feby 14. " to Presidents Ball	5.
	March, Household furniture, Plate presented by M. le Guen	500.
	Case v. Gouverneur	
	Expended at Philadelphia last Summer	100.
	April 1. Library Acct for paid towards Encyclopedia	40.20
	paid on journey to New Haven	100.
	May 1. paid Mr. Ten Eyck half year's rent ending yesterday	437.50
	Marinus Willet, this sum lent his wife	125.
	May 9. paid Dr. Belleville bill in full	12.50
	May 18. Delv^d. E. Hamilton, & paid for pistols	62.
	June 30. paid Independence Dinner	10.
	Aug. 23. paid Wyllies house & Chaise hire	30.
	Dec. 18. paid Mrs. Hamilton some time since	100.
1799.	Jan. 12. Expenses for a Demijohn of wine	20.
	Jan. 19. paid French Taylor	100.
	Jan. 29. to Military Service[1] compensation for November & December	536.70
	Febr. 12. paid for Prints	28.

[1] During the time he was inspector-general of the reorganized army.

1799. Mar. 1.   Expences for half the rent of a Country
            place last fall   37.50
         paid Isaac Jones
         Mar. 29.   United States Postage paid by Capt.
            Church   21.
         postage paid by Mrs. Williams to accountant of
            War Dept.   215.84
1802. Febr.   By Bank N. Y. overdrawn   50.
         Expence House Rent   110.
1799. Sept. 25.   Paid for horse   125.
1802. May 12.   Expenses Philip's funeral [1]   266.11
1803. Charity, Alms House   105.

The accounts of the last few years are even more condensed and less orderly, and are grouped under "Receipts &
Expenditures." Many of these refer to the building of the
Grange where he lived until his death, and to the payment
of household expenses, wages, etc.

In another part of the book appear several entries, undoubtedly in connection with the election of John Adams,
and showing that even in those days a degree of conviviality was indispensable to the exercise of the franchise.

Disbursements for Elections

1796   Paid Jones printer for printing nominating tickets Drs. 2.
         Aprl. 16.   paid R. Boyd for tavern expenses ⎱
              " Hobson   "   "   "   ⎰   15.
         pd. Hammond as my share   30.
         " Van Orden for Tavern Expenses   9.37

                    City of N. Y. in acct. with A. H.
1788. McClean Printer at different times paid an execu-
            tion agst Capt. —— on acct. of Rockets ex-
            pended in the procession.[2]

[1] His son killed by Eacker the previous year.
[2] To celebrate the ratification of the Constitution in New York.

The cost of living in this city in those days may be approximately reached by this bill for provisions for about ten days:

No. 45.   Reinhard Kahmer bot for Cornal Hamilton at Sundred times

1791

October 19th	To " 3 " bushels of potatoes at 2ˢ/9ᵈ	£0. 8. 3	
	To a ½ " peck of pears	0. 1.10½	
	To a ½ " bushel of turnips	0. 1. 3	
	To " 3 " bunches of Carrots & Cabeges	0. 0. 9	
	To " 8 " lb. beef at 3½	0. 2. 4	
	To " 12½ " lb. mutton at 4ᵈ½	0. 4. 8	
	To " " " " buns & som yearbs . .	0. 1. 8½	
20 "	To " 6 " lb. beef at 3½	0. 1. 9	
	To " 2 " bushels of Apels	0. 5. 0	
	To " 8 " lb. butter at 1/3	0.10. 0	
21 "	To " 17 " lb. beef at 6 & 1 lb. Suet at 8ᵈ	0. 9. 2	
	To " 3 " Dozen of Eggs	0. 3. 0	
	To " 13½ " lb. Mutton at 5ᵈ	0. 5. 7½	
	To a ½ " peck of pears & Spinnag .	0. 2. 3	
	To onions 5½ Endif 3ᵈ & Salrey 8ᵈ . .	0. 1. 4½	
	To . . . . a Copel of fowls	0. 2. 0	
	To . . . . a basket	0. 1.11½	
22 "	To " 7¾ " lb. Veal at 7ᵈ	0. 4. 6½	
	To " 7½ " lb. beef at 5ᵈ	0. 3. 1	
	To . . . . time & parsly	0. 1. 6	
	To . . a set of Calfs feet	0. 0. 6	
	To " 1½ " bushel of turnips at 2ᵈ/6 .	0. 3. 9	
	To . . . . Eggs & Cabeges	0. 2. 6½	
	To . . . . Quals, tripe	0. 2. 6	
	To " 13 " lb. mutton at 4ᵈ	0. 4. 0	
		£4. 4. 8	
24th	To " 9 " lb. beef at 4ᵈ	0. 3. 0	
	To " 2 " bushels of turnips 2ˢ/6ᵈ . .	0. 5. 0	
	To " 4 " fouls at 3/9	0. 3. 9	
25 "	To " 5 " bushels of potatoes at 2/9 .	0.13. 9	
	To " 10½ " lb. Corn beef at 5ᵈ . . .	0. 4. 4½	
	To " 20 " lb. pork at 4½	0. 7. 6	
	To " 14 " lb. mutton at 4ᵈ	0. 4. 8	
	To . . . . Cabeges	0. 3. 4	

October 25th　To " ½ " bushels of Cramberies　. .　o. 3. 6
　　　　　　　To " 12 " dozen of Eggs at 10 & 4 dozen
　　　　　　　　at 3–9　. . . . .　o.13. 9
　　　　　　　To " 6 " lb. butter at 1/4　. . . .　o. 8. o
　　29 "　　　To . . . a tung Salt . . . .　o. 2. 6
　　　　　　　To " 13 " lb. mutton at 4½　. . . .　o. 4.10½
　　　　　　　To " 3 " teal at 1/3 a piece & Car-
　　　　　　　　rits 6ᵈ　. . . . .　o. 4. 3
　　　　　　　To . . . Swete potatoes　. . . . .　o. o.11
　　　　　　　　　　　　　　　　　　　　　£8. 7.10

CHAPTER IX

FRIENDS AND ENEMIES

FROM an early period in the war until after the overthrow
of Louis XVI, a number of brilliant Frenchmen landed on
our shores.   Some, like La Fayette, the Duc de Lauzun,
the Vicomte de Noailles, the Marquis François Jean de
Chastellux, Rochambeau, Tousard, Pont de Gibaud, Du-
portail, Maudiut Duplessis, the Comte de la Rouarie, or
Colonel Armand as he was known to his fellows, came to
fight.

Others, like Louis Philippe, the Comte de Volney, the
Comte Alexandre de Tilly, Moreau de St. Méry, the Duc
de la Rochefoucauld-Liancourt, J. P. Brissot de Warville,
came as *émigrés*, or to travel; and the ubiquitous Bishop of
Autun, otherwise Charles Maurice Talleyrand, after stirring
up all the mischief he could in Great Britain, and starting an
Irish rebellion, came here to spy.   These, and many other
clever and witty men from different parts of Europe, among
them the veteran soldier Steuben, gave to society at the time
of the American Revolution a decided charm.   We find them
in Philadelphia, as well as at every large army camp, and
in the gloom incident to the hardship and struggles of
a poorly equipped force fighting against superior numbers
of well-trained troops, they were cheerful and welcome
visitors.   They certainly brought with them a fund of
gayety, which did much to raise the drooping spirits of the
hardy patriots, and with most of them Hamilton was on

very good terms. Of him Oliver draws this picture, which, perhaps, applies to a later period, but according to those French travellers and writers who knew him in the field, he was always fascinating: "This serious young statesman we gather to have been remarkable in private life, chiefly for his high spirits, his good looks, his bright eyes, and his extraordinary vivacity. He loved the society of his fellow-creatures, and shone in it. He loved good wine and good company and beautiful things—even clothes and ruffles of fine lace. He despised slovens and people like Jefferson, who dressed ostentatiously in homespun. He belonged to the age of manners, and silk stockings, and handsome shoe-buckles. In Bagehot's excellent phrase, 'he was an enjoying English gentleman'; companionable and loyal, gay and sincere, always masterful and nearly always dignified."[1]

Let us see, then, who were his friends. As a rule, they were men who were honorable and well educated, of good courage and good breeding, gallant and chivalrous, and who possessed the other attractions of an heroic age.

As his capacity for making lasting friends was greatly inferior to the ease with which he made enemies, this can be explained by the statement of one of his historians that "his love for his country was always greater than his love for his countrymen," and it can be easily conceived how a man with so critical a sense, and with such strong ideas regarding unselfish requirements for the public weal, must not only fail to exert himself for the mere shallow fascination of his fellow men, as did Burr, for instance, but must antagonize many men with less lofty aims.

His attachments were strangely assorted, but, as a rule, were very deep, very affectionate, and very lasting; and, as is usually the case, the less brilliant and more sober-minded

[1] *Op. cit.*, p. 430.

friends were those that remained loyal and unselfishly devoted to him until the end, and did more for his family after his death than any of the others. It may be said that they were divided into two categories: those that were drawn to him by his humorous and almost feminine traits, which were coupled with a fascinating culture and a flow of spirits that almost bubbled over; and others, who had been engaged with him in the war, and in his legal practice, and the many public affairs which were so vital at the time. These really loved him for his great intellectual gifts and his absolute sense of justice. Although Lodge has gravely declared that he had no imagination, it does, on the contrary, appear that he had a lively sense of humor, and was at times exceedingly witty.

This is shown in his letters to John Laurens, to La Fayette, and a few of his early friends, and in the rather short and unsatisfactory remaining correspondence with his wife and sister-in-law. In 1780, at a time when the condition of affairs was certainly not conducive to high spirits, we find that he wrote, in the field, to General Anthony Wayne in regard to a Rev. Dr. Mendey, "who is exceedingly anxious to be in the service, and I believe has been forced out of it not altogether by fair play. He is just what I should like for a military parson, except that he does not drink, and he will not insist upon your going to heaven whether you will or not."[1]

There is the jauntiness of the gay soldier in his few words to one of his warmest army friends, Otho Williams (1779): "Mind your eye, my dear boy, and if you have an opportunity, fight hard,"[2] but a tenderer note in his long letter to John Laurens, which is not so well known as to lose its charm by abridged repetition; probably none of his com-

[1] Wayne "Correspondence" referred to by Lodge.
[2] "Hamilton's Works" (J. C. H.), vol. I, p. 79.

rades was dearer to Hamilton than Laurens, whose untimely death was a very great blow.[1]

Cold in my professions—warm in my friendships—I wish, my dear Laurens, it were in my power, by actions, rather than words, to convince you that I love you. I shall only tell you, that till you bid us adieu, I hardly knew the value you had taught my heart to set upon you. Indeed, my friend, it was not well done. You know the opinion I entertain of mankind; and how much it is my desire to preserve myself free from particular attachments, and to keep my happiness independent of the caprices of others. You should not have taken advantage of my sensibility, to steal into my affections without my consent. But as you have done it, and as we are generally indulgent to those we love, I shall not scruple to pardon the fraud you have committed on one condition; that for my sake, if not for your own, you will continue to merit the partiality which you have so artfully instilled into me.

Fleury[2] shall be taken care of. All the family send love. In this, join the General and Mrs. Washington; and what is best, it is not in the style of ceremony, but sincerity."

One of Hamilton's most devoted friends was the Baron Frederick William August Steuben, who began his military career in Prussia as an aide to Frederick the Great, and who was afterward general of the guard of the Prince of Hohenzollern-Hechingen. This friendship began when Steuben landed in America in 1777, and joined the army at Valley Forge in 1778. Although he was Hamilton's senior by about twenty-seven years, there was something very amusing about what might be called the reversal of relations, and the almost paternal interest of the young protégé in his

---

[1] *Ibid.*, vol. I, p. 109.

[2] Vicomte Louis de Fleury, a brave officer who had served as an engineer and later joined Rochambeau. For gallantry at the storming of Stony Point he received a vote of thanks from Congress.

middle-aged instructor, for it was the baron who first taught the American troops the orderly tactics of war, and gave them the benefit of his past experience, which he had derived in the service of the great Frederick; but in spite of all his military genius he was helpless as a child in other things, and to Hamilton he looked for advice and help.

Not only were the relations of Hamilton and Steuben of a delightfully affectionate nature, but we find that Angelica Church frequently alluded to him, in her bright way, in many letters written to her sister. Nine years after the war she wrote: "I envy you the trio of agreeable men you talk of, my father and my baron and your Hamilton, what pleasant evenings, what agreeable chit-chat, whilst my vivacity must be confined to dull, gloomy Englishmen. Adieu, my dear Eliza; tell Hamilton if he does not send my Father[1] Ambassador, that I shall believe he has no influence at Court, and that I will try not to care for him. Adieu, my dear Eliza, be happy and be gay, and remember me in your mirth as one who desires and wishes to partake of your happiness. Embrace Hamilton and the Baron. Yours, A. C."[2]

Again, having met the royal family at the theatre, she said: "but what are Kings and Queens to an American who has seen a Washington!" In another letter: "This day year, my dear Eliza, I had the happiness to see you and receive the affectionate attention of you and my dear Hamilton, and the gallantries of the Baron." Indeed, Steuben was a jovial companion, most intimate with Hamilton, and an ever welcome guest at his home and that of General Schuyler. His rather extravagant ways evidently kept him embarrassed most of the time, but he knew little or nothing of the value of money, while his efforts to obtain

[1] General Philip Schuyler.
[2] London, Jan. 3, 1792.

assistance were pitiable indeed, for he appears to have been always in financial distress.

It has been stated by several historians that he often spoke of Hamilton not only as his friend, but as his *banker*, and it would seem as if the latter was much more than this, if we may infer from the number of unpaid promissory notes from the baron to Hamilton which are found among the latter's papers, among them judgments in favor of Hector St. Jean de Crevecœur[1] for various large sums. On November 23, 1785, Hamilton wrote to Washington as follows: "The poor Baron is still soliciting Congress and has every prospect of indigence before him. He has his imprudences, but on the whole he has rendered valuable services, and his merits and the reputation of the country alike demand that he should not be left to suffer want. If there could be any mode by which your influence could be employed in his favor by writing to your friends in Congress or otherwise, the Baron and his friends would be under great obligations to you."[2]

Chancellor Livingston wrote to Hamilton in regard to Steuben's affairs as follows, in a letter dated March 3, 1787:

I received your favor with the Baron's papers inclosed by the post. The letter you mention I have sent by a private hand now under me. I enclose a letter to the Baron containing my opinion tho' I confess to you that I do think that in publishing it (as he told me he purposed) he will show more resentment than prudence. He will provoke replies, he will be called upon to show what he has lost, the payments to him will be compared with what other officers have received. It will be said that Congress have failled in all their engagements from necessity, that there is nothing singular in his solicitation. In short, he will hear many

[1] Better known as the author of "Lettres d'un Cultivateur en Amérique," Paris, 1787.

[2] "Works of Alexander Hamilton," Henry Cabot Lodge, 1st ed., vol. VIII, p. 181.

things that will vex and disturb him and he will exclude himself from all hopes of a further provision. When a more liberal sperit, or a heavier purse may incline Congress to make it. If you think with me, you will use your influence with him to drop the idea of a publication that can do him no good, but may injure him.

It would appear that this brave old soldier was ultimately cared for, and the trite saying that nations are ungrateful was disproved, for through the influence of Schuyler, Livingston, and Hamilton, he was finally given a large tract of land, amounting to sixteen thousand acres, in the upper part of New York State, a portion of which he gave to Captain Ben Walker and to Generals North and Popham, and there he lived for the rest of his life, dying November 20, 1794. The State of New Jersey also gave him land, and the National Government an annuity of twenty-five hundred dollars.

The gay trio to which Hamilton and Laurens belonged was made complete by La Fayette. On the whole, there was something about them rather suggestive of the three famous heroes of Dumas, although the period of the American Revolution was less romantic than that of the Musketeers. It is true that Hamilton was urged to kidnap the English General Clinton, who insecurely held New York, but refused upon the score that the latter, because of his incompetence, could do more harm if he were suffered to remain where he was than if captured.

There is a note of romance in their friendship, quite unusual even in those days, and La Fayette, especially during his early sojourn in this country, was on the closest terms with Hamilton. He touchingly writes from Paris, April 12, 1782, as follows:[1]

---

[1] "Hamilton's Works," vol. I, p. 277.

DEAR HAMILTON: However silent you may please to be, I will nevertheless remind you of a friend who loves you tenderly, and who, by his attachment, deserves a great share in your affection.

This letter, my dear Sir, will be delivered or sent by Count de Segur,[1] an intimate friend of mine, a man of wit and of abilities, and whose society you will certainly be pleased with.

I warmly recommend him to you, and hope he will meet from you with more than civilities.

At this late day La Fayette certainly seems, to some extent, a disappointing figure in history, if his behavior at home during and after the French Revolution is considered. While his aid to the American cause, prior to his return to France and shortly before the above letter was written, entitles him to the deep gratitude of all Americans, and his career while in America was that of an unselfish and brave soldier, who gave all his energy and much of his fortune to the cause of patriots, his remarkable weakness at a time when his sovereign was in the gravest danger is almost incredible, and cannot even be explained by the fact that he had taken part in our own struggle for freedom, and had been influenced by his sympathy with the colonists, who were themselves fighting for liberty.

Hamilton certainly must have lost much of his respect and no little of his affection for his old friend for the manner in which he had acted, for in a later letter he criticised Burr's conduct in making disloyal toasts, among them one to La

[1] Segur was a distinguished Frenchman whose brilliant writings are well known. He was the French Ambassador to Berlin before August 10, 1792, and at St. Petersburg several years before that. Later he served with Napoleon and accompanied the latter to Moscow in 1812. It was Segur who wrote during the French Revolution: "Liberty, whatever its language might be, pleased us for its courage; equality, because it was so convenient. One enjoys descending as long as one pleases; without forecast, we enjoyed at the same time the advantages of aristocracy, and the sweets of plebeian philosophy."

MARQUIS GILBERT MOTIER DE LA FAYETTE

Fayette. He refers to this as an evidence of Burr's misconduct and sympathy with "the daring scoundrels of every party," and his tendency "to avail himself of their assistance, and of all the bad passions of society.[1]

But Hamilton's friendship for La Fayette was shown in late years, even after he had disappointed him by his conduct during the French Revolution, and in his connection with the Garde Nationale.[2] When captured by the Austrians after his conflict with the extreme Jacobins, he escaped across the frontier, was imprisoned in Olmütz, and treated with great brutality, owing to a desire for retaliation for the treatment by the French of the unfortunate Marie Antoinette. Here he remained secluded and unheard of until he was later joined by his wife and daughter. Through the exertions of Fox, Wilberforce, and Sheridan, as well as Washington and Hamilton, strong representations were made to the Prussian Government, though in so doing serious complications with the French were narrowly escaped. Young George Washington La Fayette, the son, who had been sent here during the Reign of Terror, was, for a time, an inmate of Hamilton's house, and was treated like a son by the latter, and acted in conjunction with others in his father's behalf.[3] In 1794 a Dr. Bollman, and Francis Kinloch Huger, of South Carolina, by a brilliant stroke, effected La Fayette's escape, but he was recaptured and taken, in chains, back to his dungeon. It was not until 1797 that he was liberated by Napoleon.

To her sister Mrs. Church wrote in 1795: "You will receive the letter by Dr. Bollman, a young gentleman of good sense and polite manners, his exertions for the Marquis de

---

[1] *Century Magazine*, vol. LX, No. 2. (See p. 253.)

[2] See his letter of temperate warning to La Fayette, written October 6, 1789.

[3] In the expense-book occurs the following item: "$16. George Washington cash, for this sum paid as expense to carry a letter to Young Lafayette."

La Fayette have been so zealous and active that every good American must honor him for his generous conduct; his friend, Mr. Huger, is also greatly entitled to praise for what he has done. I hope that my Brother will afford them his best assistance in an introduction to General Washington and our distinguished men."

La Fayette's subsequent career was interesting, by reason of the manner in which he adapted himself to the kaleidoscopic changes of French misgovernment, for his attitude was never stable or consistent. At this moment I may be pardoned for referring at length to a somewhat interesting incident, which tells how this distinguished person figured in the history of another branch of my family. In 1829 my maternal grandfather, Louis McLane of Delaware, was Minister to England, and one of his many sons was Robert M. McLane,[1] now dead. Seeking for a school, he wrote to his friend La Fayette, who replied:

I Have for some time devised an answer to your kind letter February 16th Because I wanted to take information relative to the several schools in Paris. The result of my inquiries is very favorable to the College of Louis le Grand. It appears the young men are well attended to with respect to the diet, the personal care, and that the classic studies are as well, they even say Better Conducted than in any other school of the kind. I cannot therefore but encourage the choice you are disposed to make.

Another point had a claim upon my Solicitude. I was afraid of a private Roman Catholic influence, as it is now Become a Government party affair. But I am assured that young Protestants at the College Have Had no cause of complaint in that way. Let me add, my dear Sir, that you may depend upon my earnest and tender love, not only By

[1] Robert M. McLane. Minister to China and Mexico, Governor of Maryland, and Minister to France during the administration of Grover Cleveland.

personal attention, But through men more fit than I am, to Receive minute information and act upon them in Contact with me.

We are in a critical parliamentary situation, the address to the King will be debated next Monday in committee agreeably to a very improper article of the Charter, it shall expect a letter of disapprobation of the Polignac administration; I don't question its obtaining a great majority. What will follow is very uncertain. The King, his son, and some of the ministers seem determined to go on. Whether the Chamber will be prorogued, dissolved or kept to try the continuance of a stormy session, it must be known in a few days.

Have you been pleased to ask Mr. Perkins what has become of his Pole friend Borowsky? No answer or Bill from Him Has Been received by Mr. Laweschi.

Be so kind as to present my affectionate Respects to Mrs. McLane. My son begs to be respectfully remembered, and I am, Most Cordially,

Your friend,

LAFAYETTE.

The lad was, upon his recommendation, sent to Paris where he remained; but meanwhile the Revolution of 1830 had broken out, and McLane sent Washington Irving, who was his secretary, to France to investigate, and the latter subsequently reported to the anxious father:

PARIS, August 7, 1830.

MY DEAR SIR: I arrived here last evening after a very pleasant journey through country as tranquil as England on a Sunday; nothing but the national cockade of the traduced flag displayed in every direction gave a hint of the great revolution that had taken place. On my arrival in Paris, I was struck with the unusual number of pedestrians on the streets, in pairs or in groups, all talking with great earnestness, but general good humor. I never have seen even the lively streets of Paris so animated on an ordinary evening of the week.

Today the Chambers are in session, and it is expected the question will be decided before night, who is to succeed to the vacant throne. I have not been able to see anyone who could procure me admission to the Chamber. I called on Mr. Rives,[1] but he was from home, and had gone himself to the Chamber. There appears to be some awakening among the leaders; they fear some movement among the people in favor of a republic. There has been an attempt to assemble the students before the Chamber in order to intimidate them, but it has failed. I don't see any ground for serious apprehension. The republican party is not strong. There are small parties also in favor of the Duke de Bordeaux, and the son of Napoleon, but the great mass of the people and almost all those who have property at stake, seem convinced that the weak mode of quieting the present state of excitement and restoring anything promptly to order is to call the Duke of Orleans to the throne. I have been in the open place before the Chamber of Deputies. It was filled with people, the great part young men. Precautions had been taken against any popular commotion. The interior of the Court yard was strongly garrisoned by a detachment of the garde Nationale and another detachment was stationed at the head of the adjacent bridge. I saw, however, no sign of riot among the people. The assemblage reminded me of the crowd before one of our polls, and I have never seen anything in France that so completely rebuked the populace of a free country (?). Everyone was expressing his opinion loudly and copiously, discussing men, makers, forms of government, etc. The discussions, however, were carried on without passion, with mutual civility, with acuteness and good sense; in fact, it is surprising to see the moderation, the judgment and magnanimity which have governed and still govern this vast population throughout the whole of this sudden and extraordinary situation. I feel satisfied that all will go right, and that the Duke of Orleans will be called

---

[1] William Cabell Rives, Minister to the French Court from 1829–32.

to the throne immediately, and with the general approbation of the people, though the people will take advantage of the present crisis to augment their power, and to diminish the royal prerogative.

This triumph of the Parisians has been so brilliant, prompt and decisive, and has put them in such general good humor that they seem to have lost their bitterness against the Bourbons. They speak of them with contempt rather than otherwise; they caricature, lampoon and laugh at them, and the shop windows already teem with ludicrous caricatures of Charles X. When they speak of the ministers, however, their tone changes, and they hold them accountable for all the blood that has been shed.

The battle has been fought by the very lowest people. I have been told by those who visited the scene of the combat, that the slain are generally people of the poorest classes. Was the struggle here to be achieved by the people of property, the Bourbons would have still been upon the throne.

I called this morning to see Robert at his school. He looks well and rather less like a race horse than when in London. The *soupe maigre*, in spite of his abuse of it, agrees with him. I like the looks of his school, its external appearance, the general air of its arrangements are better than any I have seen in Paris. Robert was at school when the revolution broke out. He kept tolerably quiet during the two first days, but when a third day of fighting came, it was too much for him, and he and almost a dozen other boys broke out of school and ran to set the world in order. They joined in some of the skirmishing, but had no other weapons than stones and one or two old pistols. Rob only threw stones, and on my putting him on his honor and conscience, he confessed that he could not boast of having killed a single man, but he and his band of truant revolutionists afterwards made a forage into the center of Paris, but the fighting was already over and all the killing done, so they returned quietly to their school, quite satisfied with their share of the victory. On the following Sunday he was supposed to go out to visit his friends, Paris then being tranquil. He went with the other boys, to see Genl Lafayette go in State to visit the Duke of Orleans.   The General passed through the streets escorted by his (black) guards in ragged breeches with drawn swords. The people shouted "Vive Lafayette," but Rob and his companions who were on a heap of stones cried in English, "Long live Lafayette!" and they attracted the attention of the General.   He recognized Bob, took him by the hand and they walked together the most of the way to the Palais Royal, Bob being no doubt mistaken by the populace for some surprising youth who had signalized himself in the late Victory. Bob asked me very anxiously whether it was true that the people meant to storm the Chamber of Deputies today, as such a report had prevailed in the school and the master had put them all on their honors that they would not break out. I gave him my opinion that there would be no tumult to call either for their aid or opposition, and his Zeal and anxiety seemed in some measure pacified.   He will have a good deal to tell his Mama and sisters when he returns home. They have reason to be proud of him.   I left directions with Mr. Beasley about your [illegible] which will be promptly attended to.

   With kind remembrances to Mrs. McLane and the family, I remain, my dear sir,

Yours very truly,
WASHINGTON IRVING.

   The Vicomte de Noailles, closely related to La Fayette, came here very early in the Revolution and was one of the small coterie of army friends who were with Hamilton at Yorktown.   The latter wrote to him in 1782:

   Esteem for your talents and acquirements is a sentiment which, from my earliest acquaintance with you, dear Viscount, I have shared in common with all those who have the happiness of knowing you; but a better knowledge of your character has given it, in my eyes, a more intrinsic merit, and has attached me to you by a friendship founded upon qualities as rare as they are estimable.   I cannot forbear indulging this declaration, to express to you the pleasure I felt at receiving (after an inexplicable delay), the letter you were so obliging as to write me before your departure from Boston. It was of that kind which is always produced by those attentions of friends we value; which, not being invited by circumstances nor necessitated by the form of Society, bespeak the warmth of the heart. At least my partiality for you makes me proud of viewing it in this light and I cherish the opinion.[1]

He continues in this happy vein, trusting that his friend will return. After his service here de Noailles, like La Fayette, retired to France and took the liberal side in the French Revolution, but was finally obliged to flee from the blood-thirsty sans-culottes, leaving his wife, who was afterward guillotined in 1794, together with his father and mother. He came to the United States a second time in that year, and for a time entered into business, being with Bingham & Co., the bankers of Philadelphia, and speculated so successfully that he acquired a large fortune. He again re-entered the French service and went to Santo Domingo, and afterward to Cuba, where, in an action between his ship and an English man-of-war, he was killed. During his stay in Philadelphia he saw Hamilton frequently, and their old friendship was renewed.

Another army friend was General Nathaniel Greene, who was president of the court of inquiry in the André case. After his death, Hamilton's enemies even alleged that the latter was guilty of malfeasance during the time he was Secretary of the Treasury in looking after the affairs of his dead friend, and had helped his widow out of the public funds. Greene, too, like Hamilton, at another time was assailed by the friends of Gates to whose command he succeeded.

With Richard K. Meade, who was also an aide-de-camp to Washington with Hamilton, there existed a close intimacy

---

[1] "Hamilton's Works" (J. C. H.), vol I, p. 314.

which was participated in by Mrs. Hamilton, and the Schuylers as well, and the appended extract from one of his letters is an indication of their affectionate relationship:

I have explained to you the difficulties I met with in obtaining a command last campaign. I thought it incompatible with the delicacy due to myself to make any application this campaign. I have expressed this sentiment in a letter to the General, and, retaining my rank only, have relinquished the emoluments of my commission, declaring myself, notwithstanding, ready at all times to obey the calls of the public. I do not expect to hear any of these, unless the state of our affairs should change for the worse; and lest, by any unforeseen accident that should happen, I choose to keep myself in a situation again to contribute my aid. This prevents a total resignation.

Truly, my dear Meade, I often regret that fortune has cast our residence at such a distance from each other. It would be a serious addition to my happiness if we lived where I could see you every day; but fate has determined it otherwise. I am a little hurried, and can only repeat, in addition, that you will present me most affectionately to Mrs. Meade, and believe me to be, with the warmest and most unalterable friendship,   .   .   .

It must almost appear as if Hamilton was either unaware of Talleyrand's true character, or cultivated him because of his many agreeable qualities, for it cannot be denied that, despite his absolutely unpardonable immoralities, he had an extraordinary fascination.[1] Then again, there was a sense of all that was humorous in all he did, whether in getting the best of dull-witted and pompous commissioners, or hoodwinking his less astute fellow conspirators. No one who has read his memoirs can help secretly admiring a cer-

---

[1] The reader should consult Stewarton's extraordinary memoirs of Talleyrand, which are evidently a true though prejudiced account of the life of the Bishop of Autun. The more recently published memoirs are of doubtful authenticity.

PRINCE CHARLES MAURICE DE TALLEYRAND–PÉRIGORD

tain intense mental force and cleverness, as well as a faculty for escaping from danger; but it must be confessed that it is often the same amusement and admiration that one feels after reading the story of Jonathan Wild, or those of the other heroes of the Newgate Calendar. Talleyrand came to America in 1794, after making himself so disagreeable in England that he was obliged to shift the scene of his activity to the United States, in which country the influence of the French Republic and the effrontery of Citizen Genet were being felt; thanks to the temporary co-operation of Thomas Jefferson; after a brief stay he returned to make fresh mischief with a new party in France.

His stay in Philadelphia was characterized by conduct so scandalous as to shock Pontgibaud [1] and his other countrymen, for his open immoralities and behavior with a woman of color (probably Madame Grand) led to much gossip. Nevertheless he took great interest in all public affairs of the new country, and was busy as well in scientific work, and by his eloquence and charm made many friends who were disposed to overlook his foibles. Hamilton, who always respected brains, became, in a way, attached to him. Talleyrand was an agreeable Lucifer, and it was he who said that no one who had not lived before 1789 in France had any idea of the "charm of life." He had known all the delightful great men and women of France and England in his day, and, therefore, was certainly a competent critic. He liked the young statesman and said of him, "*Je considère Napoléon, Fox et Hamilton comme les trois plus grands hommes de notre époque, et si je devais me prononcer entre les trois, je donnerais sans hésiter la première place à Hamilton. Il avait deviné l'Europe.*" [2]

---

[1] A French volunteer of the War of Independence. "The Chevalier de Pontgibaud." J. W. Bouton & Co., New York, 1897.

[2] "Etudes sur la République."

That he had, sometimes, a strong and more tender feeling is evinced by the inscription upon the back of the picture of Hamilton that he later returned, which was, "You were appreciated. He loved you and you loved him." Hamilton seems to have kept up his pleasant relations with Talleyrand until shortly before his death, for, on March 25, 1804, he wrote to the latter in regard to a cousin Alexander, who had been imprisoned in Paris, and who was then on parole, asking certain privileges for the latter.

The affection felt for him by the members of his wife's family appears everywhere in a great mass of correspondence now before me.   One of his warmest admirers was his father-in-law, who was of middle age when the young soldier married his second daughter in 1780.[1] He certainly supplied the qualities lacking in Hamilton's own father, and added to them the jealous pride of a rugged veteran. During the time Hamilton was thrown so much into contact with him at Morristown, and until the very end of his life, there was a delightful intimacy between them, both in the field and when they were engaged in the conduct of public affairs, which crops out in all of General Schuyler's letters. Hamilton's success was Schuyler's very own, and his disappointments were shared by the affectionate, proud old man, who took up the cudgels and berated Jefferson and all the others whenever he got a chance.

Hamilton's overwork brought its penalty, for, at times, his condition was such as to alarm his friends, yet he, as a rule, rarely succumbed. Nothing can be more solicitous than the following, written at a time when he was not only busily engaged in practising law, but organizing the new army, and effecting a number of far-reaching public reforms and improvements:

[1] See chapter V.

General Philip Schuyler to his daughter

ALBANY, *February* 1st, 1799.

MY DEARLY BELOVED ELIZA: I am deeply affected to learn that my beloved Hamilton is so much indisposed.   Too great an application to business and too little bodily excercise have probably been the cause of his disorders, immersed as he is in business, and his mind constantly employed he will forget to take that excercise, and those precautions which are indispensable to his restoration.   You must therefore, my Dear Child, order his horse every fair day, that he may ride out, and draw him as frequently from his closet as possible.   Keep me advised my Dear Child continually of his state of health.   If that should happily be true, try to prevail on him to quit the busy scene he is in, and to pay us a visit accompanied by you.   The journey will be of service to him, and I shall experience the best of pleasures in embracing children so dear to me.

Embrace my Dear Hamilton and your children for me. All here unite in love to you, to him and them.

God bless you my Amiable
and Dear Child.   Ever most
tenderly and affectionately Yours

PH. SCHUYLER.

He wrote to his daughter in 1795, regarding his young son, who was an inmate of Hamilton's household, as follows: "I have urged him [Philip] to copy your amiable husband as where he will see sense, virtue and good manners combined, which will endear him to all."

Hamilton's sister-in-law Angelica, as has been said, was an active correspondent, and wrote upon every possible occasion.   Shortly before the arrival of Talleyrand she sent the following letter from England to prepare for his reception:

Angelica Church to Elizabeth Hamilton

LONDON, *Feb.* 4, '94.

I recommend to your most particular care and attention, my dear and kind Elisa, my friends, Messieurs de Tallyrand and de Beaumetz; make our country agreeable to them as far as it is in your power (and your influence is very extensive). Console them by your hospitality and the image of your domestic happiness and virtues, for all that they have suffered in the cause of moderate Liberty; and you will be gratified, my dear Eliza, by rendering them services when by so doing you are also prompting the *requests* of your own Angelica.

I have for these persons the most sincere friendship. To your care, dear Eliza I commit these interesting strangers, they are a loan I make you, till I return to America, not to reclaim my friends entirely, but to share their society with you and dear Alexander, the amiable.

Speak of these gentlemen as members of the Constituent Assembly, as friends of La Fayette, and of good government, and who left their country when anarchy and cruelty prevailed.

If I have any influence with Americans who have been in England, let them shew the sense they entertain of it, by receiving well my friends, whoever cultivates their intimacy will thank me for giving them such valuable acquaintances.

A few weeks later she wrote to Mrs. Hamilton:

Angelica Church to Elizabeth Hamilton

LONDON, *February* 27, 1794.

Monsieur de Tallyrand being detained, my dear Eliza, a week longer than he expected has given me time to finish your handkerchief which may be worn either on the head or neck, the other two I beg you will send to Peggy and Cornelia.[1]

---

[1] Her sisters, Margaret and Cornelia Schuyler, who became Mrs. Stephen van Rensselaer and Mrs. Washington Morton.

It is an age since I have heard from you, pray write me news and tell me if I may hope for peace. Mr. Jefferson is said to be on his voyage to France. You will see by my last letter in how particular a manner I have requested your attention for my friend. I am sorry that you cannot speak French, or Mr. Talleyrand English, that you might converse with him, as he is extremely agreeable, and very much improves on acquaintance; he is of one of the most ancient families in France and has been a Bishop and possesses a large fortune and now obliged by the order of this court to leave England. I wish that they would oblige me to go to America for the time is not yet fixed. Adieu my dear sister,

Very affectionately yours,

A. CHURCH.

Did Mrs. Bache[1] send you a hat with purple ribband and a cap. I wish to know as she has not written me a line.

Angelica Church to Elizabeth Hamilton

LONDON, *July* 30, 1794.

I have a letter my dear Eliza from my worthy friend M. de Talleyrand who expresses to me his gratitude for an introduction to you and my *Amiable*, by my Amiable you know that I mean your Husband, for I love him very much and if you were as generous as the old Romans, you would lend him to me for a little while, but do not be jealous, my dear Eliza, since I am more solicitous to promote his laudable ambition, than any person in the world, and there is no summit of true glory which I do not desire he may attain; provided always that he pleases to give me a little chit-chat, and sometimes to say, I wish our dear Angelica was here. Tallyrand and Beaumetz write in raptures to all their friends of your kindness, and Colonel Hamilton's abilities and manners, and I receive innumerable compliments on his and your account.

---

[1] The only daughter of Benjamin Franklin, who married Richard Bache, who succeeded Dr. Franklin as Postmaster-General.

Ah! Bess! you were a lucky girl to get so clever and so good a companion.

Mr. Jay[1] has been perfectly well received at Court and by the Ministers, as yet no material business is done. The people are anxious for a peace with America, and the allied armies are beat out of Flanders and on the Rhine. These circumstances may determine the Minister to be just and wise. Mr. Jay dined with Mr. Fox[2] at our house a few days after his arrival.

Mr. Morris[3] is building a palace, do you think Monsieur l'Enfant[4] would send me a drawing of it? Merely from curiosity, for one wishes to see the plan of a house which it is said, will cost, when furnished £40,000 Sterling.

This house was built by Robert Morris, in Philadelphia, after he had resigned his office and begun his land speculations. It was an enormous palace designed by Major l'Enfant, and was afterward known as "Morris's Folly." At the time it was begun Morris was regarded as the richest man in the United States, but through reckless plunging and speculation, lost all his money and was arrested and confined in the debtor's prison for several years. Through the grandiose and impractical plan of l'Enfant and the underestimation of the cost, Morris could not meet the demands upon him. His schemes were almost like those of an insane man, and he never occupied the gigantic building which was erected in a square bounded by Walnut and Chestnut, Seventh and Eighth Streets, for it was not finished. It is said that he even imported shiploads of costly furniture, one vessel bringing five thousand guineas' worth of mirrors.

Much has been said about Hamilton's relations with Wash-

[1] John Jay, then engaged in arranging the treaty with Great Britain.
[2] Charles James Fox.
[3] Robert Morris, financier and signer of the Declaration of Independence.
[4] Major Pierre Charles l'Enfant, the distinguished French architect, who afterward designed the plan of the city of Washington.

ington, and the absence of any deep friendship between the two, and Oliver has gone so far as to observe that in not one of the former's writings is there any eulogy or even marked praise of his great commander.

Sumner makes this same assertion, and brief excerpts of letters are reproduced, the impression being that there was a stiffness and coldness, not to say a formality in his correspondence with the former which indicated a lack of attachment, and no very great admiration.

These accusations I am sure are unjust, for in the letter to Mrs. Washington written after the death of the first President, there is much that is genuine, and in his letters to Washington during his lifetime he nearly always signed himself "Yours affectionately," in those that were personal. A great deal has been made of the circumstances attending Hamilton's resignation as a member of Washington's military family, and it must be conceded that the letters he wrote to his father-in-law, General Schuyler, and McHenry are not only in bad taste, but he makes use of certain expressions which voice his short-lived anger; this, however, must be set down to his extreme youth, and some of it to the fact that he had been more or less flattered and his head, for the time, turned.[1] Like many other men, his subsequent conduct would almost look as if he had been ashamed of himself, for he plunged at once into more active military service, and per-

---

[1] In a letter to McHenry he voices his grievances. His wounded dignity was the result of a reprimand from Washington because he stopped to speak to Lafayette upon the stairs, and kept his chief waiting.

"I have, Dear Mac, several of your letters. I shall soon have time enough to write my friends as often as they please.

The Great man and I have come to an open rupture. Proposals of accomodation have been made on his part, but rejected. I pledge my honor to you that he will find me inflexible. He shall for once at least repent his ill-humor. Without a shadow of reason and on the slightest grounds—he charged me in the most affrontive manner with treating him with disrespect. I answered very decisively 'Sir, I am not conscious of it, but since you have thought it necessary to tell me,

formed an act of loyal devotion which he knew would be approved by his old commander when he made a brilliant assault upon the enemy's works at Yorktown. Before doing this he wrote to Washington as follows in 1781: "It has become necessary to me to apply to your Excellency to know in what manner you forsee you will be able to employ me in the ensuing campaign. I am ready to enter into activity whenever you think proper."

All of his subsequent relations with Washington were intimate and affectionate, and their private letters to each other show that they must have been so much in accord as to exclude any real coolness of feeling. Forgiving and generous as Washington always was, he probably felt little or no resentment toward Hamilton for his hasty action in parting from him in a manner more befitting a spoiled boy than a gallant and useful soldier, and he ever afterward relied upon his former aid, even to the extent of getting his assistance in the preparation of his Farewell Address.

It would hardly seem from the following that any of Hamilton's early resentment, and want of appreciation of Washington's kindness had survived.

so we part!' I wait till more help arrives, at present there is besides myself only Tilghman, who is just recovering from a fit of illness, the consequence of too close application to business.

We have often spoken freely our sentiments to each other. Except to a very few friends our difference will be a secret, therefore be silent.

I shall continue to support a popularity that has been essential—is still useful.

Adieu my friend. May the time come when characters may be Known in their true light.

Madame sends her friendship to you.

A. H."

Alexander Hamilton to Washington

MY DEAR SIR: The receipt two days since of your letter
of the 21st instant gave me sincere pleasure.   The token of
your regard which it announces is very precious to me, and
will always be remembered as it ought to be.

Mrs. Hamilton has lately added another boy to our
stock; she and the child are both well.   She desires to be
affectionately remembered to Mrs. Washington and yourself.

We have nothing new here more than our papers contain,
but are anxiously looking forward to a further development
of the negotiations in Europe, with an ardent desire for
general accommodation.   It is at the same time agreeable
to observe that the public mind is adopting more and more
sentiments truly American, and free from foreign tincture.

I beg my best respects to Mrs. Washington.

James McHenry, Secretary of War during Adams's administration, was one of Hamilton's most loving friends.
During the early operations of the army he saw a great deal
of the latter, and there was much that was jocular and breezy
in their conversation and correspondence.   In after years
this relation was more staid, but just as affectionate.   In
1795, after Hamilton's retirement, McHenry wrote, "Though
not writing I have not ceased to love you, nor for a moment
felt any abatement of my friendship." [2]   At an earlier period,
when Hamilton was but twenty-six, McHenry wrote, that
if he were ten years older and twenty thousand pounds
richer, he (Hamilton) might have the highest office in the
gift of Congress, and added:

Cautious men think you sometimes intemperate, but
seldom visionary. . . . Bold designs, measures calculated

[1] "Hamilton's Works" (J. C. H.), vol. V, p. 623.
[2] "Life and Correspondence of James McHenry."

for their rapid execution—a wisdom that would convince from its own weight, a project that would surprise the people into greater happiness, without giving them an opportunity to view it and reject it—are not adapted to a council composed of discordant materials or to a people which have 13 heads, each of which pays superstitious adorations to inferior divinities.

Upon the occasion of a slight difference regarding the appointment of a candidate recommended by McHenry, the latter waited until Hamilton's retirement from office and wrote:

You see how well I have persevered in this determination, and that it is only now, when I can have nothing to expect, and nothing to give, that I recall you to the remembrance of our early union and friendship. It is during this period, my dear Hamilton, that you will find unequivocal instances of the disinterested friendship I feel for you and which ought to convince you, how well I am entitled to a full return of yours. The tempest weathered and landed on the same shore, I may now congratulate you upon having established a system of credit and having conducted the affairs of our country upon principles and reasoning, which ought to insure its immortality, as it undoubtedly will your fame. Few public men have been so eminently fortunate, as voluntarily to leave so high a station with such a character and so well assured a reputation and still fewer have so well deserved the gratitude of their country and the eulogiums of history. Let this console you for past toils and pains, and reconcile you to humble pleasures and a private life. What remains for you, having ensured fame, but to ensure felicity. Look for it in the moderate pursuit of your profession, or if public life still flatters, in that office most congenial to it and which will not withdraw you from those literary objects that require no violent waste of spirits and those little plans that involve gentler exercise and which you can drop or indulge in without injury to your family. I have built houses. I have cultivated fields. I have planned gardens. I have planted trees. I have written little essays. I have made poetry once a year to please my wife, at times got children and, at all times, thought myself happy.   Why cannot you do the same ? for after all, if a man is only to acquire fame or distinction by continued privations and abuse, I would incline to prefer a life of privacy and little pleasures.

Before the war McHenry studied medicine under Dr. Benjamin Rush, of Philadelphia, and entered the army as a surgeon, but it was not long before he gave up his calling and became an aide to General Washington. He certainly took an unusual interest in the health of his friend Hamilton, and prescribed for him. According to his biographer, this was about the last professional duty that he performed, and followed shortly after his transfer, as he had been made prisoner by the British. Some of the advice given by the Revolutionary doctor would not be out of place to-day, and the directions regarding his friend's very unromantic disorder are the following:

In order to get rid of some of your present accumulations, you will be pleased to take the pills agreeable to the directions; and to prevent future accumulations observe the following table of diet. This will have a tendency also to correct your wit. I would advise for your breakfast two cups of tea sweetened with brown sugar and colored with about a teaspoonful of milk. I prefer brown sugar to loaf because it is more laxative. And I forbid the free use of milk until your stomach recovers its natural powers. At present you would feel less uneasiness in digesting a round of beef than a pint of milk.

You will not drink your tea just as it comes out of the pot; let it have time to cool. The astringuency of the tea is more than counter balanced by the relaxing quality of hot water.

For your dinner let me recommend about six ounces of beef or mutton, either boiled or roasted, with eight or ten ounces of bread. Cut the meat from the tenderest part with little or no fat. Use the natural juice, but no rancid oily gravy whatsoever. For some time I would prefer the beef, because it contains more of a natural animal stimulus than mutton. Once or twice a week, you may indulge in a thin slice of ham. Your best condiment will be salt.

You must not eat as many vegitables as you please—a load of vegitables is as hurtful as a load of any other food. Besides the absurdity of crowding in a heap of discordant vegitables with a large quantity of meat is too much of itself for the digestive powers. You may eat a few potatoes every day. Water is the most general solvent the kindliest and the best assistance in the process of digestion. I would therefore advise it for your table drink. When you indulge in wine let it be sparingly. Never go beyond three glasses— but by no means every day.

I strictly forbid all eatables which I do not mention, principally because a formula of diet for your case should be simple and short. Should this table be strictly observed, it will soon become of little use, because you will have recovered that degree of health which is compatable with the nature of your constitution. You will then be your own councellor in diet for the man who has had ten years experience in eating and its consequences is a fool if he does not know how to choose his dishes better than his Doctor.

But in case you should fall into a debauch—you must next day have recourse to the pills. I hope however that you will not have recourse to them often. The great Paracelsus trusted to his pills to destroy the effects of intemperance— but he died if I forget not about the age of 30 notwithstanding his pills. Lewis Cornare the Italian was wiser—he trusted to an egg, and I think lived to about ninety.

Hamilton's accounts show that he lived well, and that his bills for wine during the time he stayed in New York reached goodly proportions, but he probably did not exceed his friend's prescription, for his life appears to have been well-regulated and comparatively abstemious. It would be gratifying to know whether he would have lived to a ripe old age had his life not been snuffed out by the bullet of Burr. His children were all examples of longevity, for several were over eighty when they succumbed to ordinary senile conditions, and two were more than ninety. This vitality, however, might have been influenced by their mother, who was ninety-seven when she died.

I have alluded to other friends, many of whom were identified with his later life. These included his own medical advisers, Doctors Samuel Bard and David Hosack, the former of whom brought several of his children, including the first Philip, into the world, and who continued to take care of Hamilton until the end of his life. He was the son of Dr. John Bard, who had been associated with Dr. Peter Middleton, who, in 1750, made the first dissection recorded in this country. He was a graduate of the University of Edinburgh, and began the practice of his profession in America in 1765. Dr. Hosack was present at the duel with Burr, and he and Dr. Post were with Hamilton when he died.

Among other intimates were Gouverneur Morris, Rufus King, Nicholas Fish, Egbert Benson, John Laurance, Brockholst Livingston, Richard Peters, Robert Troup, William Duer, Richard Varick, Oliver Wolcott, William Seton, Charles Wilkes, Matthew Clarkson, Richard Harrison, Elias Boudinot, Thomas Cooper, Caleb Gibbs, William Bayard, Timothy Pickering, and James Kent.

Some of these men were associated with him in the army, and during the years he was in Congress and in the Treasury, and others were constantly engaged at the same time in the courts. So closely were his professional and public life connected, that we find his correspondence filled with all manner of subjects, and it is common for letters to open with an appeal to him for legal aid, and to end with some reference to politics.

Gouverneur Morris, it is quite evident, always entertained a grudge against Hamilton for his summing up and retort in the Le Guen case,[1] for Morris appears to have been very vulnerable to sarcasm, as he was a conceited, though great, man. He, however, manifested much kindness of heart when allowed to manage other people's affairs, and was perfectly amiable and often went to great lengths to help others. He was about five years Hamilton's senior, was licensed to practise law, and had much to do with the conduct of the financial affairs of the country, and the preparation and framing of the Constitution.

Rufus King, who was the first person in the United States to seriously advocate the abolition of slavery, proposed, in 1785, an act of Congress for that purpose. Negro slavery, however, seems to have been quite general, and it was not until 1799 that there was special legislation in New York, which made all children free that were born in that State after July of that year, though they were to remain with the owner, the men till they were twenty-eight years and the women till they were twenty-five. It has been stated that Hamilton never owned a negro slave, but this is untrue. We find that in his books there are entries showing that he purchased them for himself and for others.[2]

Rufus King and General Schuyler were representatives of New York in the national Senate in 1789. Under the new Constitution King was also American Minister to Great Britain, from 1798–1814, and again, for a short time, in

---

[1] See "Hamilton as a Lawyer," chapters VI and VII.

[2] *E. g.*, 1796. Cash to N. Low 2 negro servants purchased by him for me, $250. (Hamilton expense-book.)

1825, and both Schuyler and Hamilton relied upon him as an able and powerful Federalist.

Egbert Benson, the first Attorney-General for the State of New York, was a remarkably clear-headed lawyer. He had been previously a member of the Committee of Safety, and later was one of the three commissioners who were to supervise the emigration of Tories from New York to Nova Scotia, and was concerned in fixing the boundary line between the United States and British territory.

He was looked upon as an important person, and with Hamilton settled many disputed points during the post-Revolutionary period. David Howell[1] wrote from Halifax, August 31, 1796, to Hamilton:

SIR: Col. Barclay and myself after 7 or 8 days canvassing have agreed upon the Hon. Egbert Benson of New York as 3rd Commiss.

As he is your friend as well as ours, let me request your influence with him to accept this appointment. We shall never agree with any other person. The alternative is not very promising nor likely to prove satisfactory to either country.

I hope your State will suspend their claims on Mr. Benson only for a few weeks this fall—the cause, Col. Barclay and myself have agreed shall be tried in the City of N. York.

As you delight in doing public services, I assure myself of your attention to the object of this letter. I need only add that when I parted with you, I requested you to consult Mr. Benson and to write me whether he would accept or not, and that from your silence I had some reason to hope he would accept.

With great esteem and in haste,
I am Your
Very obt. Sert.

Hon. A. Hamilton.   DAVID HOWELL.

[1] David Howell (1747–1826) was professor of mathematics and law at Brown University from 1790–1824, and judge of the Superior Court. He was an authority on international law.

The Henry Barclay referred to in Howell's letter graduated at King's College, and studied law under John Jay, and was a son of the Rector of Trinity Church before the Revolution, but sided with the British, and after the war escaped, with his family, to Nova Scotia. After Jay's treaty, he was appointed one of the Commissioners in behalf of Great Britain.

Benson was in the Continental Congress from 1789–1794, and in the new Congress from 1789–1793, and from 1813–1815. He was judge of the New York Supreme Court, and of the United States Circuit Court, from 1794–1801.

John Laurance, who had been an aide to Washington, was in Congress and a State senator as well for many years. He was also a judge of the United States District Court of New York, from 1794–1796, and afterward of the Supreme Court of the United States from 1796–1800.

Brockholst Livingston had been on General Schuyler's staff, after Jay's mission to the Spanish Court, whither he also went, became a prominent lawyer and ultimately judge of the Supreme Court of New York. He, too, frequently appeared with Hamilton in court, and usually on the same side. Both he and Jonathan Dayton went to school with Hamilton at Elizabethtown.

The witty Richard Peters, after a long and honorable service in the army, and after winning distinction as an admiralty lawyer, became United States District Judge of the Pennsylvania Court from 1789 until his death. He was a curious, inventive genius, and dabbled to some extent in chemistry. He it was who introduced gypsum for agricultural purposes, and the writer is in possession of a letter containing his suggestion for the manufacture of india ink from lamp-black. His intercourse with Hamilton was most intimate, and as he was a great deal of a *farceur*, his letters are filled with evidence of this spirit.

Pickering, who was Secretary of State from 1795–1800, took an active part in the obstinate fight of the Federalists against Burr, and espoused Hamilton's side in his difference with Adams.

Oliver Wolcott was with Hamilton at the time of his death, and his two pathetic letters to his wife, describing the events, are published elsewhere. He took an active part in national affairs, and especially in those of Connecticut, his native State, where he was lieutenant-governor for ten years. Hamilton always turned to him in his political troubles, and he was sympathetic, and resourceful in his advice.

Robert Troup, who graduated at King's College at about the time Hamilton entered, seems to have been the *fidus Achates* of the latter, and many were the actions in which they were associated, Hamilton usually being the counsel. There was probably no more attached friend than Troup, and he was always ready to champion the cause of Hamilton, who was exactly his own age. Troup was made a judge of the United States Circuit Court of New York, and had much to do with the land affairs of the great Pulteney estate, the territory which was purchased from Robert Morris, who afterward had reason to regret the sale.

William Duer was Assistant Secretary of the Treasury under Hamilton, and had been Secretary of the Financial Board under Robert Morris. He, too, had been actively engaged in public affairs, and was one of the committee who drafted the first constitution of the State of New York. He married Lady Kitty, daughter of Lord Stirling, in 1779, when he was an army officer at Morristown, and was very intimate with Hamilton and his other friends. Duer, like many others, later not only became involved in unfortunate speculations, but gambled with the public funds.   This led to his ruin and incarceration by his creditors.   From all accounts he appears always to have been a lovable man and, notwithstanding his irregularities, was the recipient of much sympathy.   His downfall was a sad one, and his treatment of Pintard, a young broker who trusted him and was ruined thereby, was highly discreditable to Duer.   After his failure he was immediately sued by a number of angry people.

When he attempted to make restitution, it was found that his bank stock could not be converted into cash, and his land could not be disposed of because of the panicky nature of the times.   Hamilton had done his best to help him get financial assistance from Mr. Willing, the banker of Philadelphia, but the latter replied that he could do nothing.   The crash came, and in his distress Duer wrote to Hamilton:

William Duer to Alexander Hamilton

NEW YORK, *March* 18th, 1792.

My dear Friend: I find by a letter from Col'l. Wadsworth that news has arrived there of my having suspended payment.   The fact is that I have been compelled to do it, with Respect to a certain Description of Notes, which were issued by my agent[1] during my absence from this City—the Circumstances are too long and too painful to detail—: You shall know them on my arrival in Phila. for which Place I will certainly set off to-morrow—: Col'l. Wadsworth writes me that unless I arrive this day—a suit will Certainly be brought against me.

For Heavens Sake!   Use for once your Influence to defer this till my arrival—when it will not be necessary—My Public Transactions are not blended with my private affairs.   Every Farthing will be Immediately accounted for.   Of this I pledge my Honor.   If a suit should be brought on the Part of the Public,—under my present distrest Circumstances—

[1] John Pintard.

my Ruin is complete. I despatch this by Express—in order
that this step may not be taken—if it is I am sure that
those who pursue this Measure will in a short time lament
the Consequences.

I am your affectionate but distrest
Friend

W. Duer.

Hamilton devoted himself to the cause of his old comrade,
and wrote to one of the creditors the following letter:[1]

Alexander Hamilton to —————— ——————

Dear Sir: Poor Duer has now had a long and severe con-
finement such as would be adequate punishment for no
trifling crime. I am well aware of all the blame to which he
is liable, and do not mean to be his apologist, though I believe
he has been as much the dupe of his own imagination as
others have been the victims of his projects. But what then?
He is a man—he is a man with whom we have both been in
habits of friendly intimacy. He is a man who, with a great
deal of good zeal, in critical times, rendered valuable services
to the country. He is a husband who has a most worthy
and amiable wife, perishing with chagrin at his situation,—
your relative and mine. He is a father, who has a number of
fine children, destitute of the means of education and support, every way in need of his future exertions. These are
titles to sympathy which I shall be mistaken if you do not
feel. You are his creditor, your example may influence
others. He wants permission through a letter of license,
freely to breathe the air for five years.

Your signature to the inclosed draft of one, will give me
much pleasure.

Your ob't Serv't,

A. Hamilton.

It was at the house of William Bayard that Hamilton died,
for he and his family had always been intimate friends of

¹ Hamilton's "Reminiscences," p. 5.

the former. Bayard was a member of the firm of Bayard, LeRoy & McEvers, and had long been a client of Hamilton. Charles Wilkes was the president of the Bank of New York, for which Hamilton acted as counsel, and after the death of the latter Wilkes was one of those who made provision for his family.

It is somewhat surprising to find that the early friendship that existed between Hamilton and Edward Stevens led to no greater intimacy in later life. Stevens was one of the few friends who did not particularly distinguish himself, and about whom little is heard. He grew up to be a worthy doctor, but was a negative character, and his sole public service was rendered in a consulship to Hayti. The letters that passed between the two were of the most formal character, and there is no display of extraordinary interest in any of them, despite the promising beginning.

During Hamilton's attachment to Washington's staff he was thrown much into contact with Caleb Gibbs, who was not only the commander of the Life Guard of Washington, but in a way was *major domo* of the President's household, where he remained in command until the end of 1779. In this connection reference may be made to the troubles of the latter.

Chastellux, in speaking of his visit to Boston, refers to one John Tracy, who had strange vicissitudes of fortune in the early part of the war. At the end of 1777 he and his brother, who held letters of marque, had lost forty-one ships and were about to give up business, when a prize entered Boston Harbor which was worth about £35,000 sterling. With this windfall their fortunes changed, so that at the time of the visit of the Frenchman John Tracy was worth £120,000. He gave £5,000 to the State of Massachusetts, but his revenues were subsequently greatly diminished, and his taxes amounted to £6,000 a year—an enormous sum.

It is quite probable that the tide of his good fortune ultimately changed, for the following letter would show that he
lost, not only his own money, but that of others, among them
the funds of Gibbs who wrote to Hamilton, who had evidently befriended him and given him legal advice.

BARRE, *May* 16th, 1791.

MY BEST FRIEND: I have been honored by your much esteemed favour of the 20th ulto.

With the most pungent grief did I read your letter respecting Mr. Tracy's affairs; it is too much for me to relate. Nay
My good Hamilton (excuse the freedom) it fairly unnerved
me, and what is still more affecting to me to see my amiable
wife looking over the letter and exclaiming "is it possible, is
it possible Mr. Gibbs that you have lost that hard earned
money you friendly lent that wicked man"—indeed my
friend it was too much for her to bear, and more particularly
so considering her situation; we have been almost ever since in
a state of dispair—for I have all along held up to her the Idea,
that there was hopes of recovering my property more especially as we thought it was in your hands—but now forever
lost—not only so but *good money which I borrowed of you* to
bear my expenses thrown away in pursuit of what he owes
me, and God only knows when I shall be able to pay you.

Pray for God's sake my friend speak to the President for
me,—the Surveyorship of the Port of Boston is now vacant,
cannot you befriend me—Every one who knows (& I know
you do) that the great economy used in the Expenditures of
the General's family was in a very great degree owing to me
—Speak peace to me, drop but one drop of the balm of Comfort & Consolation. If I am worthy of another line from
you give me it as a Comforter.

I pray God to preserve you
                    & believe me yours
                              devotedly   C. GIBBS.

Something has been said of Hamilton's difficulties, and
the manner in which he contrived to bring upon his own

head the wrath of many persons with whom he was officially thrown into contact. Political differences were even more bitter than to-day, and as has been shown in a previous chapter, scurrilous abuse was quite as pungent and intolerable.

Sumner[1] says: "One of his most remarkable traits contrasting in the strongest manner with his contemporaries, was his fearlessness of responsibility. If he went upon that principle, he was sure to bear the brunt of every contest, provoked by his enterprises; and as he was always in the advance of other people, he was sure to excite their wonder, doubt and suspicion by his enterprises."

"Hamilton's methods were calculated to raise against himself very bitter opposition. He forced every issue in its most direct form. His fearlessness, openness, and directness turned rivals into enemies, irritated smaller men, and aroused their malicious desire to pull him down. At the same time, by the mass he was not understood, and in them he inspired a vague sense of alienation and distrust."

Some of this was because, as he once announced, he held popular opinion of no value—which is all in a way very true, but, as has been said, "It may have no value, but a statesman must notice that it has power."

This feeling caused him many a bitter moment, and upon various occasions he was quick to recognize the dissatisfaction which attended the disintegration of his own party, and the secession of those who did not approve of his vigorous methods. The attacks upon him were, perhaps, more bitter from the time he retired from public office until his death than at any other, and the various projects which he believed could be successfully carried out were assailed on all sides.

Madison, who had been his coadjutor in the preparation of the *Federalist*, he believed to have turned against him,

[1] *Op. cit,* p. 228.

and so stated in a letter to Carrington in 1792. Jefferson was always jealous and inimical, and lost no chance either secretly or openly to try to undermine his popular rival, although he was forced to admit the latter's greatness. His objection to the funding system and the establishment of the bank were very decided and were carried out with the assistance of Freneau, the editor of a newspaper to which reference has been made.

Hamilton seems to have been in a constant broil with many of these people, and it is a wonder how he could have kept his peace of mind and self-control, smarting as he did under the assaults, not only of Jefferson, but even of Thomas Paine, whose methods were those that had, in 1793, found so much favor with the violent National Convention. So bitter was the fight between Hamilton and Jefferson, and so far-reaching the possibilities of public demoralization, that Washington was obliged to make peace between the two, although his sympathies were clearly with Hamilton. It would seem as if there was no limit to the abuse poured out by Callendar,[1] Bache,[2] and his colleagues, they being egged on by Jefferson, and this led to a celebrated libel suit in which Hamilton appeared (the Croswell case), and was, in measure, based upon the outrageous abuse of Washington.

General Schuyler wrote from Albany August 19, 1802, to Hamilton: "If Mr. Jefferson has really encouraged that wretch Callendar to vent his calumny against you and his

---

[1] John Thomas Callendar was banished from Great Britain for seditious writings, and came to Philadelphia in 1794. He published various scurrilous sheets, among them the *Political Register*, the *American Annual Register*, and the *Richmond Recorder*. He also was the author of the "Prospect of the United States," 1797, and "History of New York," in 1796. He violently assailed Washington, Hamilton, and others, for a time finding favor with Jefferson, but was ultimately repudiated by the latter, though only after he had attacked him.

[2] B. F. Bache, a grandson of Wm. Franklin, who published the *Aurora General Advertiser*. (See chapter iii.)

predecessors in office, the head of the former must be abominably wicked and weak. I feel for the reputation of my Country which must suffer, when its citizens can be brought to elevate such a character to the first office of the republic. May indulgent heaven avert the evil with which we are threatened from such a ruler and the miscreants who guide his councils. Adieu My Dear Sir. May you enjoy health and happiness and that peace of mind which results from a rectitude of conduct."

John Adams, on one occasion, spoke of Hamilton as "the bastard brat of a Scotch pedlar," and accused him of any amount of vile things. Callendar even intimated that Hamilton regretted that the insurgents (during the Whiskey Rebellion) did not burn Pittsburg in 1794, and called him Caligula and Alva, and spread the often-repeated story that seemed to have been the chief stock in trade of his many calumniators that he was constantly attempting the establishment of a monarchy.

One of Hamilton's most venomous opponents was William Maclay, who was a United States senator from Pennsylvania between 1789–1791. At an early stage of his political career he broke with the Federalists, and never ceased, thereafter, to speak of them all in a contemptuous manner. None were free from his shafts, and his unexpurgated journal [1] has no equal as a vituperative masterpiece. His only friend for a time seems to have been Robert Morris, but later he turned upon him. He spoke of Hamilton and others at a dinner he attended, as follows: "I could not help making some remarks on our three Secretaries—Hamilton has a very boyish giddy manner, and Scotch-Irish people would

[1] "Journal of William Maclay, 1789–1791," edited by Edgar S. Maclay, A.M., N.Y., D. Appleton & Co., 1890. Maclay is spoken of as the original Democrat, and Jefferson merely as his successor.

call him a 'skite.' Jefferson transgresses on the extreme of
stiff gentility or lofty gravity. Knox[1] is the easiest man, and
has the most dignity of presence. They retired at a decent
time, one after another. Knox stayed longest, as indeed
suited his aspect best, being more of a Bacchanalian figure."

Hamilton is accused, by him, of all manner of corruption,
and even of knowingly issuing Treasury certificates which
were counterfeit. He referred constantly to Hamilton's
"tools," whom he also calls "Senatorial Gladiators," and of
his use of Washington as "scapegoat." The "Cincinnati"
was one of his machines. Much of his enmity is of the usual
kind, so characteristic of the day, as, in referring to his own
efforts to get the Senate to repudiate the indebtedness of the
country to foreign officers who had fought in the Revolution,
"I set myself to defeat it, and happily succeeded," he
said. "The consequence is, that I have all the Secretary's
[Hamilton's] gladiators upon me. I have already offended
Knox and all his military arrangements; I have drowned
Jefferson's regards in the Potomac. Hamilton, with his host
of speculators, is upon me, and they are not idle; the City
hates me, and I have offended Morris, and my place must
go. My peace of mind, however, shall not go, and, like a
dying man, I will endeavor that my last moments be well
spent." The reference to the "host of speculators" is an
assumption that Hamilton's friends had bought up the claims
of the French officers who had fought during the Revolution.

In 1776 General Charles Lee was guilty of treacherous
disobedience in refusing to re-enforce Washington, who had
ordered him to make a junction with him at Hackensack.
His idea was clearly to embarrass and put Washington in
a false position, and to profit by his failure to prevent the
British from taking Philadelphia. Not only was Lee guilty

---

[1] General Knox was the Secretary of War.

of rank insubordination, but he wrote to the Commander-in Chief two disrespectful and insolent letters.   This led to his arrest and court-martial, and he was sentenced to suspension from the army for one year.   Hamilton and the other sup-porters of Washington were, naturally, highly indignant, and the former gave very damaging testimony at the trial.   Major J. S. Eustace, one of Lee's strong friends and supporters, and a vulgar and hot-headed officer, emptied his vials of abuse in various letters to his discredited friend, and did his best to provoke Hamilton to fight a duel.   Extracts from two of his letters may be produced which show the hatred felt not only by this man, but by others.   Writing from Phila-delphia, November 29, to Lee he says:

I met Hambleton [sic] the other day in Company with the favorite Green[1] the Drunkard Stirling[2] and their class of at-tendants.   He advanced toward me on my entering the room with presented hand.   I took no notice of his polite in-tention, but sat down without bowing to him or any of the class (it happened at the Q^r. M^r. General's office at Morris-town) he then asked me if I was come from Camp—I say'd *shortly No*, without the usual application of SIR, rose from my chair—left the room, and him *standing before the chair*. I could not treat him much more rudely—I've repeated my suspicions of his *veracity* on the *tryall* so often that I expect the s—— of a b—— will challenge me when he comes.   If he does he will find me as unconcerned as he can possibly be anxious.

And again he wrote to Lee:

I speak of you here *openly* and *loyally*, and I give my senti-ments of your affairs, with all the warmth of a *young man—* tho' without the *prudence* of an *old one*.   I said 'tother night I thought *Colonel Hamilton was perjured*—that I could con-

---

[1] General Nathaniel Greene.   [2] General Lord Stirling.

vince himself of IT, by reading over the Tryall to him—and if that was not *sufficient evidence*, it might rest on *matter of opinion*, and he decided as he chose, there were several officers present but they said nothing in reply—tho' I am confident they'll tell him & I've no objections.[1]

The involuntary praise of some of his most important antagonists was the greatest tribute. Jefferson called him the "Colossus of the Federalists," and upon one occasion, when Hamilton had written articles for Fenno's paper signed Marcellus, he wrote to Madison, informing him by whom they were produced, with the remark that they promised "much mischief." Madison was urged to exert himself against "this champion. You know the ingenuity of his talents, and there is not a person but yourself who can foil him. For Heaven's sake then, take up your pen and do not desert the public cause altogether."

Much criticism has been indulged in, by those inimical to Hamilton, regarding a letter written by Hamilton to Gouverneur Morris on July 27, 1802, shortly after the movement had been started to impeach several of the circuit judges by the anti-Federalists. This was at a time when the scurrilous sheets were filled with abuse of the opponents of Burr and Jefferson, and when Hamilton was well-nigh distracted by the machinations of the Democrats in his own State. "Mine is an odd destiny," he said; "perhaps no man in the United States has sacrificed or done more for the present constitution than myself; and contrary to all my anticipations of its fate, as you know from the very beginning, I am still laboring to prop the frail and worthless fabric, yet I have the murmurs of its friends no less than the curses of its foes for my reward. What can I do better than withdraw from the

[1] Both of these letters are printed in the N. Y. Historical Society's Collections (Lee Papers), vol. III, 1873.

scene? Every day proves to me more and more that this American world was not made for me." As a rule his enemies ignore and neglect to quote a later paragraph which is as follows: "The time may ere long arrive when the minds of men will be prepared to make an effort to *recover* the Constitution, but the many cannot now be brought to make a stand for its preservation. We must wait a while." This is almost prophetic when we consider the re-establishment of national faith in this great instrument which followed the disorderly reign of Jefferson and his followers, down to a time when civil strife led to a new order of dignity and unswerving devotion to the original laws of our national organization.

CHAPTER X

THE YEARS FROM 1790 TO 1800

In the fall of 1790, as has been said, Hamilton went to Philadelphia with his family, and applied himself assiduously to his financial work which had been commenced in New York. The obligations of the nation were great indeed, and consisted not only of its original indebtedness to France, but of debts incurred in the campaign of St. Clair against the Indians in the North-west, and for various other purposes. Much of his official labor was connected with two prospective foreign loans which entailed great trouble and worry, and met with unlooked-for opposition from Giles, a Virginian, whom Hamilton, however, had often befriended in the past. This man, acting upon instructions from Jefferson and his friends, did all he could in Congress to hamper Hamilton in his continued efforts to prevent the nation from becoming bankrupt, accusing him of irregular practices, and among other things, of favoritism to certain banks.

Hamilton, as usual, had no trouble in thoroughly vindicating himself and presenting ample documentary evidence of the perfect order of all his transactions. So that his enemies were again discomfited.

About this time a new and very serious condition of affairs had to be met, for the international complications of the young republic were many. Hardly secure in her new footing in the family of nations, her adjustment to the ways of her older sisters was slow and difficult. Some of this was due to the jealousy of the two great countries, from the control of one of which she had freed herself a few years previously, and some to the chagrin that that nation naturally felt in the apparent success of French influence. It is true that "a definitive treaty of peace and friendship between His Britannic Majesty and the United States of America was signed at Paris, the 3d day of September, 1783, in the name of the Most Holy and Undivided Trinity," but this was apparently insufficient, and Great Britain had not only left much undone, but had continued, among other things, to infringe upon the rights of the emancipated colonists.

John Adams had been sent abroad, had signed the first treaty of peace, and later attempted fresh negotiations with England, but he was treated discourteously, though he did all in his power to conciliate the mother country. He returned, however, empty-handed, without having accomplished anything. England was not disposed to fulfil her obligations in paying us for the negroes she had carried away near the close of the Revolution, and in many ways was arrogant and unjust. The American jingoes had no warm welcome for Mr. Adams, and a historian of the time said, "after Mr. Adams' return from England he was implicated by a large portion of his countrymen as having relinquished the Republican system, and forgotten the principles of the American revolution which he had advocated for nearly twenty years." [1]

From the overthrow of Louis XVI until 1800 and later, the United States not only suffered internal dissensions, but her relations with both England and France were of the most discouraging kind. Hamilton's energies were first directed to the establishment of a more perfect reconciliation with the

---

[1] "History of the Rise, Progress, and Termination of the American Revolution," by Mrs. Mercy Warren. Boston, 1805.

people speaking our own tongue, and with established institutions of the kind best calculated to benefit his own country.
Indeed, our success and prosperity were, at an early period,
attracting the attention and respect of Great Britain, and
the first evidence of a tardy *rapprochement* was the arrival
of George Hammond, who was sent as diplomatic agent to
join in negotiations for a treaty.   Hamilton's exertions were
unremitting.   He disregarded the aggression and the enemy
that we and others had just defeated, for he recognized the
advantages of harmonious relations with an important, rich,
and powerful commercial nation.   As early as 1790, both
Hamilton and Adams showed that the trade regulations
of Great Britain were more favorable to the United States
than those of France, although the latter had been our
ally.

Owing to Jefferson's sympathy with the French, and his
dislike of England, Hamilton's efforts at conciliation and an
orderly adaptation to new conditions were, with difficulty,
carried on.   A new and disturbing influence which made
itself manifest about this time was the absolute change in
our attitude toward France after her Revolution.

After the War of Independence America bought freely
from England, but not from France, much to the disappointment of the latter.   Then, again, the debt of the United
States to France had been incurred at a time previous to the
revolt and overthrow of the king, and it was seriously questioned, even by Hamilton himself, whether the obligation
should not be repudiated so far as the new government, which
he never willingly recognized, was concerned.

His sentiments are embodied in a paper hitherto unpublished which I cannot identify.   It is a fragment, but was
probably written at a time when great pressure was being
brought by Jefferson, Paine, and others, to have the United

States take up the cause of the French Republic, and establish an *entente* with France.

All this was and is seen, and the body of the people of America are too discerning to be long in the dark about it. Too wise to have been misled by foreign or domestic machinations, they adopted a constitution which was necessary to their safety and to their happiness. . . . Too wise to be ensnared by the same machinations, they will support the government they have established, and will take care of their own peace, in spite of the insidious efforts, which are making to detach them from the one and to disturb the other. . . .

The information, which the address of the Constitution contains, ought to serve as an instructive lesson to the people of this Country. It ought to teach us not to overrate *foreign friendships* . . . to be upon our guard against *foreign attachments*. The former will generally be found hollow and delusive; the latter have a natural tendency to lead us aside from our true interest and to make us the dupe of foreign influence.[1]

Foreign influence is truly the Grecian horse to a republic. We cannot be too careful to exclude its entrance. Nor ought we to imagine that it can only make its approaches in the gross form of direct bribery. It is then most dangerous, when it comes under the patronage of our passions, under the auspices of national prejudice and partiality. . . .

I trust the morals of the country are yet too good to leave much to apprehend on the score of bribery. Careless condescentions, flattery, in unison with our prepossessions, are infinitely more to be feared; and as far as there is opportunity for corruption, it is to be remembered, that one foreign Power can employ this resource, as well as another, and that the effect must be much greater, where it is combined with the other means of influence, than where it stands alone.

The observations and facts contained in this paper, while they lead to the conclusions just drawn, serve also to dem-

---

[1] They introduce a principle of action, which, in effect, if the expression may be allowed, is *anti-national*.

onstrate, that as far as the conduct of France towards us in our late revolution created a claim to our acknowledgement and friendship[1] these dispositions were *immediately* due to the then sovereign of the country and could not justly have been withdrawn from him to be placed elsewhere.

Gratitude alone therefore would not have recommended our assisting the French Nation against him. . . . As far as that principle was allowed to have any operation;—this, upon a just estimate,would have been the result; that we ought not to take part against the person on whose sole will the assistance we received had depended—that we ought not to take part with him, against the nation whose blood and whose treasure had been the means in his hands of that assistance.

"But Louis the XVI was a Tyrant. By his perjuries and his crimes he forfeited his crown and his life, and with these his title to our esteem and sympathy.—Besides—he is now no more . . . whatever competition may have before existed ceased with his death. The claim to our gratitude has by this devolved exclusively upon the Nation."

That Louis was a Tyrant is contradicted too emphatically by the whole tenor of his life to be credited without better evidence than has yet been produced. That he was guilty of the crimes which were the pretexts of his death remains still to be proved to an impartial world. Against the presumption of his guilt, this strong argument, independent of other topics which might be urged, presents itself. . . . "If the Convention had possessed *clear proofs* of the guilt ot Louis, *they would have promulgated them to the world in an authentic and unquestionable shape:* Respect for the opinion of mankind, regard for their own character, the interests of their cause made this an indispensable duty, and would have produced a correspondent effect, if the case had admitted ot it—The omission is a satisfactory indication that the means of doing it were not possessed; and that the melancholy catastrophe of Louis XVI was the result rather of a supposed political expediency than of real criminality."

In a case so circumstanced, does it consist even with our

---

[1] Which under a certain aspect has been conceded.

justice or humanity to participate in the angry and vindictive passions, which are endeavored to be excited against him?

Hamilton then goes on to question the propriety of extending the "refined and beneficient sentiment of gratitude" to the successors of the murdered king, and says:

Shall we not be more sure of violating no obligation of that sort, of not implicating the delicacy of our national character, by taking no part in the contest, than by throwing our weight into either scale?

But the cause of France is the cause of Liberty. 'Tis our own cause; and it is our first duty to countenance and promote it—Whatever foundation there may be for this suggestion, it is entirely foreign to the question of gratitude—It turns upon a principle wholly distinct. Gratitude has reference only to kind offices received. The obligation to and the cause of liberty has reference to the abstract intrinsic merits of that cause—It is possible that the benefactor may be on one side—the defenders and supporters of liberty on the other. Gratitude may point that way . . . the lover of liberty this . . . . There is a necessary distinction to be made.

How far the last mentioned consideration ought to operate with us will be hereafter examined.[1]

As usual, any attempt upon his part to even tolerate things British was misunderstood, and he was forever accused of acting against the national interests, and being an Anglophile. In this connection it is curious to find that he was not only unjustly judged at home, but the same fairness which impelled him to fight the Trespass Act many years before, protecting the rights of the Tories themselves, led to the assumption by the representative of England that he was really in improper sympathy with Great Britain, because he appeared in court in Tory cases.

[1] It is sufficient to let it be said here that it is not connected with the question of gratitude.

Mr. Barclay,[1] the English Consul in New York, said after Hamilton's death, in a letter to a Mr. Merry: "July 13, 1804. By the public papers you will be informed of the unfortunate death of General Hamilton, one of the most reputable characters of this State, and a gentleman of eminent talents. I consider him even as a loss to His Majesty and our Government from the prudence of his measures, his conciliatory disposition, his abhorence of the French Revolution and all republican principles and doctrines, and his great attachment to the British Government."

After much delay and obstruction John Jay, who was then the Chief Justice, was sent to England with a treaty. Lord Grenville had already paved the way by a conciliatory speech, and at length there seemed to be some hope that advantageous commercial relations might be attained. Hamilton, who had first been named as an envoy, appreciating the opposition of those at home, and believing he could do more good in his own country by meeting the intrigues and hostile schemes of Randolph and Monroe, and at least keeping and exercising control of the Treasury, remained at his post. In spite of the attacks of Burr and the other anti-Federalists, Jay's nomination in the Senate was confirmed, and he ultimately embarked. His mission was beset with difficulties, for offensive and irritating measures directed against Great Britain were proposed, and it is said that the very ship that conveyed the American representative carried insulting papers which were not calculated to help the treaty or to insure Jay a warm welcome.

Congress had extended the embargo on English vessels, and did all it could to thwart the negotiations by all manner of petty proceedings. Another faction of the Democratic party sent tactless, congratulatory messages to the disor-

---

[1] "Correspondence of Thomas Barclay." New York, 1894.

derly French revolutionists, and fomented the lawless feeling
at home, which not only led to the persecution of those favor-
ing the treaty, but to actual personal assaults.   The so-called
Jacobin clubs burned Jay in effigy and paraded the streets,
and even brutally stoned and assaulted Hamilton when he
attempted to speak in public.

A French vessel loaded with gunpowder was permitted to
pass the embargo, but was captured by the British vessels
of war, and this also aroused new agitation.   When Jay arrived in England, he was directed to demand compensation
for losses through unlawful depredations; to insist that no
armed force should be maintained by either party on the
Great Lakes; that more liberal opportunities should be given
to trade with the Indians living in the territories of either
country; in fact, that they should not be encouraged to fight
or be supplied with munitions of war or unusual stores.

Besides these, compensation should be given for negroes
carried away by the British, and various minor commercial
and territorial concessions were demanded, some of which
had relation to the surrender of posts.   In its turn the United
States agreed to indemnify the mother country for losses
arising from legal obstructions interposed to the recovery of
the ante-Revolutionary debts not exceeding in the whole a
certain sum to be named.[1]   Upon Jay's arrival on June 15,
1794, he at first met with opposition, but the treaty, with
slight modifications, was agreed to, and signed by Jay and
Lord Grenville, on November 19, 1794, though not received in
Philadelphia until almost six months later.   The enmity and
bad feeling still existed, together with much disorder, but the
treaty was finally ratified by only four votes in 1796.   Washington's attempt to enforce it met with fresh lawlessness.
A timid Congress was disposed to thwart its operations.   It

[1] See Morse's "Life of Alexander Hamilton," vol. II.

was then that Hamilton and his father-in-law were strongly alarmed—for, under the circumstances, Great Britain had shown an extraordinary amount of forbearance. It was, therefore, thought best to stir the citizens of their own State as well as others to a sense of danger and the possible consequences of bad faith. General Schuyler at once circulated a broadside, of which a fac-simile is given herewith, and in a letter to Hamilton told of his efforts to accomplish something.

He also wrote to Hamilton, April 25, 1796:

Philip Schuyler to Alexander Hamilton

DEAR SIR: Unadvised of the measures pursuing at New York, relative to the treaty with Britain, It was not deemed prudent to convene the citizens here on the subject, until we received information from your city. On Saturday morning the mail arrived, and the *Herald* announced what had been done. About forty citizens were immediately convened, and unanimously agreed to petition in the words of the New York petition, with no other variation than what was requisite to accommodate It to the people in this quarter. 500 copies were immediately printed, proper persons appointed to invite the signature of the Citizens individually. Before sunset this was compleated, all having subscribed Except about ———— who declined. Many decided Antifederalists concurred and signed.

A circular letter was prepared, directed to the Supervizors, assessors and town Clerks, of the several towns in this and the counties to the Eastward, Northward and Westward of this. Several of these, with copies of the petition, are already dispatched, and the residue will be sent today.—We believe the subscribers will be numerous.

The petition from this city will be sent to Philadelphia by this day's mail.—

We are anxious to hear the result of the Application to the citizens of New York, and If favorable, will It be communicated in a formal manner, by the New York committee.—

The inclosed is copy of the letter, which accompanies the copy of the petition to the several towns.

Pray drop me a line, advising me of the latest intelligence from Philadelphia, on this important subject.

Adieu.   My love to all

Yours most affectionately

PH. SCHUYLER.

Alexander Hamilton, Esq.

This action seems to have been amply justified, for the strain was indeed great, and upon previous occasions acute trouble had been imminent, because of the presence of foreign men-of-war in New York harbor.   *The Daily Advertiser*, two years previously, contained a proclamation of Governor George Clinton, in which he forbade "all ships and vessels of foreign nature except those engaged in Commerce to approach the City nearer than one mile southward of the Southern-most Point of Governor's Island, and all War vessels above this point to retire."

Shortly after the signing of the treaty, and when popular unrest had subsided, Hamilton wrote, urging the Churches to return.   It is somewhat amusing to find that the popular disapproval regarding Mr. Jay's arrangements had had its influence, more or less, upon the sister-in-law of its most earnest defender.

"Adieu my dear and naughty Brother," wrote Angelica Church; "it will be impossible for me to charter a vessel, for how can I bring out furniture when I do not know the number of rooms my house contains.   What an agreeable amiable fellow! Mr. Jay's WISE treaty turned into a defender of what he never would himself have deigned to submit to. *Voilà mon sentiment* change to *si vous voulez*."

Friends and Fellow-Citizens !

Y OUR attention is called to a fubject involving your in-tereft, your happinefs, and your peace.---Appearances indicate, that a dif-pofition prevails in a majority of the Houfe of Reprefentatives of the United States, not to make the requifite provifion, for carrying into effect the Trea-ty lately concluded with Great Britain, altho ratified on the part of the Uni-ted States, by the Conftitutional Authorities thereof.

Should our apprehenfions, excited by fuch a difpofition be verified, an expenfive WAR, with all its attendant calamities, will probably be the refult ---Indeed the very profpect of it, has already diminifhed the price of our agricultural produce, to a confiderable extent---the depreciation will doubt-lefs encreafe ; while the price of the neceffary foreign articles of confumption will certainly rife. Under thefe impreffions, and others. arifing from cir-cumftances equally important, the Citizens of many of the States, ar ; pre-paring remonftances on the fubject to the Houfe of Reprefentatives. The Citizens of New-York, have already concluded on their addrefs ; and have recommended to you and to us, to afford our aid on this ferious occafion ; the inclofed copies are now fubmitted for fignature, by the Citizens of this city---and will, we truft, meet with general approbation, as Citizens of every political party are equally interefted in the refult.

Will you be pleafed to lay it before the Citizens of your town, for their determination, and if it meets with their approbation, to intreat their fignatures: and when figned, to tranfmit it at an early day to us.

By order,

Ph: Schuyler, Chairman.

ALBANY, April 23, 1796.

To the Supervifor, Affeffors and Town-Clerk, of the
town of   in the county of

Facsimile of original Broadside.

Hamilton's interest in France and Frenchmen, up to 1792, appears to have been continuous and intense before the ascendancy of the republic.   Speaking and writing the language with great facility, he not only made friends very readily, as has been shown, with the host of those who, for various reasons, espoused the American cause, but upon several occasions was sent to meet the naval and military commanders upon their arrival.   It was he who welcomed d'Estaing, and who acted as the representative of Washington in arranging the details of active co-operation with our force. Possibly he healed internal dissensions, averted the consequences of petty jealousy, and finally sent them home in good spirits, for there is no doubt that the French officers were not always agreed, or upon the best terms with each other.   The establishment of the Society of the Cincinnati, for which he was responsible, and which led to so much criticism upon the part of the "American Jacobins," did much to cement the *entente* between the American officers and their French comrades in arms.

Philadelphia had become the rendezvous of expatriated Frenchmen, and, as a rule, they were clever, capable, and uncomplaining, though they had to adapt themselves to a serious change of fortune, incident to the loss of all they possessed.   Mention has been made of some of these.   Angelica Church wrote, July 4, 1793, and her final outburst of patriotism is characteristic:

Pray write to me a line to say that you are well for it is an age since I have seen your signature.

I wrote yesterday and recommended to the protection of our *dear Minister* General Valence who has served in the French army, and who married a Daughter of the celebrated Madame de Genlis who has written many and useful volumes on female Education.   I hear my dear that you

will give our Hamilton a hint to invite him to dinner, and
to be civil to him for I have promised half a dozen pretty
French women to recommend him to you.

Mrs. Bache is to return to America next month. I shall
see her before she goes, that she may have an opportunity of
chatting to you, for she is a sensible and reserved person and
cannot talk without a good subject.

Adieu my dear Sister. Pray where is Cornelia? She
never does me the favor to write me a line.

My love to Angelica and the Children, embrace my dear
Hamilton for me à la Française.

Farewell my dear Sister.

July the 4th, 1793,
        Vive la république!

A few months earlier she had written to Hamilton:

MY DEAR BROTHER: You will receive this from a friend
of mine and an admirer of your virtues and your talents.
He goes to America to partake of that Liberty for which he
has often exposed his life, and to render it all the services
his knowledge of Europe and of the emigration about to take
place to America, give the opportunity of doing.

The Count de Noailles requires less recommendation than
most people, because he is well known to you my friend.
When you and he have talked over Europe and America,
spare a few moments to the recollection of your faithful friend

And affectionate sister,

ANGELICA CHURCH.

London, February 17th, 1793.
Alexander Hamilton, Esq.

The Chevalier de Pontigibaud,[1] who had fought in the war
and subsequently went back to France, returned at its
conclusion to collect the pay due him for his services, and his

---

[1] "Memoirs," pp. 146–150.

account of an interview throws light upon the social conditions at the time.   He said:

I was glad to meet some of my old comrades in arms, both French and Americans; amongst others the brave and wise Colonel Hamilton, the friend of Washington, and who was afterwards unfortunately killed in a duel by Colonel Burgh [sic].   Hamilton, who had quitted the army and returned to civil life, was a lawyer, and pleaded in the courts and gave consultations.   We often talked together,—much to my profit,—of the causes of the war, the actual condition of the United States, and the probable destiny of the nation. Anyone who had heard us talking about events which were then a matter of history, would have taken us for two of the speakers in Lucian's or Fénelon's "Dialogues of the Dead."   "The American War," I said, "began in a very singular manner, and was carried on in a way yet more singular.   It seems to me, on summing up all my observations, that the English made a mistake in sending troops against you, instead of withdrawing those which were already in the country, as did you submit at once you must have inevitably ended by winning sooner or later.   You gained experience and discipline in the indecisive engagements which were fought, and the scholars were bound to finish by becoming as clever as their masters.   Look, for instance, at the Swedes under Charles XII. and the Russians under Peter the Great."

"You are right, no doubt," he replied, "but their second fault was to give the two brothers Howe each a command. The general undertook scarcely anything by land in order to allow his brother, the admiral, the chance to distinguish himself at sea.   All that the English need have done was to blockade our ports with twenty-five frigates and ten ships of the line.   But, Thank God, they did nothing of the sort."

"Thank God, indeed," I said, "for I believe that America would have come to terms with the mother country.   I am the more inclined to believe this, as I notice there are a great many Tories in your country, and I see that the rich families still cling to the King's Government."

"Yes; and thus it happens," he replied, with a smile, "that though our Republic has only been in existence some ten years, there are already two distinct tendencies,—the one democratic, the other aristocratic. In Europe they always speak of the American Revolution, but our separation from the mother country cannot be called a revolution. There have been no changes in the laws, no one's interests have been interfered with, everyone remains in his place, and all that is altered is that the seat of government is changed. Real equality exists among us at present, but there is a remarkable difference of manners between the inhabitants of the Northern and Southern States. The negro is free at Philadelphia, but he is a slave in Virginia and Carolina. Large fortunes are made in the Southern States, because the Country is rich in production; but it is not the same in the Northern States."

"Yes," I said, "those who claim to look into the future may see in some nation,—as you say,—two diverging tendencies; the one towards democracy, the other towards aristocracy; but if some separation of these elements could be made quietly and without strife, would the people be any the happier? Territorial possessions are, there is no doubt, but lightly esteemed in your country, which is perhaps owing to the fact that the British or Anglo-American of today only dates back to Penn and his colony, or only a hundred years or so. An estate over here rarely remains ten or twelve years in the same hands."

"That is partly due," answered he, "to the facilities for changing our place of residence, and to the fact that land which is relatively dear near the great cities, is much cheaper at some distance from them. Besides we are essentially business men; with us, agriculture is of small account; commerce is everything."

"That is true," I said, "many persons believe they have but to land in the United States to make a fortune, and the first question that is put to you when you arrive, is 'Do you come here to sell or buy?'"

I have given, as nearly as I can remember it, all that passed between the soldier-lawyer and me at this interview, but I cannot forget the singularly wise reflection that I heard him make one day, on the subject of the French interference in the American War.

"Considering the question by itself," I said to him, "the Cabinet of Versailles would seem to have committed a political fault in having openly supported the Americans in the War of Independence, and more particularly for having sent over here all the young nobility of the Court, who returned embued with republican principles. It has been maintained that the proper action for France was to remain neutral and take advantage of the difficulties of England, to occupy, and thus make her restore Canada, which has always remained French at heart. This double opportunity of war, or re-occupation, would have furnished an outlet for surplus population, which, failing that, has overflowed in the form of a revolution on our own monarchy, and has then inundated Europe."

This speech made him think of the young nobles, who had overrun America like the sheep of Panurge, without, however, reducing the surplus population of France, and Colonel Hamilton could not help laughing as he replied:

"You are right. I am speaking in opposition to our own interests, for it is to the French arms that we owe our independence, but your Government would, perhaps, have done better if it had sent us your lower orders instead of your upper."

Great was the distress and misery of the people who crowded here to escape the persecution at home. The Count de Tousard was a brave artillery officer during the war of the Revolution, and later entered the reorganized army in 1799.

At the time when the disrupting influence of the French Republic had even extended across the Atlantic and did so much harm here, Tousard, who had, meanwhile, paid a visit to his native country, returned just before the cruel persecution of suspected persons became so great. He wrote to Mrs. Hamilton the following:

Louis Tousard to Elizabeth Hamilton

WILMINGTON, *June* 4th, 1794.

MADAM: Too great was my trouble when I had the honor to meet with you a few days ago in the city; and perhaps you could not understand all the unfortunate events which I related to you.

My sister-in-law [Mrs. Tousard's eldest sister] flying from under the *guillotine* which has destroyed most of all her family, guilty of no other crime but of having married a man of nobility, has just landed in this Continent, but the ship which brought her in was unhappily cast away on the Eastern shores of New Jersey; her and her children's life saved but her goods and even cloathes all lost—the news of her sister's death overwhelmed her entirely.

I hastened her home, foreseeing that after so much trouble both of mind and body she would not be long without getting sick, and indeed two days after, feeling great pains in her body she was soon reduced so very low by the ague and spitting of blood that it is but since yesterday that we see some relaxations in her pains and in our uneasiness on her account; but alas! I fear that she keeps in her bosom the principle of the disease which has carried off the dear Madame de Tousard. I have given her the cloathes of her sister. She is not in want, but the three children are most naked and the rigourous season is coming very fast, my resources entirely exhausted in helping so many others exist no more—a circumstance which concerns me so nearly though I was far from foreseeing it.

In such a critical conjuncture for me, I had a mind to apply to Col. Hamilton and to deposite in his friendly heart all my anxieties and sollicitudes, but being not yet certain of his return at home and knowing that there is not a sentiment in one of your hearts which is not felt by the others, I did not hesitate to apply to you, Madam, and recommend to your sensibility those three unfortunate children.   The two daughters are something more than Martine and Caroline, the son is seven years old.   I wish I could send him to college and the two daughters to Mrs. Mitchell at Burlington, but it is out of my power to advance the necessary money for it.   If any generous soul of your acquaintance could supply my deficiency at this moment, I hope that in a few years my sister-in-law would be able to return together with gratitude the money advanced to enable her children not to lose so precious a time for their education.   I beg your pardon, Madam, for troubling you so often with the account of my countrymen's misfortunes; but in the same time, I cannot but rejoice myself in having found a heart so compatient with them and your name will be for ever engraved in theirs.

   I have the honor to be with respect

Madam   Your most humble and obedient
                                 servant
                                              DE TOUSARD.

   With the overthrow of Louis XVI and the formation of the national Committee of Safety serious trouble was inevitable, and the doctrines, if they might be so called, of the savage rabble found a fertile soil here for the incubation of revolutionary disorder.   Here the unstable followers of Jefferson, already hating the Federalists, were quite ready to adopt the wild, anarchistic ideas of those who kept the guillotine so busy, and were ever drunk with the blood lust. Thomas Paine, Bentham, and a host of religious reformers, atheists, and communists had preached their extreme and socialistic doctrines.   Within a few months after the murder of the king a note was addressed to a number of individuals, both here and elsewhere, making them "citizens" of the French Republic.   The list of people thus honored included the names of "Georges Washington, James Maddison, Anacharsis Klootz, Jeremy Bentham, Joseph Priestly and

'Jean' Hamilton." The first document was signed by Danton. The second by Roland. Hamilton's endorsement upon the back of the folio he received is indicative of the contempt he felt. It is as follows:

> "*Letter from Government of French Republic transmitting me a Diploma of Citizenship mistaking the Christian name.*
> *Oct.* 1792.
> *curious example of French finesse.*"

The communication is the following.

Paris: le 10 Octobre 1792, l'an 1 de la République Françoise.

J'ai l'honneur de vous adresser ci-joint, Monsieur, un imprimé revêtu du sceau de l'Etat, de la Loi du 26 Août dernier, qui confère le titre de Citoyens François à plusieurs Etrangers. Vous y lirez, que la Nation vous à placé au nombre des amis de l'humanité et de la société, aux quels Elle à déféré ce titre.

L'Assemblée Nationale, par un Décret du 9 Septembre, a charge le Pouvoir exécutif de vous adresser cette Loi; j'y obéis, en vous priant d'être convaincu de la satisfaction que j'éprouve d'être, dans cette circonstance, le Ministre de la Nation, et de pouvoir joindre mes sentimens particuliers à ceux que vous témoigne un grand Exemple dans l'enthousiasme des premiers jours de la liberté.

Je vous prie de m'accuser la recéption de ma Lettre, afin que la Nation soit assurée que la Loi vous est parvenue, et que vous comptez également les François parmi vos Frères.

Le Ministre de l'Intérieur
de la République Françoise   ROLAND.

M. Jean Hamilton, dans les Etats-Unis de l'Amérique.[1]

---

[1] Paris, the 10th October, 1792, the First Year of the French Republic.
I have the honor, Monsieur, to herewith address you a printed document invested with the Seal of State, of the Law of the 26th of last August, which confers

As a result of his sympathy with the French cause, Joseph Priestley,[1] one of those honored by the certificate of citizenship, found his stay in England so uncomfortable that he came here in 1794. An English mob had attacked his laboratory, wrecked his house, and violently assaulted him so that he barely escaped with his life. He appears to have known Mr. Church in London, and came with a letter of introduction.

Angelica Church to Alexander Hamilton

MY DEAR BROTHER: You will have the pleasure to receive this letter by Dr. Priestley, a man dear to virtue and to science. Without the advantage and satisfaction of his acquaintance, I revere him for his works, and take a particular interest that he should be well received in America. That happy country which seems reserved by Providence as an Assylum from the crimes and persecutions which make Europe the pity and disgrace of the age.

You my dear Brother will receive with distinguished kindness this worthy stranger, (if he whose breast teems with the love of mankind may anywhere be called a stranger) and make our country so dear to him as to cause him to forget that which he leaves at an advanced period of Life and which he has most ably served.

the titles of French Citizens upon several Foreigners. In it you will read that the Nation numbers you amongst those friends of humanity and Society upon whom it confers this title.

The National Assembly, by a Decree of the 9th September, instructs the Executive Power to present you with this Law; I obey it, entreating you to believe in the satisfaction I feel in being, upon this occasion, the Minister of the Nation, and in being able to unite my private sentiments to those conveyed to you by a great people in the enthusiasm of its first days of liberty.

I beg that you will acknowledge the receipt of my letter, so that the Nation may be sure the Law has reached you, and that you likewise consider the French as your Brethren.

Minister of the Interior of the French Republic,

ROLAND.

Mr. Jean Hamilton,
    in the U. S. of America.

[1] The discoverer of oxygen gas.

Mr. Church is under the first attack of the Gout. He unites in love to you and dear Eliza.

I am my dear Brother

your affectionate sister

ANGELICA CHURCH.

England had declared war upon France, and this was not without its influence upon the democrats or French sympathizers, as well as the patriots abroad. Angelica Church wrote from London: "My heart beats with anxiety and fear. The Americans here speak of a war between this country and one a thousand fold dearer to me which Heaven avert. In consequence of this an order from the British Court has been issued to take all ships heading for France or her Colonies. Show this to Hamilton and bid him write to me for he is too silent."

This action led, not only to much interference with commerce, but much injustice was done to American subjects.

The interference with American shipping by English cruisers never entirely stopped, and during the war with France this was often most offensive. Mr. Richard Olive was a prosperous merchant in New York, but after the French Revolution he attempted to take his family back for a visit, with disagreeable results which he communicated to his friend, Alexander Hamilton, who was also his lawyer, in this pathetic letter:

Richard Olive to Alexander Hamilton

DARTMOUTH, *Sep.* 1801.

There could not possibly be two more astounding contrasts for us than that from New York to Dartmouth to which place we have been brought after 35 days' passage; the interest and kindness with which you have honored my family make it my duty to give you a faithful account of the events that have happened to us since we left happy America, that beautiful part of the world in which Providence has placed men who do honor to humanity!

We were sailing with perfect security under a flag that we believed to be more than ever respected in Europe, since generous America had covered the ocean with her vessels in order to succour England by sending her the large quantity of provisions she lacked. Personally I was perfectly tranquil [undisturbed?] being provided with a passport from Col. Barclay,[1] under whose protection I thought to be secure from all persecution in regard to the time at which I had emigrated; at the entrance to the Channel we were met by the British Cruiser *Fly*, Captain Thomas Duval, homeward bound from the African Coast; he sent Captain Jan Landon on board the *Georgia* to examine all her papers with strict attention, having found them all correct he allowed us to proceed; the examining officer told Captn Duval that there was a French family on board, and that Mme Olive had not left her bed since leaving N. York; we were quite close to the English frigate; it was perfectly calm; Captn Duval came on board with his surgeons to offer assistance to Mme Olive with a grace that yet adorns mankind. To this gallant and generous officier of His Majesty I showed all that I must naturally feel in such circumstances; he was short of provisions, I had the satisfaction of offering him half of mine, and during the 5 days that we were within reach there was a continual engagement of proceedings in no wise hurtful and that leave no trace but those of reciprocal esteem; Monsieur Duval, a young officer whose merit shows itself in spite of great modesty, is that one sent by Lord Nelson overland to India after the battle of the Nile, and who went and returned so promptly; this fact alone proves that he is one of the most distinguished officers; I have infinite pleasure Monsieur, in giving you these details before telling you their hideous contrast.

The *Fly* was nearly out of sight when we were stopped by

[1] Thomas Barclay, H. B. M. Consul General at this time and until 1812.

two cutters, calling themselves cutters of the King. They sent two boats aboard; they examined our papers and having found them all correct ordered us to proceed. Captain Landon was working the ship ahead, when upon second thoughts he was ordered to stop, and soon after they boarded us in numbers in order to take us into Dartmouth, which we reached the evening of the 17th August. I could fill twenty pages with the account of the barbarous treatment my family endured from the two lieutenants commanding these two cutters, armed by private individuals and hired out to the King. We were confined to the ship twelve days and twelve nights, without holding any communication with anyone whatsoever; Mme Olive and her daughters were searched in their beds and themselves searched to the skin; they forced themselves into the cabin where my sick wife lay, in order to rob her for three days of the only servant she had; I was then escorted to land; in short, towards us they violated the Rights of Nations, the Rights of Men, the protection of passports, the Rights of decency and even the rights of humanity! In vain I asked to see the Governor, the Commander, the Magistrates, with tears of rage and despair; our two tyrants replied with an insulting smile that it was the way of the service; at last I managed to get a letter to Monsieur Rufus King, your Ambassador, telling him in the confusion of my grief that I had no claim upon his protection except that my family had the honor of his acquaintance, and that two of my children were born in his country; he did not lose a moment and applied to Lord St. Vincent with an interest and kindness that filled me with sentiments that no words can express; thus even in Europe, Monsieur, America still protects my unfortunate family; what do we not owe this second fatherland!

Thanks to Mr. King and to Monsieur Duval who also took measures, we are on land, and are meeting with comforting tokens of kindness on the part of all the reputable inhabitants of Dartmouth, and even from the people, who have been told of the severity of the two men who are a disgrace to their society.

The governor has taken in my two eldest daughters and we are now amongst noble and generous English, awaiting orders from the Admiralty.

Captain Landon left three days ago for London, he was held prisoner several days; this estimable Captain redoubled his consideration, exertions and attentions towards my family in our distress. I and mine owe him eternal gratitude. Without the slightest ceremony they deprived me of all my books, my private papers, not leaving me a single one, and that without taking an inventory, without a receipt, without a soul to represent me during the examination. They are at the mercy of the two lieutenants in a lodging house; dead oak leaves could not be neglected with less care.

I expect justice from the Government, if necessary I will go to London to obtain it; if not for myself for those who in the future might experience similar persecution.

I should not know Europe again, ah! Monsieur, how it is all changed! This town had 150 ships. At this moment nine only are being equipped for Newfoundland; the people are tired of war, they sigh and long for peace; everything is at a standstill; children and old men—such would describe the inhabitants of the town. Everyone speaks with a kind of envy of the prosperity of the United States, in all conversation it is disputed and asked which country offers the greatest resources? as if each one had thoughts of leaving; I am telling you the exact truth; I also expect to find many changes in my own country, but I had no idea of all that I see here. I beg you to present the most respectful regards from my family to Madame Hamilton and to Mme Church, whose kindness will never be effaced from our hearts.

With assurance of profound respect Monsieur, I am

Your very humble & obedient servant,

RICH^D. OLIVE.

All this time revolutionary clubs were forming, and a large part of the community was in sympathy with the "sister republic." [1]

Angelica Church wrote, January 1, 1793, to her sister from London:

The French are mad, but I have a great curiosity to be well informed in what light they are regarded by the majority of America and what is the opinion of the discerning few. You have intelligence at hand. Alexander can tell you all. I hear the Jacobins have already made a thrust at him, but that he defended himself with vigour.

A year later she wrote:

If you ever meet Mr. Bache the printer pray tell him that in France they say that Jacobin clubs are the center of sedition and they are suppressed by the Convention amid the applause and blessings of the people—this will be a very agreeable article to his supporters the Jacobin democrats.

Jefferson's life in France admirably fitted him as leader for the so-called "Republican" party at home. In his "Notes on Virginia" his contemptuous state of mind is ap-

---

[1] The *Gazette Nationale* or *Moniteur Universelle*, No. 276, October, 1793, contained the following:

"Jacobin Society.
Coupe de Loise in the Chair.

The Republican Society of *Charleston* in *Carolina*, one of the United States of *America*, demand of the Jacobin Club its adoption.

HAUTIER: "We have spilt our blood for the establishment of American liberty. I think that the Americans ought to do the same for us, before we grant them adoption."

A CITIZEN: "Before engaging them to intermeddle in our war, it is necessary to understand one another, to come to an agreement, with them. I do not see, then, a more efficacious way for the previous reunion than an adoption of this society."

Collot d'Herbois after making some general observations says: "Nevertheless, we should not neglect the advantages which may arise from this advance. I conclude that we agree to this adoption."

parent, and on his return he began the attack on the so-called "monarchical party," in other words, the Federalists. Imbued with more or less of the discontent and revolutionary feelings of those in France who had just murdered their king, he was quite ready to lend himself to the disorder that had been stirred up by the French agents in the United States. Edmond Charles Genet,[1] representing the French Republic, landed in Charleston, South Carolina, April 9, 1793, with his pockets filled with blank commissions and appointments, and fitted out the privateer *Embuscade*, which patrolled the coast and captured an English merchantman, which it took into Philadelphia. This city, which was then full of *émigrés* and French sympathizers, including the redoubtable Talleyrand, was in a state of mind to eagerly welcome the swashbuckling Genet, who tied his vessel up to the Market Street wharf, all decorated with the insignia of the revolutionists at home. The bow, stern, and top of the foremast of the *Embuscade*, we learn, were adorned with liberty caps, while inscriptions were attached to other parts of the ship, all breathing of extravagant promises of liberty, equality, and fraternity. A body of leading citizens, headed by Jefferson and Governor Mifflin, and including Clement Biddle, Rittenhouse, Dallas, Dulonceau, and others, heartily welcomed the French minister with salvos of artillery and fulsome speeches; and, without waiting until he had presented his credentials to President Washington, he accepted an invitation to dinner, which was a remarkably disorderly event. Washington's reception of the man was dignified but freezing, and Genet's

---

[1] Gouverneur Morris had taken Genet's measure before he came to the United States, and in a letter to Washington written January 6, 1793, said: "I have seen M. Genet and he has dined with me since I had the pleasure of writing to you on the 28th of last month. He has, I think, more of genius than ability, and you will see in him at first blush the manner and look of an upstart. My friend the Maréchal de Ségur had told me that M. Genet was a clerk at £50 per annum in his office while Secretary of War."—"Diary and Letters of Gouverneur Morris," vol. II, p. 25.

embarrassment was further increased by finding pictures of
the dead king upon the walls of the executive mansion.   His
indignation knew no bounds, and this "insult" was only
made bearable by the kind sympathy of his new friends, and
another public dinner, which must have been a veritable
saturnalia.   One of the dishes was a roast pig, which Genet
proceeded to stick with his knife, meanwhile crying, "Tyrant! tyrant!" He then placed upon his own head a liberty
cap, which was transferred to the heads of the others in
turn, while the "Marseillaise" was sung by the half-crazed
party.

The state of popular feeling was incredible, and the Jacobin
clubs, which represented the disorderly majority, lost no
opportunity of praising Genet, and encouraging him in his
obstinate course of fitting out privateers to prey upon English
commerce.   So bad did this become that Chief Justice Jay
was obliged to issue a warning, and declared it the duty of
all grand juries to prosecute persons guilty of such violations
of the laws.   English prizes were restored to their owners,
and even Jefferson, who had silently encouraged the rabble,
slowly realized that he was Secretary of State, and tardily
admonished Genet.

The incredible arrogance and impudence of this individual
was such that he threatened to appeal from the President
and his advisers to the people; but luckily the noisy mob
was then really in the minority, and cooler reason prevailed.
Before this point had been reached, however, Genet attempted to fit out the English prize that had been seized by
the *Embuscade*, which he called the *Little Sarah* or *Petit
Democrat*.   Hamilton, who had stood shoulder to shoulder
with Washington, here asserted himself.   The situation is
summed up in a letter, written by the Secretary of the Treasury to Rufus King:

Alexander Hamilton to Rufus King[1]

PHILADELPHIA, *Aug.* 13, 1793.

DEAR SIR: The post of to-day brought me your letter of the 10th, but I was too much engaged to reply to it by return of post.

The facts with regard to Mr. Genet's threat, to appeal from the President to the people, stand thus:

On Saturday, the 6th of July last, the warden of this port reported to Governor Mifflin that the brig *Little Sarah*, since called the *Petit Democrat* (an English merchant vessel, mounting from two to four guns, taken off our coast by the French frigate the *Ambuscade*, and brought into this port), had very materially altered her military equipments, having then fourteen iron cannon and six swivels mounted, and it being understood that her crew was to consist of one hundred and twenty men.

Governor Mifflin, in consequence of this information, sent Mr. Dallas to Mr. Genet to endeavor to prevail upon him to enter into an arrangement for detaining the vessel in port, without the necessity of employing for that purpose military force.

Mr. Dallas reported to Governor Mifflin that Mr. Genet had absolutely refused to do what had been requested of him, that he had been very angry and intemperate, that he had complained of ill-treatment from the government, and had declared that "he would appeal from the President to the people;" mentioned his expectation of the arrival of three ships of the line, observing that he would know how to do justice to his country, or, at least, he had a frigate at his command, and could easily withdraw himself from this; adding that he would not advise an attempt to take possession of the vessel, as it would be resisted.

The refusal was so peremptory that Governor Mifflin, in consequence of it, ordered out 120 men for the purpose of taking possession of the vessel.

[1] "Hamilton's Works" (J. C. H.), vol. V, p. 574.

This conversation between Genet and Dallas was *in toto* repeated by General Mifflin to General Knox the day following, and the day after that the governor confirmed the declaration with regard to appealing to the people, owned that something like the threat to do justice to his country by means of the ships of the line was thrown out by Mr. Genet, but showed an unwillingness to be explicit on this point, objecting to a more particular disclosure, that it would tend to bring Mr. Dallas into a scrape.

Mr. Jefferson, on Sunday, went to Mr. Genet, to endeavor to prevail upon him to detain the *Petit Democrat* until the President could return and decide upon the case, but, as Mr. Jefferson afterwards communicated, he absolutely refused to give a promise of the kind, saying only that she would not probably be ready to depart before the succeeding Wednesday, the day of the President's expected return. This, however, Mr. Jefferson construed into an intimation that she would remain. Mr. Jefferson also informed that Mr. Genet had been very unreasonable and intemperate in his conversation (though he did not descend to particulars), and that Dallas had likewise told him (Mr. Jefferson) that Genet had declared he would appeal from the President to the people.

The *Petit Democrat*, instead of remaining as Mr. Jefferson had concluded, fell down to Chester previous to the Wednesday referred to, where she was when the President returned. A letter was written to Mr. Genet, by order of the President, informing him that the case of the vessel, among others, was under consideration, and desiring that she might be detained until he should come to a decision about her, but this requisition was disregarded. She departed in defiance of it.

I give this detail that you may have the whole subject before you, but I cannot authorize you to make use of it all. The circumstance of the letter may be omitted. It may be said generally that a requisition was made of Mr. Genet, by order of the President, for the detention of the vessel. All that part, however, which is scored or underlined, may be freely

ALEXANDER HAMILTON: AGE 45
From a painting by John Trumbull

made up. This part is so circumstanced as to take away all scruples of personal or political delicacy. 'Tis not so much with the rest. It can therefore only be confidently disclosed to persons whose discretion may be relied on, and whose knowledge of it may be useful.

It is true (as you have heard) that things, if possible still more insulting, have since been done by Mr. Genet; but of this at present no use can be made, no more than of some antecedent transactions nearly, if not quite, as exceptional. The mass would confound Mr. Genet and his associates. Perhaps it may not be long before a promulgation will take place.

I am of opinion with you that the charge ought to be insisted upon.

P. S.—The case does not require the naming General Knox or myself, and it will therefore not be done. It is to be observed that the equipments of the *Petit Democrat* are, in strictest sense, an original fitting out. She was before a merchant vessel; here she was converted into a vessel commissioned for war, of considerable force.

General Schuyler, who was in Albany, wrote from that place, December 15, 1793, to his son-in-law:

My Dear Sir: I am happy that the children are safely arrived with you. I hope that you and my Eliza are in health.

The president's message of the 5th has reached us. I am rejoiced that he has been so explicit relative to the French anarchists. The parties here who had boldly asserted that the imputation of an appeal to the people was a fabrication to injure the French cause, stand abashed,—and I am persuaded that Genet's intemperance has served the Federal interest instead of injuring It.

We are all in health and join in love. My Angelica is perfectly happy, and very lively.

I am Sir Your Affectionate

PH. SCHUYLER.

Genet's offensive methods were such that, in 1793, the President issued a proclamation of neutrality, referred to in Schuyler's letter, and which, though distasteful to the Democrats who called it an "edict of royalty," put an end to his activities. He was succeeded by Jean Antoine Fauchet, a less explosive and more rational man, who represented the republic in 1794-95, and by Pierre Augustus Adet in 1795-97. This latter made an issue of the treaty of 1778, and presented a note from the Directory which "declared that the flag of the republic would treat all neutral flags as they permitted themselves to be treated by the English."

It is somewhat remarkable that Washington, with all his experience of Genet, should have received either of the two later representatives of the republic as he did. The papers of the day refer to the presentation by Adet of a "beautiful flag of silk—the tri-color," and print Washington's fraternal and sympathetic response to Adet's speech; but it is to be supposed that diplomacy of this kind was a necessity, though a distasteful concession to a cause which both he and the Federalists generally abominated. The activity of the press at the time was ceaseless, and no occasion was lost to lampoon, either in letter, press, or caricature, the government or its opponents, Jefferson even coming in for his share. He was held up to ridicule in a broadside entitled *Observations on the Dispute between the United States and France* by Harper, which contained an especially stinging caricature. Numerous other broadsides also appeared—one of them bearing the title, "The Guillotine—or a Democratic Dirge," which was published by Thomas Bradford in Philadelphia, in 1796.

It is difficult to conceive the discomfort of those who had daily to witness the low imitation of the doings in Paris during the Reign of Terror. Sympathy with the specious and picturesque doctrines and teachings of the French was evi-

dent in the adoption of all the horrors except the guillotine.
The high and low were all *citizens* or *citizenesses*, and the
marriage notices in the Philadelphia newspapers invariably
gave these appellations to the contracting parties. It was
"Citizen Brown," or "Citizenesse Jones," and this continued
until it became too ridiculous to be tolerated.

Upon the occasion of Genet's dinner, one of the taverns
showed a painting of the gory body of Marie Antoinette, and
the sheets covering it were decorated with the tri-color.

Herman Le Roy was a prosperous merchant of New York,
and a partner of Bayard McEvers.   He, like others who were
sane citizens, suffered from persecution not only at home, but
in France, and on March 29, 1793, he wrote to his friend and
lawyer, Hamilton, suggesting an ingenious method of reimbursement for this seizure of his property by those in control
of France at the time:

DEAR SIR: A part of the Estate which my Father has left
consists in French Funds, while from the distracted situation
that Country is in, neither principal or interest can be procured upon same.   Since the United States are indebted to
France, and they are now actually discharging same, pray
would it not be possible to indemnify us, as American Citizens, out of the debt due them, by producing the Funds at
their Charge, which can be proved have been in the family
for upwards of half a Century?   Some of our Law Characters
here have suggested the possibility of such a scheme being
practicable, which alone induces me to sollicit the favor of
your giving me your kind advice and opinion upon the subject, in doing of which you will render me a particular service, which on all occasions I shall be always happy to repay
with sincere gratitude.

I am ever with Sincere esteem & respects
         Dear Sir   Your humble Servant,
                                        HERMAN LE ROY.
Alex. Hamilton, Esq.

When the Hamiltons went to Philadelphia with the other members of the Cabinet they found themselves in a merry throng of agreeable people who entertained frequently and lavishly. The Binghams and their connections were chief among the non-official set—William Bingham had married the beautiful young daughter of Thomas Willing, and after their return from England built a grand house, and hither flocked the charming society which Chastellux, and other writers, declared to be far more gay and agreeable than that of New York. The President occupied the Morris house, and immediately entered upon the social duties of his office. Levees, drawing-rooms, and dinners were in order, and in their way were elaborate and attractive, although it is stated by one carping critic, a lady who had been abroad, that the rooms were "despicable" and "etiquette was not to be found."[1] At these functions we find the "ladies of the Court," as they were called by Mrs. John Adams, and these include the wives of the Cabinet—the Binghams, Willings, Morrises, the Misses Allen and Chew, "Sally" McKean, daughter of the Chief Justice, and "Dolly" Madison, Mrs. Stewart, Henry Clymer, James Greenleaf, George Clymer; the delightful French gentlemen who were in Philadelphia, and Van Berkle, Lord Wycombe, the eldest son of the Marquis of Lansdowne, who, as Lord Shelburne, did so much to further the treaty of 1783, and the Spanish and Portuguese ministers. Neither Genet, Adet, nor Fauchet seemed to be in good favor, because of their offensive conduct.

Theophilus Bradbury described a men's dinner, given by the President, in 1795, as follows: "In the middle of the room was placed a piece of table furniture about six feet long and two feet broad, rounded at both ends. It was either of wood gilded or polished metal raised only about one inch,

[1] Mrs. John Adams.

with a silver rim round it like that round a tea-board. In the centre was a pedestal of plaster of Paris with images upon it and on the end figures male and female of the same. It was very elegant and used for ornament only. The dishes were placed all around and there was an elegant variety of roast beef, veal, turkey, ducks, fowl, ham, puddings, jellies, oranges, apples, nuts, almonds, figs, raisins and a variety of wines and punch. We took our leave at six, more than an hour after the candles were introduced. No lady but Mrs. Washington dined with us. We were waited on by four or five men servants dressed in livery." [1]

It may, perhaps, have been this very dinner of which the ascetic William Maclay, senator from Pennsylvania, in his "Sketches," said: "Dined with the President of the United States. It was a dinner of dignity. All the Senators present, and the Vice-President. I looked often around the company to find the happiest faces. Wisdom, forgive me if I wrong thee, but I thought folly and happiness were the most nearly allied. The President seemed to bear in his countenance a settled aspect of melancholy. No cheering ray of convivial sunshine broke through the cloudy gloom of settled seriousness. At every interval of eating and drinking he played on the table with a fork and knife like a drumstick."

On May 5, 1789, at the request of General Washington, Hamilton, who was then Secretary of the Treasury, prepared a code of etiquette for the use of the President. This he prefaced: "The public good requires, as a primary object, that the dignity of the office should be supported. Whatever is essential to this ought to be pursued though at the risk of partial or momentary dissatisfaction. But care will be necessary to avoid extensive disgust or discontent. Men's

---

[1] *Pennsylvania Magazine*, VIII, p. 226.

minds are prepared for a pretty high tone in the demeanor of the executive, but I doubt whether for so high a tone as in the abstract might be desirable. The notions of equality are yet, in my opinion, too general and too strong to admit of such a distance being placed between the President and other branches of the government as might even be consistent with a due proportion. The following plan will, I think, steer clear of extremes, and involve no very material inconveniences."

He then suggested that there should be a "levee day once a week for receiving visits," and that the President should remain half an hour. During this time he "may converse cursorily on indifferent subjects." A mode of introduction through particular officers is insisted upon, and no visits are to be returned. Upon the anniversary of important events of the Revolution formal entertainments are to be given, but these are not to exceed in number "twice or four times a year." If the former number, the Fourth of July and the Inauguration Day are to be those selected.

If an entertainment is to be given four times, the day of the treaty alliance with France, and that of the definitive treaty with Britain are to be added to the other. He then went on to recommend the "method practiced in some European Courts," which involves the entertainment of foreign ministers and other distinguished strangers. Suggestions as to the issuance of invitations, the character of the dinnerparties, and the question of rank are fully gone into, and the matter of precedence is discussed, so far as the members of the Senate and the House of Representatives are concerned, and, with few changes, these conventions have been practically observed up to the beginning of the past decade.

Washington appeared to have been very grateful to Hamilton for all this, and in a reply sent the same day he said:

DEAR SIR: I beg you to accept my unfeigned thanks for your friendly communications of this date, and that you will permit me to entreat a continuation of them as occasions may arise.

The manner chosen for doing it is most agreeable to me. It is my wish to act right; if I err, the head and not the heart shall, with *justice*, be chargeable.

With sentiments of sincere esteem and regard,

I am, dear Sir

Your obed^t. Serv't

GEO. WASHINGTON.

The domineering conduct of the French finally became unendurable. This was a natural result of a variety of causes—not the least of and important of which was the supineness and venal trickery of Edmund Randolph who, when Secretary of State in 1794, weakly gave way to the impudent demands of Fauchet and Adet as far as he could, despite the opposition of Hamilton and the outraged members of the Cabinet.

Randolph's undoing occurred in a dramatic manner, and, despite his attempts at vindication he failed completely, and left the public service a defaulter. During his connivance with Fauchet, he wrote a letter to the latter, in which he alleged that for a money consideration certain interests could be turned to the French; that owing to Hamilton's activity in suppressing the Whiskey Rebellion he was hated by every one, and, in fact, it was but a plot upon his part and that of the Federalists to exploit himself and declare for a monarchy, and that France could easily count upon popular support. These and other absurd statements were embodied in the foolish letter. Unfortunately, when on its way to Fauchet, the vessel which carried it was captured by an English vessel, and the original letter was sent to Mr.

Hammond, the Minister from Great Britain, who delivered it to Washington. The situation that followed can well be conceived.

The depredations of the French privateers along our coasts were apparently unceasing, and there was scarcely a harbor into which some prize was not brought every few days by the impudent and high-handed Frenchmen. The Secretary of the Treasury had instructed the Collector of Customs, in a letter written August 4, 1793, to prevent the fitting out of privateers in ports of the United States, and they were required to "visit in the strictest manner, not only all privateers, but all vessels entering or going out of American Ports." Notwithstanding the most energetic measures the law was violated, and the courts of the country were kept busy. After Washington's proclamation *La Cassius, L'Ami de la Point à Petre, L'Amour de la Liberté, La Vengeance, La Montague, Le Vanqueur de la Bastile, La Carmagnole, L'Espérance, Citizen Gênêt,* and *Sans Pareil* were the worst offenders, and Dutch, English, and Spanish vessels were captured and taken to New York, Newport, and Norfolk. Fights were even frequent between English and French vessels within the confines of the same harbor. Callender, in his mischievous way, tried to increase popular sympathy for the French cause, and, to create prejudice against the English, referred to the fact that certain members of American crews were "pressed" by English cruisers in the West Indies.

Adet was constantly stirring up mischief—one of his complaints being that he and Fauchet had been snubbed and discriminated against on ceremonial occasions. "The French Ministers," he said, "have always enjoyed the precedency as to those of England, not only in the United States, but throughout the World, and France, as a republic, has pos-

sessed and will preserve the rank she has had in the Diplomatic Corps under her ancient regime." [1]

Hamilton had already left the Cabinet, but was alive to
all of the interference with our rights as a nation, and felt the
insults very keenly. Adams had sent Gerry, Marshall, and
Pinckney to France to obtain compensation for the depredations on commerce; but they returned after submitting
to indignities forced upon them by Talleyrand and his mistress, who acted as his representative, and they declined to
pay a *douceur* to the latter to gain the favor of her impudent protector.

About this time General Schuyler wrote to Hamilton:

Philip Schuyler to Alexander Hamilton

ALBANY, Monday, *April* 10th, 1797.

MY DEAR SIR: The Governor left this on the day of the
date of your letter enclosing one for him,—which as it is now
useless I do not return to you.

I am so much indisposed that I apprehend I shall not
be able to attend Congress at the opening of the Session,
If at all.

In the present posture of our affairs France seems to have
left us no alternative but a mean and Ignominious submission to her despotic caprice or a dignified resentment. Under
my present feelings I am for the latter, even at the risk of an
open rupture, for I believe it better manfully to meet a war
than to degrade the national character by a pusillanimous
acquiescence to Insult and injury.—Our Commerce will
suffer, but It suffers already as much or nearly as much as
It would were war actually proclaimed.—Our seaports too
will be exposed to insult, they are so already—and we have
no means of protecting them, unless we seek aid where only
It is to be found as well for the protection of our commerce
as of our ports, I mean by an alliance with Britain. It is

[1] Letter to Timothy Pickering.

not now and I believe never will be the interest of that nation to see France domineer over us.—It cannot be the interest of the former ones to attempt to annex their states to her dominions. I believe we are more valuable to her, Mutual good will as independent states than we would be as colonies. —Indeed the attempt by other nations to subjugate us appears to me must most certainly fail.

I hope to have the pleasure of seeing you, My Dear Eliza and the Children here at the close of this or early in next week.

> God bless you all
> Yours most affectionately
> Ph. Schuyler.

When, in 1799, Adams sent Vans Murray, who was generally regarded as a weak and incompetent man, to France to continue negotiations there was much dissatisfaction. General Schuyler again addressed Hamilton, March 20, 1799: "The President's nomination of ambassador to France appears to me a measure replete with weakness and inconsistency, and has in my opinion degraded himself and his country,—and if he was previous to the nomination advised that French agents were to be sent from Hamburgh to sow discord, and create insurrection in this country, his conduct merits epithets much more severe than weakness and inconsistency."

France had, meanwhile, grown tired of the trouble, and possibly hesitated because of the energetic preparation for war that had been already undertaken in the United States. Murray was really sent in response to a hint from Talleyrand, who saw the drift of things, and the advisability of avoiding an expensive war. Hamilton, whose policy had been to proceed in such a way as to make France see the error of her ways and herself make diplomatic overtures, was already planning defensive measures. He, as well as the other Federalists, was naturally incensed when Adams supinely sent some one to actually sue for peace, thus humiliating the nation he represented.

Upon the ignominious return of the original commission, whose unsuccessful efforts only widened the breach that had previously existed, the exasperation of an insulted people passed all bounds and a general popular movement was started to furnish ships and munitions of war. Of this commission, Marshall appears really to have been the only member who saved its face, while Gerry, by his weakness, greatly compromised his fellow members.

Washington, who already in 1798, had been appointed Commander-in-Chief, insisted that Hamilton should, as Major-General, come after him, while Generals Pinckney and Knox were to follow in the order named. President Adams, who even then disliked Hamilton intensely, would not endorse Washington's choice, insisting that Knox should be the second in command. "He refused to admit that Hamilton was the man best fitted for the post, and was so considered by the Public; he plunged himself and his party into a bitter, personal quarrel, and all because he disliked Hamilton and was enraged at the opposition of the Cabinet to himself." [1] The ultimate result was that Washington gave his ultimatum that Hamilton should have the place or he would resign. This was too much for Adams and he reluctantly gave Hamilton the first command.

[1] Lodge's "Alexander Hamilton," p. 207.

Alexander Hamilton to George Washington

NEW YORK, *9th August,* 1798.

MY DEAR SIR: A necessary absence from this City prevented the receipt of your letter of the 9th instant till yesterday.

It is very gratefull to me to discover in each preceding occurrence a new mark of your friendship towards me. Time will evince that it makes the impression it ought on my mind.

The effect which the course of the late military appointment has produced on General Knox though not very unexpected is very painful to me. I have a respectful sense of his pretentions as an officer—and I have a warm personal regard for him—My embarrasment is not inconsiderable between these sentiments, and what I owe to a reasonable conduct on my own part, both in respect to myself and to the public.

It is a fact that a number of the most influencial men in our affairs would think in waving the preference given to me I acted a weak part in a personal vein—And General Knox is much mistaken if he does not believe that this sentiment would emphatically prevail in that Region, to which he supposes his character most interesting, I mean New England.

Yet, My Dear Sir, I can never consent to see you seriously compromitted or embarrassed.—I shall cheerfully place myself in your disposal, and facilitate any arrangement you may think for the general good—It does not however seem necessary to precipitate anything—It may be well to see first what part General Pinckney will act when he arrives.—

The Secretary at War has sent me a copy of General Knox's letter to him on the subject of his appointment.—It does not absolutely decline, but implies the intention to do it, unless a Rule of the late Army giving in cases of promotions on the same day privately according to former relative rank is understood to govern. I have advised a reply, of which a copy is inclosed.—

The Commissions have issued so that no alteration can be now made as between Generals Knox and Pinckney—if there were not the serious difficulties in the way which you seem to have anticipated.—

The Secretary at War has proposed to the President a change of the plan announced in the first instance—which may bring into immediate activity the Inspector General and General Knox.—In this case you may depend upon the best efforts in my power with a peculiar attention to the objects you mention and you shall be carefully and fully advised of whatever it interests you to know.

Col. Walker resides at present in the Western parts of this place. He is occupied in some important agencies for persons abroad which render it doubtful whether he would now accept Military employment. He has been written to and will be proposed for the command of a Regiment—is in many respects very desirable in the capacity you mention. But you are I presume aware of the impracticability of his temper.—With the most respectful and affectionate attachment I have the honor to remain—

My dear General your very
obedt. servt.

ALEXANDER HAMILTON.

The papers sent by you are now returned.

Timothy Pickering, then a member of Adams's Cabinet, later wrote to James A. Hamilton, a letter which has not, until now, been published. It refers to a conversation held with Adams in July, 1798.

Timothy Pickering to James A. Hamilton

SALEM, *June* 14, 1821.

DEAR SIR: I forgot whether I did or did not mention to you and your mother, at my house, what passed between President Adams and me, in July, 1798, in relation to the command of the little army which Congress were then about authorizing to be raised.

A. "Whom shall we appoint Commander-in-Chief?"

P. "Colonel Hamilton."

On a subsequent day:

A. "Whom shall we appoint Commander-in-Chief?"
P. "Colonel Hamilton."

On a third day:

A. "Whom shall we appoint Commander-in-Chief?"
P. "Colonel Hamilton."
A. "O no! It is not his turn by a great deal. I would sooner appoint Gates, or Lincoln, or Morgan."
P. "General Morgan is now here in Congress, a very sick man, with one foot in the grave. He distinguished himself as a brave and good officer in the Revolutionary War; and his present informities may be owing, in part, to the hardships then endured: but his talents would never entitle him to rise beyond the command of a brigade"—"as for Gates, he is now an old woman—and Lincoln is always asleep."

To my answers, in these short dialogues, Mr. Adams made no reply, except once, as just recited. My answers marked with double commas, are *verbatim* as I uttered them. My observations on Morgan, as above stated, exhibit precisely the ideas I expressed; but I cannot undertake to give the very words; tho' I am sure they were substantially as above written.

It was from these occurrences that I first learned Mr. Adams's extreme aversion to or hatred of your father.

General Washington was appointed to the chief command, I wrote him a letter to apprise him of the necessity of his interposition to secure to your father that place in the army to which he was entitled—the second when he was present, and the first in his absence. This first letter on the subject was followed by others of considerable length; when Mr. Adams attempted to derange the order in which Washington had designated the three major Generals—Hamilton—Pinckney—Knox; and to make it Knox—Pinckney—Hamilton. And because this inversion was not effected, Knox refused to serve. I am, Sir, your obed^t Servt

TIMOTHY PICKERING.

General Schuyler, on July 16, 1798, wrote to his daughter:

Many have been the conjectures as to my dear Hamilton's visit to Philadelphia. Some believed it was to assist in *preventing* a bill for the punishment of seditious persons others that he wished to converse with the president previous to accepting a military appointment. Time will develop the cause of his journey. General Washington's acceptance of the command of the army affords great satisfaction to the friends of order, and is doubtless chagrining to those of a contrary complexion. The former wishes Col° Hamilton second in command as that would place them perfectly at ease as to our military operations.

Hamilton now started in upon his work of reorganizing an army. Fifteen years had elapsed since the war of the Revolution, and it was a difficult matter to gather together a serviceable body of men in an emergency. However, he applied himself to his difficult task.

He was favored almost immediately by offers of service from many of his old comrades in arms.

Major Tousard, to whom reference has already been made, applied at once, in the following letter, for a position next to his old chief.

Lewis Tousard to Alexander Hamilton

PHILADELPHIA, *August* 7th, 1798.

DEAR SIR: I was extremely sorry that my being on a public mission at Baltimore prevented my waiting on you when you were lately in Philadelphia, and presenting you, or rather to the whole Army, my most sincere congratulations on the choice the President has made of you for an Inspector general.

Entirely devoted to the carreer which I have followed from my youth, which your kind interest procured me to enter in this country again; I would feel highly gratified to be more intimately attached to you and receive your immediate orders. I have often mentioned it to my friend Gen¹ McPherson¹ and even wrote to him upon the subject. The last Law of the United States presents a favourable opportunity for it by the creation of an Inspector of Artillery which is to be taken from amongst the corps of Artillerists and Engineers. The relations of that office must be entirely dependent on the Inspector General and consequently ought to be the man of your choice.

I will only mention my long services in that branch of the military duty which is contemplated by the Law, to determine your choice and claim your friendship but in case of indecision between myself and another officer. It was a natural consequence of my ambition and application to my duty, that all the principles of Artillery which I have been taught since the year 1765, all the instructions of our schools, all the Duty I have seen in that part should recurr to my mind, more especially since I am diverted of any other kind of business. The several memoirs and observations which I wrote upon the subject, and presented to the Secretary of War to be laid before the Committee of defence; the works I am compleating at Fort Mifflin; the plans I have presented to be executed at Baltimore; those I am ordered to fix at Tammany hill at Rhode Island are the proofs that I have not been thought unworthy the confidence of the Secrʸ of War. He has before him all my commissions without interruption from the year 1765 that I was admitted at the school of Artillery at Strasburgh; Elève of Artillery in 63; 1st Lieut. of Artʸ canonneers in 69; 1st Lᵗ of Bombardiers in 72; Captⁿ of Artʸ in 76; Major of Artʸ in 80; Lᵗ Col. in 1784. I leave aside all the other commissions of commandant in the several parts of St. Domingo, of General in chief of three different armies marching against the Rebels; My intention only is to show that I have been regularly brought up an officer of Artillery and taught all the details of their instruction. How

¹ William McPherson, in 1799, appointed brigadier-general in the Provincial Army. In the Revolution he commanded a company known as "McPherson's Blues." He put down Frie's Rebellion.

far I have profited by, is what I wish you would try, in attaching me intimately to you and presenting me to the office of Inspector of Artillery.   My zeal will redouble by serving under your command and the desire of justifying the interest of an officer whose appointment excited so deserved transports in the whole Army.

I hope you will excuse my troubling you with so long a letter, and attribute it to my desire of being placed in a situation to claim your esteem and glory myself in it as I do in the friendship you constantly honoured me with.

With great respect
I have the honor to be

Dear Sir

Your most humble and very
obed^t Servt

LEWIS TOUSARD.

General North, the intimate friend of Steuben and a brave and experienced officer, wrote later:

William North to Alexander Hamilton

DUANESBURGH, *Nov.* 12, 1799.

You were right, my dear General, in saying that a soldier should have no other wife than the service; and I will add, that he should have neither children nor landed property nor be a guardian, nor a director of a turnpike road, nor plaintiff, nor defendant against a rascal who every day brings fresh actions, for seven years together.   Either of these things forms an impediment sufficient to make one lose sight of the point of view, but when they are combined, they so twist and turn a man head and heels, that it is almost impossible for him to get forward in any line whatever; to suppose that he can in the new French method, look straight forward and keep his alignment, is nonsense.   In truth, was it not for the point of honor, which like a will o' the wisp intices him to the front, and the prick of ambition which goads him in his rear, he never would advance at all.   Fortunately, I have cleared my way of everything but my wife and children, with whom, as it would be unsoldierly to abandon them, I hope to be in New York by the 25th of this month, and when there I shall do whatever Heaven, and your Honour may think best for the service of our dear Country, without further let, or hindrance.

Please to offer my respects to Mrs. Hamilton and believe me to be

Dr. General
Your obd^t H^{ble} Servt
W. North.

As soon as the prospect of war became generally appreciated other applicants for office from New York State presented themselves. Their names were submitted to Hamilton, who went carefully over them considering the fitness of the candidate and making such comments as he saw fit. This is the list:[1]

APPLICANTS	REMARKS
1. Nathaniel Paulding,	Probably a good Lieutenant,
2. John Treat Irving,	Unknown
3. Timothy——[2]	Unworthy,
4. William——	Drunkard,
5. Cornelius C. Van Allen, ✕,	Democratic, but upon the whole eligible as Second Lieutenant,
6. G—— I. S——	Unworthy,
7. E.—— H.——	Drunkard,
8. Michael G. Howdin,	A deserving man, but superannuated,
9. —— Kirkland,	Unknown, probably bad,
10. Gerret Hellenback, 11. Nicholas Hilton	Sons of Mechanics little known but it is believed would make tolerable Ensigns.
12. W—— R——	Unworthy,
13. Prosper Brown, 14. John Cuyler (Surgeon)	Unknown,

[1] This was asked for by James McHenry, who was Secretary of War.
[2] The full names are omitted by the writer for obvious reasons.

APPLICANTS	REMARKS
15. Dowe J. Fonda,	A good Ensign in the late War is worthy of a Captaincy but a majority would be too much now.
16. Volkart Dow,	A good Second Lieutenant,
17. Samuel B. Berry,	The same,
18. E.—— H.—— [1]	Drunkard
19. Christopher Backuet ×	Brother in law of Governor Trumbull probably a good first Lieutenant
20. B.—— H.——	Drunkard (not certain) but probably of slender qualifications— expects a Majority.
21. William Elsworth, ⎫ 22. James Washbos, ⎭	Unknown,
23. John M. Lawrence,	(Son of the Senator) Clever young man good first Lieutenant,
24. Robert Heaton Junior,	Clever fellow probably a good Captain
25. George W. Kirkland,	Probably a good Captain,
26. J.—— K.——	Worthless,
27. Francis Drake, ×,	Probably a good second lieutenant,
28. William Scudder,	Served last War, pretty negative character perhaps a first lieutenancy,
29. W.—— B. V.——	Worthless.
30. Thomas W. Williams ⎫ 31. Benjamin C. Curtis ⎭	Unknown,
32. William Cocks,	Pretty good Lieutenant,
33. A.—— R.——	Gambler,
34. Harmanus P. Schuyler,	A clever fellow—probably a good captain,
35. J.—— S.——	Drunkard,
36. Richard Baldwin, ×	Good ensign
37. Richard L. Walker,	Very violent Jacobin,
38. Fitch Hale,	probably a respectable Captain,
39. John H. Carr,	pretty good second Lieutenant,
40. Samuel Hoffman,	probably a good Second Lieutenant,

[1] E. H. seems to have been passed upon twice.

APPLICANTS	REMARKS
41. Adrian Kiffan,	of good connection and character —probably a good Captain,
42. Joseph C. Cooper, ✕	good Ensign,
43. Andrew Van Wort, ✕	good Ensign,
44. Alexander Macomb Junior	the same,
45. John Starns (surgeon) 46. John White, 47. William B. Peters 48. Rowland Colton, Additional	Unknown
49. Philip Church,	A good Captain of Infantry,
50. William Maurice Thompson ✕	A good Cornet or Second Lieutenant,
51. William Neilson,	A young gentleman of Education and sense probably a very good first Lieutenant,
52. John W. Patterson,	A young gentleman of family worth and spirit—seems not willing to accept less than a company—probably a good Captain,
53. Frederick N. Hudson,	probably a good Lieutenant,
54. Robert LeRoy Livingston,	Good Second Lieutenant,
55. Jacob Manlius 56. Jacob C. Ten Eyck	Good Ensigns,
57. Jeremiah Landon,	probably a good Captain,
58. William W. Wand,	good Lieutenant,
59. Garret De Bow,	Young man tolerably recommended without much education, may make a good Ensign,
60. John Duer,	probably a very good Ensign,
61. Joseph Kellogg ✕	good Lieutenant,
62. David Leavenworth (Junior)	
63. J.—— H.——	cannot be recommended.
64. Philip Cortlandt	well recommended,
65. Frederick A. DeZeng,	formerly in German service—a good Captain of Horse now a citizen and married among us,
66. Warren Delancy, ✕	formerly British Lieutenant would make a good Captain
67. Jacob C. Ten Eyck	good Ensign,

APPLICANTS	REMARKS
68. John Bleeker,	pretty well recommended as Captain,
69. Stephen Haynes,	The same,
70. John Terrill ×	desirous of a Lieutenancy of Artillery in preference well recommended and probably a good Lieutenant,
71. Nicholas R. Kirby ×	good second Lieutenant,
72. William A. Giles, ×	a good ensign
73. John McKinney,	good Surgeons Mate Platt
74. David Jones,	a good first Lieutenant, Talbot,
75. Thomas Tresdale,	recommended as a Capt. by General H. Livingston but otherwise unknown
76. Philip S. Schuyler,	Nephew of General Schuyler a promising young man worthy of a Lieutenancy
77. William Gilliland, ×	very respectfully recommended for a Lieutenancy
78. Andrew White,	a good Captain high up in seniority,
79. Samuel Young,	probably a good first Lieutenant
Thomas Asbeck,	
Henry W. Ludlow,	

General Schuyler shared Hamilton's dislike of Adams, who was undoubtedly regarded by both as a fussy, interfering, and incompetent executive who was likely to meddle with the organization of the Army. The views of the former are embodied in the following letter. The McHenry alluded to was then Secretary of War, and Hamilton's friend. Although Schuyler's criticism is rather severe, it cannot be denied that at times McHenry showed very little push and executive ability.

Philip Schuyler to Alexander Hamilton

ALBANY, *August* 6th, 1798.

I am not surprized My Dear Sir that you found much had not been done in the execution of the important objects, for I have some time since perceived that Mr. McHenry had not a mind sufficiently extensive & energetic to embrace and execute all the objects incident to the war department and I foresee that you will be under the necessity to direct the principle operations of that department, to avoid those embarrassments which must otherwise inevitably result from incompetency in the officers, indeed I see no alternative, for I doubt much if a man of adequate abilities can be found properly to discharge the duties of an office, on which so much depends, even should the present incumbent resign.

Who is to be quarter master General? and who commissary General? If these are not men of business, If they cannot form a system by which to conduct their departments, we shall experience all that confusion and waste which distressed and disgraced us in the revolutionary wars—the President's ideas of the importance of these offices, is probably inadequate, and with the best intentions he may be led to improper appointments, unless advice is interposed by those who are capable of offering it, and to whose recommendations he ought to yield.

The principles and spirit from which have emanated the address to the president, and that attention which has been paid him could not fail of affording him solid satisfaction and yet not without some alloy, persuaded as I was that every disaster which might befall the first executive would be deeply Injurious to my country in the present critical juncture. I dreaded lest the injected Gas should become so highly inflammable as to injure the upper works of the machine, but It is not surprizing that the old Cock should be elated and crow audibly for

The young oak which must prevail at length
has grown with his growth, strengthened with his strength.

A report via Boston prevails, which advises that Guille-man is dismissed, and that we shall have no war—I hope the latter is unfounded for I feel that war with all Its calamities, would be less Injurious to my country, than a peace which might be followed, and probably would be with the rein-troduction of the pernicious and destructive principles which prevail in France.

Harmanus P. Schuyler, a distant relative of mine, believes he could raise a company of foot If he was honored with a commission. He has been long and is now a captain of Militia in the Albany regiments,—is about thirty five years old, discreet and sober, he has been a protege and a pupil of mine in [illegible]. If a commission can be obtained for him It would be pleasing to me, his politician.

God Bless you My Dear Sir, take care of your health, for without It you cannot sustain the labors your devotion en-tails. Let my Children share with you in that tender affec-tion which I feel with so much force.

Ever Your Serv.

PH. SCHUYLER.

Hon. Genl. Hamilton.

The danger of war was finally averted and the excitement of the moment was superseded by that of the political agita-tion of 1800 and the practical overthrow of the Federal party. Hamilton, during the short time he was virtually at the head of the army, had perfected the military system and es-tablished certain means of national defence, which are in existence to-day. He even suggested, and prepared plans for the Military Academy at West Point.

Although all thought of war with France was ended, he recognized and deplored the mischief that had been wrought in the last decade of the eighteenth century, and mourned over what he regarded as a form of early degenera-tion in the young republic when Jefferson and his party came into power. He was sincere and expressed his fears and des-peration in a letter to Gouverneur Morris, which has elsewhere been printed. He believed in the moral decay of the United States—the loss of religious principle in consequence of the teachings of Paine, and those of irresponsible fanatics who had done so much to unsettle the simple faith of the early patriots. The future to him was threatening, and he sought for a means of regeneration.

A great deal of canting speculation has been indulged in by various persons as to Hamilton's religious faith, for it was alleged that he died without belief. Bishop Moore's account of his death, on the contrary, shows that he was a man of earnest, simple faith, quite unemotional in this respect, so far as display was concerned, but his belief was very strong.

He who had all his life made his way by more or less militant methods, or by appeals to reason, by careful and subtle argument, and diplomatic manœuvres, conceived, in his fear for the future welfare of his country, the establishment of a vast religious body to be called "The Christian Constitutional Society." With his keen insight he knew that even the mob could be swayed by such an organization, and that the mental epidemic that was caused by "the poisonous French Doctrines" might be replaced, perhaps, by a movement of a healthy and uplifting kind.

To Bayard he wrote: "Unluckily for us in the competition for the passions of the people, our opponents have great advantages over us; for the plain reason that the vicious are far more active than the good passions; and that, to win the former to our side, we must renounce our principles and our objects, and unite in corrupting public opinion till it becomes fit for nothing but mischief. Yet, unless we can contrive to take hold of, and carry along with us some strong feelings of the mind, we shall in vain calculate upon any substantial or durable results. Whatever plan we may adopt, to be successful, must be founded on the truth of this proposition, and perhaps it is not very easy for us to give it full effect; especially not without some deviations from what, on other occasions, we have maintained to be right.   But, in determining upon the propriety of the deviations, we must consider whether it be possible for us to succeed, without, in some degree employing the weapons which have been employed against us, and whether the actual state and future prospects of things be not such as to justify the reciprocal use of them.   I need not tell you that I do not mean to countenance, the imitation of things intrinsically unworthy, but only of such as may be denominated irregular; such as, in a sound and stable order of things ought not to exist.   Neither are you to infer that any revolutionary result is contemplated. In my opinion, the present constitution is the standard to which we are to cling.   Under its banners *bona fide* must we combat our political foes, rejecting all changes but through the channel itself provided for amendments.   By these general views of the subject have my reflections been guided. I now offer you the outline of the plan they have suggested. Let an association be formed to be denominated 'The Christian Constitutional Society,' its object to be 1st: The support of the Christian religion.   2d: The support of the United States."   He then unfolded a scheme which advocated the diffusion of information.   "The use of all lawful means in concert to promote the election of fit men," and various means for the education of public opinion.

To him the growing influence of the "Jacobins" and their party meant only ruin and disaster, and though he, perhaps, did not fully share Horace Binney's later expressed sentiment that he "believed Jefferson was the full incarnation of Satan," he had good reason to dread the influence of a man and his supporters who had done so much to weaken the respect for the Constitution of the United States.

CHAPTER XI

BUILDING A HOME

THE same yearning for rest in the country which seems to have been felt by so many men at the termination of a busy public career, came to Hamilton as well, and a few years before his death he wrote: "To men who have been so much harassed in the base world as myself, it is natural to look forward to complete retirement, in the circle of life as a perfect desideratum. This desire I have felt in the strongest manner, and to prepare for it has latterly been a favorite object. I thought I might not only expect to accomplish the object, but might reasonably aim at it and pursue the preparatory measures."

It is true that these sentiments were directly provoked by his political disappointments, as well as a realization that he must make provision for his old age, but it may be assumed that the time had come for the enjoyment of the comforts of a house of his own in the quiet country. Possibly his familiarity with Virgil's bucolics, and especially the First Eclogue, had filled his mind with sylvan longings; or, again, there may have been the influence of his early life, spent in a clime full of beauty and restfulness, that prompted him to look about for a retreat which was far enough removed from the bustle and affairs of men to enable him to find relaxation in the happiness of seclusion. It is somewhat difficult to-day to realize that the isolated place he then selected, which was eight miles from the Bowling Green, is now a somewhat crowded part of a great city which extends several miles further north. At that time stage-coaches ran but three days in the week to a point which now corresponds with 42d Street and Broadway, and is a congested thoroughfare, although through service to Albany then enabled one to descend at Hamilton's gate. He had, during the summer and fall of 1798, leased and occupied, in company with his brother-in-law, John B. Church, a country house in the neighborhood of what was afterward his own estate.

Although his professional income at that period was comparatively large, his earnings being twelve thousand dollars annually, he was obliged, before he got through building, to make financial arrangements which would enable him to meet the demands of masons and builders, and early in 1804 his warm friend and client, Louis Le Guen, loaned him five thousand dollars on bond and mortgage. After some search he found a tract of land to his liking which, to-day, is that roughly bounded by St. Nicholas and Tenth Avenues, and which extends from 141st to 145th Streets, but formerly was much larger in extent, the western limit being the Hudson River. The Albany or Bloomingdale Road which passed diagonally through it has, of course, now entirely disappeared, but undoubtedly divided the part upon which the house stood from the farm on the easterly side. General Ebenezer Stevens, who was then a prosperous merchant, had, at the time, a country place in the vicinity, and to him Hamilton wrote, making inquiry as to available property:

Alexander Hamilton to Ebenezer Stevens

25th of October, 1799.

If the owner of the ground adjoining you will take Eight Hundred pounds (£800) for sixteen acres including a parcel of the woodland, and lying on the water the whole breadth, you will oblige me by concluding the bargain with him, and I will pay the money as soon as a good title shall appear.   If he will not sell a part at this rate, I request you to ascertain whether he will take Thirty pounds an acre for the whole tract and let me know.

If I like it, after another view of the premises, I shall probably take the whole at this price.   But I can only pay one half down, a quarter in six months and the remaining quarter in a twelve month.   He shall be satisfied on the score of security if he desires.

Yrs with regard,
A. Hamilton.

The building itself which is now in existence, although moved from its original position, stood for a long time at the corner of 142d Street and Tenth Avenue, but within recent years has been moved so that it adjoins St. Luke's Episcopal Church, and is used as a school.   It is little the worse for age, despite all it has gone through, and was never an architectural triumph, although it is a type of the comfortable country house of the period.   It is a square structure two stories high, and had verandas on both the north and south sides as it originally stood.   The main entrance was on the west.   Near the southwest corner was a group of thirteen gum trees, planted in a circle by Hamilton, one for each of the original States, but they were so closely set that they never attained a great size, and all eventually languished and died, their destruction being hastened by the depredations of the relic hunters.

The house was designed by John McComb, one of the leading architects and builders of the time, and was constructed by Ezra Weeks,[1] who superseded a builder named Putnam.   McComb's excellent work which remains to-day

[1] See p. 185.

is the old City Hall, which shows the artistic influence of Sir Christopher Wren, and, in some ways, is one of the most charming old buildings in the country.[1] It is quite probable that Hamilton himself worked at the plans, and was frequently in consultation with General Schuyler, who manifested his interest by furnishing timber from his own estate at Saratoga.   In this connection he writes to his son-in-law:

Philip Schuyler to Alexander Hamilton

ALBANY, Monday, *August* 25th, 1800.

MY DEAR SIR: Your favor of the 13th instant with the plan of your intended house was delivered me on Thursday last, that of the 18th by the mail I received yesterday. I have delivered Mr. Putnam the builder, the plan, and a paper of which you have a copy on the other side, and expect his answer tomorrow. If the house is boarded on the outside, and then clap boards put on, and filled in the inside with brick, I am persuaded no water will pass to the brick. If the clapboards are well painted, and filling in with brick will be little if any more expensive than lath and plaister, the former will prevent the nuisance occasioned by rats and mice, to which you will be eternally exposed if lath and plaister is made use of instead of brick.

The partitions between the apartments in the interior of the house, if made of joice and then lathed and plaistered also have vacancies as receptacles for rats and mice. It is a little but not much more expensive to have the partitions of plank of 2 or 2½ inches thick set vertically from floor to ceiling and joined together, but not planed, on these planks the lathes and plaister are to be put, and thus a solid partition is formed. In the bill of scantling which you have sent me I do not find any timbers for the gutters, perhaps this has been ommitted.

Should Mr. Putnam refuse to contract unless for the whole

---

[1] The design was that of Major L'Enfant.

house in all its parts, except the masonry, I will receive his proposals on a statement which I shall make and transmit it to you without delay, or should he be extravagant in his demand, I shall as soon as Cornelia is brought to bed, go up and contract for the timber and purchase the boards and planks, and if possible I will cause the boards and planks to be put into water for two months and then piled up with decks between them that they may be seasoned before they are worked up.

It will save very considerable expense if the clap boards and boards for the floors were sawed to the proper breadth and thickness at the sawmills, I therefore wish you to send me how many of each Mr. —— thinks will be wanted, their breadth and thickness. I rejoice, my dear Son, that my Philip[1] has acquitted himself so well, and hope that his future progress may correspond with your and my wishes.

All here unite in love to you, my Eliza and the children. I am my dear Sir

Ever most affectionately yours,

PH. SCHUYLER.

Honble M. Gen. Hamilton.

On August 22d, 1802, he wrote to Mrs. Hamilton:

I am anxious to visit you and to participate in the pleasure of your country retreat which I am informed is fast reaching perfection. Embrace my dear Hamilton and the children. He and they participate with you in your mother's and my warmest affections. May health and happiness be the portion of all. God bless you my dearly beloved child.

I am ever, most tenderly and affectionately, yours,

PH. SCHUYLER.

From Albany he again wrote to her on April 23, 1803:

DEAR CHILD: This morning Genr. Ten Broeck informed me that your horses which went from hence were drowned,

---

[1] Alexander Hamilton's eldest son, who was then at Columbia College.

and that you had lost paint, oil, &c to a considerable amount, —Supposing this account to have been truly stated to the General, I send you by Toney my waggon horses of which I make you present.

I intended to have your house painted If you cannot re- cover the paint, purchase no more as I will have the house painted.

When an opportunity offers send my saddle and bridle which Toney will leave.—

Your Sister unites with me in love to you and Eliza.

I am Dr child

Your affectionate parent

PH. SCHUYLER.

As an illustration of how dwelling-houses were built in New York at the time, the mason's specifications may be produced.

Proposal for finishing General Hamilton's Country House——Viz.

To build two Stacks of Chimneys to contain eight fire-places, ex- clusive of those in Cellar Story.

To fill in with brick all the outside walls of the 1st and 2nd stories, also all the interior walls that Separate the two Octagon Rooms— and the two rooms over them—from the Hall and other Rooms in both Stories.

To lath and plaster the side walls of 1st and 2nd stories with two coats & set in white.

To plaster the interior walls which separate the Octagon Rooms in both Stories, to be finished white, or as General Hamilton may chose.

To lath and plaster all the other partitions in both Stories.

To lath and plaster the Ceiling of the Cellar Story throughout.

To plaster the Side walls of Kitchen, Drawing Room, Hall & passage, & to point & whitewash the Stone & brick walls of the other part of Cellar Story. To Point the outside walls of Cellar Story and to fill in under the Sills.

To lay both Kitchen hearths with brick placed edge ways.

To put a Strong Iron back in the Kitchen fire-place five feet long by 2 ½ 9″ high.

To put another Iron back in the Drawing Room 3′-6″ by 2′-9″.

To place two Iron Cranes in the Kitchen fire Place—& an Iron door for the oven mouth.

The Rooms, Hall, and Passage of the first Story to have neat Stocco Cornices—Those of Octagon Rooms of Best Kind (but not inriched).

To put up the two setts of Italian Marble in the Octagon Rooms, such as General Hamilton may chose—and Six setts of Stone Chimney pieces for the other Rooms.

The Four fireplaces in the two Octagon rooms & the two rooms over them, to have Iron Backs and jambs, and four fire places to have backs only.

To lay the foundations for eight piers for the Piazza.

Mr. McComb to find at his own expense all the Material requisite for the afore described work and execute it in a good & workmenlike manner for one thousand Eight Hundred & Seventy five Dollars.

General Hamilton to have all the Materials carted and to have all the Carpenters' work done at his expense—

General Hamilton is to find the workmen their board or to allow ———— shillings per day for each days work in lieu thereof.

New York 22nd June 1801.

JOHN McCOMB Jun

To build the Stew holes and a wall for the sink.

The whole to be completed by————?

The chimneys, which were very large, were a source of much anxiety to Hamilton and his advisers. At that time Count Rumford [1] was an authority on everything scientific in this country, and his experiments on the domestic application of artificial light and heat attracted almost as much attention as did the inventions of Benjamin Franklin, whose stoves were coming into general use. Finally the matter

---

[1] Benjamin Thompson was born in Woburn, Mass., and was really a patriot. He was not regarded with favor, however, by his townsmen, who did not approve of his conservatism, which they mistook for disloyalty, and he was obliged to flee, and later actually entered the British service. He afterward went to Bavaria, and after very distinguished public service was given the title of the Count Rumford. He always devoted himself to science, and rendered great service to mankind by his discoveries, and their application to everyday life. He ultimately returned to America, and when he died, left bequests both to Harvard University and the Royal Society of England.

was settled, and the comfort of the inmates of the house assured by the adoption of a proper chimney.

Plan of a Chimney on Rumford's principles.

The whole width in opening in front of the fire place 39 inches of which thirteen to from back side at an Angle of about 135 Degrees and thirteen the back.

From these dimensions the depth results—

The height from the floor to the throat about three feet and the throat about four inches wide—and central to the base or perpendicular over the fire.

Thus

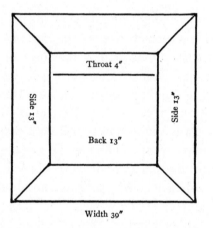

In this connection it is interesting to read of Burr's later opinion of Rumford's invention, and his own attempts to keep warm in a foreign city. Aaron Burr in his diary,[1] in describing his room in Paris which he occupied in 1810, said:

"The fireplace (more like an oven) is three feet deep, and five feet wide, and of course smokes perpetually. Having endured this now more than two months, and finding my eyes worse for it, sent today for one of those scientific men

[1] "The Private Journal of Aaron Burr" (Bixby Publication).   Vol. II, p. 77.

called *fumistes*. Showed him the evil and proposed a remedy.
'*Mais sur quelles principes mons. sont fondés vos idees.*' In
vain did I take on myself the hazard of the result. '*Non
c'est decarter de tous les principes,*'[1] and so we parted. Nineteen out of twenty of the chimnies of Paris (of France I
might say) smoke always, and the other twentieth occasionally. In vain have Franklin and Rumford shown by fact
and experiment how chimnies should be built. Their obstinacy and stupidity passes belief. And so I sit envellopped
in smoke, or as you have it, sit like the gods in the
clouds."

Hamilton kept minute accounts of the cost of labor and
material, and it is curious to note the rate of wages paid one
hundred years ago, long before the days of labor unions.
We find that one Thomas Costigan, who had, apparently,
been engaged in building the house, and afterward became
a man-of-all-work, received, for services rendered for three
and one-half years, the sum of four hundred and twenty-four
dollars and fifty cents. Thomas Dunnevan was another
workman upon the place, and in an entry in the expense-
book it is stated that he was paid one hundred and fifty-two
dollars and eighteen cents by wages, from the 8th of March,
1802, to the 4th of August, 1803, "when the poor worthy
fellow was drowned. Sixteen months and twenty-seven days
at 9d." This bill was receipted by Edward Kerhal, who
was next of kin.

The entire cost of building the house was £1,550, and this
sum was paid to Ezra Weeks.

Hamilton always had a taste for gardening and farming,
and one of his friends who did much to encourage him was

---

[1] Throughout the diary Burr indulges in abbreviations, and takes extraordinary
liberties with the various languages he quotes. It was his evident aim to be
mysterious.

Dr. David Hosack, a distinguished and fashionable physician of the time. In 1796 Dr. Hosack became a partner of Dr. Samuel Bard, and these two were Hamilton's physicians and friends. Later, upon the death of his son Philip, Bard wrote a most tender letter of sympathy to his dear friend Hamilton from his country house in Hyde Park, where he passed the remainder of his days. Dr. Hosack, whose education had been undertaken in part in Europe, had become deeply interested in botany. This led, on his return, to his appointment as professor of botany and afterward materia medica in Columbia College. For a time he became connected with the Rutgers Medical College, having associated himself with Dr. Valentine Mott and Dr. Francis, but later returned to the old college. In 1798 he formed the idea of providing a large botanical garden which could be used in connection with his teaching, and applied to Columbia College for funds,[1] but without success. He then bought four plots of the so-called "common land" on the middle road (now Fifth Avenue), between 47th and 51st Streets, extending to a point a hundred feet west of Sixth Avenue. This was in 1801, and in 1804 he paid for the property.

Upon this space he laid out a diversified garden, afterward erecting glass-houses and raising a great variety of tropical and sub-tropical plants. It was his idea as well to raise vegetables for the supply of his fellow townsmen. Hamilton, who was fond of horticulture, shared Hosack's enthusiasm, and as he daily drove from his own place several miles north, was in the habit of stopping to compare notes with his enthusiastic family doctor, who donated cuttings and bulbs.

[1] See an article by Adrian Brown in the "Bulletin" of the New York Botanical Society, vol. V, No. 18, February 8, 1909.

Available correspondence conveys an idea of the great pleasure the cultivation of his place gave him.

He wrote to his old comrade-in-arms, General Pinckney of South Carolina, from the Grange:[1]

Alexander Hamilton to Charles Cotesworth Pinckney

December 20, 1802.

"MY DEAR SIR: A garden, you know, is a very usual refuge of a disappointed politician. Accordingly I have purchased a few acres about nine miles from town, have built a house, and am cultivating a garden. The melons in your country are very fine. Will you have the goodness to send me some seed, both of the water and musk melons? My daughter[2] adds another request, which is for three or four of your paroquets. She is very fond of birds. If there be anything in this quarter, the sending of which can give you pleasure, you have only to name them. As farmers, a new source of sympathy has arisen between us, and I am pleased with everything in which our likings and tastes can be approximated. Amidst the triumphant reign of democracy, do you retain sufficient interest in public affairs to feel any curiosity about what is going on? In my opinion, the follies and vices of the administration have as yet made no material impression as to their disadvantages. . . .

Adieu, my dear Sir
Ever Yours,
Alexander Hamilton

A few months later Pinckney replied:[3]

Charles Cotesworth Pinckney to Alexander Hamilton

CHARLESTON, *March* 6th, 1803.

MY DEAR SIR: I wrote you a few lines yesterday and sent you some watermelon seeds and musk-melon seeds by the brig *Charleston Packet* which sails this morning. I for-

---

[1] "Hamilton's Works" (J. C. H.), vol. VI, p. 551.   [2] Angelica.
[3] "Hamilton's Works" (J. C. H.), vol. VI, p. 554.

merly sent some to Mrs. Washington, at Mount Vernon, but she told me they did not answer so well as some she got in the neighborhood; perhaps had she planted the seeds from the melons which were produced from the Carolina seed the subsequent year, they would have adapted themselves to the climate and produced good fruit. It was by this means we obtained our fine cotton, which has been of such advantage to our State. The first year it produced but three or four pods; by planting the seed of these pods the second year, they produced thirty; and by following the same method, the third year they were thoroughly naturalized, and bore from one hundred and fifty to two hundred pods.

I will also send you by the *Industry* a few seeds of the salvia cocinea, or scarlet sage, which I believe you have not with you, and of the erytherina herbacea, or coral shrub; also a few seeds of the Indian creeper, and some of a beautiful purple convolvulus.

I will endeavor to obtain some paroquets for Miss Hamilton. I have not seen any for some years; ours are the large kind, by no means equal in beauty to the small African species. . . .

Hamilton left, after his death, certain memoranda regarding the arrangement of his garden, which show that he was more than an amateur. Whether he had availed himself of Batty Langley's "New Principles of Gardening,"[1] which was Washington's horticulture guide and a well-known authority in those days, is not known; yet he seems to have had a practical knowledge of what was needed, and a few of the notes left by him may be appended to show what is meant.

1. Transplant fruit trees from the other side of the stable.
2. Fences repaired. (Worn away) repaired behind stable. The cross fence at the foot of the hill? Potatoes Bradhursts?

[1] "New Principles of Gardening, or the Layout and Planting of Pastures, Groves, Wildernesses, Labyrinths, Avenues, Parks, etc., after a More Grand and Rural Manner than has Been Done Before. Illuminated with a Variety of Grand Designs," by Batty Langley. London, 1728.

Ground may be removed and used for this purpose. Cows no longer to be permitted to range.

3. The sod and earth which were removed in making the walks *where it is good* may be thrown upon the grounds in front of the House, and a few waggon loads of the compost.

4. A *Ditch* to be dug along the fruit garden and grove about four feet wide, and the earth taken and thrown upon the *sand hill* in the rear.

After referring to the arrangement of flower beds and the laying out of a vegetable garden he proceeded:

2. The Gardener, after marking these out and making a beginning by way of example, will apply himself to the planting of Raspberries in the orchard. He will go to Mr. Delafield for a supply of the English sort and if not sufficient will add from our own and some to be got from our neighbors.

3. If it can be done in time I should be glad if space could be prepared in the *center* of the flower garden for planting a few tulips, lilies, hyacinths, and [missing]. The space should be a circle of which the diameter is Eighteen feet: and there should be nine of each sort of flowers; but the gardener will do well to consult as to the season.

They may be arranged thus: Wild roses around the outside of the flower garden with laurel at foot.

If practicable in time I should be glad some laurel should be planted along the edge of the shrubbery and round the clump of trees near the house; also sweet briars and [illegible]

A few dogwood trees not large, scattered along the margin of the grove would be very pleasant, but the fruit trees there must be first removed and advanced in front.

These labours, however, must not interfere with the hot bed.

Life at the Grange was undoubtedly a merry one, for within its hospitable walls were gathered many of those clever people with whom Hamilton had so much to do during his many years of busy, official life. Gouverneur Morris often came from Morrisania, while Rufus King drove over from Jamaica in Long Island to discuss politics or gossip

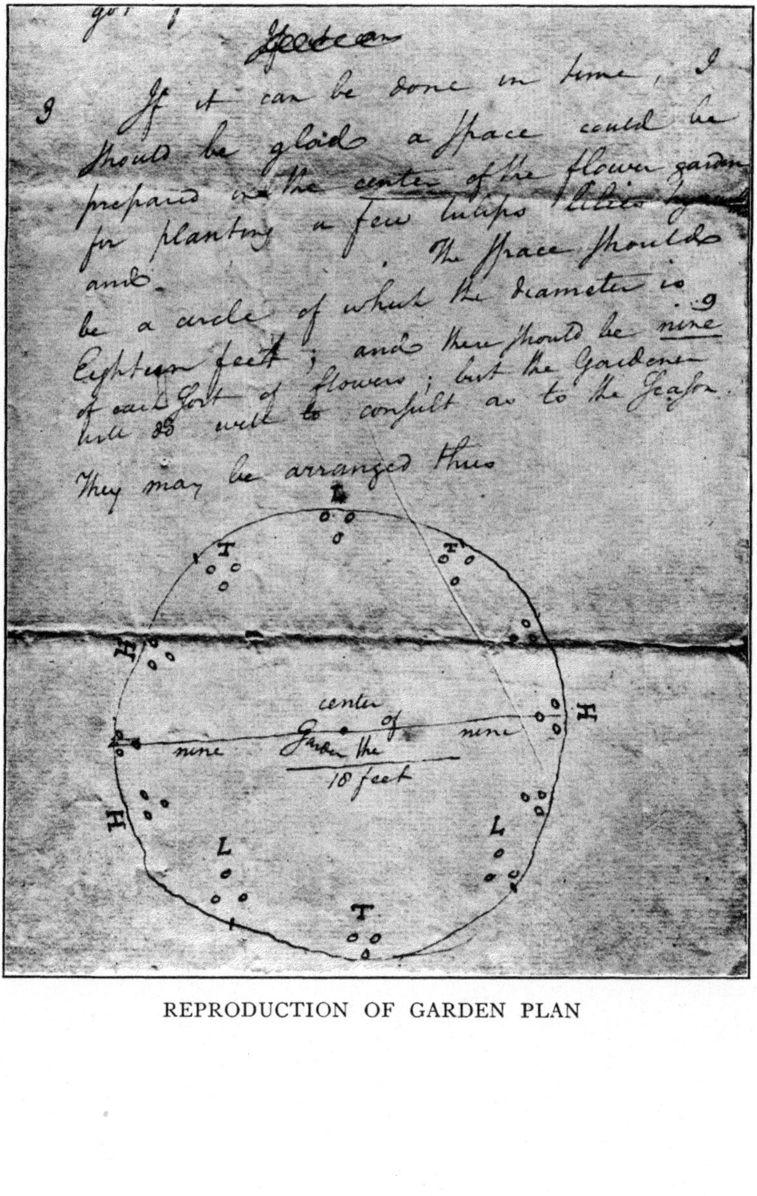

REPRODUCTION OF GARDEN PLAN

with the former Secretary. The Schuylers, too, came frequently, and sent good things from the Albany homestead, and in many of the General's letters are references to prodigious gifts of vegetables and fruit, which were consigned to his daughter by way of the river sloops, while in the winter it was rare for a beef to be slaughtered without a quarter finding its way to the Grange.

The Hamilton family was often invited to Albany, and alluring accounts of what awaited them were drawn by the devoted father-in-law. General Schuyler wrote from Wood Creek, where he was journeying July 15, 1802: "We have excellent mutton here, and as fine and fat salmon as ever were dished and I believe as cheap as Cod at the New York market. I gave half a dollar for a very fine one weighing a little more than nineteen pounds. They are taken four miles from here."

In Hamilton's periods of relaxation he was to be seen wandering through the woods of Harlem with a single-barrelled fowling-piece, on the lookout for woodcock or other game, or he found his way to the wooded shores of his estate in search of an occasional striped bass in the clear water of the North River. Before his death he gave this gun to Trumbull, the artist, and it ultimately came into the writer's possession. On the stock are roughly carved the letters "A. Hamilton, N. Y.," and this was evidently his own work. When occasions were favorable, the worries of professional work, and possibly the importunities of builders, were escaped by a visit to the theatre, Hamilton and his wife going to the city, where they were the guests of many of their old friends, and they still kept a house in Partition Street. About this time the New or Park Theatre was under the management of Hallam, or Hodgkinson, or Cooper. According to the contemporary press it appeared that the most generous and varied kinds of entertainment were there offered. Among the plays produced we find the "Tragedy of Alexander the Great with a Grand Heroic Spectacle of the Siege of Oxydrace," "The Positive Man," the "Duenna," "The Lyar," "The Manager in Distress," "Count Benyowski, or the Conspiracy of Kamskatka," and upon one occasion, "Paul & Virginia, the Plot from M. de St. Pierre's very popular novel of the same with new scenery and machinery never before exhibited,— Dance by the Negroes, the Whole to Conclude with the representation of a Tornado in which Virginia is shipwrecked, who is seen struggling in the Water while the Ship is Burnt by Lightning."

In the New York *Evening Post* of March 8, 1802, there is an advertisement headed "The Theatrical Curiosity." "The Two Samuels which arrived a few days since from Senegal we understand will be introduced into the Triumphal Procession on Monday Evening at *Mr. Cooper's Benefit*, being it is presumed their first appearance on any stage."

Hamilton also attended the meetings of the Philharmonic Society, which were held at Snow's Hotel at 69 Broadway.

General Schuyler's visits to the Grange, during the latter part of his life, became less and less frequent because of his ill health. Referring to the illness of his little grandson, one of Hamilton's boys, he wrote from Albany, December 20, 1802: "I hope he is now perfectly recovered, and that I shall embrace him here, as Mr. Rensselaer says you intend to accompany the General in the next month when he must be here. This will afford us additional pleasure, and the journey be of service to you, and if the wound in my thigh and the Gout which has seized on one of my feet will permit, we will accompany you to the Grange, of whose beauties the Patroon speaks with rapture."

In this letter he refers to his grandson, Philip, his name-sake, and writes: "It affords me great pleasure to be advised that he is attentive to his studies. I hope that he may make eligible Progress and become a man of Virtue." In April, 1804, a few months before Hamilton's death, he received a visit from Chancellor Kent who, in a letter to his wife, described his stay at the Grange:

"I went out with General Hamilton on Saturday, the 21st, and stayed till Sunday evening. There was a furious and dreadful storm on Saturday night. It blew almost a hurricane. His house stands high, and was much exposed, and I am certain that in the second story, where I slept, it rocked like a cradle. He never appeared before so friendly and amiable. I was alone, and he treated me with a minute attention that I did not suppose he knew how to bestow. His manners were also very delicate and chaste. His daughter,[1] who is nineteen years old, has a very uncommon simplicity and modesty of deportment, and he appeared in his domestic state the plain, modest, and affectionate father and husband."[2]

Hamilton's professional engagements about this time took him often to Albany, and he either went by sloop or mail stage, the latter leaving New York every morning at six and reaching Albany the third day after. The passengers, meanwhile, during the intervening nights lodged at Peekskill or Rhinebeck. This line was managed by William Vandervoort, and the stages departed from the corner of Cortlandt and Greenwich Streets. The proprietors of the stage line were Potter, Hyatt & Company. The fare charged was eight dollars for the entire journey, or six-pence a mile for way passengers. On these journeys Hamilton wrote frequently to his wife, and he was undoubtedly kept informed

[1] Angelica.
[2] *Op. cit., p.* 143.

NEW-YORK AND ALBANY
MAIL STAGE,
LEAVES New-York every morning, at 6
o'clock, lodges at Peekskill and Rhinebeck,
and arrives in Albany on the third day. Fare of
each passenger through eight dollars, and 6d per
mile for way passengers. For Seats apply to *William
Vandervoort*, No.48, corner of Courtland and Greenwich streets, New-York, and of *T. Witmore*, Albany.
February 13 tf   POTTER, HYATT & Co.

of all that went on during his absence.   He certainly found
time to direct those in charge of the improvements at home.

Alexander Hamilton to Elizabeth Hamilton

CLAVERACK, *Oct.* 14, 1803.

MY DEAR ELIZA: I arrived here this day, in about as good
health as I left home though somewhat fatigued—

There are some things necessary to be done which I omitted
mentioning to you.   I wish the Carpenter to make and insert
two Chimnies for ventilating the Ice-House, each about two
feet square & four feet long half above and half below the
ground to have a cap on the top sloping downwards so that
the rain may not easily enter—The aperture for letting in
and out the air to be about a foot and a half square in the
side immediately below the cap (see *figure* on the other side.[1])

Let a separate compost bed be formed near the present one,
to consist of 3 barrels full of the *clay* which I bought, 6
barrels of *black moulds* 2 waggon loads of the best clay on the
Hill opposite the *Quakers plain* this side of Mr. Verplanks

[1] It is regretted that in the original letter, which is in the Ford Collection in the
New York Public Library (Lenox), the plan has been cut out at some time and
therefore cannot be produced.

(the Gardener must go for it himself) and one waggon load of pure cowdung—Let these be well and repeatedly mixed and pounded together to be made up of hereafter for the Vines.

I hope the apple trees will have been planted so as to profit by this moderate and wet weather. If not done, let *Tough* be reminded that a temporary fence is to be put up along the declivity of the Hill from the King's bridge road to the opposite wood so as to prevent the cattle injuring the young trees—the fence near the entrance to the Helicon Spring ought for the same reason to be attended to—The materials of the fence taken down in making the Kitchen Garden & some rubbish, which may be picked up will answer—

Remember that the piazzas are also to be caulked & that additional accommodations for the pidgeons are to be made—

You see I do not forget the Grange—No that I do not; nor any one that inhabits it. Accept yourself my tenderest affection—Give my love to your Children & remember me to Cornelia.

Adieu my darling

A. H.

Mrs. H.

To Mrs. Elizabeth Hamilton,
    No. 58
        Partition Street.

PEEKSKILL, October 16.
Saturday.

I have just arrived here and shall stay till tomorrow.

It has always appeared to me that the ground on which our orchard stands is much too moist. To cure this, a ditch round it would be useful, perhaps with a sunken fence as a guard. But this last may be considered at a future time.

If you can obtain one or two more laborers, it may be advisable to cut a ditch round the orchard—three feet deep by three feet wide at the bottom. The clay that comes out of the ditch will be useful to give firmness to our roads and may be used for this purpose.

Yet you will consider this merely as a suggestion and do as you think best after you shall have ascertained whether you can procure any better materials for the purpose.   But remember that mere *sand* and stones will not answer.

Very affectionately my beloved,

Yrs, A. H.

Mrs. Elizabeth Hamilton
> at Haerlem,
>> New York.

I was extremely disappointed, my dear Eliza, that the Monday's post did not bring me a letter from you.   You used to keep your promises better.   And you know that I should be anxious of your health.   If the succeeding post does not rectify the omission of the former, I shall be dissatisfied and pained.

Adieu my beloved, and be assured that I shall not lose a moment to return to you.

Yours tenderly,

A. H.

Saturday 2nd of October.

Mrs. Elizabeth Hamilton
> at Haerlem
>> New York.

Sunday Morning.

I was much relieved, my dear Eliza, by the receipt yesterday morning of your letter of Monday last.   How it came to be so long delayed I am unable to conjecture.   But the delay gave much uneasiness in consequence of the imperfect state of health in which I had left you.   I thank God you were better—for indeed, my Eliza, you are very essential to me. Your virtues more and more endear you to me and experience more and more convinces me that true happiness is only to be found in the bosom of ones own family.

I am in hopes, that I may be able to leave this place sooner than I had counted upon, say on Friday or Saturday.   But I may be disappointed and may be detained till Sunday morning.   This at all events I trust will bring me home on Tuesday following.   The stage is three days in performing the journey.

I am anxious to hear from Philip. Naughty young man! But you must permit nothing to trouble you and regain your precious health.

Adieu my beloved.

A. H.

The returns from his farm seem to have been trivial; a few baskets of strawberries, cabbages, and asparagus were sold in 1802, the returns from the same being £7.10.2. And the experience of the amateur farmer then seems to have differed but little from that of most of us to-day.

After the sad turn of events which followed the duel, we find the widow loath to leave the happy home, but struggling on to keep her little family together and clinging as long as possible, to the place so sanctified by tender memories. Brave to a degree and unusually masterful, she managed the estate and directed the workmen. Although the elder boys, Alexander, James, and John, were, respectively, eighteen, sixteen, and twelve years, they could be of little help to her, while all the others, except Angelica, were of tender age. Her devoted sister, Angelica Church, did her utmost to persuade her to give up the country place and come to New York, which she eventually did, but meanwhile she made a brave fight. In a letter written to her daughter in the early years of her bereavement, she said: "I rode up in the carriage that was formerly mine, and you know how very easy it was. The boat did not arrive until late in the evening. I am now in the full tide of occupation, four men to attend to, fine morning with the place looking lovely. A carriage dearest and yourself, with the house in order, would be delightful to have."

When staying later in Warren Street she received a letter from her sister, who wrote: "Your brother deems it the most prudent that you remain where you are, as it is utterly impossible for you to be at the Grange without horses, and their expense will pay your house rent. He thinks the Grange might be let. If you please early on Saturday morning—say at seven o'clock—I will be ready to attend you to the Grange."

It was soon after this that her necessities forced her to dispose of the home she and Hamilton had planned and built together, which was to be to their children what the Schuyler home had been to them.

Despite the generous efforts of Hamilton's friends, and even of General Schuyler himself, who died a few months after his son-in-law, no such comparative luxury was possible as that which had hitherto been enjoyed. When not visiting the Albany relations, Mrs. Hamilton made New York her home, where she brought up her children as best she could— the two elder boys receiving help from friends and acquiring the father's profession.

CHAPTER XII

HAMILTON AND BURR

HAMILTON's prejudice against duelling was sincere, and the result of his growing conviction, which he reluctantly disregarded under the pressure of the exigencies of the time and the feeling that his prestige, as the head of a great though demoralized party, would suffer by his refusal to meet his adversary. Nearly two years before he had told his son Philip to fire his first shot in the air when he was called upon to meet Eacker at Paulus Hook, and his several communications leave no doubt as to his extreme reluctance to run the risk of taking the life of another. In fact, during the years 1798 and 1799 he had, among other reforms, advocated anti-duelling laws. In earlier years the duel was so much a matter of course, and so necessary an institution of social life, that we find he not only appeared as a second, but gave advice to others who contemplated this method of vindicating their honor. As is known, he was the second of the younger Laurens, when he met General Charles Lee on June 28, 1778, after the battle of Monmouth, when the latter had spoken disrespectfully of Washington. Hamilton's attitude upon this occasion was extremely fair and sensible, and he did his best to adjust matters without a resort to extreme consequences. Major Edwards attended Lee. When six paces apart the principals fired simultaneously, and Lee received a slight wound. When he proposed a second exchange of shots, and Laurens agreed, Hamilton said that, "unless the General was influenced by motives of personal enmity, he did not think the affair ought to be pursued any further; but as General Lee seemed to persist in desiring it, he was too tender of his friend's honor to persist in opposing it. It was then that Major Edwards interfered, and explanations were made that were satisfactory." A minute narrative of the entire proceedings, concluding with the statement that, "upon the whole, we think it a piece of justice to the two gentlemen to declare that after they met their conduct was strongly marked with all the politeness, generosity, coolness and firmness, that ought to characterize a transaction of this nature," was drawn up by Hamilton and agreed to by Edwards.[1]

In 1779 Hamilton, when a lieutenant-colonel, was slandered by a Reverend Doctor William Gordon,[2] of Jamaica Plain, Massachusetts, who spread a story to the effect that Hamilton, at a "public coffee house," had abused Congress. This was at a time when the latter was withholding the pay of the army, and when there was much discontent among the troops, although there was more trouble in 1781. Hamilton was reported to have said, in the presence of other officers, "that the army would, by-and-by, turn their arms upon the country and do themselves justice," and again, "that it was high time for the people to rise, join General Washington and turn Congress out of Doors." Hamilton was apprised of this alleged seditious language imputed to him by a Lieutenant-Colonel Brooks, and he quickly traced the

[1] See "Notes on Duelling," by Lorenzo Sabine, p. 228. London, Sampson Low, Son & Co., 1855.
[2] William Gordon (1730–1807) was the chaplain of the Provincial Congress in Massachusetts. He was dismissed from this position, "as the Legislature regarded his prayers as intended rather to dictate their measures than to implore the divine direction to them." Appleton's "Cyclopædia of American Biography, vol. II, p. 687.

libel to Francis Dana,[1] who, however, denied the responsibility for the accusation, and gave the name of Gordon as
that of the culprit. When cornered, the latter admitted the
existence of a mysterious witness and informant, and his
letters to Hamilton were notably evasive and exasperating.
Two are presented, one of which embodied the clergyman's
determination that Hamilton should not be permitted to
challenge his traducer, and another from Hamilton which
shows, even at this early date, that he did not look upon a
duel as an adequate cure for wounded honor.

It appeared that nothing came of all this correspondence,
and that Gordon was a fussy mischief-maker. Colonel
David Henly,[2] who was Hamilton's representative, had a
poor opinion of the clergyman, for in a letter of September
1, 1779, he said: "I do think Col. Hamilton you will find
Doctr. Gordon the cause of this mischievous and false
Report—the other Day he was prov'd a Lyar in the publick
Street, and had it not have been for his Cloth, I am sure
would have been more severely dealt with—he more than
once has occasioned Quarrels by his Conduct." And again,
"Yesterday I delivered your Letter to Doctr. Gordon and
hope you will receive such satisfaction, as is due you either
in wounding him in his honor, or by treating the man with
contempt that has endeavored to injure your Reputation."

---

[1] Francis Dana (1743–1811) played an important part in early American affairs.
In 1780 he went to Great Britain as the secretary of John Adams, to negotiate the
Treaty, and remained for some years abroad engaged in diplomatic work. In 1785
he was appointed Chief Justice of Massachusetts, and in 1786 was a delegate to
the Annapolis Convention.

[2] A colonel in a Massachusetts regiment in 1776. In 1777 commander of troops
at Cambridge.

Reverend William Gordon to Alexander Hamilton

SIR: Upon my return home from a visit on the Monday evening I received yours without a date. However *common* the principle may be, on which you urge me, to *an immediate direct and explicit answer* as tho' *the least hesitation* or reserve might give *room for conjectures, which it can be neither your wish nor mine to excite*—it is certainly a *false* one.

In many cases a gentleman may receive information from persons of indisputable character which it may be highly proper for him to communicate, without discovering the informer; and I am convinced you will think with me, when you have been more conversant with the world and read *mankind* more. Neither will such gentleman, when conscious of his own integrity and of established character regard the conjectures of those who are almost or altogether strangers to him.

I do not mean by advancing those sentiments to refuse you aid in detecting the inventor of a calumny. Mr. Dana mentions his having the declaration, alluded to in his letter from me. He communicated to me Col. Brook's letter to you, and yours to himself and the substance of what he intended to write. I objected to nothing regarding myself, excepting its being said *public coffee house* in which I supposed him mistaken. I understood it was a *public house,* but rather thought it was not the coffee house. That excepted the sentiment was as he had represented, whether the words were identically the same or not. I am glad to find by what you have wrote, that you have lost all remembrance of it; as it serves to shew that it was the effort of a *sudden transport,* and not of a depraved judgment. You will infer from hence, that I supposed the sentiment to have been spoken. I do: upon the belief, that my informer was a person of veracity, and could not be mistaken. The reasons are these, his general character, and his declaring that it was

uttered in his hearing. I saw him on his way from Philadelphia. He left the City sometime after the inhabitants
had been undivided by Mr. Dean's[1] imprudent address, in
which he promised us great discoveries, tho' he had made
none; and by which he raised a jealousy of Congress, and
put many upon clamouring against them. In this crisis, and
I conjecture thro' conversation leading to it, you was betrayed
into a speech tantamount to the representation made me.
You was not the only one that spoke unguardedly all this
season. Persons of equal or with superior talk are known
to have done it, and many in the military department having
been soured by the hardships they had undergone and an
apprehended neglect of their grievance and on the part of
Congress backwardness, to redress them, seemingly took a
part with Mr. Dean; and the unguarded expressions that
fell from them, then and afterwards, proved alarming to
weak but good minds. I was much hurt in my own feelings
because of the wrong, I am convinced, it led some to do his
Excellency, in fearing that such sentiment were dropt in his
presence, without meeting with a further check. My informer told me, that he took notice to you of the unsuitable-
ness of such like expressions, with which you was rather displeased, but that he insisted further upon it, and that then
it ended. I should infer from its representation given me
that, there were others in Company. I have not mentioned
his name; but if you cannot possibly recollect having said
anything like what he reported; continue to view it as a
calumny; and insist upon knowing him, I do not imagine
he would object to it, but, whether he do or not, shall mention him, upon your assuring me upon your honour, that you
will neither give nor accept, cause to be given nor accepted,
a challenge upon the occasion, nor engage in any recounter

[1] Silas Dean. After his return from France, where he had made contracts with several French officers who subsequently fought in the American Revolution, he returned to Philadelphia. Congress immediately found fault with him for his alleged
financial irregularities and extravagance, and he returned to France to obtain
documents to prove his case. Meanwhile his written criticisms of the French were
such as to make him a *persona non grata,* and he fled to Holland, and afterward went
to England, where he died.

that may produce a duel—for tho' do not in general produce more than the honorable settlement of a dispute, yet they may be the unhappy cause of the publick's losing good and useful members; and upon the principles of religion I am totally averse to them. You must further assure me, that you will admit of the matter's being thoroughly examined into by Congress, or individuals of the first character. The oversight of individuals too often raise prejudices against a whole body. It is common, and yet commonly condemned. I am convinced that notwithstanding the natural tendency of martial manners, there are as good citizens *in* the military line, as out of it; and I hope that the event will ever shew that by far the majority of our officers love the liberties of citizens more than any earthly command whatsoever. I as earnestly wish, that the citizens of the United States may do justice to the army, and their own engagements by keeping it up to the spirit of them wherein it is possible, that so our brave brothers may not have any just cause of complaint when affairs are brought to a settlement.

Sir

Your most obedient humble servant

WILLIAM GORDON

Alexander Hamilton to the Rev. William Gordon

DEAR SIR: I have received your letter of the 25th of August which you will probably not be surprised to hear is by no means satisfactory. Instead of giving up the author of the accusation, you charitably suppose me guilty, and amuse yourself in a stream of conjecture (which whatever *ingenuity* it may have was certainly unnecessary)—about the manner in which the affair happened and the motives that produced it. Your entering a volunteer to apologize for me is no doubt a mark of your condescension and of your benevolence, and would make it ungrateful as well as indecent to suspect, that the conditions with which you fetter a compliance with my request, proceed from any other cause than a laudable, though perhaps in this instance, an officious zeal, for the interests of religion and for the good of society. It shall never be said, that you had recourse to a pitiful evasion, and attempted to cover the dishonor of a refusal under a precious pretence of terms, which you know as a gentleman, I should be obliged to regret—I venture however with every allowance for the sanctity of your intention and with all possible deference for your judgment to express my doubts of the propriety of the concessions you require on my part, as preliminaries to a discovery, which I still think you are bound to make as an act of justice. This is a principle from which I can never depart; and I am convinced I shall have the common sense and feelings of mankind on my side. An opinion of my *inexperience* seems to have betrayed you into mistakes—Whatever you may imagine Sir, I have read the world sufficiently to know that though it may often be *convenient* to the propagator of a calumny to conceal the inventor, he will stand in need of no small address to escape the suspicions and even the indignation of the honest and of the disinterested. Nor can I but persist in believing that, notwithstanding the confidence which from a very natural partiality you place in your own character, the delicacy of your sentiment will be alarmed at the possibility of incurring this danger and will prevent your exposing yourself to it, by refusing, or delaying any longer to comply with so reasonable a demand.

It often happens that our zeal is at variance with our understanding. Had it not been for this, you might have recollected, that we do not now live in the days of chivalry, and you would, have then judged your precautions on the subject of duelling, at least useless—*The good sense of the present times has happily found out, that to prove your own innocence, or the malice of an accuser, the worst method you can take is to run him through the body or shoot him through the head.* And permit me to add, that while you felt an aversion to duelling on the principles of religion, you ought in charity to have supposed others possessed of the same scruples—of whose impiety you had had no proofs. But whatever may be my final determination on this point, ought to be a matter of indifference. Tis a good old maxim, to which we may safely adhere in most cases, that we ought to do our duty and leave the rest to the care of heaven. The crime alleged to me is of such enormity, that if I am guilty it ought not to go unpunished, and, if I am innocent, I should have an opportunity of vindicating my innocence. The truth in either case should appear, and it is incumbent upon you, Sir, to afford the means, either by accusing me to my civil or military superiors, or by disclosing the author of the information.

Your anxiety to engage me "to *admit* of the matter's being thoroughly examined into by Congress or individuals of the first character" was equally superfluous. I am at all times amenable to the authority of the state and of the laws; and whenever it should be the pleasure of Congress, the means of bringing me to justice for any crime I may have committed are obvious and easy, without the assistance of a formal stipulation on my side. I shall not expose myself to the ridicule of self-importance by applying to Congress for an inquiry, nor shall I invite the charge of impertinence, by promising to do what I have no power to refuse. I shall only declare for my own satisfaction, that so far as concerns myself, nothing would give me greater pleasure than to undergo the strictest scrutiny in any legal mode in the rectitude of my conduct, on this and on every other occasion as a soldier or as a citizen. With respect to an examination by individuals of character, whenever I have it in my power to confront my accuser, I shall take care to do it in presence of witnesses of the first respectability, who will be able from what they see and hear, to tell the world that I am innocent and injured and that he is a contemptible defamer.

It is, no doubt, unfortunate for me that you have prejudged the case and are of a different opinion. You profess to give credit to the story, because, you say, your informer "is a man of veracity and *could not be mistaken.*" From this description he is probably not a soldier, or you would have been more inclined to suppose him *fallible.* But whoever he may be you have certainly shown a facility

in believing that does honor to your credulity at the expense
of your candour.   I protest, Sir, this is the first time I have
heard my own veracity called in question.   Had you not
given a sanction to the contrary by your example, I should
have indulgently flattered myself, that I had as much right
to be believed as another, and that my denial was a counter-
ballance to the assertion of your informant, and left the
affair in suspense to be decided by the future circumstances.
You persue a different line, and in the overflowing of your
pious hatred to political heresy, have determined, that I must
be guilty at all events.   You ascribe the denial to a deficit of
memory, and pretend to think it more likely that I should
have lost all recollection of the fact, than that you should
have been misinformed.   Far from accepting, I absolutely
reject the apology you make for me, and continue to believe it
impossible, I could have made a declaration similar to the
one reported; for I abhor the sentiment, it contains, and am
confident it never could have had a momentary place in my
mind, consequently never could have dishonored my lips.
The supposition is absurd, that I could have used the expressions when I cannot recognize the remotest trace of
an idea, at any period, that could possibly have led to
them.

In this consciousness, I again appeal to you, and demand by all the ties of truth, justice, and honour, that you
immediately give up your author.   I stake my life and reputation upon the issue, and defy all the craft of malevolence,
or of cabal, to support the charge.   If you decline a discovery, I shall then not have it in my choice to make any
other than *one conclusion*.

You have blended several matters foreign to the purpose,
which might as well have been omitted.   I shall only answer
in general, that I religiously believe the officers of the army
are among the best citizens in America, and inviolably attached to the liberties of the community; infinitely more so,
than any of those splenetic patriots out of it, who endeavour
for sinister purposes, to instil jealousies and alarms, which
they themselves know to be as groundless as they are impol-

itic and ridiculous. But if any individuals have been imprudent, or unprincipled, let them answer for themselves. I am responsible only for my own conduct. Your fears for the injury which the indiscretion of such persons might do to the general, were kind, but I hope unnecessary. The decided confidence of Congress, and the hearts of the people of America, are the witnesses to his integrity. The blame of the unmeaning petulance of a few impatient spirits, will never rest upon him; for whoever knows his character, will be satisfied, that an officer would be ashamed to utter, in his hearing, any sentiments, that would disgrace a Citizen.

West Point, Sep. 5, 1779.
The Rev. Dr. Gordon, Esq.

Hamilton, when practising law in New York, was appealed to for advice by Lieutenant-Colonel Stephen Rochefontaine while the latter was in command at West Point. Rochefontaine had been a brilliant engineer officer, and had distinguished himself at Yorktown, but seems to have been unpopular with his comrades and, at times, hyper-sensitive. General Joseph Gardner Swift, the first graduate of the United States Military Academy, ambiguously said of him:

"It is to be admitted that whatever may have been the talents of Colonel Rochefontaine, he had occupied many good positions with his narrow redoubts, and also that such works were more commensurate with the views of Congress at the time, than in accordance with those of the Colonel." [1] Quarrels at West Point seem to have been frequent, and as a rule were settled by a passage at arms. There probably was some friction between the French and American officers, and the fighting proclivities of one of the latter were notorious. This was Lieutenant William Wilson, then at West Point,

---

[1] "The Memoirs of Genl. Joseph Gardner Swift, LL.D., etc., 1800–1865," p. 75, by H. Ellery. Privately printed, 1890.

who seems to have been a very disagreeable person. In 1795 he was tried by court-martial, ordered by Major Lewis Tousard, but escaped punishment.[1]

A year later Rochefontaine had a quarrel with him growing out of the court-martial, and wrote two letters to Hamilton, but it is to be regretted that the responses of the latter are not available.

Lieutenant-Colonel Stephen Rochefontaine to Alexander Hamilton

WEST POINT, *April* 28th, 1796.

DEAR SIR: Give me leave to apply to you for advice in a very disagreeable case which happened to me here a few days ago, it perhaps has been misrepresented to you by those who form a party against me in the corps, but you may rest assured that my honor has not been stained in the least; and I hope that if you find me guilty, it will only be of imprudence, and of no dishonourable act.

The cause of dislike of the officers to me may be ascribed to their being collected at West Point, while I was absent, and altho' unknown to most of them, they took such a wrong turn against me, that I hardly did receive marks of common

---

[1] Proceedings of a general Court Martial of the Corps of Artillerists and Engineers commanded by Lieutenant-Colonel Rochefontaine held at West Point this 15th day of June 1795, by order of Major Lewis Tousard at West Point.

LIEUT. JOHN McCLALLIN, *Pres't.*
Members: LIEUT. J. P. HALE, LIEUT. N. FREEMAN,
    LIEUT. GEDDES, LIEUT. MUHLENBURGH

The Court having met agreeably to the order of Major Tousard, having been duly sworn and having appointed Lieut. J. P. Hale recorder, are of opinion that they cannot proceed to the trial of Lieut. Wm. Wilson as there has not been produced an arrest before them, and as he has been at this Garrison for more than the space of eight days, they do in consideration of the 16th Article of the administration of Justice, recommend to the Commanding officer, that the Sword of Lieut. Wilson be returned to him.

JNO. McCLALLIN, *Lieut,*
President.

(Copies from Orderly Book No. 1, Corps of Artillerists and Engineers, commenced at West Point, May 7, 1795.)

politeness when I first came to join them here last January;
add to that the general antipathy of most of the individuals
of this country for any sort of subordination, and you will
know pretty near the principle of that great and most general
dissatisfaction of the officers towards me. A Mr. Wilson,
Lieut. in the Corps, as contemptible a character as can be
found anywhere, was particularly charged with the honourable trust of provoking me. (Mr. Wilson has killed a
Brother officer in a Duel about a 12 months ago.)

On the 21st of this month, two officers only were at Parade and 2 were absent without cause; instead of acting
with the Rigidity of the Law, I sent from Parade a message
to the absents, one only came, and the others refused to ac-
cede to the request.

After the Evening Roll Call, as I was returning home
passing before Mr. Wilson's quarters, I saw him out of his
window calling very loud to the Major who was also in sight,
by the name of John, his christening name, adding some
injurious expressions to it. At last my own name was pronounced with the epithet of *Damned Rascal*, and other expressions intended to be very provoking. I thought Mr.
Wilson intoxicated, or at least out of his senses, two officers
within the Room were exciting Mr. Wilson by loud fits of
Laughing. I felt very much discontented, and for an hour
I did remain uncertain about the part I should take;—a
court martial composed of officers contrary to me, would not
find any proofs of my accusation against Wilson, and it
would only be giving publicity to gross Insults, which an
officer dared to offer without any punishment. I thought the
mode of punishing him by a private Interview, which would
deter other officers from further insults of that kind was
preferable. As I was going to impart my resolution on that
head to Major Rivardi, I met Mr. Wilson taking a Walk by
himself—he stopped at a little distance from me, expecting
as I suppose, that he would be spoken to by me. I called on
him and I Inquired of him if he was the man who an hour
before that, had so loudly and so shamfully expressed himself in pronouncing my name; his answer was that he did not.

I told him that I was very glad that he did deny it, or else it would have been pronouncing himself a vilain and a scoundrell,—that if had something against me he might call on me at any time, and may be assured that I would grant him any redress that a gentleman might wish from another gentleman & a brave man. Mr. Wilson had a Small Cane in his hands, and at the expression of Scoundrell, which I suppose he did think himself very deserving of, he lifted it up as to strike at me. I had a Sword *Sheathed in the Scabbard, and raped over with a Large belt*, provoked by the former Insult, by the shameful denial of Expressions intended to be very publick outrages, for I heard them 300 yards off,—and they were issued out in presence of a Dozen of Servants or Waiters playing in front of the house, and Enraged at the Idea that he was going to strike me, I discharged once on his shoulder a Blow with the hilt of my Sword. I felt instantly that I had been imprudent, and to repair it as well as it lay'd in my power, I did offer him on the Spot the satisfaction that he might wish for, the moon shone very bright, and I observed that if he had had his Sword on as a Man who has Insulted another ought always be ready to give satisfaction, I would fight him. He called to his servant to bring him his Sword, but he did observe that he did not know how to make use of it. I proposed him then to fight him with any weapons he wished to propose, and pistols were agreed upon, and 15 minutes were required before we met with a Second on each side; the agreement after we met was, that in order to avoid the formality of a Duel, we should settle the dispute by a Rencounter with two loaded pistols each and a Sword. The fires were to be given at pleasure and the distance be such as it suited the two adversaries; the first fire went off almost at the same time on both sides. My second Pistol went off unaware and I remained against my antagonist who had yet a Loaded pistol against me. He came up to me within three steps and missed fire, it is a general rule in such occasions to lose the chance when the pistol has not gone off, yet my adversary cocked up and missed his fire a second time, in order to prevent his firing a third time, I fell on him to try to prevent him from cocking his piece, but he did it notwithstanding, and his pistol missed fire again, the muzzle touching my breast. The two wittnesses came up then and separated us, my noble adversary enraged at not assassinating me on the spot, was furiously asking powder of his second, to kill said he *that S—— of a B——*, this was his noble expression on that occasion.

It is to be remarked that that affair which among men of honour is generally kept a Secret, was known thro'out the garrison, and we were immediately surrounded by people whom Mr. Wilson had informed of it, the reason why would be impossible for me to guess at.

We all retired to our quarters, my second and myself persuaded that the Rencounter having taken place, it put a stop to all further proceedings, and had made up all difficulties agreeably to stipulation. Two days afterwards I received a written challenge from Mr. Wilson thro' his former second. I answered him that according to our agreement, we had made up for the Insults and that I requested he would not mention that matter any more.

Here begins the perfidious agency of the officers who form a Party against me. Mr. Wilson, tho' a man of a very contemptible character, has been pushed forward and promised the support of all the officers if he would prosecute that affair against me. They assembled together upon my answer, and then Informed me that on hearing of my refusing satisfaction to Mr. Wilson, my Brother officer, for a gross Insult offered to him, they were going to publish my infamous conduct to the world. I refused that paper because it was not signed, and it did not bear any mark of authenticity about it. They did not return it. Sunday last was the day it was brought to me. Mr. Lovel one of the Ring Leaders, went on that day to New York—perhaps to have it published; on Monday—a Mr. Elmer another Ring Leader, went up to Goshen to begin against me, as I understand, a civil prosecution for the blow. On that same day I did inform the officers that I was sorry that they had not had confidence enough in me to let me know the object of their meeting, and that in explaining to them the affair, with its causes and all the circumstances, I might have prevented the Breach from opening between us, and that they perhaps would have been convinced that a full atonement had been granted for the Insult, agreeably to stipulation, and that it was unjust to carry judgments without hearing but one party, but at all events, I proposed a way to come regularly and without passion to a Settlement,—which was to leave the matter to the decision of three officers of the army well acquainted with the rules generally observed in affairs of honor, and that if they did determine that I owed farther satisfaction to Mr. Wilson I would follow their decision to all its extent, upon that proposition they altered their former plan and changed it into an accusation before the Secretary of War.

I am now arrived to a few Queries which I would wish you to favor with your opinion upon and as soon as convenient, in order that I may avoid if possible the Inconveniency of a writ, which may be served against me upon the application of my adversaries.

When two military characters happen to have a difference between them, which has been the cause of a Breach of the law short of murder, and when that affair of honor has been agreed upon as a Sufficient atonement, is one of the two Liable to be prosecuted by the other before the Tribunals of the State?

Is an offense passed on a Spot within the territory of the United States as West Point is, amenable before the tribunal of the State of New York?

Is an officer accused before a Military Tribunal for an offense, by the person who received it, liable to be prosecuted at the same time before the civil authority, by the same person or by anybody else for him?

If an officer is tryed before a Military Tribunal, and acquitted or condemned, is he liable to be prosecuted again before the civil tribunal?

Can I with the challenge which I have possession of, check the writ against me, if any there is? I must own to you Sir, that I would consider that Mode of clearing myself as Shameful, the perfidy of the act perpetrated against me would be the only reason that would make me pass over it, and the disagreeable situation of being under the weight of an arrest from the Civil Authority would be a further reason in favor of it.

I will dispense Sir, with any further Queries upon the subject laid before you, I have tried to detail it as much as I could, in order that you may be led by the circumstances, and that you may give me explanations upon points which, the essential, I have not perhaps insisted on or even perceived.

The most delicate point which I would be glad you would favor me with your opinion upon, is that of honor, my firm determination is to give full and ample satisfaction if wanted, even was it unasked, for I conceive that a man is the most unhappy of wretches, if he is convinced that his honor and delicacy have received a check.

I am with great Esteem and Respect, Dear Sir
You obedt. humble Servant
STEP. ROCHEFONTAINE
Lt. Col. Com'dr. of the
Artr. & Engr.

Alex. Hamilton, Esqe.,
Attorney-at-law, New York.

On May 10 he again wrote:

WEST POINT BY PEEKSKILL.

DEAR SIR: I have had the honor to transmit to you in the course of last week, a letter detailing the affair which passed between Mr. Wilson, a Lieut. in the Corps, and myself; the Injuries offered on both sides had been settled agreeably to the rules of honor adopted by gentlemen, and in consequence of a Particular agreement made by the two Seconds. Two days after I received a challenge from Mr. Wilson by his second, Mr. Lovel, a Lieut. also,—my answer was that I looked on that affair as settled. Some of the officers who are far from being my friends, and who are too Prudent to

Expose themselves without danger,—they assembled the
officers who, thro' hatred to me, others thro' fear of their
Brother-in-Arms, many without any other motive but insubordination, which is generaly impregnated in the minds
of the people under a Free Government, signed a sort of libel
in which they declare that they will publish to the world,
that after insulting Mr. Wilson, I refused to give him satisfaction; I refused the paper which was not authenticated
by any signature and I did not receive it back, but they sent
me a copy of some charges laid against me before the Secretary of War.

Mr. McHenry has sent me the copy of the accusation, and
has not informed me yet what plan he expected to proceed
upon,—I desired him by this post to grant me a Court of Inquiry instead of a Court Martial. The Court of Inquiry
may investigate the whole affair which will throw the accusation to the ground,—a Court Martial on the contrary cannot conceive any disposition upon facts, let them be so near
related to the head of accusation, if they are not materialy
in the charges, it begins also by a Punishment, the arrest.
This is at least the principle upon which our officers have
acted, for they are most of them Lawyers of the worst Kind,
viz: full of those low means, which are dishonorable in the
eyes of an honest man. I have another evil to contend with,
that of preventing the officers from gaining or otherwise
hindering the witnesses that I may call upon to prove certain facts, from telling what they saw or heard. The general
saying among those people is, that it will bring trouble unto
those who will take any part for me.

I will not take up any more of your time to read my scribbling, my first letter has gone as fully as I thought necessary
on the details of that affair,—I wish you would oblige me
with your advice, both as to my conduct towards the civil or
military prosecution, to avoid the evils prepared against me
by baseness, and cowardice; any expense attending the
prosecution of my enemies and my defense upon the delicate
point of honor, I will bear with a great deal of pleasure, I
wish therefore you would inform me what will be necessary,

and the Sums will immediately be forwarded thro' the Bank at New York.

I wish very much for your answer, and I am very anxious to know if you will condescend to take my defense in that affair, in which I may again assure you that my honor has not received the least attack or blemish.

I am with great Respect
        Dear Sir
            Your most obedt. Servant
                    STEP. ROCHEFONTAINE.
                    Lt. Col. Com'd'r. of 7th Corps of
                                Art'r. & Eng'rs.

It does not appear that anything came of all this, and it is probable that through Hamilton's efforts matters were adjusted.

From this time on he underwent a decided change of heart regarding this method of settling personal difficulties. Many of the old army and some of his friends had fallen in the field of honor, for toward the end of the century encounters of this kind were too often the result of trivial affronts and tavern brawls. When his own beloved firstborn perished in this way his horror of the duello became so great that he, whenever possible, forced his clients and those who consulted him to settle their difficulties in some less extreme way.[1]

Brave as he was, it may be, therefore, perceived how his encounter with Aaron Burr was one that he was reluctantly drawn into, and quite inconsistent with the stand he had taken for the last two years before his death.

---

[1] There is a reference in Hamilton's papers to an occasion in 1787, when he acted as peacemaker in a quarrel between a Major Pierce and a Mr. Auldjo, who came very near fighting. To one of these gentlemen he wrote: "I can never consent to take up the character of a second in a duel till I have in vain tried that of mediator. Be content with *enough*, for *more* ought not to be expected." Referred to by Lodge, vol. IX, p. 421. (Constitutional Edition.)

Though much misconception exists as to the relations of Hamilton and Burr, it cannot be denied that destiny shaped their lives in such a way that their paths forever crossed, and that one always affected the other in some manner during their eventful careers. The thought certainly suggests itself to the fatalist that the subsequent death of Hamilton and the disgrace and poverty of Burr were preordained. A study of the parallel of their lives becomes, therefore, one of interest. They were born within a year of each other. Burr entered Princeton College in 1769 when but thirteen, and graduated in 1772. He, subsequently studied the Gospel, but eventually became an atheist. Hamilton entered the Continental Army when seventeen, Burr when nineteen.

Both were brave and dashing young soldiers. Burr accompanied Arnold in his expedition to Quebec, and was present at the famous assault on the city, although he later quarrelled with General Montgomery. From May, 1776, he was, for a few weeks, a member of Washington's staff, where he must have been associated with Hamilton. Here he was detected in "immoralities" by Washington, and his resignation as an aide demanded. He subsequently tried to injure the Commander-in-Chief by taking sides with Gates and Lee, and being proxy to their treachery. He behaved well at the battle of Monmouth.

Hamilton's military duties undoubtedly brought him in close contact with Burr, as he, too, was attached to Washington's staff.[1] His disagreement with the Commander-in-Chief occurred, but because of nothing worse than wounded vanity, and he was not only loyal, but we find that he attacked both Lee and Gates in defence of Washington. Physically Ham-

---

[1] According to Worthington Ford, Burr was never an *aide-de-camp* of Washington's. His name does not appear in the list, but it is possible he was detailed for a time, and not regularly appointed. See "The Writings of George Washington," vol. XIV, p. 452. New York, G. P. Putnam's Sons, 1893.

ilton and Burr were slight men, and both gifted with extraordinary powers of fascination. As Oliver has pointed out, Burr exercised this gift to win any one and every one. Hamilton discriminated, and charmed the worthy minority.[1]

After the war, both began the practice of law in the same year, and were associated or opposed to each other in many local cases. According to his biographers Burr had no rival but Hamilton. He finally, after eight years in the Legislature, came to New York and took a magnificent house known as Richmond Hill. From the first he prospered, not only in Albany, but in New York, and lived luxuriously, while Hamilton was not so well favored, and got along as well as he could on much smaller emoluments, bringing up his large family. When the former began his legal practice in Albany he was twenty-six. Hamilton was twenty-five.

In political life Burr was always a consistent and bitter anti-Federalist, although, for a time, he pretended a half-hearted attachment to this party. Later he was more or less of a sycophant to Jefferson, until the latter grew tired of him. His atheistic ideas made him a warm partisan of the cause of the French Republic. Hamilton detested the French

---

[1] Burr's peculiarly attractive manner was sketched by a person who remembered him, and communicated his impressions to a member of my family. "I was brought up," he said, "with a horror towards Colonel Burr. I remember well the first time I saw him. I met him when walking with my mother in Broadway when I was about seven years old. I was attracted by this peculiar, foreign-looking man in the old-fashioned costume of tights and powder, and turned to gaze at him. He had also turned and stood looking at us. Always after, when we met him, I found that he looked after us with Curiosity. When I was old enough to understand the dreadful fate of his only child, to hear how lovely she was, these few meetings touched me sensibly. You know how fascinating he was to young men. Two very distinguished men of our State, who were much noticed by him when quite young, have told me of his rare attraction. When I inquired in what it consisted, one of them replied—'In his manner of listening. He seemed to give your thoughts so much value by his manner of receiving, & to find so much more meaning in your words than you had intended; no flattery was more subtle.' "

revolutionists. Burr was selfish, Hamilton altruistic, devoting his talents to the good of all.

So far as is known, Burr never openly wrote anything, and there are no literary remains except his diary, which is a curious and eccentric production. All unite in praising his eloquence, his shrewdness and cleverness, his "dauntless resolution," and his great self-possession.

His engaging manners, which have been referred to, gave him all the power of a demagogue, and, for a time, he was a master of men, such as they were. "In his case," says a critic, "the finest gifts of nature and fortune were spoiled by unsound moral principles, and the absence of all genuine convictions. His habits were licentious. He was a master of intrigue, though to little purpose." [1]

In later years the paths of the two men diverged to a still greater degree, the course of Burr being marked by flagrant trickery and conscienceless immorality. In contrast to this was Hamilton's purity of motive and honest consistency.

Though Burr and Hamilton were nearly always on opposite political sides, this was most marked during the end of the eighteenth century, when the Federalists were effectually overthrown and beaten. Though defeated by General Schuyler in 1797, when the latter was elected senator, Burr in 1800 became Vice-President, and Jefferson President, there being a tie which was broken by the election of the latter to chief office. It was at this time that Hamilton's pent-up indignation found the fullest vent in a series of letters both from his pen and those of his friends.

Burr was a member of the convention to revise the Constitution, and was unanimously elected chairman. While it is true that Hamilton for a time favored Jefferson's election as President, his advocacy was half-hearted, and the mis-

[1] "Appleton's Cyclopedia of American Biography," p. 467.

taken idea arose from political exigencies, for he could not
tolerate Burr or his methods.

In this connection he wrote to Theodore Sedgwick, in
December 22, 1800:[1]

I entirely agree with you, my dear sir, that in the event of
Jefferson and Burr coming to the House of Representatives,
the former is to be preferred. The appointment of Burr as
President would disgrace our country abroad. No agreement with him could be relied upon. His private circumstances render disorder a necessary resource. His public
principles offer no obstacle. His ambition aims at nothing
short of permanent power and wealth in his own person.
For heaven's sake, let not the federal party be responsible for
the elevation of this man!

It is unfair to say that Burr was only a "respectable lawyer
and speaker," as has been alleged. He was really brilliant,
able, and full of resources.[2] Hamilton was associated with
him in many cases, and Burr often had a great deal to do with
the ultimate success of the particular action—the Le Guen
case being an example—and he took good care to get the
lion's share of compensation.

While Hamilton's chief success was before juries, it would
appear, from the few carefully reported cases that went to
appeal, that Burr was more often successful there.

In the early days of the acquaintance, and even for many

---

[1] "Hamilton's Works," vol. VI, p. 495.

[2] Oliver's opinion of Burr is of interest as that of an impartial historian:

"It is impossible, moreover, to resist the conclusion that Aaron Burr, with all his
great and admirable qualities, was, in fact, a sham. Chesterfieldian maxims are not
the best foundation for a real human character. His manner and his pose were
magnificent. His attitude in the face of the world was sublime. But we have
the feeling all the time that he was acting; that in public affairs his eye was fixed
upon the pit and the stalls, or, at any rate, upon the critics rather than upon the
subject. He made no vulgar appeal to a mean audience. We feel indeed that
often his sole admirers—pit, stalls, and critics—consisted of himself, and he was a
severe judge. But it was acting all the same."—*Op. cit.*, p. 416.

years after, their relations were not unfriendly, and Hamilton, doubtless, admired and respected the mental qualities of his adversary, and was fair enough to admit it; but he was placed, upon many occasions, in the disagreeable position of appearing against Burr for clients who had been the victim of the latter's dishonest practices.

Much speculation has been indulged in regarding Hamilton's action in meeting Burr, despite his strong and oft-expressed prejudices against duelling, and many conscientious people are inclined to censure him for this. There can be no doubt, however, that he deliberately sacrificed himself for his patriotic principles, and I prefer to take the view held by a few persons that he met Burr only because he knew that his future usefulness as the leader of his party would have been hurt by any exhibition of what might have been, in any degree, regarded by the mob as the white feather. It is unnecessary to call attention to the obligations of the code in those days. In fact, until a very late period in the history of some States, the refusal to accept a challenge would have been paramount to a confession of cowardice. Even forty years later the kind-hearted and peaceful-minded Abraham Lincoln prepared himself to fight a duel with broadswords, and actually went to meet his adversary, who ingloriously retired when he saw his huge opponent slashing the grass with his enormous weapon.[1] As Lodge has intimated, Hamilton knew that the time might come when civil war, or the insults of the French nation, would precipitate a conflict, and that as one likely to be major-general his prestige as a commander would be seriously hurt if he had not gone out to

---

[1] The challenge was sent by one James Shields, a boastful and pompous person, who had been ridiculed in a local newspaper called the *Sangamo Journal* by Lincoln and others. A full account of this proceeding may be found in "Abraham Lincoln —A History," by John G. Nicolay and John Hay, vol. I, p. 203. New York, The Century Company, 1890.

fight with Burr.   Although Hamilton, in his later life, hated
the very idea of settling disputes of personal wrongs in this
way, he, as a soldier, could not entirely free himself from the
customary obligations of his profession.

Rufus King,[1] a temperate and cool-headed man, did his
best to stop the duel, and in a letter to Charles King, April 2,
1819, said: "You cannot my Dr. Sir, hold in greater abhorrence than I do, the practice of duelling.   Our lamented
friend was not unacquainted with my opinion on the subject, but with a mind the most capacious and discriminating
that I ever knew, he had laid down for the government of
himself certain rules upon the subject of Duels, the fallacy
of which could not fail to be seen by any man of ordinary understanding; with these guides it is my deliberate opinion
that he could not have avoided a meeting with Col. Burr, had
he even declined the first challenge."

After the duel, and even to-day, it is hard for some admirers of Burr to believe all this, and it has been repeatedly
asserted that Hamilton did not throw away his first shot.
Not only is this erroneous, but every utterance and action
shows that he had absolutely no intention of shooting Burr,
and though his pistol was discharged it was an involuntary
act.[2]   The account of Dr. Hosack contains references to
this, and his own letters and papers are convincing witnesses
of his sincere good faith.   In the statement Hamilton drew
up before he fought he speaks not only of his desire to avoid
the interview upon "religious and moral" grounds, the pos-

---

[1] Also "Rufus King's Life and Letters," pp. 398 et seq., vol. IV.
[2] Both Burr and Van Ness always said that Hamilton fired first by a second.
Judge Pendleton, after Van Ness's dissatisfaction with the report, went to Weehawken a day or two after and inspected the duelling ground.   He stated that
Hamilton's bullet hit a branch twelve and one-half feet above the ground, four
feet to the right, and thirteen feet from where Hamilton stood—the contestants
stood eleven paces apart.   This was considered proof by him that Hamilton's
pistol was accidentally discharged.

sible loss to his family, and a sense of obligation to his creditors, but he says: "It is also my ardent wish that I may have been, and that he [Burr] *by his future* conduct may show himself worthy of all confidence and esteem, and prove an ornament and blessing to his Country." If these words are not an indication that he believed Burr would survive, and intended he should, they mean nothing. Again, in the two last letters to his wife, there is a clearly expressed idea that he would himself fall.

This paper, written by him, is again worthy of reproduction and goes to prove all this:

On my expected interview with Col. Burr, I think it proper to make some remarks explanatory of my conduct, motives and views.

I was certainly desirous of avoiding this interview for the most cogent reasons.

1. My religious and moral principles are strongly opposed to the practice of duelling, and it would ever give me pain to be obliged to shed the blood of a fellow creature in a private combat forbidden by the laws.

2. My wife and children are extremely dear to me, and my life is of the utmost importance to them, in various views.

3. I feel a sense of obligation towards my creditors; who in case of accident to me, by the forced sale of my property, may be in some degree sufferers. I did not think myself at liberty as a man of probity, lightly to expose them to this hazard.

4. I am conscious of no *ill will* to Col. Burr, distinct from political opposition, which, as I trust, has proceeded from pure and upright motives.

Lastly, I shall hazard much, and can possibly gain nothing by the issue of the interview.

But it was, as I conceive, impossible for me to avoid it. There were *intrinsic* difficulties in the thing, and *artificial* embarrassments, from the manner of proceeding on the part of Col. Burr.

Intrinsic, because it is not to be denied, that my animadversions on the political principles, character, and views of Col. Burr, have been extremely severe; and on different occasions, I, in common with many others, have made very unfavorable criticisms on particular instances of the private conduct of this gentleman.

In proportion as these impressions were entertained with sincerity, and uttered with motives and for purposes which might appear to me commendable, would be the difficulty (until they could be removed by evidence of their being erroneous), of explanation or apology. The disavowal required of me by Col. Burr, in a general and indefinite form, was out of my power, if it had really been proper for me to submit to be so questioned; but I was sincerely of opinion that this could not be, and in this opinion, I was confirmed by that of a very moderate and judicious friend whom I consulted. Besides that, Col. Burr appeared to me to assume, in the first instance, a tone unnecessarily peremptory and menacing, and in the second, positively offensive. Yet I wished, as far as might be practicable, to leave a door open to accommodation. This, I think, will be inferred from the written communications made by me and by my direction, and would be confirmed by the conversations between Mr. Van Ness and myself, which arose out of the subject.

I am not sure whether, under all the circumstances, I did not go further in the attempt to accommodate, than a punctilious delicacy will justify. If so, I hope the motives I have stated will excuse me.

It is not my design, by what I have said, to affix any odium on the conduct of Col. Burr, in this case. He doubtless has heard of animadversions of mine, which bore very hard upon him; and it is probable that as usual they were accompanied with some falsehoods. He may have supposed himself under a necessity of acting as he has done. I hope the grounds of his proceeding have been such as ought to satisfy his own conscience.

I trust, at the same time, that the world will do me the

justice to believe that I have not censured him on light grounds, nor from unworthy inducements. I certainly have had strong reasons for what I may have said, though it is possible that in some particulars, I may have been influenced by misconstruction or misinformation. It is also my ardent wish that I may have been more mistaken than I think I have been, and that, he, by his future conduct, may show himself worthy of all confidence and esteem, and prove an ornament and blessing to the country.

As well because it is possible that I may have injured Col. Burr, however convinced myself that my opinions and declarations have been well founded, as from my general principles and temper in relation to similar affairs, I have resolved, if our interview is conducted in the usual manner, and it pleases God to give me the opportunity, to *reserve* and *throw away* my first fire, and I *have thoughts* of even *reserving* my second fire—and thus giving a double opportunity to Col. Burr to pause and to reflect.

It is not, however, my intention to enter into any explanations on the ground—Apology from principle, I hope, rather than pride, is out of the question.

To those, who, with me, abhorring the practice of duelling, may think that I ought on no account to have added to the number of bad examples, I answer, that my *relative* situation, as well in public as private, enforcing all the considerations which constitute what men of the world denominate honour, imposed on me (as I thought) a peculiar necessity not to decline the call. The ability to be in future useful, whether in resisting mischief or effecting good, in those crises of our public affairs which seem likely to happen, would probably be inseparable from a conformity with public prejudice in this particular.

A. H.

CHAPTER XIII

THE DUEL

THERE need be no speculation as to the cause of the duel. What has been said in previous chapters shows the forces that were at work for a very long time, but in a more pronounced way for at least two years before the event. Even if he had not wished to do so, Hamilton was unwillingly obliged, in the practice of his profession, to expose Burr's corrupt practices and the manner in which he swindled his clients; he had no choice. In political antagonism the worst offence was given, for Hamilton's attacks had been unremitting and bitter, and though undertaken because he believed the welfare of the nation demanded the defeat of Burr, he could expect no other ending than that which followed.

While the correspondence directly connected with the sending of the challenge seemed forced and disingenuous upon Burr's part, and the issue was directly precipitated by the latter, he was undoubtedly goaded on by Hamilton's scathing denunciation, and it is surprising that he did not force the duel upon some much earlier occasion, as Hamilton was always free in his criticism, and wrote many letters and inspired many bitter newspaper attacks. What could be more provoking than the letter addressed to John Rutledge, and found afterward among the papers of Francis Hopkinson ?[1]

[1] *Century Magazine*, vol. IX, p. 250.

Alexander Hamilton to John Rutledge

(Confidential)

NEW YORK, Jany. 4, 1801.

My DEAR SIR: My extreme anxiety about the ensuing election of President by the House of Representatives will excuse to you the liberty I take in addressing you concerning it without being consulted by you. Did you know M^r. Burr as well as I do, I should think it unnecessary. With your honest attachment to the Country and correctness of views, it would not then be possible for you to hesitate, if you now do, about the course to be taken. You would be clearly of opinion with me that M^r. Jefferson is to be preferred.

As long as the Federal party preserve their high ground of integrity and principle, I shall not despair of the public weal. But if they quit it and descend to be the willing instruments of the Elevation of the most unfit and most dangerous man of the community to the highest station in the Government—I shall no longer see any anchor for the hopes of good men. I shall at once anticipate all the evils that a daring and unprincipled ambition wielding the lever of Jacobinism can bring upon an infatuated Country.

The enclosed paper exhibits a faithful sketch of M^r. Burr's character as I believe it to exist, with better opportunities than almost any other man of forming a true estimate.

The expectation, I know, is, that if M^r. Burr shall owe his elevation to the Fœderal party he will judge it his interest to adhere to that party. But it ought to be recollected, that he will owe it in the first instance to the Antifœderal party; that among these, though perhaps not in the House of Representatives, a numerous class prefers him to M^r. Jefferson as best adapted by the boldness and cunning of his temper to fulfil their mischievous views; and that it will be the interest of his Ambition to preserve and cultivate these friends.

M^r. Burr will doubtless be governed by his interest as he views it. But stable power and wealth being his objects— and there being no prospect that the respectable and sober fœderalists will countenance the projects of an irregular Ambition or prodigal Cupidity, he will not long lean upon them—but selecting from among them men suited to his purpose he will seek with the aid of these and of the most unprincipled of the opposite party to accomplish his ends. At least such ought to be our calculation—From such a man as him, who practices all the maxims of a Catiline, who while despising, has played the whole game of, democracy, what better is to be looked for. T is not to a Chapter of Accidents, that we ought to trust the Government peace and happiness of our country—T is enough for us to know that M^r. Burr is one of the most unprincipled men in the U States in order to determine us to decline being responsible for the precarious issues of his calculations of Interest.

Very different ought to be our plan. Under the uncertainty of the Event we ought to seek to obtain from M^r. Jefferson these assurances 1 That the present Fiscal System will be maintained 2 That the present neutral plan will be adhered to 3 That the Navy will be preserved and gradually increased 4 That Fœderalists now in office, not being heads of the great departments will be retained. As to the heads of Departments & other matters he ought to be free.

You cannot in my opinion render a greater service to your Country than by exerting your influence to counteract the impolitic and impure idea of raising M^r. Burr to the Chief Magistracy.

Adieu My Dear Sir Yrs with sincere
　　　　affecn & regard
　　　　　　　　　　　　　A. HAMILTON.

J. Rutledge Esqr

(The inclosure, also in Hamilton's Handwriting.)

(Confidential)

A BURR

1–He is in every sense a profligate; a voluptuary in the extreme, with uncommon habits of expense; in his profession extortionate to a proverb; suspected on strong grounds of having corruptly served the views of the Holland Company, in the capacity of a member of our legislature;[1] and understood to have been guilty of several breaches of probity in his pecuniary transactions. His very friends do not insist upon his integrity.

2 He is without doubt insolvent for a large deficit. All his visible property is deeply mortgaged, and he is known to owe other large debts for which there is no specific security. Of the number of these is a Judgment in favour of M[r]. Angerstien for a sum which with interest amounts to about 80,000 Dollars.[2]

3 The fair emoluments of any station, under our government, will not equal his expenses in that station; still less will they suffice to extricate him from his embarrassments. He must therefore from the necessity of his station have recourse to unworthy expedients. These may be a bargain and sale with some foreign power, or combinations with public agents in projects of gain by means of the public moneys; perhaps and probably, to enlarge the sphere—a war.

4 He has no pretensions to the Station from services. He acted in different capacities in the last war finally with the rank of L[t]Col in a Regiment, and gave indications of being a good officer; but without having had the opportunity of performing any distinguished action. At a critical period of the war, he resigned his commission, assigning for cause ill-health, and went to repose at Paramus in the State of New Jersey. If his health was bad he might without difficulty have obtained a furlough and was not obliged to resign. He was afterwards seen in his usual health. The circumstance excited much jealousy of his motives. In civil life, he has never projected nor aided in producing a single measure of important public utility.

5 He has constantly sided with the party hostile to fœderal measures before and since the present constitution of the U States—In opposing the adoption of this constitution he was engaged covertly and insidiously; because, as he said

[1] This refers to Burr's attempt to modify the laws of the State of New York, permitting aliens to hold and dispose of land.　　[2] Hamilton was Angerstien's lawyer.

at the time "it was too strong and too weak" and he has been uniformly the opposer of the Fœderal Administration.

6 No mortal can tell what his political principles are. He has talked all round the compass. At times he has dealt in all the jargon of Jacobinism; at other times he has proclaimed decidedly to total insufficiency of the Fœderal Government and the necessity of changes to one far more energetic. The truth seems to be that he has no plan but that of getting power by any means and keeping it by all means. It is probable that if he has any theory t is that of a simple despotism. He has intimated that he thinks the present French constitution not a bad one.

7 He is of a temper bold enough to think no enterprise too hazardous and sanguine enough to think none too difficult. He has censured the leaders of the Fœderal party as wanting in vigour and enterprise, for not having established a strong Government when they were in possession of the power and influence.

8 Discerning men of all parties agree in ascribing to him an irregular and inordinate ambition. Like Catiline, he is indefatigable in courting the young and the profligate. He knows well the weak sides of human nature, and takes care to play in with the passions of all with whom he has intercourse. By natural disposition, the haughtiest of men, he is at the same time the most creeping to answer his purposes. Cold and collected by nature and habit, he never loses sight of his object and scruples no means of accomplishing it. He is artful and intriguing to an inconceivable degree. In short all his conduct indicates that he has in view nothing less than the establishment of Supreme Power in his own person. Of this nothing can be a surer index than that having in fact high-toned notions of Government, he has nevertheless constantly opposed the fœderal and courted the popular party. As he never can effect his wish by the aid of good men, he will court and employ able and daring scoundrels of every party, and by availing himself of their assistance and of all the bad passions of the Society, he will in all likelihood attempt an usurpation.

8 [sic] Within the last three weeks at his own Table, he drank these toasts successively 1 The French Republic 2 The Commissioners who negotiated the Convention 3 Buonaparte 4 La Fayette: and he countenanced and seconded the positions openly advanced by one of his guests that it was the interest of this country to leave it free to the Belligerent Powers to sell their prizes in our ports and to build and equip ships for their respective uses; a doctrine which evidently aims at turning all the naval resources of the U States into the channel of France; and which by making these states the most pernicious enemy of G Britain would compel her to go to war with us.

9 Though possessing infinite art cunning and address— he is yet to give proofs of great or solid abilities. It is certain that at the Bar he is more remarkable for ingenuity and dexterity, than for sound judgment or good logic. From the character of his understanding and heart it is likely that any innovation which he may effect will be such as to serve the turn of his own power, not such as will issue in establishments favourable to the permanent security and prosperity of the Nation—founded upon the principles of a strong free and regular Government.[1]

This letter, and those addressed to James A. Bayard, James Ross, and Theodore Sedgwick, as well as others, must have become public property, or at least have been known to reach Burr. Although the two men for a long time naturally hated each other, there does not appear to have been any very marked outward expression of this animosity. It is stated, that at a meeting of the Cincinnati, a few days before the duel, Hamilton entertained the company with a song, and that Burr, who was present, was observed to be silent and gloomy, gazing with marked and fixed earnestness at Hamilton during this song.[2] It is not

---

[1] Also see "Life and Correspondence of McHenry," p. 485.

[2] Morse, II, 364. The song is supposed by some to have been "The Drum," but by others one of Wolfe's songs called, "How Stands the Glass Around." See a pamphlet by I. E. Graybill, entitled, "Alexander Hamilton," Nevis, Weehawken.

difficult to believe that this was one of those cases when one man breeds in the other a species of fascination and affection—distinct as it were from another self that becomes so hateful and insupportable, that destruction is the only relief. How the words of Brutus suggest themselves!

The first intimation of the duel was a letter written by Burr to Hamilton, June 18, 1804, and delivered to the latter by W. P. Van Ness, a legal friend of both. The attention of Hamilton was called to an alleged assertion made by a Dr. Cooper of Albany in effect that he (Cooper), "could detail a still more despicable opinion which General Hamilton has expressed of Mr. Burr." In this communication Burr reminded Hamilton that "he must perceive the necessity of a prompt unqualified acknowledgment or denial" of the use of these expressions. In a letter written by Hamilton to Burr, June 20, 1804, the former says:

I have maturely reflected on the subject of your letter of the 18th inst., and the more I have reflected the more I have become convinced that I could not without manifest impropriety make the avowal or disavowal which you seem to think necessary. The clause pointed out by Mr. Van Ness is in these terms, "I could detail to you a still more despicable opinion which Hamilton has expressed of Mr. Burr." To endeavour to discover the meaning of this declaration, I was obliged to seek in the antecedent part of this letter for the opinion to which it referred, as having been already disclosed: I found it in these words, "General Hamilton and Judge Kent have declared in substance, that they looked upon Mr. Burr to be a dangerous man, and one who ought not to be trusted with the reins of government."

The language of Dr. Cooper plainly implies, that he considered this opinion of you, which he attributes to me, as a despicable one, but he affirms that I have expressed some other, still more despicable; without, however, mentioning to whom, when, or where. 'Tis evident that the phrase "still more despicable" admits of infinite shades from very light to very dark. How am I to judge of the degree intended? or how shall I annex any precise idea to language so indefinite?

Between Gentlemen, despicable and more despicable are not worth the pains of a distinction: when, therefore, you do not interrogate me, as to the opinion which is specifically ascribed to me, I must conclude that you view it as within the limits to which the animadversions of political opponents upon each other may justifiably extend, and consequently as not warranting the idea of it which Doctor Cooper appears to entertain.

Repeating that I cannot reconcile it with propriety to make the acknowledgment or denial you desire, I will add that I deem it inadmissible on principle, to consent to be interrogated as to the justice of the inferences which may be drawn by others from whatever I may have said of a political opponent in the course of a fifteen years' competition. . . . I stand ready to avow or disavow promptly and explicitly any precise or definite opinion which I may be charged with having declared of any Gentleman. More than this cannot fitly be expected from me; and especially it cannot be reasonably expected that I shall enter into an explanation upon a basis so vague as that which you have adopted. I trust on more reflection you will see the matter in the same light with me. If not, I can only regret the circumstance and must abide the consequences.

The publication of Doctor Cooper was never seen by me 'till after the receipt of your letter.

I have the honor to be, &c.,   A. HAMILTON.

Col. Burr.

In reply to this letter, on June 21, Burr said:

Your letter of the 20th instant has been this day received. Having considered it attentively, I regret to find in it nothing of that sincerity and delicacy which you profess to value.

Political opposition can never absolve gentlemen from the necessity of a rigid adherence to the laws of honor and the rules of decorum. I neither claim such privilege nor indulge it in others. . . .

Your letter has furnished me with new reasons for requiring a definite reply.

The New York *Evening Post*, in the issue of July 12, says: "On Saturday, the 22d of June, Gen. Hamilton, for the first time, called on Mr. P. [Pendleton] and communicated to him the preceding correspondence. He informed him that in a conversation with Mr. V. N. [Van Ness] at the time of receiving the last letter, he told Mr. V. N. that he considered that letter as rude and offensive, and that it was not possible for him to give it any other answer than that Mr. Burr must take such steps as he might think proper. He said further, that Mr. V. N. requested him to take time to deliberate, and then return an answer, when he might possibly entertain a different opinion, and that he would call on him to receive it. That his reply to Mr. V. N. was, that he did not perceive it possible for him to give any other answer than that he had mentioned unless Mr. Burr would take back his last letter and write one which would admit of a different reply. He then gave Mr. P. the letter hereafter mentioned of the 22d of June, to be delivered to Mr. V. N. when he should call on Mr. P. for an answer, and went to his country house."

The correspondence was continued at length, being chiefly between W. P. Van Ness and Nathaniel Pendleton, who also had several conversations together, as representatives of their principals in the difficulty. The final letter, from Mr. Van Ness, dated June 27, concluded as follows: "The length to which this correspondence has extended, only proving that the redress, earnestly desired, cannot be obtained, he [Col. Burr] deems it useless to offer any proposition except the simple message which I shall now have the honor to deliver."

It is added, by the *Evening Post*, that, "with this letter a message was received, such as was to be expected, containing an invitation which was accepted, and Mr. P. informed Mr. V. N. he should hear from him the next day as to further particulars."

There was a delay caused by General Hamilton's professional engagements in the Circuit Court, but "on Friday, the 6th of July, the Circuit being closed, Mr. P. gave this information, and that Gen. Hamilton would be ready, at any time after the Sunday following. On Monday the particulars were arranged."

The attitude of Hamilton toward his family must have, for many days, been extremely embarrassing, for the meeting with Burr appears to have been postponed from time to time. Meanwhile he lived with his wife and children at the Grange, and, apparently, attended to his affairs in the city with his accustomed regularity. He wrote his wife two farewell letters, one on July 4, and another on July 10, at 10 P.M., but how these letters reached her, or by whom they were delivered, is not known. They were preserved by her and were probably carried about and reread many times, judging by their tattered appearance, and to-day one of them is scarcely legible. The first letter was possibly written after he had attended the meeting of the Society of the Cincinnati—perhaps after he had rendered the jovial song the night before the duel, at some place in the city itself.

Alexander Hamilton to Elizabeth Hamilton

This letter, my very dear Eliza, will not be delivered to you unless I shall first have terminated my earthly career, to begin, as I humbly hope, from redeeming grace and divine mercy, a happy immortality.

If it had been possible for me to have avoided the interview, my love for you and my precious children would have been alone a decisive motive. But it was not possible, without sacrifices which would have rendered me unworthy of your esteem. I need not tell you of the pangs I feel from the idea of quitting you, and exposing you to the anguish which I know you would feel. Nor could I dwell on the topic lest it should unman me.

The consolations of Religion, my beloved, can alone support you; and these you have a right to enjoy. Fly to the bosom of your God and be comforted.

With my last idea I shall cherish the sweet hope of meeting you in a better world.

Adieu best of wives—best of women.

Embrace all my darling children for me.

Ever yours   A. H.

July 4, 1804.
Mrs. Hamilton.

Alexander Hamilton to Elizabeth Hamilton

My beloved Eliza: Mrs. Mitchel is the person in the world to whom as a friend I am under the greatest obligations. I have not hitherto done my duty to her. But resolved to repair my omission to her as much as possible, I have encouraged her to come to this country, and intend, if it shall be in my power, to render the evening of her days comfortable.

But if it shall please God to put this out of my power, and to enable you hereafter to be of service to her, I entreat you to do it, and to treat her with the tenderness of a sister.

This is my second letter.

The scruples of a Christian have determined me to expose my own life to any extent rather than subject myself to the guilt of taking the life of another. This much increases my hazards, and redoubles my pangs for you.

But you had rather I should die innocent than live guilty.

FAC-SIMILE OF LETTER FROM ALEXANDER HAMILTON TO MRS. HAMILTON

Heaven can preserve me, and I humbly hope will; but in the contrary event I charge you to remember that you are a Christian. God's will be done!

The will of a merciful God must be good. Once more, Adieu, my darling, darling wife.

A. H.

Tuesday Evening, 10 o'Cl.
Mrs. Hamilton.

Early the next morning he was shot.

The story of the meeting has been so often repeated that it seems unnecessary to again publish the familiar details, yet even to-day there is much misconception. I shall, however, present the well-attested facts, to which I purpose to add others in my possession. The available and established data concerning the duel seem to be those which follow.

On Friday, July 6, 1804, Mr. Pendleton informed Mr. Van Ness that General Hamilton would be ready at any time after the eighth. On Monday the particulars were arranged; on Wednesday the parties met on the Jersey shore at seven o'clock in the morning.

The details of the actual meeting were printed by the New York *Evening Post* of July 12,[1] and the account is that furnished by the seconds. It may be stated in this connection that the conclusions of these gentlemen were not harmonious, as may be seen by a comparison of the newspaper account with Mr. Pendleton's notes, which are now for the first time published. The language of the published statement essentially agrees with that in " Paper 2 " in the Pendleton memoranda; but there is an abrupt hiatus after the words

---

[1] As well as the *Morning Chronicle*, which was established in 1802, and edited by Dr. Peter Irving. (See Hudson's " History of Journalism," p. 263.)

"The fire of Colonel ——." [1] It would appear as if Van Ness, after agreeing to the statement, had changed his mind the day after the duel.

Col. Burr arrived first on the ground, as had been previously agreed: When Gen. Hamilton arrived the parties exchanged salutations, and the seconds proceeded to make their arrangements. They measured the distance, ten full paces, and cast lots for the choice of position, as also to determine by whom the word should be given; both of which fell to the second of Gen. Hamilton. They then proceeded to load the pistols in each other's presence, after which the

---

[1] Memorandum of original papers connected with duel between General Hamilton and Colonel Burr, fought on the 12th day of July, 1804. [The interlineations and corrections are as contained in originals.]

No. 1. The following paper is in the handwriting of Nathaniel Pendleton, Esq., General Hamilton's second:

"1. The parties will leave town tomorrow morning about five oClock, and meet at the place agreed on. The party arriving first shall wait for the other.

"2. The weapons shall be pistols not exceeding eleven inches in the barrel. The distance ten paces.

"3. The choice of positions to be determined by lot.

"4. The parties having taken their positions one of the seconds to be determined by lot (after having ascertained that both parties are ready) shall loudly and distinctly give the word 'present'—If one of the parties fires, and the other hath not fired, the opposite second shall say one, two, three, fire, and he shall then fire or lose his shot. A snap or flash is a fire.

"Monday.

"11 July 1804."

No. 2 is a paper in Mr. Pendleton's handwriting which evidently was read over to Mr. Van Ness, Colonel Burr's second, and abruptly ends, for the reason that the seconds could not agree on the concluding part of it. It is endorsed, as appears on the back, "Facts agreed between N P. & Wm. V. Ness," which shows that, so far as it went, it was agreed upon. This paper is as follows:

"Colo. Burr arrived first on the ground, as had been previously agreed—When General Hamilton arrived the parties exchanged salutations, and the seconds proceeded to make their arrangements.

"They measured the distance ten full paces, and cast lots for the choice of position, as also to determine by whom the word should be given, both of which fell to the Second of General Hamilton. They then proceeded to load the Pistols in each others presence after which the parties took their stations. The Gentleman who was to give the word then explained to the parties the rules which were to govern them in firing, which were as follows: 'The parties being placed at their stations, the second who gives the word shall ask them if they are ready—being answered in

parties took their stations.[1]   The gentleman who was to give
the word then explained to the parties the rules which were
to govern them in firing, which were as follows:

The parties being placed at their stations the second
who gives the word shall ask them whether they are ready;
being answered in the affirmative, he shall say *'Present!'*
after this *please* . . . If one fires before the other, the opposite
second shall say one, two, three, fire . . . and he shall then
fire or lose his fire."   He then asked if they were prepared;
being answered in the affirmative, he gave the word *present*,
as had been agreed upon, and both parties presented and

the affirmative he shall say "present" after which the parties shall present & fire
when they please.   If one fires before the other the opposite second shall say, one,
two, three, fire, and he shall fire or lose his fire.   The Gentleman who was to give
the word asked if they were prepared, being answered in the affirmative he gave
the word "present."   Both the parties presented.   The Pistols were both discharged
succesively (but the time intervening between the two is not here stated the seconds
not agreeing in that fact) The fire of Col⁰.' "——
On July 13, 1804, Mr. Van Ness, Colonel Burr's second, wrote Mr. Pendleton a
letter, which shows that there was some discussion as to completing the statement.
The letter is as follows:

"D SIR: I left you for the purpose of procuring and examining my own papers
relative to the late unfortunate affair, and was sorry to find on my return that you
had left Dr. Hosack's—The statement which you hastily read to me contained one
or two things that rendered it desirable for me to recur to my own notes—As I
presume no publication will be made in the morning papers, I will have the honor
of seeing you again on my return to the City, which will be at an early hour in the
morning—
                    "I have the honor to be
                      "Your most obt & very
                        "hm Svt
                                                    "W. P. VAN NESS.
"Nath. Pendleton, Esq.
  "July 13, 1804."

No. 4 is two slips of paper, apparently originally one piece, which has been accidentally torn apart at one of the foldings.   This is in Mr. Van Ness's handwriting,
and is evidently intended as a proposed correction of the published account of the
duel in the paper.   This is without date.   There is nothing on it to show that it

---

[1] An incident of the duel, afterward related by Burr, was that Hamilton asked for
a moment's delay before the signal was given to wipe his eyeglasses.   This is untrue, as Hamilton never wore eyeglasses.   (A. McL. H.)

fired in succession—the intervening time is not expressed, as the seconds do not precisely agree on that point.

The fire of Colonel Burr took effect, and General Hamilton almost instantly fell. Col. Burr then advanced toward General Hamilton, with a manner and gesture that appeared to General Hamilton's friend to be expressive of

was sent to Mr. Pendleton, but the fact that it was found among Mr. Pendleton's papers would indicate it had been sent to him by Mr. Van Ness. The paper is as follows:

(First piece:) "It is agreed by the Gentlemen who attended Genl Hamilton & Col. Burr in the late unfortunate affair that the following Document No. 13 in the statement which appeared in the *Morning Chronicle* of yesterday should be corrected in the following manner."

(Second piece:) "In the interview between Genl Hamilton & Col. Burr, both parties agreeably to the word of command *presented*, this term should therefore be employed as more correct than the expression 'took aim' inserted in document No. 13 of the statement published in the *Morning Chronicle* of yesterday——"

There is also in Mr. Pendleton's handwriting a letter addressed to Mr. Van Ness, dated July 16, 1804, which evidently shows there had been some disagreement in regard to the matter of the publication. This letter is evidently a draft which was kept by Mr. Pendleton as his copy of the letter he sent; the original doubtless was copied out fairly in accordance with the corrections here shown and sent to Mr. Van Ness. The letter is as follows:

"July 16, 1804.
"½ after one

"DEAR SIR

"It will not be possible for me to see you in time to give you another opportunity of seeing the statement I before showed you, before it is printed,—as The arrange-
to have it appear   this day having reserving
ments were so made that the Statement should appear reservedly a few lines of
after
until ∧ the hour you mentioned;
addition for your examination ∧ as to which too we had before conversed. I have
by you   I offered from Gen H.
added in explicit terms the reason assigned ∧ for not receiving the last paper ∧—
no   as you seem to desire
I could by ∧ means consent to omit the paper I read to you ∧ as you must have
particularly
supposed it was deemed ∧ a material subject by having been put into writing. I
will
trust you ∧ find no reason to complain of any want of accuracy or precision in the publication I have authorised.

"I am Sir, have the honor
"to be Yr &c

"Wm. P. Van Ness, Esq."

The above memoranda were given to the writer by Francis K. Pendleton, Esq., a great-grandson of Nathaniel Pendleton.

regret, but without speaking, turned about and withdrew, being urged from the field by his friend, as has been subsequently stated, with a view to prevent his being recognized by the surgeon and bargemen, who were then approaching. No further communication took place between the principals, and the barge that carried Col. Burr immediately returned to the city. We conceive it proper to add that the conduct of the parties in this interview was perfectly proper as suited the occasion.

William Coleman, of the *Evening Post*, gives his version as follows:[1]

It was nearly seven in the morning when the boat which carried General Hamilton, his friend Mr. Pendleton, and the Surgeon mutually agreed on, Doctor Hosack, reached that part of the Jersey shore called the *Weahawk*. There they found Mr. Burr and his friend Mr. Van Ness, who, as I am told, had been employed since their arrival, with coats off, in clearing away the bushes, limbs of trees, etc., so as to make a fair opening. The parties in a few moments were at their allotted situations. When Mr. Pendleton gave the word, Mr. Burr raised his arm slowly, deliberately took his aim, and fired. His ball entered General Hamilton's right side. As soon as the bullet struck him, he raised himself involuntarily on his toes, turned a little to the left (at which moment his pistol went off), and fell upon his face. Mr. Pendleton immediately called out for Dr. Hosack, who, in running to the spot, had to pass Mr. Van Ness and Col. Burr; but Van Ness had the cool precaution to cover his principal with an umbrella, so that Dr. Hosack should not be able to swear that he saw him on the field.[2]

---

[1] This account, and much of what is to follow, is from "A Collection of the Tracts and Documents Relative to the Death of Major General Alexander Hamilton, with Comments Together with the Various Orations, Sermons, and Eulogies, etc.," by the editor of the New York *Evening Post*. New York, Hopkins & Seymour, 1804.

[2] The Federalist press, in July, 1804, teemed with stories more or less absurd in regard to the behavior of Burr. Some of these had, undoubtedly, a slight foundation, but most of them were preposterous. *The Balance and Columbian Repository*[1]

[1] Vol. III, No. 33, p. 267, Tuesday, August 14, 1804.

What passed after this the reader will have in the following letter from Dr. Hosack himself:

Dr. David Hosack to William Coleman

August 17th, 1804.

DEAR SIR: To comply with your request is a painful task; but I will repress my feelings while I endeavor to furnish you with an enumeration of such particulars relative to the melancholy end of our beloved friend Hamilton, as dwell most forcibly on my recollection.

When called to him, upon his receiving the fatal wound, I found him half sitting on the ground, supported in the arms of Mr. Pendleton. His countenance of death I shall never forget. He had at that instant just strength to say, "This is a mortal wound, Doctor;" when he sunk away, and became to all appearance lifeless. I immediately stripped up his clothes, and soon, alas! ascertained that the direction of the ball must have been through some vital part.[1]

---

published an account of the accidental discharge of a pistol in the hand of "M. E. L. Schieffelin, Druggist, in Pearl Street," who was firing at a mark. The muzzle of the weapon was but twenty inches from his foot, yet when the ball struck the top of the foot near the ankle, a trivial wound only was made. This was explained by the fact that Mr. Schieffelin wore ribbed silk stockings, and "not a thread of the stocking was broken"—the ball being forced into the foot and the stocking "made a sort of bag for it." The editor also refers to an English case when the presence of a silk handkerchief on the breast of a young woman saved her life when a pistol was accidentally discharged. The editor goes on to say: "The extract from the London paper above quoted in regard to the resistibility of silk appeared in the *Morning Chronicle* about ten days previous to the fatal interview. We know that Mr. Burr practised shooting at a mark, but we are not sure the *Morning Chronicle* quotation was 'put' into his hands, and that he tried the experiment of shooting at silk in order to ascertain how he could best preserve himself from the ball of his illustrious victim in case he fired. Facts, however, warrant conjectures very unfavorable to Mr. Burr. After the challenge was accepted, Mr. Burr wrote a note to his tailor, Mr. Francis Davis, requesting that he would make him a *silk coat* (having already the undergarment of silk) by Monday evening, and adding that unless it was then brought home it would be of *no use*, as on *Tuesday morning, by four o'clock, he was to leave town!* Special directions were given to make the coat *unusually large*. It was made according to order, and delivered to Mr. Burr on Monday evening. In this coat, which was *black*, he killed General Hamilton."

[1] "For the satisfaction of some of General Hamilton's friends, I examined his body after death, in presence of Dr. Post and two other gentlemen. I discovered that the ball struck the second or third false rib, and fractured it about in the middle;

His pulse was not to be felt; his respiration was entirely suspended; and upon laying my hand on his heart, and perceiving no motion there, I considered him as irrecoverably gone. I, however, observed to Mr. |Pendleton, that the only chance for his reviving was immediately to get him upon the water. He therefore lifted him up, and carried him out of the wood, to the margin of the bank, where the bargemen aided us in conveying him into the boat, which immediately put off. During all this time I could not discover the least symptom of returning life. I now rubbed his face, lips and temples, with spirits of hartshorne, applied it to his neck and breast, and to the wrists and palms of his hands, and endeavored to pour some into his mouth. When we had got, as I should judge, about 50 yards from the shore, some imperfect efforts to breathe were for the first time manifest; in a few minutes he sighed and became sensible to the impression of the hartshorne, or the fresh air of the water: He breathed; his eyes, hardly opened, wandered, without fixing on any objects; to our great joy he at length spoke: "My vision is indistinct," were his first words.

His pulse became more perceptible; his respiration more regular; his sight returned.

I then examined the wound to know if there was any dangerous discharge of blood; upon slightly pressing his side it gave him pain; on which I desisted. Soon after recovering his sight, he happened to cast his eye upon the case of pistols, and observing the one that he had had in his hand lying on the outside, he said, "Take care of that pistol; it is undischarged, and still cocked; it may go off and do harm; Pendleton knows, (attempting to turn his head towards him) that I did not intend to fire at him." "Yes,"

---

it then passed through the liver and diaphragm, and, as nearly as we could ascertain without a minute examination, lodged in the first or second lumbar vertebra. The vertebra in which it was lodged was considerably splintered, so that the spiculæ were distinctly perceptible to the finger. About a pint of clotted blood was found in the cavity of the belly, which had probably been effused from the divided vessels of the liver."

said Mr. Pendleton, understanding his wish, "I have already made Dr. Hosack acquainted with your determination as to that." He then closed his eyes and remained calm, without any disposition to speak; nor did he say much afterwards, excepting in reply to my questions as to his feelings. He asked me once or twice, how I found his pulse; and he informed me that his lower extremities had lost all feeling; manifesting to me that he entertained no hopes that he should long survive. I changed the posture of his limbs, but to no purpose; they had totally lost their sensibility. Perceiving that we approached the shore, he said, "Let Mrs. Hamilton be immediately sent for—let the event be gradually broken to her; but give her hopes." Looking up we saw his friend Mr. Bayard standing on the wharf in great agitation. He had been told by his servant that Gen. Hamilton, Mr. Pendleton and myself had crossed the river in a boat together, and too well he conjectured the fatal errand, and foreboded the dreadful result. Perceiving, as we came nearer, that Mr. Pendleton & Myself only sat up in the stern sheets, he clasped his hands together in the most violent apprehensions; but when I called to him to have a cot prepared, and he at the same moment saw his poor friend lying in the bottom of the boat, he threw up his eyes and burst into a flood of tears and lamentation. Hamilton alone appeared tranquil and composed. He then conveyed him as tenderly as possible up to the house. The distresses of this amiable family were such that till the first shock was abated, they were scarcely able to summon fortitude enough to yield sufficient assistance to their dying friend.

Upon our reaching the house he became more languid, occasioned probably by the agitation of his removal from the boat. I gave him a little weak wine and water. When he recovered his feelings, he complained of pain in his back; we immediately undressed him, laid him in bed, and darkened the room. I then gave him a large anodyne, which I frequently repeated. During the first day he took upwards of an ounce of laudanum; and tepid anodyne fomentations were also applied to those parts nearest the seat of his pain. Yet were his sufferings, during the whole of the day, almost intolerable.[1] I had not the shadow of a hope of his recovery, and Dr. Post, whom I requested might be sent for immediately on our reaching Mr. Bayard's house, united with me in this opinion. General Rey, the French Consul, also had the goodness to invite the surgeons of the French frigates in our harbour, as they had had much experience in gunshot wounds, to render their assistance. They immediately came; but to prevent his being disturbed, I stated to them his situation, described the nature of his wound and the direction of the ball, with all the symptoms that could enable them to form an opinion as to the event. One of the gentlemen then accompanied me to the bedside. The result was a confirmation of the opinion that had already been expressed by Dr. Post and myself.

During the night, he had some imperfect sleep; but the succeeding morning his symptoms were aggravated, attended however with a diminution of pain. His mind retained all its usual strength and composure. The great source of his anxiety seemed to be in his sympathy with his half distracted wife and children. He spoke to her frequently of them. "My beloved wife and children" were always his expressions. But his fortitude triumphed over his situation, dreadful as it was; once, indeed, at the sight of his children brought to the bedside together, seven in number, his utterance forsook him, he opened his eyes, gave them one look, and closed them again, till they were taken away. As a proof of his extraordinary composure of mind, let me add, that he alone could calm the frantic grief of their mother, "*Remember, my Eliza, you are a Christian,*" were the expressions with which he frequently, with a firm voice, but in a pathetic and impressive manner, addressed her. His

---

[1] "As his habit was delicate and had been lately rendered more feeble by ill health, particularly by a disorder of the stomach and bowels, I carefully avoided all those remedies which are usually indicated on such occasions."

words, and the tone in which they were uttered, will never
be effaced from my memory. At about two o'clock, as the
public well know, he expired.

Incorrupta fides—nudaque veritas
Quando ullum invenient parem ?
Multis ille quidem flebilis occidit.

I am, Sir,

> Your friend & humble serv't
>
> DAVID HOSACK.

Wm. Coleman, Esq.

The house where Hamilton died belonged, at the time, to
his friend William Bayard, and was situated at 80–82 Jane
Street, but has long since disappeared, having gone the way
of all the old buildings of New York; when last described
it was a squalid tenement. It stood near the corner of
Greenwich Street, and the garden is said to have extended
to the North River. Hamilton died in a large, square room
on the second floor of the building. Burr was landed at the
foot of Canal Street, and hurried to his home at Richmond
Hill, which was at the present crossing of Varick and
Charlton Streets. A courier was immediately despatched
for Mrs. Hamilton, who was at the Grange, quite oblivious of
all that had occurred, and she was able to get to her husband's bedside at noon. Before Mr. Hamilton died she
was joined by her children, my father being a baby of two
years, who was kissed by his father, who recognized them
all. With Mrs. Hamilton was her sister Angelica, who
wrote to her brother Philip at once as follows:

> AT MR. BAYARD'S, GREENWICH.
> Wednesday Morning.

MY DEAR BROTHER: I have the painful task to inform
you that Gen. Hamilton was this morning wounded by that
wretch Burr, but we have every reason to hope that he will

recover. May I advise that you repair immediately to my father, as perhaps he may wish to come down.

My dear sister bears with saintlike fortitude this affliction. The town is in consternation, and there exists only the expression of grief and indignation.

Adieu, my dear brother

Ever yours, A. CHURCH.

Oliver Wolcott, one of Hamilton's closest friends, who afterward did much to straighten out his affairs, wrote to his wife, both on the 11th and 13th of July, leaving the bedside of his dying friend for the purpose.

Oliver Wolcott to Mrs. Wolcott

I had prepared to set out to see you tomorrow morning, but an afflicting event has just occurred which renders it proper for me to postpone my journey a few days. This morning my friend Hamilton was wounded, and as is supposed *mortally* in a duel with Col°. Burr. The cause the old disagreement about Politicks.

I have just returned from Mr. Wm. Bayards—where Hamilton is—I did not see him—he suffers great pain—which he endures like a Hero—Mrs. Hamilton is with him, but she is ignorant of the cause of his Illness, which she supposes to be spasms—no one dare tell her the truth—it is feared she would become frantic.

Gen'l Hamilton has left his opinion, in writing, against Duelling, which he condemns as much as any man living— he determined not to return the fire of his adversary—and reasoned himself into a belief, that though the custom was in the highest degree *criminal*, yet there were peculiar reasons which rendered it proper for *him*, to expose *himself to Col. Burr in particular*. This instance of the derangement of intellect of a great mind, on a single point, has often been noticed as one of the most common yet unaccountable frailties of human nature.

Gen¹ Hamilton has of late years expressed his conviction of the truths of the Christian Religion, and has desired to receive the Sacrament—but no one of the Clergy who have yet been consulted will administer it.¹

¹ This was an erroneous statement, as Bishop Moore not only administered the communion but remained with him until his death. Undoubtedly the reluctance upon the part of certain clergymen that Wolcott mentions arose from an extreme ecclesiastical narrowness and intolerance of duelling that existed in that day. Bishop Moore, in a letter to William Coleman, wrote:

Yesterday morning, immediately after he was brought from Hoboken to the house of Mr. Bayard, at Greenwich, a message was sent informing me of the sad event, accompanied by a request from General Hamilton, that I would come to him for the purpose of administering the holy communion. I went; but being desirous to afford time for serious reflection, and conceiving that, under existing circumstances, it would be right and proper to avoid every appearance of precipitancy in performing one of the most solemn offices of our religion, I did not then comply with his desire. At one o'clock I was again called on to visit him. Upon my entering the room and approaching his bed, with the utmost calmness and composure he said: "My dear sir, you perceive my unfortunate situation, and no doubt have been made acquainted with the circumstances which led to it. It is my desire to receive the communion at your hands. I hope you will not conceive there is any impropriety in my request." He added, "It has for some time past been the wish of my heart, and it was my intention to take an early opportunity of uniting myself to the Church, by the reception of that holy ordinance." I observed to him that he must be very sensible of the delicate and trying situation in which I was then placed; that however desirous I might be to afford consolation to a fellow-mortal in distress, still, it was my duty as a minister of the Gospel to hold up the law of God as paramount to all other law; and that, therefore, under the influence of such sentiments, I must unequivocally condemn the practice which had brought him to his present unhappy condition. He acknowledged the propriety of these sentiments, and declared that he viewed the late transaction with sorrow and contrition. I then asked him, "Should it please God to restore you to health, sir, will you never be again engaged in a similar transaction? And will you employ all your influence in society to discountenance this barbarous custom?" His answer was, "That, sir, is my deliberate intention."

I proceeded to converse with him on the subject of his receiving the communion; and told him that, with respect to the qualifications of those who wished to become partakers of that holy ordinance, my inquiries could not be made in language more expressive than that which was used by our Church: "Do you sincerely repent of your sins past? Have you a lively faith in God's mercy through Christ, with a thankful remembrance of the death of Christ? And are you disposed to live in love and charity with all men?" He lifted up his hands and said: "With the utmost sincerity of heart I can answer those questions in the affirmative. I have no ill-will against Colonel Burr. I met him with a fixed resolution to do him no harm. I forgive all that happened." I then observed to him that the terrors of Divine law were to be announced to the obdurate and impenitent, but that the consolations of the Gospel were to be offered to the humble and contrite heart; that I had no reason to doubt his sincerity, and would proceed immediately to gratify his wishes. The communion was then administered, which he received with great devotion, and his heart afterwards appeared to be perfectly at rest. I saw him again this morning, when, with his last faltering words, he expressed a strong confidence in the mercy of God through the intercession of the Redeemer. I remained with him until two o'clock this afternoon, when death closed the awful scene. He expired without a struggle, and almost without a groan.

Whilst there is life there is Hope, but that is all which can be said. Thus has perished one of the greatest men of this or any age. I am as well as could be expected, considering how my mind is agitated by this event & I will come to you as soon as the issue is decided.

Kiss the children and believe me

Affectionately yours,

OLIV. WOLCOTT.

P. S. Hamilton spent the afternoon & evening of Monday with our friends at my House in Company with Mr. Hopkinson of Phil^a. He was uncommonly cheerful and gay. The duel had been determined on for ten days. Monday was first proposed—it was then postponed till Tuesday—& took effect this Morning. Judge Pendleton was his second.

If Mr. King is at Litchfield tell him I have written to him at Hartford.

Mrs. Elizabeth Wolcott
    Litchfield,
        Connecticut.

And again:

Oliver Wolcott to Mrs. Wolcott

Yesterday Genl Hamilton expired in the midst of his family, who are agonized beyond description. No person who witnessed their distress will ever be induced to fight a duel—unless he is a person wholly insensible to every sentiment of humanity.

Nothing can present a more humiliating idea of the imperfection of human nature, than the scene we have witnessed. A man of the first endowments of mind, the most strict probity, the greatest sincerity, and the most tender attachments, has for a considerable time been deliberately settling his affairs, in contemplation of the event which has happened, as one highly probable—he has left his family in perfect health, as if proceeding on ordinary business & with the same deliberation has rec^d a mortal wound—thus proving his respect for justice in comparatively small matters, & at the same time disregarding its obligations on points of the first importance. This inconsistency has moreover happened in compliance with a custom, which he deemed wholly immoral & indefensible, by which he had lost a darling son, in the prime of life, and with which he had resolved never to comply, except in respect to the disposal of his own existence. The defence of all this conduct, is, that there was a chance for an Escape, & that it would be wrong to torture his family with unnecessary anxiety. This excuse is weak & unsatisfactory, & it proves, that on certain points, the most enlightened men are governed by the most unsound reasons.

Tomorrow the funeral will be attended, & I have supposed, that you would think it my duty to be present.

I feel the most sincere regret at the delay & more so, as I am concerned to hear that you are unwell. I will come the next stage at all events. Give my love to Mary, the Children & my Brothers family, & be assured of the attachment of y^{rs}

OLIV. WOLCOTT.

The pistols which were used figured in more than one affair of honor. With them John Barker Church, it is said, met Aaron Burr, the challenge following some scandal arising from a report that the Holland Land Company had cancelled a note held by the latter in consideration of legislative services rendered by him. Little is known of this duel, which is said to have been also fought at Weehawken Sept. 2, 1799, but it is only a tradition in the Church family. They are also said to have been used by young Philip Hamilton in his encounter with Eacker, his cousin Philip Church, a son of John Barker Church, being his second. It is also stated that they were used in a duel between James Wadsworth of Geneseo and a Colonel Kane of Philadelphia when Philip Church was Wadsworth's second, but I am unable to confirm this.

THE PISTOLS USED BY HAMILTON AND BURR

The pistols were restored to their owner, John Barker Church, by Mr. Pendleton after the duel, and were inherited by his grandson, Richard Church, Esq., to whom they now belong. They are of English make, and bear the name WOGDEN. The barrels are nine inches long and of admirable workmanship. They were purchased by Mr. Church in London, in 1795 or 1796, and used by him in an English duel.[1]

Coleman's "Collections," and the newspapers of the day, were full of accounts of the funeral, which attracted much attention. The procession started from Mr. Church's house in Robinson Street, at eleven o'clock in the morning, and was composed of the Society of the Cincinnati, the Sixth Regiment of militia, the gentlemen of the bar, the Lieutenant-Governor of the State, the corporation of the city of New York, the foreign consular agents, army and navy officers of the United States, as well as of the foreign services who were in New York, the Chamber of Commerce and officers of the various banks, the port wardens and masters of vessels in the harbor, the president, professors, and students of Columbia College in mourning gowns, the St. Andrews, Tammany, Mechanics, and Marine societies, and a large number of people who followed the coffin through Beekman, Pearl, and Whitehall Streets, up Broadway to Trinity Church.

On top of the coffin was General Hamilton's hat and sword, and his boots and spurs were reversed across the horse, which was a gray one. It was dressed in mourning, and led by two negro servants in white, with white turbans trimmed with black.

---

[1] There are numerous other pistols in existence that are said to have been those used by Hamilton, but none are genuine. The writer has frequently been approached by venders who have produced "documentary proof," but investigation has shown this to be valueless.

During the procession there was a regular discharge of minute guns from the Battery, by a detachment from the regiment of artillery, and the different merchant vessels in the harbor wore their colors half-mast.

The British ship of war *Boston*, Captain Douglass, at anchor within the Hook, appeared in mourning during the morning, and at ten o'clock commenced firing minute guns, which were continued for nearly an hour. The British packet, *Lord Charles Spencer*, Captain Cotesworth, also was in mourning, and fired an equal number of guns. The French frigates *Cybelle* and *Didon* were also in full mourning, with yards peaked, and fired minute guns during the procession.

The family at Albany were naturally thrown into a condition of great distress and anxiety, and General Schuyler wrote at once to his daughter:

Philip Schuyler to Elizabeth Hamilton

Monday Morning, 13 *July*, 1804.

MY DEAR DEARLY BELOVED AND AFFECTIONATE CHILD: This morning Mr. Church's letter has announced to me the severe affliction which it has pleased the Supreme being to inflict on you on me and on all dear to us. If aught under heaven could aggravate the affliction I experience, it is that incapable of moving or being removed I cannot fly to you to pour the balm of comfort into your afflicted bosom, to water it with my tears, to solace yours and mine in this depressing situation. Under the pressure of this most severe calamity let us seek consolation from that source where it can only be truly found, in humble resignation to the will of heaven. Oh my Dearly Beloved Child let us unanimously entreat the Supreme being to give you fortitude to support the affliction, to preserve you to me, to your dear children and relations. Should it please God so far to restore my strength as to enable me to go to you, I shall embrace the first moment to do it, but should it be otherwise, I entreat you my beloved Child to come home as soon as you possibly can,

GENERAL PHILIP SCHUYLER
From the painting by John Trumbull, 1792

with my dear Grandchildren.   Your sisters will accompany
you.   May Almighty God bless and protect you and pour
the balm of consolation into your distressed soul is and will
always be the prayer of
                Your affectionate and distressed parent.
                                              PH. SCHUYLER.
    Mrs. Hamilton.

And again, on Tuesday, 17th July, 1804, to Mrs. Church,
who was with her sister:

The dreadful calamity my Dearly Beloved Child which
we have all sustained affected me so deeply as to threaten
serious results, but when I received the account of his
Christian resignation my afflicted soul was much tranquillized.   Oh may heaven indulgently extend fortitude to
my afflicted, my distressed, my beloved Eliza.   I trust that
the Supreme being will prolong my life that I may discharge
the duties of a father to my dear child and her dear children.
My wounds bear a favorable aspect, and the paroxisms of the
gout have not been severe for the past two days, and yesterday I was able to sit up all day.   God grant that my recovery may be accelerated, to enable me to go to New York
and embrace my distressed children.   Should however my
restoration be retarded, I wish to see you all here.   The
change of scene may perhaps tend to soothe my distressed
Eliza and her children.   She knows how tenderly I loved
My Dear Hamilton, how tenderly I love her and her children.
Much I feel all the duties which are devolved on me.   The
evening of my days will be passed in the pleasing occupation of administering comfort and relief to a Child and
Grand-Children so highly entitled to my best exertions.
    My Kitty is most deeply affected.   Her tears have flowed
incessantly.   She begins to be more composed, and unites
with me in love to your distressed Sister and all so dear to us.
    I do not write to day to my Eliza lest it should create a fresh
paroxism of grief.   May she become calm.   Her piety will I
trust sustain her and her life be preserved that her parent, her
children and relations may not sustain an additional calamity.

Your Brother Philip was on his way home and missed my letter. He is now here and sets out immediately for New York.

Excuse me to Mr. Church for not writing him today. Adieu my Dearly beloved Child. May God bless and preserve you all is the constant prayer of your

Afflicted parent

PH. SCHUYLER.

Mrs. Church.

Fail not my Beloved to let me daily know the state of your afflicted sister. My anxiety on her account rends my heart.

In the following November her father again wrote:

"What your afflictions my dear dearly beloved child have added to mine, was the natural result of a parent's tenderness for a dutiful and affectionate child, as he invariably experienced from you." This was the last letter he wrote the bereaved widow, for he died a short time after.

The public excitement was great indeed, and all classes turned out to do Hamilton honor; even the most rabid political enemies were silent for a time, and some of them grudgingly admitted his worth. Coleman, who had preserved and published all the comments of the press of the day, also reproduced the funeral and other orations. Gouverneur Morris, Eliphalet Nott, and Harrison G. Otis delivered eulogies, and the sermon of Nott is one of the most eloquent and forceful examples of rhetoric. Even the vituperative *American Citizen*, that had bitterly assailed Hamilton during his life, now praised him, and the editor said: "Death has *swallowed up* in *victory*, cruel and fatal victory, the narrow isthmus that separated from this great luminary, those with whom I act."

In fact, all newspapers of both parties united in honoring his memory. Poets of both sexes contributed verse to the daily press, some of considerable excellence, but not a little of the turgid kind of the period; all however were sincere.

His will was made two days before he died, and is as follows:

LAST WILL AND TESTAMENT OF ALEXANDER HAMILTON

In the name of God, Amen!

I, Alexander Hamilton, of the State of New York, counsellor at law, do make this my last will and testament, as follows:

First: I appoint John B. Church, Nicholas Fish, and Nathaniel Pendleton, of the city aforesaid, esquires, to be executors and trustees of this my will, and I devise to them, their heirs and assigns, as joint tenants, and not tenants in common, all my estate, real and personal, whatsoever and wheresoever upon trust, at their discretion to sell and dispose of the same at such time and times, in such manner, and upon such terms, as they the survivors and survivor shall think fit, and out of the proceeds to pay all the debts which I shall owe at the time of my decease, in whole, if the fund shall be sufficient, proportionally, if it shall be insufficient, and the residue, if any there shall be, to pay and deliver to my excellent and dear wife, Elizabeth Hamilton.

Though, if it please God to spare my life, I may look for a considerable surplus out of my present property; yet if he should speedily call me to the eternal world, a forced sale, as is usual, may possibly render it insufficient to satisfy my debts. I pray God that something may remain for the maintenance and education of my dear wife and children. But should it on the contrary happen that there is not enough for the payment of my debts, I entreat my dear children, if they or any of them shall ever be able, to make up the deficiency. I without hesitation commit to their delicacy a wish which is dictated by my own. Though conscious that I have too far sacrificed the interest of my family to public avocations, and on this account have the less claim to burthen my children, yet I trust in their magnanimity to appreciate, as they ought, this my request. In so unfavorable an event of things, the support of their dear mother, with the most respectful and tender attention, is a duty all the sacredness of which they will feel. Probably her own patrimonial resources will preserve her from indigence. But in all situations they are charged to bear in mind that she has been to them the most devoted and best of mothers. In testimony whereof, I have hereunto subscribed my hand, the ninth day of July, in the year of our Lord one thousand eight hundred and four.

ALEXANDER HAMILTON.

Signed, sealed, published, and as and for his last will and testament in our presence, who have subscribed our names in his presence.

. DOMINICK T. BLAKE
GRAHAM NEWELL
INEZ B. VALLEAU.

Though Hamilton at the time of his death had a large legal practice, his old obligations and the demands upon his purse were very great. The Grange, which he had just built, was an expensive place, and the outlay for its completion was considerable. From his account books, which were kept to July 11, 1804, the day before his death, it appears that his expenditure for the preceding six months was $11,840.27. The outstanding indebtedness of his clients was only $2,510,[1] and the list of debts assigned to J. B. Church by the deed of July 9, 1804, was $1,940. This deed, which has never been published, is an indication of his business precision and system, and was executed but two days before he was killed. Not many men, under these circumstances, would even remember their laundress.

NEW YORK, July 9, 1804.

Know all Men by these Presents, That I, Alexander Hamilton, of the City of New York, Counsellor at law, in consideration of one Dollar to me in hand paid by John B. Church, Esquire, (the receipt whereof is hereby acknowledged) have bargained, sold, assigned and conveyed, and hereby do bargain, sell, assign and convey to the said John B. Church all and singular the debts due owing and payable to me; which are specified in the schedule hereunto annexed to be by him collected and the proceeds applied first toward the payment of all and every the debt and debts which I owe to my household and other servants and labourers and to the woman who washes

---

[1] See Appendix I.

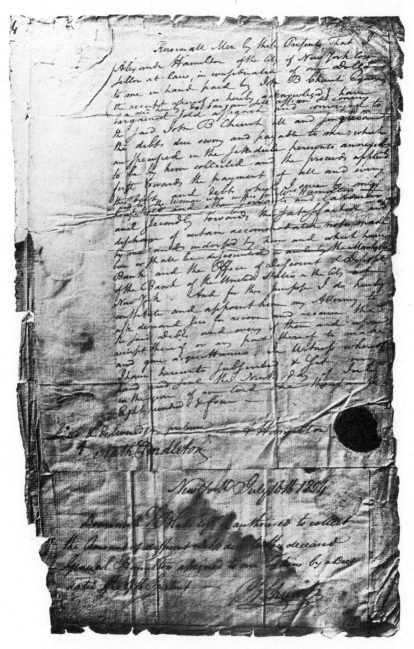

FAC-SIMILE OF POWER OF ATTORNEY

for Mrs. Hamilton, and secondly towards the satisfaction and discharge of certain accommodation notes made by me and endorsed by him and which have been or shall be discounted in and by the Manhattan Bank and the Office of Discount and Deposit of the Bank of the United States in the City of New York. And for this purpose I do hereby constitute and appoint him by Attorney to ask, demand, sue for recover and receive the said debts and every of them and upon receipt thereof or any part thereof to make and give acquittances. In Witness whereof I have hereunto subscribed and set my hand and seal the ninth day of July in the year of our Lord One thousand Eight Hundred and four.

A. Hamilton.

Dated and delivered in presence
   of
    Nath[l]. Pendleton.

Dominick T. Blake, Esq[re] is authorized to collect the amount of different Debts due to the deceased General Hamilton assigned to me by him by a Deed dated the 9th Instant.

J. B. Church.

The wretched condition of Hamilton's affairs now became a matter of solicitude to his friends, and on July 16, 1804, just three days after his death, Wolcott wrote to James McHenry:[1]

Oliver Wolcott to James McHenry

My dear Sir: I have recd. your favor of the 14th; The afflicting event you anticipated has occurred: Hamilton is no more: I will not attempt to describe my feelings: you will learn all the circumstances & the last acts of his life will elevate the character of our late Friend, though they must produce conflict of emotions, to which your bosom has been a stranger.

 Genl. Hamilton left a will in which all his property real and personal is vested in Trustees for the payment of his Debts: This property consists almost entirely of real estates, chiefly

---

[1] McHenry's "Life," p. 530.

new Lands,[1] and a valuable Country Establishment nine Miles from this City: This property cost about 80,000 Dollars[2] & owed about 55,000 Dollars—the Lands are rising in value but wholly unproductive of Revenue; he was apprehensive & I believe justly, that a forced Sale, would leave nothing for his family & perhaps not even produce enough to pay his debts: A number of Gentlemen here have resolved to raise a Fund among the Friends of the decd. for the payment of these debts & to provide for the Children. The design is, that number of Gentlemen of easy Fortunes, shall, without much eclat & publicity, subscribe what may be sufficient. I have been desired to make this intention known, to a select number of Friends and before I recd. your Letter had determined to address you & Mr. Gilmore, leaving it to your judgment to whom the communication ought to be made in Baltimore & not doubting your disposition to co-operate.

> I am Dr Sir, with high Esteem
> & sincere affection, yr. friend
> OLIV. WOLCOTT.

From New York on August 2, 1904, Wolcott again wrote:[3]

Oliver Wolcott to James McHenry

MY DEAR SIR: I addressed you a hasty Letter the 16th. ultimo, at the request of several Gentlemen of this City, who have proposed to raise by contribution, a pecuniary Aid for the family of our departed Friend Genl. Hamilton. Understanding that doubts have existed in Philadelphia, whether this proposal did not originate without the knowledge of the Connections of the Family and might, therefore, offend the sensibility of those it was intended to benefit, I have found it necessary to make certain explanations known there, which I presume will be fully satisfactory. It being possible that

---

[1] Principally in the Ohio Company's territory, and other parts of the then Far West.

[2] Probably an overestimate.   [3] *Op. cit.*, p. 531.

similar impressions have been entertained at Baltimore, I must take the liberty to address you again on this Subject.

The property left by Genl. Hamilton, consists almost entirely of new Lands and a Country Seat Nine Miles from this City. The whole valued by himself at about 80,000 Dollars. The debts are chiefly Notes discounted at the Banks & Monies borrowed on Mortgage amounting to about 55,000 Dollars. The difference is £10,000 New York Currency.

This brief Statement will enable you fully to understand the enclosed Paper, which is a copy of one left by Genl. Hamilton & which is now entrusted to you, on the condition expressed in Mr. Pendelton's Letter to me. There is no doubt, that the anticipations of our Friend, respecting the consequences of forced Sales to raise Money to discharge $55,000 in debts, would be verified. All the property would be sacrificed & his Children deprived of every Memorial of the labour of their illustrious Parent, except his reputation.

Mr. Govr. Morris, Genl. Clarkson, Mr. Gracie, Mr. Bayard &c &c have consulted on this Subject & their joint opinion is, that it is in every Respect, fit, proper, & necessary, that a number of Gentlemen of Fortune, should come forward & pay these debts & provide handsomely for the family. A sum of 100,000 Dollars is the amount proposed.

It would be an Error to consider Genl. Hamilton's Family, as objects of public Charity, but though this is not their Situation, it is certain that they might reasonably expect advancement in Life, from the exertions of our departed Friend. These hopes must, however, be totally disappointed, unless the proposed aid is obtained. It is true that the provision ought in justice to be made by Congress, or by the State of New York, but no person acquainted with the present State of public affairs, will place the least reliance on this resource. Instances of similar benefactions in antient & modern times must be familiar to your mind & it is certain that they have always been considered equally honourable to the Receivers & Givers. The suggestion that the Family would be offended by such proof of the Gratitude & Attachment of the respectable part of the Community, is here well understood to be unfounded.

The mode of giving Effect to the proposed design has been considered & it is supposed that a medium course between the ostentation of a public indiscriminate subscription, & the secresy of private donation would render the provision most munificent & of course most honourable for all Parties concerned. All that is proposed may be easily affected without any sensible burthen & when the enclosed document is perused & it is considered how greatly the men of Property are indebted to the labours of General Hamilton, they must doubtless be affected by his declaration, that those *"labours have amounted to absolute sacrifice of the Interests of his Family."*

Not doubting your disposition to exert your influence in giving effect to the benevolent object of this letter, I remain,

Dr Sir, with sincere Esteem
& true Attachment
yrs

OLIV. WOLCOTT.

Hamilton's interest in the Ohio Company was not, really, very valuable, as it turned out, and consisted of five shares conveyed by Rufus Putnam, Manasseh Cutler, Robert Oliver, and Griffin Green, directors of the Ohio Company, May 14, 1792. As the result of Wolcott's efforts, an indenture entered into April 25, 1806, between Gouverneur Morris, Rufus King, Egbert Benson, Oliver Wolcott, and Charles Wilkes, conveys this land to William Dean and John Lovett for the sum of one dollar, and it is evident difficulty was found in selling it.[1]

Hamilton himself calculated, some time before his death, that his property stood him in about ten thousand pounds, and the surplus beyond his debts was double that sum if all of it could be sold to advantage. Yet he doubted if a forced

[1] Appendix J.

sale were made if it would be sufficient to meet them. He
thought that his holdings should bring him an annual income of at least twelve thousand dollars.[1]

My expenses while the first improvements of my country
establishment were going on have been great, but they would
this summer and fall reach the point at which it is my intention they should stop, at least till I should be better able
than at present to add to them; and after a fair examination
founded upon an actual account of my expenditures, I am
persuaded that a plan I have contemplated for the next and
succeeding years would bring my expenses of every kind
within the compass of four thousand dollars yearly, exclusive of the interest of my country establishment. To this
limit I have been resolved to reduce them, even though it
should be necessary to lease that establishment for a few
years. In the meantime, my lands now in a course of sale
and settlement would accclerate the extinguishment of my
debts, and in the end leave me a handsome clear property.
It was also allowable for me to take into view collaterally the
expectations of my wife; which have been of late partly realized. She is now entitled to a property of between 2,000
and 3,000 pounds (as I compute), by descent from her
mother, and her father is understood to possess a large estate. I feel all the delicacy of this allusion, but the occasion, I trust will plead my excuses, and that venerable
father, I am sure, will pardon. He knows well all the nicety
of my past conduct.

Viewing the matter in these different aspects, I trust the
opinion of candid men will be that there has been no impropriety in my conduct, especially when it is taken into the
calculation, that my country establishment, though costly,
promises, by the progressive rise of property on this island
the felicity of its situation, to become more and more valuable. My chief apology is to those friends who have from
mere kindness endorsed my paper discounted at the banks.
On mature reflection I have thought it justifiable to secure

[1] Lodge's "Hamilton," vol. VIII, p. 630 *et seq.*

them in preference to other creditors, lest perchance there should be a deficit. Yet, while this may save them from eventual loss, it will not exempt from present inconvenience. As to this I can only throw myself upon their kindness and entreat the indulgence of the banks for them. Perhaps the request may be supposed entitled to some regard. In the event which would bring this paper to the public eye, one thing at least would be put beyond doubt. This is that my public labors have amounted to an absolute sacrifice of the interests of my family, and that in all pecuniary concerns the delicacy no less than the probity of conduct in public stations has been such as to defy even the shadow of a question.

Indeed, I have not enjoyed the ordinary advantages incident to my military services. Being a member of Congress while the question of the commutation of the half pay of the army for a sum in gross was in debate, delicacy and a desire to be useful to the army by removing the idea of my having an interest in the question, induced me to write to the Secretary of War and relinquish my claim to half pay, which or the equivalent I have never received. Neither have I even applied for the lands allowed by the United States to officers of my rank. Nor did I ever obtain from this State the allowance of lands made to officers of similar rank. It is true that having served through the latter periods of the war on the general staff of the United States and not in the line of this State I could not claim the allowance as a matter of course; but having before the war resided in this State, and having entered the military career at the head of a company of artillery raised for the particular defense of this State, I had better pretensions to the allowance than others to whom it was actually made, yet it has not been extended to me.

A. H.

After Hamilton's death a law was passed by Congress, in 1816, giving his widow back pay and she received about ten thousand dollars.[1] Among his papers was found a small

[1] The following case stated by the auditor is submitted by the Secretary of the Treasury to the Attorney-General for an opinion: "Alexander Hamilton was a

land allotment of a quarter section for which he had never applied. It is a matter of fact that many of his expenses incurred in the equipment of his company of artillery, and his visits to Annapolis to attend the meetings of the Constitutional Conventions, and other places, were unpaid by the government.

In 1810 Mrs. Hamilton heard from her sister, Mrs. Church, who said, "we had the pleasure to hear that you were safe arrived at Philadelphia, and your letter of yesterday from Washington removed all apprehensions; if anything is to be done, your presence is better than twenty agents and I sincerely hope that for your case and for the honor of

Lieut. Colonel in the Army of the Revolutionary War but is understood to have retired from service towards the close of the year, 1781, and in the month of November, 1782, took his seat in Congress as a member from the State of New York. Does the act for the relief of Elizabeth Hamilton, widow of Alexander Hamilton, passed on the 29th of April, 1816, place her on an equal footing with the officers entitled to Commutations under the Resolution of Congress of March, 1783, or, in other words, does the spirit and true meaning of the said act require that interest be allowed for the five years' full pay therein granted?"

Richard Rush, who was Attorney-General June 29, 1816, replied: "I think it does. I am given to understand that it has not been the practice in the accounting offices of the Treasury Department to allow Interest upon an account directed to be settled or paid by an act of Congress, unless there be in the act itself special words to that effect. This rule, taken as a general one, it is not my part to controvert, nor is it supposed that the above opinion will imply any contradiction. I grant it on the peculiar words of the act of April 29, 1816, which, taken in connection with the Resolution of March 22, 1783, appears to me in full consideration to confirm the construction that it was the intention of Congress, not merely to make an independent grant to Elizabeth Hamilton, but to place her upon a footing of equal advantage in all respects with the officers entitled to commutation under that Resolution."

"The consequence will be that as was the case with the officers themselves (none of whom it is believed received the amount in money.) She, too, will be entitled to interest at 6 per centum, the rate specified in the Resolution."

Mrs. Hamilton therefore received five years' full pay for the services of her husband as lieutenant-colonel in the Revolutionary War, being the commutation of his half-pay for life allowed by the act of the 29th of April, 1816, at 60 dollars per month . . . . $3,600.
To interest on the above from the 16th of November, 1783, when the commutation became payable until the day, say April 29, 1816, the date of the act at 6 per cent. per annum, 32 years, 165 days . 7,009.64

$10,609.64

my native country, a liberal allowance will be made." The sum allowed enabled her to provide in measure for the support and education of her growing family, the property left by her father having been greatly depleted.

Burr's indifference regarding the duel seems to have impressed so biassed a biographer as Parton, who ventures the opinion that he did not *know* what he had done.[1] As has been stated, when Burr landed in New York on the morning of July 11, he proceeded to his home, and was there found by one of his young relations who had just come from Connecticut to visit him. When shown into the library he found Burr. The latter was engaged in his "usual avocations," and showed no indication of what had occurred an hour or two previously. He was, in every respect, as usual, and did not manifest in his "manner or conversation any concern." The guest was surprised, when he left the house and went to another part of the city, to find all the existing excitement and to learn, for the first time, that Hamilton had been killed by his imperturbable cousin.

Burr himself was hardly prepared for the attitude of the public, for, secure in his office as Vice-President, which he had gained after discomfiting the very man he had shot, he felt he was more popular than the departed Hamilton, who, after all, in his opinion, was only a dead Federalist.

Even Burr's own friends were shocked and horrified, and John Adams is reported to have said, "No one wished to get rid of Hamilton in *that* way." Two days afterward Burr wrote to Alston, his son-in-law: "General Hamilton died yesterday. The malignant Federalists or Tories, and the embittered Clintonians, unite in endeavoring to excite public sympathy in his favor, and indignation against his antagonist. . . . I propose leaving town for a few days, and meditate

---

[1] "The Life of Aaron Burr," by John Parton, vol. II, p. 13. Boston, 1882.

also a journey of some weeks, but whither is not resolved. . . . Our most unprincipled Jacobins are the loudest in their lamentations for the death of General Hamilton, whom, for many years, they have uniformly represented as the most detestable and unprincipled of men—the motives are obvious. Every sort of persecution is to be exercised against me. A Coroner's jury will sit this evening, being the *fourth* time. The object of this unexampled measure is to obtain an inquest of murder. Upon this a warrant will be issued to apprehend me, and if I should be taken, no bail would probably be allowed. You know enough of the temper and principle of the generality of the officers of our State Government to form a judgment of my position." He also complained that the statement of his second, Van Ness, had not been shown him, and intimated that the publication in the *Morning Chronicle* was garbled, and "several circumstances not very favorable to the deceased are suppressed—I presume for holy reverence for the dead."

So bitter and excited were the feelings of every one that he did not leave Richmond Hill for eleven days. Meanwhile it was suggested that Bishop Moore and Dr. Mason or Dr. Hosack should give the needed testimony, and the coroner's jury brought in a true bill.[1]

CITY AND COUNTY OF NEW YORK, ss.:

An Inquisition indented, taken for the People of the State of New York at the Third Ward of the City of New York, the thirteenth day of July, in the year of Our Lord One thousand eight hundred and four, and contained by adjournment until the second day of August in the year aforesaid, before me, JOHN BURGER, Coroner for the said City and County of New York, on view of the body of Alexander Hamilton, then and there to wit, on the said thirteenth day of July, in the year

---

[1] Matthew L. Davis, a merchant of 49 Stone Street, one of Burr's devoted friends, went to Weehawken and saw the duel but would not testify when summoned by the Coroner. He it was who subsequently published Burr's Journal.

last aforesaid, at the Ward, City and County aforesaid, lying dead. Upon the oath of Alexander Anderson, George Minuse, John A. Hardenbrook, Peter Bonnett, Elam Williams, John Coffin, John Mildeberger, David A. Brown, David Lydig, Abraham Bloodgood, Samuel Cummings, Amos Curtis, Isaac Burr, Benjamin Strong and John D. Miller, good and lawful men of the said City and County of New York, duly chosen, and who being then and there duly sworn and charged to inquire for the People of the State of New York, when, where and by what means the said Alexander Hamilton came to his death, do, upon their oath, say that Aaron Burr, late of the Eighth Ward of the said City, in the said County, Esquire, and Vice-President of the United States, not having the fear of God before his eyes, but being moved and seduced by the instigation of the devil, on the eleventh day of July, in the year last aforesaid, with force and arms, in the County of Bergen and State of New Jersey, in and upon the said Alexander Hamilton, in the peace of God and of the People of the said State of New Jersey, then and there being feloniously, wilfully and of his malice aforethought, did make an assault and that the said Aaron Burr a certain pistol of the value of One Dollar charged and loaded with gun-powder and a leaden bullet which he, the said Aaron Burr, then and there had held in his right hand, to, at and against the right side of the belly of the said Alexander Hamilton, did then and there shoot off and discharge, by means whereof he, the said Aaron Burr, feloniously wilfully and of malice aforethought did then and there give unto him, the said Alexander Hamilton, with the leaden bullet aforesaid, so as aforesaid, shot off and discharged out of the pistol aforesaid by the force of the gun-powder aforesaid, upon the right side of the belly of him, the said Alexander Hamilton, a little above the hip, one mortal wound penetrating the belly of him, the said Alexander Hamilton, of which said mortal wound he, the said Alexander Hamilton, from the said eleventh day of July, in the year aforesaid, until the twelfth day of July in the same year, as well in the County of Bergen in the State of New Jersey aforesaid, as also at the Eighth Ward of the City of New York, in the County of New York aforesaid, did languish and languishing did live, on which twelfth day of July in the said year the said Alexander Hamilton, at the said Eighth Ward of the said City in the said County of New York, of the mortal wound aforesaid died, and the Jurors aforesaid, on their oath aforesaid, do further say that William P. Van Ness, late of the First Ward of the City of New York, in the County of New York aforesaid, attorney at law, and Nathaniel Pendleton, late of the same place, counsellor at law at the time of committing the felony and murder aforesaid, feloniously, wilfully and of their malice aforethought were present, abetting, aiding, assisting, comforting and maintaining the said Aaron Burr to kill and murder the said Alexander Hamilton in manner aforesaid.

And so the Jurors aforesaid, upon their oath aforesaid, do say the said Aaron Burr, and the said William P. Van Ness and Nathaniel Pendleton, him, the said Alexander Hamilton, in manner and by the means aforesaid, feloniously, wilfully and of their malice aforethought, did kill and murder against the peace of the People of the State of New York and their dignity.

IN WITNESS WHEREOF, as well the aforesaid Coroner as the Jurors aforesaid, have to this Inquisition put their seals on the second day of August, and in the year One thousand eight hundred and four and at the place aforesaid.

JOHN BURGER, Coroner.   L.S.

ALEXR. ANDERSON.	L.S.
GEO. MINUSE.	L.S.
JOHN A. HARDENBROOK.	L.S.
PETER BONNETT.	L.S.
ELAM WILLIAMS.	L.S.
JOHN COFFIN.	L.S.
JOHN MILDEBERGER.	L.S.
DAVID BROWN.	L.S.
DAVID LYDIG.	L.S.
ABM. BLOODGOOD.	L.S.
SAMUEL CUMMINGS.	L.S.
AMOS CURTIS.	L.S.
ISAAC BURR.	L.S.
B. M. STRONG.	L.S.
J. D. MILLER.	L.S.

At the end of eleven days Burr was spirited away by his intimate and faithful friend, John Swartout, and embarked Saturday night, July 21, in a barge. After an all-night's row they reached the house of Commodore Truxton at Perth Amboy. Here he stayed until the following Monday, when he again pushed southward, reaching Philadelphia, finding refuge at the house of A. J. Dallas, another old friend who, it will be remembered, was so prominent in welcoming Genet.

When he heard of the finding of the coroner's jury, it was on August 2, and he knew that warrants had been issued for his arrest and that of Pendleton and Van Ness.

Fearing extradition he left Philadelphia and, accompanied by Samuel Swartout and a faithful slave, he fled to St. Simon's Island on the Georgia coast, where Major Pierce Butler had an estate. His stay at Philadelphia, it is reported, was enlivened by a pleasant renewal of a flirtation with one Céleste, who was an old flame, and it was only because fearful of apprehension that he reluctantly sought a more secure hiding-place. After a visit paid to his daughter Theodosia, in South Carolina, which was undertaken after great exposure and hardship, he having travelled four hundred miles in an open boat, and feeling sure that the excitement had blown over, he proceeded to Washington to preside over the Senate, but stopped *en route* at Petersburg, Va., where he received an "ovation," a public dinner being tendered him by the "Republicans." Burr was cheered and toasted, and made much of. When he reached Washington he found that both New York and New Jersey had issued indictments against him, but he was not prosecuted, as political and personal influence was brought to bear. About this time the case of a certain Judge Chace, who was to be tried by the Senate for malfeasance in office, came up for trial. Burr, as the Vice-President, took charge of the proceedings, and his attitude was such as to cause a certain newspaper to say that "he directed the trial with the dignity and impartiality of an angel and the vigor of a devil." The issue of the duel was forgotten, and there was a reaction in his favor, but he could never regain his position. It was shortly after this that he resigned public office, first delivering an emotional and fetching speech, which caused his hearers to melt into tears. Probably at no time in his career was he so eloquent. Ruin succeeded his extravagant and blasted life. Richmond Hill was pressed for sale, and brought twenty-five thousand dollars, which was insufficient to pay his debts, and as he was liable to arrest at any time, and as his practice had gone and he was without earning power he was obliged to flee. It was then that he sought Louisiana, soon becoming involved in new trouble. The history of his subsequent life both in America and abroad need not be dwelt upon. He always spoke lightly of the duel, and seemed to be without concern or remorse. He was bitter, and keenly felt the censure of others, and in his diary[1] on October 24, 1808, when in Hamburg said:

"I find that among the great number of Americans here and *there*, all are hostile to A. B.—all—what a lot of rascals they must be to make war on one whom they do not know; on one who never did harm or wished harm to a human being. Yet they, perhaps ought not to be blamed, for they are influenced by what they hear. I learn further that A. B. is announced in the Paris papers in a manner in no way auspicious."

Many anecdotes are told of him, illustrating not only his casual feeling in regard to serious things, but what I have just mentioned. It is said that in a letter written when yellow fever was rife in New York, he cynically observed: "We die reasonably fast. Mrs. Jones died last night; but then Mrs. Smith had twins this morning; so the account is even."[2]

Upon one occasion he referred to "my friend Hamilton, whom I shot." Upon another, a foreigner asked, in Burr's hearing, if Hamilton was a gentleman. Burr resented the question and replied with hauteur, "Sir, *I* met him."[3] Upon

---

[1] "Private Journal," vol. I, p. 274.
[2] "Parton," vol. II, p. 19.   [3] Oliver, *op. cit.*, p. 417.

another he is said to have visited the duelling ground with a friend, and in the words of the latter, "He justified all he had done; nay, applauded it."

This and other statements of the kind are, possibly, exaggerations, or even lies, for vituperation and misrepresentation were active at the time. For over one hundred years few historians have been found who were willing to accord to Burr a single virtue; yet, in spite of certain grave defects of character, there is, after all, much that appeals to the just and fair-minded critic. No one who is conversant with the history of his middle and old age, can help admiring those traits of generosity and a certain tenderness that are shown, especially in his letters to his daughter Theodosia and some others. Doubtless, in a way, he greatly liked Hamilton, so long as the latter did not cross his political path, for in early years they were much together, and Burr was a frequent visitor at Hamilton's house, and upon more than one occasion was the messenger between husband and wife. They had a great deal in sympathy, the same sense of humor, and capacity for witty retort; and the ability to appreciate the amiable weaknesses of others. If such existed, it is a pity that none of their correspondence has been preserved, for it would be the best index of the feeling underneath that might have existed at some time.

While these good traits did not compensate for a great deal that was absolutely vicious, it is not right to invariably speak of Burr as a monster—even if his moral sense was in many ways defective or even deficient. There is something in the misery of the man during his exile that is very touching, and his life abroad, where he was an Ishmaelite, was filled with bitterness which he endured, meanwhile showing a stubborn courage. His diary is a strange mixture of accounts of dissipation and references to his daughter which betray that, at heart, there was one tender point in his nature. The pages devoted to the account of his wretched and uncomfortable trip to Boston in a slow and dreary packet, after pawning the little gifts for Theodosia and escaping the land sharks with just enough to reach America, throw light upon the character of a man who, no matter what he had done, was proud and self-reliant in his adversity. Oliver [1] is most charitable, and in speaking of Burr says: "Two things about him passed the bounds of acting—his generosity and his affection. He had at all times many creditors, and it cannot be said of him that he was depressed by the weight of his obligations. Strictly he was an immoral citizen, because he flouted the sanctity of contract and gave away upon an impulse what was already hypothecated to others. But at least he did not spend upon himself. . . . He gave because he could not resist appeals, because he could not help giving. . . . His charity was of the heart, spontaneous, promiscuous, and usually misdirected. . . . In his old age the habit amounted to a mania. He fancied himself rich, and gave still more recklessly—a more amiable and a less common trait in septuagenarians than to fancy themselves poor and hoard. . . . Lovers of Hamilton and of a settled order— Federalist partisans and outraged Democrats—have drawn the picture of Burr which is accepted in history books. It is only natural that the shadows have been overblackened."

Burr died in 1836, and his body lies near that of his father and grandfather at Princeton. Hamilton was buried in the churchyard of old Trinity, within a few hundred yards of the site of the first house he occupied when he came to New York, and of Federal Hall, while the graves of Elizabeth Hamilton and himself are really located in the very commercial centre of the United States. Every one who hurries

[1] *Op. cit.*, pp. 417–418.

up the great street that extends from the venerable church to the East River can, if he chooses, always see the humble monument which covers all that is left of the first Secretary of the Treasury of the United States.

After the growth of more than a century, our country, with all its present greatness, calmly weighs the part played by those early patriots who brought it into life. The individual influence of the "Makers of America" is every day showing itself, and as our institutions become more and more firmly established we constantly and steadily thrive as a nation. It is hardly necessary to say that those principles that are most firmly dependent upon an adherence to the precepts of the Constitution have been the best. This has been tested and proved over and over again. That great "system of fundamental principles" has ever served and saved us in times of national peril, and when its provisions have been ignored, or it has been disregarded, we have, at times, been perilously near demoralization, for then the rights of *all* the people for which Hamilton really fought have been jeopardized, but not for long. Happily these instances have been rare, and those men who have tampered with it have usually been wrong-headed meddlers or demagogues.

After the many years that have elapsed since the creation of the Constitution of the United States, it is not saying too much to assert that to Hamilton belongs most of the credit for its preparation and adoption, and that it is to-day the best monument of his greatness.

The rancor of personal abuse, so prevalent during the early part of the last century, does not now concern or interest a great people, and whatever were his faults—which, by the way, were only those of an impetuous nature—the persistent and prophetic work of his short life is now making itself felt, and its results are admitted, by those more competent and worthy than myself, to be beyond improvement. Jefferson, Callender, and Cheatham are gone. Freneau's scurrilous diatribes are forgotten, and, to-day, able and impartial historians, both here and abroad, are according him the tardy acknowledgment of what he has done for the United States and for the World.

Perhaps his most impartial and grateful critics and admirers are the millions who, denied liberty elsewhere, have availed themselves of the complete protection embodied in an instrument with which his name is so intimately identified.

The Grave of Alexander Hamilton.

APPENDIX A

(PAGE 8)

HAMILTON OF CAMBUSKEITH AND GRANGE [1]

"THE progenitors of the Hamiltons of Cambuskeith, now called the *Mount*, were derived by Crawfurd and Wood, from Walter, second son of Sir David, filius Walteri de Hamilton, the third in the line of succession from Gilbert de Hamildun, the founder of the ducal house of Hamilton. Crawfurd further states that *Hamilton* of *Grange*, in Ayrshire, was the representative of the Cambuskeith Hamiltons. This is very probable, although neither Crawfurd, nor the writer of the family genealogy in Robertson's *Ayrshire Families*, proves it to be the fact. We shall, however, follow the latter account, said to be drawn from family writs, so far as it appears to be correct.

"The first recorded in these documents is:

"I.   David Hamilton, of Cambuskeith, who had a charter of the lands of Blairmead from his uncle (patruus) Alan Hamilton of Lethberd, which was confirmed by the over lord, Archibald, Earl of Douglas, Lord of Galloway and Annandale, at Peebles, on the 29th January, 1411.

"II.   James Hamilton of Cambuskeith, who was served heir to his father David in 1436. He married Margery, daughter of Sir James Hamilton of Preston, by Margaret, daughter of Sir James, afterward Lord Hamilton, by whom he had his successor,

"III.   John Hamilton of Cambuskeith, who married Marion, daughter of Sir John Maxwell of Calderwood, by whom he had a son,

"IV.   Alexander, who was served heir to his father John in 1489. His name occurs as one of the assize in a criminal case in 1512; and he was amerciated for intercommuning with the Sheriff of Ayr, in 1527. He married Marion, daughter of Sir Adam Cuninghame of Caprington, by Isabel, daughter of Sir Malcolm Craufurd of Kilbirnie, by whom he had a son,

"V.   John Hamilton of Cambuskeith, who in 1542 appears in the

[1] Prepared from "History of Ayrshire and Its Families," by James Paterson, vol. II, pp. 201, 202, 203.

Scots Acts of Parliament as one of the curators of John Hamilton of Fynart. He was killed on the Muir of Glasgow, May, 1544. He married Margaret, daughter of Cuninghame of Leglane, by whom he had a son,

"VI. John Hamilton of Cambuskeith, who was served heir to his father, John, in 1546. He did not, however, long enjoy the property, as he died intestate in September, 1547. His relict, Joneta Muntgumery, was confirmed *executores* datein, the following January. He left issue:

  1. John, 'his son and heir apparent.'
  2. Elizabeth, 'his daughter.'

"'William Hammiltone, Tutour of Cammiskeyth,' was charged with celebrating mass, and attempting to restore Popery at Kirkoswald in 1563,

"VII. John Hamilton of Cambuskeith. It was this John, probably, who married Catherine Farquhar, daughter of the Laird of Gilmilnscroft, by whom he had two sons:

  1. John, his successor.
  2. William, afterward Sir William Hamilton of Sorn.

"VIII. John Hamilton of Cambuskeith, who was served heir to his father, John, in the lands of Cambuskeith in 1561, and to his grandfather, John, in the lands of Pophill, Burnhill, and others, near to Craufurdland and Kilmarnock Castles, on 1st May, 1572. He married, first, Jane Montgomerie, daughter of the Laird of Haiselheid, by whom he had his successor, and probably a daughter, Elizabeth; secondly, he married Janet Stewart, daughter of Mr. Matthew Stewart of Minto, by whom he had a son, according to the writer in Ayrshire Families, David of Ladyton, which lands he obtained from his father in 1571, and who married Marion Campbell, daughter of the Laird of Ducathall.

"IX. John Hamilton of Cambuskeith or Grange. He was retoured heir to his great-grandfather, John, in the lands of Overmure and Carlingcraigs, 3d Nov., 1603. He married Janet, daughter of William Cuninghame of Caprington, by whom he had no issue. His brother-in-law, William Caprington, is said to have obtained, unfairly, a charter under the Great Seal of the ten-pound land of Cambuskeith in 1598. 'Johanne Hamiltoun of the Grange of Kilmarnock' is mentioned as one of the assize in a criminal case in 1608. He died before 1615, in which year 'umquhile, John Hamiltoun of Grange,' occurs as a debtor in the testament of 'Mr. Johnne Luif,' Kilmarnock. He was alive in 1612, so that his death must have occurred between the years 1612 and 1615. The writer in

Robertson states that the representation of the family now devolved on his brother David of Ladyton. No proof is adduced of this, but it seems probable from the fact that Ladyton was the property of the family. It does not appear, however, that David succeeded his brother, or that he was ever styled of Grange, as we find.

"X. 'Alexander Hamilton of Greng,' mentioned in the testament of John Hutchesoun in Bog, Galston Parish, in June, 1616. He was retoured heir to his father, David, in the lands of Grange, 10th January, 1617. He married Agnes (not Elizabeth) Craufurd, niece of the Laird of Lochnorris, by whom he had two sons:

    1. John, who is erroneously said to have died young.

    2. Robert, said to have been the successor of his father.

"XI. John Hamilton of Grange. His name occurs in various documents. In 1618 John Hamilton of Grange disposed of his annual rent on the lands and barony of Kilmarnock to the Boyd family, which he seems to have again acquired, for, in 1634, John Hamilton of Grange has in festment of the annual rent furth of the lands and baronies of Kilmarnock and Grougar. He may have been succeeded by his brother,

"XII. Robert Hamilton of Grange, who was retoured heir to his father, Alexander, 19th December, 1661. He married Margaret Hamilton, daughter of the Laird of Neilsland, by whom he had a son,

"XIII. John Hamilton of Grange, who married Elizabeth Craufurd, daughter of the Laird of Craufurdland, by whom he had two sons and six daughters, of the latter of whom, Margaret, was married in 1675, to Robert Hunter of Kirkland. He was succeeded by his eldest son,

"XIV. John Hamilton of Grange, who, in 1677, was retoured heir of his father, John. By a deed, dated June, 1677, he disposed of the 'forty-shilling land of old extent of the Kirkland of Kilmarnock, with the glebe lands thereof,' to the Earl of Kilmarnock. In 1685, he acquired part of the lands of Stevenston-Campbell from Robert Cuninghame of Auchenharvie; and about this time also he acquired the barony of Stevenston-Cuninghame from the Glencairn family; the mansion-house of which, Kerilaw, under the name of *Grange*, became the residence as well as the title of the family.[1] He married Rebecca Cuninghame, daughter of Alexander Cuninghame of Craigends, by whom he had issue a daughter, Janet, married to William Warner of Ardeer, and an only son,

[1] Kerilaw Castle continued to be the mansion-house of this family till about fifty years ago, when the present house of Grange was built on a fine situation at a little distance from the old Castle of Kerilaw. Stat. Ac. of Scot.

"XV. *Alexander Hamilton of Grange, who succeeded him, and married, about the year* 1730, *Elizabeth Pollock, eldest daughter of Sir Robert Pollock of that Ilk, by Annabella, daughter of Walter Stewart of Pardovan, by whom he had issue:*

1. *John* } *successively Lairds of Grange.*
2. *Robert* }

3. *Alexander. He married Rachel Cuninghame, daughter of James Cuninghame* of Collellan, *by whom he had a son, Alexander, and four daughters:*
    1. *Elizabeth, married Robert Cuninghame of Auchenharvie, and had issue.*
    2. *Margaret, married Rev. Thomas Pollock, minister of Kilwinning, and had issue.*
    3. *Joana, married Edward M'Cormick, Esq., advocate, late Sheriff Depute of Ayrshire, and had issue.*
    4. *Jane, died unmarried.*

4. *James, a proprietor in the West Indies, and father of General Hamilton, the celebrated statesman and patriot in the United States, who fell, greatly regretted, in a duel with a Mr. Burr.*

5. *Walter* } *both died unmarried.*
6. *George* }

7. *William, married Jean, daughter of Robert Donald, Esq., and had issue.*

8. *Joseph.*

9. *William, who died in infancy.*

"Of his two daughters, one died in infancy, and the other, Elizabeth, was married to Alexander Blair, Esq., surveyor of the customs at Port Glasgow, son of William Blair, of Blair, and had issue.

"XVI. John Hamilton of Grange, the eldest son, succeeded. He died unmarried, and was succeeded by his brother,

"XVII. Robert Hamilton of Grange, who, dying also unmarried in 1774, was succeeded by his nephew, son of Alexander Hamilton, the third brother.

"XVIII. Alexander Hamilton of Grange, advocate and Lieut.-Col. of the late 2d Regiment of Ayrshire Local Militia. He disposed of the Grange, in 1792, to Miss Scott, afterward Duchess of Portland, who had previously, 1787, purchased Cambuskeith, the more ancient property of the family. He built the new house of Kerilaw, previous to 1790, and died in 1837. Dying without issue, the representation of this ancient family descended to Captain John Brown, of the 23d Fusileers, his grand-nephew, only son of the marriage between Major George Vanbrugh Brown of Knockmarloch and Elizabeth Cuninghame, eldest daughter of the marriage between Robert Cuninghame of Auchenharvie and Elizabeth Hamilton, eldest sister of the second Alexander Hamilton.

"ARMS: Gules, a lion rampant, argent (for the Earldom of Ross); betwixt three cinque foils, ermine (for Hamilton). *Crest:* An oak tree proper. *Motto*, in an escroll above, VIRIDIS ET FRUCTIFERA."

APPENDIX B

(PAGE 19)

KERILAW CASTLE

In "Cunninghame" (Topographized by Timothy Pont An. 1604–1608, with Continuations and Illustration Notices by the late James Dobie of Crummock, F.S.A., Scot., edited by his son John Sheddon Dobie, Glasgow, 1876[1]), we find a description of this ancient property.

"Kary-law Castle or Steninstoune Castell, a fair stronge building belonging to ye Earls of Glencairne quoho had ye said Castell barroney parisch and Lordschipe by the marriage of ye Douglass heretrix thereof it belonged in A° 1191 to ye Lockharts."

"The ivy-mantled ruins of Kerilaw Castle show it to have formed in its later days a quadrangular pile of building of about thirty yards square. Its situation on the eastern side of the Stevenston burn is not one of much natural strength, for though the ground around is prettily broken and undulating, the site itself is flat and easily approachable on three sides, while to the rear its walls arose from the edge of the low but rocky and precipitous brink of the stream. This side of the castle has almost entirely disappeared, and was, most probably, the oldest part of the building. The doorway in the northeast front is directly approached through a double line of noble old trees forming a shady avenue of about a quarter of a mile in length. The greater part of this wall, which is still standing, shows few of the defensive accompaniments common to the more ancient baronial buildings, but the lower apartments in it in the corresponding wing have been vaulted. The south-east front, which faces into the present gardens, appears to have been a more modern addition, its central doorway and window on the eastern side being of the Gothic style, and of much larger and airier proportions than those in the

[1] Also see "A Topographical Dictionary of Scotland and the Islands of the British Seas," vol. II, 1813, "A Genealogical Account of the Principal Families in Ayrshire, More Particularly Cunningham," by George Robertson, vol. I, Irvine, 1823.

wall fronting the avenue; above, in the second story, is a tier of square-headed mullion-divided windows, and the other wall is finished by a battlement. The ancient hall of Kerilaw Castle was said to have been ornamented with the coats-of-arms of the Scottish nobility, taken from the Abbey of Kilwinning after its destruction at the Reformation. If so, retribution has followed on Kerilaw. The spoils of Kilwinning have entirely disappeared, and their existence there is known only by tradition. From Kilwinning, the approach to the present mansion, which stands on the opposite side of the burn, keeps the line of the old avenue, crossing the stream by the bridge thrown over its course immediately underneath the line of the back wall of the ruins."

"This bridge, which detracts somewhat from the sole original strength of the position, adds to the picturesque effect, and the banks of the clear, rapid little stream are here over-arched by wide-spread old forest trees."

APPENDIX C

(PAGE 64)

THE RIVINGTON TRACTS

THE series of tracts issued chiefly from Rivington's press, in New York City during 1774 and 1775, consisted of twenty pamphlets and rejoinders from the Patriots, and in the beginning preceded the movement to send delegates from the Province of New York to the General Congress in Philadelphia. According to Evans,[1] the secret service fund of the British Government was largely drawn upon to subsidize the printing office of the Tory printer. This writer says: "The friends of American Liberty found arrayed against them an opposition made up of the Church of England. In fact, in its controversial phases, the struggle for civil liberty in the American Colonies assumed something of the nature of religious warfare, in which dissenting churches were opposed by the Established Church of England." This was, undoubtedly, a further evolution of the spirit of antagonism that, in the seventeenth century, led to the exodus of the little band of Englishmen who landed in Massachusetts Bay. It was, therefore, to be expected that the Tory opposition would be represented by a clergyman, and we find the Rev. Myles Cooper, the president of King's College, taking an active part.

He it was whom Alexander Hamilton helped to escape from the infuriated patriots who surrounded the college, during Hamilton's fiery and eloquent speech delivered from the doorstep. Cooper, after listening with indignant surprise from a window above, reluctantly made his exit from a back door, and sought the protection of the English man-of-war in the harbor. Cooper's first pamphlet was signed "A North American," and was entitled "*The American Querist.*" This inflamed the already exasperated "Sons of Liberty," and he was in danger of violent treatment, and ultimately left the country. Shortly afterward Bishop Seabury of Connecticut wrote several tracts taking the Tory side. His first was entitled "*A Friendly*

---

[1] "American Bibliography," by Charles Evans, vol. V, 1774–1778, p. ix *et seq.* Privately printed for the author by the Hollister Press, Chicago, 1909.

Address to All Reasonable Americans on the Subject of our Political Confusions," and was answered by Philip Livingston by *"The Other Side of the Question, or a Defense of the Liberties of North America."* The pseudonym chosen by Seabury was "A. W. Farmer," his purpose having been to turn the agricultural class against the proposed measures that were to be introduced into the coming Congress, and to convey the idea that he was an actual farmer of Westchester County. Meanwhile General Charles Lee wrote *"Strictures on a Pamphlet Entitled a Friendly Address to all Reasonable Americans, etc.,"* with the quotation from Shakespeare, "Let's canvass him in his Broad Cardinal's Hat." This was published by the Bradfords in Philadelphia.

Subsequently Seabury wrote *"Free Thoughts on the Proceedings of the Continental Congress Held at Philadelphia, Sept. 4, 1774."* This drew forth Hamilton's *"Full Vindication, etc.,"* to which reference has been made. In two or three weeks Seabury published, under his original pseudonym, *"The Congress Canvassed; or, an Examination Into the Conduct of the Delegates at the Grand Convention Held in Philadelphia, Sept. 1st, 1774."* In 1775 Hamilton issued his second rejoinder to Seabury, under the title of *"The Farmer Refuted or a More Impartial and Comprehensive View of the Dispute Between Great Britain and the Colonies, Intended as a Further Vindication of the Congress.* In the meantime spirited attacks were indulged in, and other tracts were published. One of these was entitled *"An Alarm to the Legislature of the Province of New York occasioned by the Present Political Disturbance in North America,"* and was issued from Rivington's press. Another was entitled *"What Think Ye of the Congress Now?"* erroneously attributed to the Rev. Thomas Bradbury Chandler. Joseph Galloway, who had joined the American troops, but had deserted and espoused the Tory side, wrote *"A Plan of a Proposed Union Between Great Britain and the Colonies,"* and *"A Candid Examination of the Mutual Claims of Great Britain and the Colonies; with a Plan of Accommodation on Constitutional Principles."* He also later published other tracts in England.

After Hamilton's *"Farmer Refuted"* appeared, it was answered by Isaac Wilkins, who, under the pseudonym of "A Country Gentleman," prepared a tract called *"The Republican Dissected; or, the Anatomy of an American Whig."* This, however, did not, at the time, appear, for a company from Connecticut descended upon Rivington's premises, wrecked his presses, and scattered Wilkins's proofsheets. In some way, however, a copy found its way to England, where it was reprinted. Other pamphlets that appeared in 1774 and furthered this controversy were those of Henry Barry, an English officer in Boston who attacked Lee, and of Jonathan Boucher. The latter was the author of "*A Letter from a Virginian to the Members of the Congress to be Held in Philadelphia on the First of September,* 1774."

APPENDIX D

(PAGE 71)

INDICTMENT OF WILLIAM DUANE FOR SEDITION

Pleas before the Honorable The Judges of the Circuit Court of the United States in and for the District of Pennsylvania in the Third Circuit at Philadelphia.

BE IT REMEMBERED that at a Circuit Court of the United States holden at the City of Philadelphia in and for the District of Pennsylvania in the Third Circuit on the Eleventh Day of October A.D. 1800—and in the twenty-fifth year of the Independence of the said United States   Before the Honorable William Paterson one of the associate Justices of the Supreme Court of the United States and the Honorable Richard Peters Judge of the District Court of the United States in and for the said District assigned to hold the said Circuit Court—by the oaths of John Jones—John Dunlap—George Plumstead—John C. Stecker—John Miller Jun—John Leamy—George Bickham—John Curwen—Anthony Hearn—Derick Petersen—John Holmes and John B. Gilpin—

And by the affirmations of Edward Garrigues Nathan Schoefield and Cadwallader Evans—good and careful men of the said District —then and there impannelled sworn or affirmed and charged to enquire for the said United States and for the Body of the said District—

IT IS THUS PRESENTED.

In the Circuit Court of the United States of America in and for the District of Pennsylvania of the Middle Circuit—

THE GRAND INQUEST of the United States of America in and for the District of Pennsylvania upon their respective oaths and affirmations.   Do Present that William Duane late of the District of Penn-

443

sylvania aforesaid Yeoman on the nineteenth day of February in the
year of our Lord One thousand eight hundred at the District aforesaid he being a malicious and seditious man and also wickedly de-
ceitfully falsely and maliciously contriving to Detract scandalize and
vilify and to represent the Senate of the United States of America in
Congress assembled as actuated by factions and improper views and
motives, as governed by Intrigue and the influence of private secret
meetings as unfit to be trusted with the duties and high authority ap-
pertaining to the Senate of the United States aforesaid and to bring
the said Senate and many of the members thereof into an ill opinion
hatred and contempt with all the good Citizens of the said United
States and to represent the said members of the Senate aforesaid as
corrupt persons, and for the purposes aforesaid the said William
Duane did at the District aforesaid the day and year last aforesaid
with Force and arms wickedly falsely and maliciously print and publish and cause to be printed and published a certain false scandalous and malicious libel following—to wit—

PHILADELPHIA—Wednesday, *February* 19, 1800.

"In our paper of the 27th ult. we noticed the introduction of
a "measure into the Senate of the United States by Mr. Ross"
(James Ross Esquire a Senator of the Said United States for the
State of Pennsylvania meaning) "calculated to influence and
affect the approaching Presidential Election" (meaning the
Election of President of the United States) "and to frustrate in
"a particular manner the wishes and interests of the People of
"the Commonwealth of Pennsylvania"—in which Said Libel of
and concerning the said Senate of the United States, and many
members thereof, and of and concerning a certain Bill introduced into the said Senate is contained among other things,
diverse scurrilous false feigned seditious and malicious matters
according to the tenor following to wit— "the opponants of In-
"dependence and Republican Government who supported Mr.
"Ross, in the contest against Governor McKean are well known
"by the Indecency, the slander and the falsehood of the meas-
"ures they pursued—and it is well known that they are all de-
"voted to the Federal Party which we dissected on Monday—
"Mr. Ross" (James Ross Esquire member of the Senate of the
"United States for the State of Pennsylvania meaning) "proposed
"this Bill in the Federal Senate (how consistently with the
"Decency of his Friends will be seen), a committee of five was

"appointed to prepare a Bill on the subject on this committee
"Mr. Pinckney of South Carolina was appointed on Thursday
"morning last (the Caucus held the preceeding Evening) "Mr.
"Ross" (the said James Ross Esquire Senator as aforesaid
meaning) "informed Mr. Pinckney that the Committee had
"drawn up a bill on the subject" (meaning thereby that James
Ross Esquire Member of the Senate of the United States for the
State of Pennsylvania had informed Mr. Pinckney a member
of the said Senate from the State of South Carolina) "that the
"said Committee of the said Senate had drawn up a bill on the
"subject of their said appointment when in fact Mr. Pinckney
"had never been consulted on the subject though a member of
"the Committee the Bill was introduced and passed as below."

And the said William Duane in the said Libel inserted in a
certain newspaper called *Aurora General advertiser*—did then
and there print and publish of and concerning the said Senate
and the members thereof among other things diverse false
scandalous and malicious matters according to the tenor following to wit: "On this occasion it may not be impertinent
"to introduce an anecdote which will illustrate the nature of
"caucuses and shew that our popular government may in the
"hands of a faction be as completely abused as the French
"Constitution has been by the self-created Consuls."

"In the summer Session of 1798—when federal thunder and
"violence were belched from the pestiferous lungs of more than
"one despotic minion a caucus was held at the house of Mr.
"Bingham in this City" (the house of William Bingham Esquire
member of the said Senate for the State of Pennsylvania meaning").

It "was composed of members of the Senate and there
"were present seventeen members—The Senate consisting of
"32 members this number was of course a majority and the
"session was a full one—

"Prior to Deliberation on the measures of war, navy, army,
"Democratic proscription, &, &, it was proposed and "agreed
to that all the members present should solemnly "pledge
themselves to act firmly upon the measures to be agreed "upon
by the majority of the persons present at the Caucus.

"The measures were perfectly in the high tone of that ex-
"traordinary Sessions. But upon a division of the caucus it was
"found that they were divided nine against eight. This ma-
"jority however held the minority to their engagement, and the

"whole seventeen voted in Senate upon all the measures dis-
"cussed at the Caucus

"Thus it is seen that a secret self-appointed meeting of 17
"persons dictated laws to the United States and not only that nine
"of that seventeen had the full command and power over the
"consciences and votes of the other eight, but that nine possessed
"by the turpitude of the eight actually all the power which the
"Constitution declares shall be vested in the majority *only*.

"In other words a *majority* of nine members of the Senate
"*rule* the other twenty three members.

"It is easily conceivable, as in the recent changes in France
"that this spirit of Caucusing may be conducted in progression
"down to two or three persons, thus three leading characters may
"agree to act upon measures approved by any two of them—
"these three may add two others, and they would be a majority
"of five, and those adding four others would be a majority of
"nine, and this nine possess all the power of a majority of 23 ! ! "

"Yet such is the way we" (meaning the Citizens of the United
"States) "are treated by those who call themselves Federalists"
(meaning the said Senate of the United States and the aforesaid
members thereof) "The following Bill is an offspring of this
"spirit of Faction secretly working (in the Senate of the United
"States meaning) and it will be found to be in perfect accord
"with the outrageous proceedings of the same party in our State
"Legislature who are bent on Depriving this state of its share
"in an election that may involve the fate of the Country and
"posterity—"

And the said William Duane afterwards to wit—on the nineteenth
day of May in the Year of our Lord One thousand eight hundred at
the District aforesaid in a certain newspaper called *Aurora General
Advertiser* of which he the said William was then and there the publisher did wickedly print and publish a certain false scandalous and
malicious Libel and did then and there cause to be published a certain false scandalous and malicious Libel of the Senate of the said
United States and of the members thereof in which said Libel among
other things is contained diverse false scandalous and malicious
matters according to the tenor following to wit—Monday May 19,
1800.

"Parties—We sometime since gave an analysis of the Parties
"which prevail in the United States under the general object of
"their Union and Designs—These we then divided into Re-
"publicans the friends of the President and the followers of

"Alexander Hamilton since the late explosion in the cabinet
"some carnal changes have taken place as the Senate (of the
"United States meaning) has been the principal Focus of the
"antirepublic parties we now give a statement of the parties as
"they stood in the Senate (the Senate of the United States mean-
"ing) upon the close of the Session.   They are thus designated
"Republicans—consisting of a firm body of men devoted to our
"form of Government.   Aristocrats, consisting of two descrip-
"tions or factions devoted to men and measures hostile to our
"form of Government, beside these there are a few who trim be-
"tween the different parties with which they occasionally act,"
and the said William did then and there in the said Libel print
and publish the following false scandalous and malicious things
of the said Senate and the members thereof falsely and maliciously according to the tenor following to wit.

"Light as such insignificant beings as Fenno are in the scale
"by them the weight and bias of Political parties, are oftentimes
"clearly discovered—And it is now more obvious than ever that
"what is now called the Pickeronian party was the ruling and in-
"fluential body which set in motion all the intrigues and it may
"be said without exaggeration, all the downright villany that has
"been practiced for a long time let any man examine the charac-
"ters which compose Faction and can there be any difficulty in
"forming a decisive opinion—Let the measures of only the last
"Session be examined and it will be found that the Pickeronian
"Columns either led or directed every obvious measure which
"has been brought forward."

"The attempt to encrease the at present excessive salary of
"members of Congress was made by Goodhue" (meaning Benjamin Goodhue Esquire a member of the Senate of the said
United States from the State of Massachusetts). "That audacious
"attempt to introduce a fourth Branch in the Government was
"originated by Ross" (James Ross Esquire member of the said
Senate for the State of Pennsylvania meaning).   "The Star
"chamber proceedings by Dayton and Tracy supported by Read"
and the said William did then and there in the said newspaper
falsely scandalously and maliciously print and publish of the said
Senate and the members thereof the following false scandalous
and malicious words and matters following to wit—"The system
"of speculation has been deeply interwoven with their views"
(meaning the said Senate and the members thereof and their
views) "pecuniary and personal aggrandizement subserviency

to British machinations and the most fatal of all the sacrifice of "some of our own states through factious hatred and revenge. "In the Interdiction of our trade with france, the southern States "alone were vitally affected, while the Eastern were secured by "artful provisions. The Eastern States to which such large boun- "ties are given from the national coffers to stimulate and encour- "age their maritime industry were sedulously guarded, while the "planting states were thrown at the Mercy of British Monopoly "and cut off from the best market in Europe."

And the said Inquest upon their oaths and affirmations re- spectively Do further present that the said William on the sec- ond day of May in the year last aforesaid at the said District did print and publish a Libel in which was contained among other things the following false scandalous and malicious mat- ters and expressions of and concerning the Congress of the United States and also the Directors of the Bank of the United States as follows—"We have before us a very able and an "energetic exposition of our funding System, it is from the "Pen of one of the most original and forcible writers of the "present day, a writer who when he confines himself to "measures and facts illuminates instructs and informs more "than any of his contemporances it is the author of the Po- "litical progress of Great Britain. The following is an ex- "tract from a work now in the Press by that able writer. On "March 2^d 1791, the Act past for incorporating the Hamilton "Bank—The Tenth Section says that 'neither shall the said "corporation take more than at the rate of six per centum per "annum for or upon its loans or discounts.' The Constitu- "tion gives Congress no power to regulate the interest of money. "But if they did make such a rule they should have paid some "attention to the getting of it observed. Instead of this the "following practice is said to be common in Philadelphia—The "Bank refuses to discount at the regular price—you then apply "to a broker who is in correspondence with one of the directors "of the Bank (meaning one of the directors of the said Bank of "the United States) through him" (meaning one of the said di- "rectors aforesaid) "you receive Bank notes, at two or three per "cent per month and the Broker and the Director" (meaning the "Directors of the said Bank as aforesaid) "divide the spoil— "Congress takes no cognizance of this practice so disreputable "in itself and so destructive to Commerce nay, several of its "members are Directors each has a Credit with the Bank for at

"least thirty thousand Dollars. The Directors are twenty-
"five in number. The sum total of their personal credit comes
"by the smallest computation to seven hundred and fifty thou-
"sand dollars At Three per Cent per month that sum gives two
"hundred and seventy thousand Dollars a year to the Directors
"payable monthly whereas by the Charter of the Bank the bor-
"rowers are entitled to an equal quantity of Bank notes for one
"sixth part of that money. In the affair the blame does not fall
"upon the Brokers, but upon the Directors" (meaning thereby
the "Directors of the said Bank) "who practice and the Congress"
"(meaning thereby the Congress of the said United States) "who
"suffer such extortion. The Silence of the Republican party
"in both houses upon this Subject places in a strong light the
"negligence with which they perform their Duty."

To the Great scandal of the said Senate and Congress of the
said United States of America and by the said members of the
said Senate and Congress who are in the said Libel aspersed, to
the evil example of all others in the like offending against the
form of the Act of Congress of the said United States in such
case made and provided against the peace and Dignity of the
said United States.

> JARED INGERSOLL, *Attorney*
> *of the United States*
> *for the District of*
> *Pennsylvania—*

And thereupon the said William Duane saith that he is not guilty
of the Premises in the said Indictment above specified and charged
upon him and of this he puts himself upon the County and Jared
Ingersoll Esquire the Attorney of the United States in and for the said
District doth the like—

And the said William Duane prays leave to Imparle therein here
until the Eleventh day of May next and he hath it. The same day is
given to the said United States. At which Day to wit the Eleventh
day of May Anno Domini One thousand eight hundred and one, the
aforesaid William Duane — — — — — — — — —
comes into Court and prays leave further to imparle therein here
until the Eleventh day of October next and he hath it.

The same day is given to the said United States. Afterwards to
wit on the twenty-eighth day of July A.D. one thousand eight hun-

dred and one. The United States by Alexander James Dallas Esquire, their attorney come and say that they will no further prosecute.

UNITED STATES }
DISTRICT OF PENNSYLVANIA }

I CERTIFY the foregoing to be a true and faithful copy of the Record and Proceedings in the Circuit Court of the United States in and for the District of Pennsylvania in the Third Circuit on a Certain Indictment for a Libel against William Duane.

> IN TESTIMONY whereof I have hereunto subscribed my name and affixed the seal of the said Circuit Court at Philadelphia this twenty-eighth day of June A.D. 1803, and in the Twenty-seventh year of the Independence of the said United States.
> D. C. ALDWETZ, *Clk.*

UNITED STATES }
DISTRICT OF PENNSYLVANIA }

I CERTIFY that the foregoing attestation is in Due form of Law.
RICHARD PETERS
One of the Judges of the
Circuit Court, U. S.

APPENDIX E

(PAGE 81)

THE EARLY PERIODICAL PUBLICATION
OF THE FEDERALIST

I AM indebted to Wilberforce Eames, Esq., Librarian of the Lenox Library, for the following list of the issues of the newspapers in which the Federalist first appeared:

The Federalist, No. 1–85. (*In the New York Packet*, from No. 745, Oct. 30, 1787, to No. 828, Aug. 15, 1788. *New York: Samuel and John Loudon*. F°.)

*** The library's file of *The New York Packet* lacks Nos. 749, 750, 753, 760, and 764, containing Nos. 5, 6, 11, 12, 24, 25, 31, and 32 of the *Federalist*. There was no No. 77. In the collected editions some change was made in the numbering: No. 35 became 29, Nos. 29 and 30 became 30 and 31, No. 31 was divided to make 32 and 33, Nos. 32–34 became 34–36, and Nos. 36–76 became 37–77, all the other numbers remaining unchanged.

According to P. L. Ford, Nos. 8, 12, 16, 18, 20, 22, 27, 29, 30, 32, 56, 64, 70, 72, and 75 first appeared in print in *The New York Packet*, most of the other numbers having been printed first in the *Independent Journal*, or in *The Daily Advertiser*, or in the first collected edition.

"THE NEW YORK PACKET"
THE FEDERALIST

No. 1, Oct. 30, 1787.   No. 745.
No. 2, Nov. 2,   "   No. 746.
No. 3, Nov. 6,   "   No. 747.
No. 4 (marked 3), Nov. 9, 1787.   No. 748.
No. 5, Lacking in library file.
No. 6,   "   "   "
No. 7, 8, Nov. 20, 1787.   No. 751.
No. 9, 10, Nov. 23,   "   No. 752.

No. 11, 12, Lacking in library file.
No. 13, 14, Nov. 30, 1787. No. 754.
No. 15, 16, Dec. 4, 1787. No. 755.
No. 17, 18, Dec. 7, 1787. No. 756.
No. 19, 20, Dec. 11, 1787. No. 757.
No. 21, 22, Dec. 14, 1787. No. 758.
No. 23,   Dec. 18, 1787. No. 759.
No. 24, 25, Lacking in library file.
No. 26, 27, Dec. 25, 1787. No. 761.
No. 28, 29, Dec. 28, 1787. No. 762.
No. 30,   Jan. 1, 1788. No. 763.
No. 31, 32, Lacking in library file.
No. 33, 34, Jan. 8, 1788. No. 765.
No. 35,   Jan. 11, 1788. No. 766.
No. 36, 37, Jan. 15, 1788. No. 767.
No. 38, 39, Jan. 18, 1788. No. 768.
No. 40, 41, Jan. 22, 1788. No. 769.
No. 42, 43, Jan. 25, 1788. No. 770.
No. 44, 45, Jan. 29, 1788. No. 771.
No. 46, 47, Feb. 1, 1788. No. 772.
No. 48, 49, Feb. 5, 1788. No. 773.
No. 50, 51, Feb. 8, 1788. No. 774.
No. 52, 53, Feb. 12, 1788. No. 775.
No. 54,   Feb. 15, 1788. No. 776.
No. 55, 56, Feb. 19, 1788. No. 777.
No. 57, 58, Feb. 22, 1788. No. 778.
No. 59, 60, Feb. 26, 1788. No. 779.
No. 61,   Feb. 29, 1788. No. 780.
No. 62,   Mch. 4, 1788. No. 781.
No. 63, 64, Mch. 7, 1788. No. 782.
No. 65, 66, Mch. 11, 1788. No. 783.
No. 67, 68, Mch. 14, 1788. No. 784.
No. 69, 70, Mch. 18, 1788. No. 785.
No. 71, 72, Mch. 21, 1788. No. 786.
No. 73,   Mch. 25, 1788. No. 787.
No. 74,   Mch. 28, 1788. No. 788.
No. 75,   Apr. 1, 1788. No. 789.
No. 76,   Apr. 4, 1788. No. 790.
No. 78,   June 17 and 20, 1788. No. 811, 812.
No. 79,   June 24, 1788. No. 813.
No. 80,   June 27 and July 1, 1788. No. 814, 815
No. 81,   July 4 and 8, 1788. No. 816, 817.

No. 82,   July 11, 1788. No. 818.

No. 83,   July 15, 18, 22, and 25, 1788. No. 819, 820, 821, 822.

No. 84,   July 29, Aug. 8 and 12, 1788. No. 823, 826, 827.

No. 85,   Aug. 15, 1788. No. 828.

APPENDIX F

(PAGE 83)

THE INFLUENCE OF HAMILTON'S WORK IN SOUTH AFRICAN UNIFICATION.

SIR WALTER HELY-HUTCHINSON, late Governor of Cape Colony, wrote to the author in January, 1910, as follows:

"When South African Union first seemed to be coming within the range of practical politics, and it began to be generally discussed as a possibly practical issue—about four years ago—it soon became evident that, apart from questions of racial difference and of 'native' policy, the main point as to which opinions differed was whether the union should be on a basis of federation, or of unification—whether the existing colonies should be treated as separate States, retaining their own governments and legislatures; or whether the South African Union, with legislatures deriving their powers from the main government or parliament; whether the main government should be entrusted with certain specific duties and powers, the State governments to possess the rest—or whether the provincial governments should be entrusted with certain specified duties and powers, the Union Government to possess the rest. As you know, the result of the Convention proceedings, as ratified by the British Parliament, has been 'unification with safeguards.' The whole of the power, in the ultimate resort, being in the hands of the Union Government and Parliament, the provincial governments and councils being, however, entrusted with certain specified powers and duties of which they cannot be deprived, either in whole or in part, without certain special proceedings which are intended to prevent any modification of the Constitution by anything like a scratch vote, or by bare majorities.

"Those of us who had been thinking over the subject of union for many years, and had no special interests, pecuniary or otherwise, to bind us to any particular locality or colony in South Africa, had made up our minds that the ideal form of union for South Africa was unification—but when union became the subject of public discussion,

454

and it began to look as if union, in one form or another, might possibly come about, a considerable feeling in favour of federation and
maintenance of State rights arose.   I need not go into the motives
which underlay this feeling—they were partly sentimental, partly
racial, partly pecuniary.   Enough to say that the feeling, in many
quarters, was strong, and was so articulate that it seemed even
stronger than it probably really was—and it did look, at one time,
as if federation, not unification, might carry the day.

"People in official positions, like myself, could do nothing in
public—but, fortunately, some of the leading men in politics, and
the ablest of them, especially Botha, Merriman and Smuts, were
convinced unificationists, and used all their influence in favour of
unification and a band of clever young Britishers, foremost among
whom were Patrick Duncan, Lionel Custis, Philip Kerr, and others,
devoted themselves to a regular propaganda, in favour of unification.   Closer 'Union Societies' were formed all over South Africa.
The unificationists went about, so to speak, with a copy of Alexander Hamilton's 'Life' in one pocket, and a copy of the *Federalist* in
the other, preaching unification, and advising their friends to read,
before making up their minds against unification, about the birth-
throes of the Constitution of the United States; and to note Hamilton's words of wisdom both as to the weakness likely to arise from
over-assertion of State rights, and as to the folly of rejecting a Constitution which was, of necessity, a compromise, merely because some
of its provisions did not square with one's own particular or par-
ticularist views.

"As the result, the 'Life' was widely read, and the *Federalist* was
considerably studied.   In conversations about the draft Constitution, you would often hear, 'I suppose you have read the "Life" of
Alexander Hamilton?'   'Oh, yes!'   'And the *Federalist?*'   'Well,
I've studied it a good deal.' . . .

"I am, of course, far from saying that the study of your grandfather's life brought about unification, but there is no doubt that it
was one of the influences which materially contributed to that end."

APPENDIX G

(PAGE 87)

MEMORANDUM OF PAPERS RELATING TO FAREWELL ADDRESS MADE BY JAMES A. HAMILTON

Copy of a letter from Washington to Madison, May 20, 1792.
Hamilton to Washington, May 10, 1796.
Washington to Hamilton, May 15, 1796.
A draught in Washington's handwriting.
Abstract of points, to form an address, in Hamilton's handwriting.
Endorsed "Original Draft," considerably amended, in Hamilton's handwriting.
Washington to Hamilton, dated May 15, 1796.
Washington to Hamilton, June 26, 1796.
Hamilton to Washington, July 5, 1796.
Hamilton to Washington, July 30, 1796.
Washington to Hamilton, August 10, 1796.
Hamilton to Washington, August 10, 1796.
Second draft enclosed in above letter.
Washington to Hamilton, August 25, 1796.
Washington to Hamilton, September 1, 1796.
Hamilton to Washington, September 4, 1796.
Hamilton to Washington, September 5, 1796.
Washington to Hamilton, September 6, 1796.
Hamilton to Washington, September 8, 1796.

APPENDIX H

(PAGE 153)

NOTES FOR ARGUMENT IN THE TRES-
PASS CASE

ARGUMENT

A. Introduction.
    Question concerns National faith—character—
    safety—Confederation
B. Serious because wrong judgment good cause
    of war
C. Present case somewhat new—*law of reason*
    Public good
    · ubi lex tacet judex loquitur
D. Question embraces whole law of nations—
    Reason
E. Where found? Answer ∧ *Opinions* of *Writ-*
    ers Practice of Na.
    Objection Writers differ: Ans. *So do men in*
    every thing.
    Hardw Jay civil law not bind: Civil law not
    Law of N.
F. *Jus gentium & Jus belli*, part of common law
    Coke 15 great heads!

Pul: p. 2 to 7
part 6–17–22

G. Divided into *Natural, Necessary, Internal,*
    Positive external
    Last
H. Subdivided Voluntary—customary Conven-
    tional
I. Voluntary defined=System of Rules &
    And is intrinsically obligatory; enjoyed by
    necessary
K. Two sorts of obligations *internal, external,*

457

L.   Internal like obligation to pay a debt barred by Statute of limitations.

Or to observe Parol agreement not binding St. fraud

M.   By natural, party in the wrong acquires no rights in War

By the voluntary both parties equal rights
       Effects on both sides same——

The Rule has different objects—Peace of Nations security of purchases——

—Acknowleged universally thought and efferent princ——

Some ascribing to a positive law
       Tacit Consent in making peace
       Necessity true Rule——

HENCE justice or Injustice of the war— makes no diff:

N.   Objection this not a Solemn war

—Answer by the best opinions & Practice no diff——

Date Bynker Stroeck!

But the War between G.B. &.U.S. was a solemn war
       Formalities arbitrary

Act of Parliament authorizing hostilities

Declaration of Ind. admits open War

Congress by a formal resolution authorizes against British——

O.   2. Objection no war between Independ: Nations

Journals of Cong.
P. 245

objection not good in our Mouths

Public acts contradict: claim sanction

Best opinions to the contrary.

3 Obj.

P.   State of New York has no Common law of Nations

—Answer 1. This result from Univ. law

2. Our constitution adopt common law

3. The United States have formally assented for us.

what are the effects of War!
GREAT INQUIRY

Q. Ea quae & true rule: *Molloy: Plead*
Moveables for ever
Immoveables & fruits during possession:
ROMANS 5
No Precedent of an Action
      —Reconcile Authors———
Common law: Prisoner: Real property
      —Proves that justice or injustice not
        considered
For the Civil law of every Country presumes
    its Sovereign in the right

R. Objection: Vatel says property of immove-
    ables not complete till peace
    This means full right of domain to aliens.

S. Postliminum what?
        Regulates rights of Natives within
           itself
        Has nothing to do with claim of dam-
           ages,
        Rights of contending parties or neu-
           tral nations.

OBSERV: The laws of war permit the Conqueror to take
    all the profits of the land:
        to which right in practice has suc-
          ceeded
        Contribution.
But most mitigated hostility permit making
    use of deserted property——

CONS ———
The enemy having exercised this right through
    Def. he cannot be answerable

———————————

T. Nor can it be done without a violation of the
    Treaty of peace.
Which includes Amnesty

CONS ———
Object: Congress had no right
Answer Then Cong: nothing
But Congress had a right
Our Sovereignty began by a Federal act
—Externally exists only in the Union

Declar of Ind: which is FUND,[1] constitution of each State asserts the Power of Congress to *levy war conclude peace, contract alliances*

Proceedings P. 12
New York Convention approves, not authenticates Congress, this had in fact complete Sovereignty——

Art. 30——
—Union know in the Constitution.

ART. IX
Cong: thou Abrig^m leaves Congress full powers of War Peace and Treaty

POWER of making Peace implies power of making conditions

"Lex est cuicunque aliquis aliquid concedit concedere videtur et id sine quo res ipsa effe non potuit" 16 Coke 52

Does not include power of dismembrement but of making all reasonable conditions

And without remission of damages, war continues

Q. How give away rights of CITIZENS OF NEW YORK

Ans. Citizens gave them that power.

Vatel B. 2 (7
§ 81 p. 147
The Power too results from the Eminent domain

Hence injury from the Government authorizes taking the property of innocent subjects.

Hence claim of damages for Injuries to Individuals is in the Public

Obj:
Those Injuries only forgiven which are in relation to the war——

Relationship to the War consists in the Capture of the City.

———

Lastly it would be a breach of the Confederation

—Congress have made a treaty

A breach of that would be a breach of their constitutional authority

Power of Treaty Legislative,

Proclamation a law

———

([1] Fundemental)

Sovereign authority may violate Treaties

Obj.
—Bold Ground admits the Intention

But within, Each State has no such power

Having delegated the management of its foreign concerns to Congress

To whom alone the consideration of these, reason of State belongs

As well a County may alter the laws of the
State as the State those of the Confederation.

Obj.
It has been said Legislature may alter laws of
Nations

Elen. Jurispruden:
Not true in theory

p. 62
Vatel B 3
C12 p. 76
§ 3
Example of Ramsom bill, nothing to the pur-
pose.

If such a power does exist in our Government
'tis in Congress.

OBJECT
Accession to Conf: was act of Legislature why
may not another act alter it?

ANs:
UNION preexisted

And
Act of accession not a law but a CONTRACT
which one part cannot release itself from

One part of an Empire may dismember itself,

But this supposes dissolution of the Original
contract

While Confed: exists its cons: Autho: paramount

But how are the JUDGES to decide?

Ans: Cons: giving Ind: Power only in prize
causes in all others

Judges of each State must of necessity be
judges of United States——

And the law of each State must adopt the laws
of Congress.

Though in relation to its own Citizens local
laws might govern, yet in relation to foreigners those of United States must prevail.

It must be conceded Leg: of one State cannot
repeal law of United States

All must be construed to Stand together!

De In: L 4 No. 145
And here the rule of Cicero

"Primus Igetur leges oportet contendere com-
parando utra lex ad Majores hoc est ad
utiliones ad honestiones ac magis neces-
sarios res pertineat, ex quo confissitur ut si
leges duae aut si plures aut quot quot
erunt conservari non possunt qua discrep-
ent inter se ea maxime conservanda sunt
quae ad maximas res pertinere videatur."

Many of these Argument suppose Trespass as
repugnant to the law of nations—It may
however receive a construction consistent
with all.   And to give it this Construction
is the duty of the Court.

We have seen that to make the Defendant liable
would be

TO VIOLATE the laws of nations and forfeit
character

To violate a solemn treaty of peace & revive
state of hostility

To infringe Confedered & endanger peace of
the union

CAN we suppose all this to have been intended by the Legislature

The LAW cannot suppose it

And if it was intended the act is void!

PRINCIPLES

A New case must be determined by the law
of Nature and the Public good.

Ubi lex *tacet*   Judex loquitur!!!

viner *Title Law* 1st
p. 51 Letter C p. 3
Year Books Ed. 4
P. 12

Mirror Cap 2 § 3

Says that cases were judged according to
Equity before the customs of the realm
were written & made certain, Vide
     1 Chan. Reports, 8 page. of Vindica-
tion of the Court of Chancery

Molloy B 1 Chap: 2
§ 5 = 6 = 12

2. A judgment contrary to the laws of Nations is a
good cause of war.

Coke. Lytt. P. 11 b
4 Black Com: P
66 & 67
3 Burrows Rep.
      P. 1480 }
       1481 }

3. The *jus gentium* and *jus belli* are part of the
common law.

Vatel's Preliminaries
P. 8 § 28
Book 3 Chap. 12 ⎱
particularly § 192 ⎰

Grotius B 3ᵈ Chap. 10
Vatel Preliminaries
Page 5 § 16—17
    6

5. The *voluntary* law of Nations is as intrinsically
    obligatory as the necessary law; which en-
    joins its observance.

4. Nations are under two kinds of obligation
    internal and *external*—the one founded on
    the necessary the other on the voluntary
    law of nations.

6. By the necessary, the party making an unjust
    war acquires in foro conscientiae no right,
    and is bound in foro conscientiae to make
    restitution for all damages——

Vatel Book 3 Ch 12
before quoted
Idem C 13 § 195 & 196
Molloy B 1 Ch. 1
P. 12 to 14 § 12 and
13—

Burlamaque Vol 2
P. 302 § 33 to 37—
Grotius B 3 Ch 6
P 500 § 2

Rutherford Vol 2 B 2ᵈ
Ch 9 Page 508 to
512—Quare

7. But by the voluntary law the party in the wrong
    has equal rights with the party in the right:
    and the effects of war on both sides are the
    same.

Rutherford
Book 9 Ch 9 p. 563
              564
578—to 580

Bynkershoeck Liber
1 Caput, 11 P

Hutcheson Vol. 2 P.
357

Burla: Vol 2 p. 263
§ 44

Cunningham Pos In-
suram P. 276
Hales H. P. C. Vol 1
P. 160 to 164

Burlamaque p. 271 21

8. And this is the Case by the better opinion in
    wars not solemn as well as in solemn
    wars——

Vatel B 3 Ch 18 P.
111 § 295
Burlam: P 302 33 to
37

The formalities which constitute a solemn **war**
are arbitrary.

Inst Ins: Lib II Id I
17
Molloy Book 1st Ch 1
Page 14 § 13
Grotius 500 Read be-
fore   581
Idem P 586 Note 5
Domal Vol 1 P. 455
§ 17

The effects of war are the same between two
great parts of the same empire as between two Independent nations.

The general proposition of the *jus belli* is that
"ea quae ab hostibus Capimus statim
jure gentium nostra sunt.

Burla: Vol 2 P, 290
§ 1

Viner Title Lawful
Prize Pl 1 &° 2
2 Black Comm.
       P. 401 No. 1
          402
Brooke Title Prop-
ertie P 161 C No. 18
     167 – No. 30
Grotius B 3 Ch 20
§ 22 P. 701
Hutchison Vol. 2 P.
363 &° 364
Vatel B 4 C 3 § 30
Page 123
Register P. 102
Brooke Title Prop-
ertie Page 161b N°. 18
     167   30
Year Books 7 Ed 4
Page 14 fol. 5

Grotius Lib 3ᵈ Ch 20
§ 22 Page 701 Eng ⎱
       907 Latin ⎰

Idem Lib 3 Ch 9 § 13
N°. 2 page 868

Justinians Institutes
Lib II Til IV Intere

§ 21 procedure ⎱
proves this— ⎰

Burl: Vol 2 P 295 to
98

Grotius B 3ᵈ Ch 6
§ 4—1 p 583 C 20 § 12
= 2 P 699

☞

Vatel B 3 C 14 P 83
§ 204

Moveable goods belong to the Captor for ever
after the battle is over; or according to
some common law, adjudication if fresh
perfect be not made the same day. Ante
occasum solis

And the fruits of immoveable goods while in
possession.

The common law carries the rights of war so far
Individual
as to give the ∧ Captor a property in the
Prisoner—and even transfers the absolute
right of real property.

How settle Grotius' meaning about the *profits*
☞ *fructus usufructus*

Usufructus is nearly equivalent to an *issue* at
common law.
The Idea that in one place he speaks of a new
grant in another of restitution is not accu-
rate——
The Context in both Cases relates to restitution.
And the verb *CONCEDERE* is as applicable to *surrender* as to a *new grant*.
Vatel understands Grotius in the same sense for
he refers to him!

The right over real property commences according to some from the time of Capture——
According to others when there is a firm possession which consists in the land being
enclosed by fortifications.
Postliminum is "that right in virtue of which
persons and things taken by the enemy are
restored to their former state when coming
again under the power of the nation to
which they belonged."

Burl: Vol 2 P 583 § 7
1   3
Grotius B 3ᵈ C 20
§ 15 P 699
Barbeyrars note
thereupon Vatel B
4 Ch 2 § 18 19 20 &
21 P. 120 & 121

Vide Proceedings of
Con. P. 12

Article 30 p. 26

Vide Article 9ᵗʰ.

Vatel B 2 C 7 § 81
Page 147

Elements of Juris-
prudence p. 62

Vatel B 3 C 12 p. 76
para: 3

4 Coke Rep. P. 13a
B ditto page 118
a & b

10 Mod. 245 Bacon
Title Statute 648

Venir Title Maximo
Letter pa. 351 fol 1
4 Rep. 71
Raymond 7 Coke Lyt-
tleton 49 B 1: C 59

Reports Lib 4 p 71 a
venir Title Statutes p
514 fol 27 . 30 . 31
Idem 524 par 119
Idem 527 par 145
Idem 528 par 154 &
156
1 Showers par 455

Domat Vol. 1 P. 7
§ 2
Puff B 5 C 12 fol 61

Every treaty of Peace includes an *Amnesty Express* or *virtual*

The Convention of New York does not pretend to give validity to the act of Independence but merely to approve it.
The United States are known in the Constitution.

                                  exclusively
Congress by the Confederation reserve ∧ all the powers of War peace & Treaty
The property of all the Individuals of a State is the property of the State itself in regard to other Nations.
            This is what is called the right of Eminent domain.
In theory one nation has no right to alter the general law of nations.

RULES OF CONSTRUCTION OF STATUTES

A Statute against Law and reason especially if a private Statute is void.

Statutes are to be construed by the rules of the common law.
And if against the *general policy* of the common law are to be *qualified* . . . and *controuled* by it.

Especially if the *provisions are general* in which case construction may be made *against the letter* of the Statute to render it agreeable to natural justice.

☞

Many things within the letter of a Statute are not within its equity and *vice versa.*
Laws giving remedy where there was none before are to be construed strictly. ☞

Bacon Title Statute
fol 653 N°. 92

No Statute shall be construed so as to be inconvenient or against reason.

Statutes to be construed according to the Intention of the Legislature, which intention is
to be ascertained by supposing the framers

Plowder 466 & 467

of the law wise and honest and well acquainted with all the merits of the case to
be determined upon, and under this supposition asking ourselves what could be the
intention of wise, honest and well informed
men in this particular case?

---

vide Examples from P. 16 to Page 18.

Celebrated instance of law of Bologna NO
INTERPRETATOR

Statute Gloucester bishops Norwich all Bishops
Bonhame Case 8ᵗʰ Coke several strong
examples in which Statutes have been ad-
judged void.

STATUTE OF FRAUDS executory Contracts.

STATUTE de donis Fine ipsa jure nullus:
Discontinuances

STATUTES of bankruptcy: All persons in
autre droit excepted: contrary to words of
the Statute James 1, as D. H. acknowledges.

STATUTE OF GLOUCESTER alienation by
father unless by sons &

DAMAGES dissuse Out of Entry: *person
found tenant*

Construed not to extend to tenant by act of
another or of law.

STATUTE MUST have several exceptions.

'INVOLUNTARY trespass

American Officer in Quarters!

American Vessels Captured at Sea in hands of
Neutrals
          Condemnation makes no diff

General Howe, Clinton otherwise state of War
continues.

Objection   Where Stop but where laws of Nations stop us.

This would render act Nugatory
Ans: No objection if it did.
But 'twould not.
Court here need only pay BRITISH subjects
    not included
Might still operate against our own citizens

———

Act would still answer several purposes
To give Remedy against
Assignees of Deserters
For EXECUTORS for injuries to real prop-
    erty
AGAINST EXECUTORS for Inj. both to real
    & personal.
IMAGINATION must influence
Note law respecting taking oath of allegiance to
    commence a suit.
Charter of New York holds pleas real, personal
    & mixed as fully as any Court of record of
    G. B. or Colony of New York
Never construed to extend to granting New
    trials, etc.

CONSTITUTION every male Inhabitant
IN LAW as in Religion, Letters &c.

———

CERTAINTY of the act in vain contended
    for——
Phrase "Military order" vague——

———

Not passport safe Conduct parole
Permission to occupy

———

Our justification is public enemy
hiring house for value Conf.

———

But the greater implies the less——
This is reasoning by Equity

———

We claim benefit of posterior law
                        FIDES etc.

APPENDIX H

Jacob Law Diction-
ary Title 'Inhabitant'
6 Reports 60 a

The word Inhabitant means

Nothing can be a Trespass which is involuntary

Latches Reports P 13
Miller v Dovey
Stiles 65 Smith v.
Stow Dyer 66 b

Cok Rep Book 2
Lefford's Case p. 51
Bacons Ab. Title R:
Letter L P. 367

By several authorities the Assignees of Des-
sertors could not maintain an action of
trespass.

*Nor Executors nor heirs for injuries to real
property.*

APPENDIX I

(PAGE 414)

LIST OF DEBTS ASSIGNED TO JOHN B. CHURCH, ESQUIRE, BY ALEXANDER HAMILTON, PER DEED DATED 9TH JULY, 1804.

James & William Sterling	$75.00
Isaac Clason	100.00
William Bell (Robinson and Hartshorne)	50.00
Miss Jenkins (Riggs)	50.00
Pierre Van Cortlandt late L^t. Governor	40.00
P. Jay Monroe	40.00
Champlin & Smith T. L. Ogden	50.00
Grillet & Bell	40.00
Outdoor Underwriters including Hallet & Bowne Administr. Jenks (Pendleton)	200.00
Assignee of Wm. L. Vandervort is successful 250 *more* 400 by J. J. V.	200.00
Assignees of J. Roget (Tintado)	50.00
De Peyster (Jones)	40.00
Abijah Hammond P. A. Ogden	40.00
Robert Cummings	75.00
John McVickar	30.00
Isaac Kibby	25.00
Hubbard (Riggs)	50.00
Alexander Stewart	65.
Assignees of Kirkpatrick (T. L. Ogden) by P. A. Camman	40.

George Stanton		30.
Louis Simond		50.
John Hackely	100.	Paid by Pendleton
(Riker)		
Ebenezer Stevens		50.
George Suckly		50.
Bank of N. York		100.
James Arden		50.
William Thomas		25.
William Cooper		75.
William Byron		100.
William & Silvester Robinson		250.
William Neilson		50.
James Shuter		50.
(T. L. Ogden)		
Gouverneur including Insurance Cause of Baure settled by compromise		100.
(T. L. Ogden)		
John Stewards for Note		50.
Do.		2490.
Henderson & Varick		20.
Dr.		2510.

Particulars will better appear by
Account Book endorsed
M E M
———
A. H.
July 9, 1804.

APPENDIX J

(PAGE 418)

THE SUBSCRIPTION FOR THE RELIEF OF HAMILTON'S FAMILY.

THERE does not appear any documentary evidence of the success of Wolcott's proposition to raise $100,000 by subscription. The only practical measures consisted in the contribution of shares of various land companies which were then very popular, and the later conversion of these into cash. In Boston a number of prominent gentlemen met and proposed the following plan:

"Having in remembrance the exalted worth, and pre-eminent services of the late General Hamilton—his extraordinary and truly patriotic exertions which contributed so much to save our Country from the greatest impending calamities—his able, disinterested and successful efforts to inculcate the wisdom, justice and advantage of all those maxims of jurisprudence which render sacred the rights of property and which are inseparable from true liberty—and especially recollecting that the devotion of his time and talents to the public interests has operated to deprive his Family of a common share of those pecuniary advantages, which his labours, if applied to them, would have easily made abundant. We, therefore, whose names are subscribed, to testify in some degree our sense of departed excellence and our gratitude for benefits conferred on our Country, do engage that we will pay into the hands of the Honble George Cabot, Thomas Davis, and Theodore Lyman, Esquires, the sums of money set against our respective names, to be by them applied to the benefit of the Children or Family of General Hamilton, in any manner they shall judge proper.

"And whereas we, whose names follow, are proprietors of certain parcels of land in Pennsylvania, which were purchased in A. D. 1801 of Timothy Pickering, Esquire: in shares of one hundred dollars each, which lands are not yet divided or formally conveyed.

"We do hereby authorize and request the said Timothy Pickering, Esquire to convey by a quit-claim deed, to such person or

persons as shall be named to him for that purpose, by the before-
mentioned George Cabot, Thomas Davis, and Theodore Lyman,
Esquires, or any two of them so many of our shares in said Lands
as we have set against our respective names. George Cabot 8
shares, Theodore Lyman and Wm. Gray, Jr., twenty shares, Eben
Parsons Stephen Higginson Stephen Higginson, Jr. Saml. P. Gardner
Tim^o. Williams Benj. Pickman, Jr. John Norris each ten shares.
Joseph Lee, eight shares. Thomas Davis, Nat^l. C. Lee, William
Pratt, Kirk Booth, James Perkins by J. H. P., John Parker, Daniel
Sargent, Jr., James Lloyd, Junr., Isaac P. Davis, Jos. Lee, Junr.
Israel Thorndike, Gorham Parsons, Jno. Lowell by F. C. Lowell,
Att'y, Benj. Joy, David Sears, Simon Elliot, William Orme, Wil-
liam Prescott, Simon Forrester, Samuel Blanchard, David Sears,
Att'y, and F. Dickinson, Jr., five shares. Samuel Gray, four shares.
"BOSTON, *Nov.* 16, 1804."

APPENDIX K

FACTS RELATIVE TO THE CAREER OF MRS. REYNOLDS

NOTHING has hitherto been known about the Reynolds Scandal except the pamphlet issued by Hamilton himself. As the following letter from Richard Folwell, a publisher, to one C. W. Jones, has recently come into the author's possession, he deems it worthy of reproduction as corroborative evidence of the Clingman and Reynolds conspiracy.

PHILADELPHIA, August 12, 1797.

C. W. JONES,

Having observed, by a Perusal of the History of the United States, that Odium was levelled at the Character of Col. Hamilton, and hearing that he intended to answer the Charges, I thought I possessed the Knowledge of some Traits in the Character of the Persons with whom he seems to be in Company with in that Work, that would in some Measure remove, if known, the Imputations levelled at the public Character of that Gentleman. Wishing, therefore, to see Right prevail, and Innocence protected, I suggested my Knowledge of the most material Incidents that would render improbable, in my Opinion, the Imputations contained in that Work. By your Request, I roughly summoned them up; and am sorry, lest some material Point does not strike my Mind, that these Details have never come to the Hand of Col. Hamilton. To remove, however, this Disappointment, I will invoke my Recollection, and enter on the Particulars.

A few Days after Mrs. Reynolds' first appearance in Philadelphia, a Relation of hers requested my Mother to receive her for a few Days, into our House, as she was a Stranger in the City, and had come here to endeavour to reclaim a prodigal Husband, who had deserted her and his Creditors at New York. This was readily consented to when her innocent Countenance appeared to show an innocent Heart. Not more than two Days after she was at our House. She found her Husband was here—had been in Gaol, and

473

was but just liberated. In a Day or two after she said, they had an Interview, but, could not come to Terms of Pacification. Her Mind, at this Time, was far from being tranquil or consistent, for, almost at the same Minute that she would declare her Respect for her Husband, cry, and feel distressed, they would vanish, and Levity would succeed, with bitter Execrations on her Husband. This Inconsistency and Folly was ascribed to a troubled, but innocent and harmless Mind. In one or other of these Paroxysms, she told me, so infamous was the Perfidy of Reynolds, that he had frequently enjoined and insisted that she should insinuate herself on certain high and influential Characters,—endeavour to make Assignations with them, and actually prostitute herself to gull Money from them. About five Days after she first came at our House, Mr. Reynolds had an Interview; and we, while she commanded Commiseration, were induced to warn her to depart, that a Character so infamous as her Husband should not enter our House. She moved to a reputable Quaker Lady's at No. — North Grant Street; where they lived together; but, so the Family said, did not sleep together.

Lately I have understood that Letters were frequently found in the Entry inviting her Abroad;—and that at Night she would fly off, as was supposed to *answer* their Contents. This House getting eventually too hot for them, they made their Exit. During the Period of their Residence there, she informed me she had proposed pecuniary Aid should be rendered by her to her Husband in his Speculations, by her placing Money in a certain Gentleman's Hands, to buy of him whatever public Paper he had to sell, and that she would have that which was purchased given to her,—and, if she could find Confidence in his future Prudence, she would eventually return him what he sold. From this House, if I recollect, they made their Exit for a short Time from Philadelphia; but soon returned; and gave me an Invitation to wait on them at No. — North Sixth Street. At this Time he wanted me to adventure with him in Turnpike Script,—to subscribe for which he was immediately to embark for Lancaster. The first Deposit for which was but trifling a Share—whether one or ten Dollars I do not recollect. Some considerable Time after (if necessary, Data can be procured) they removed and lived in stile in a large House in Vine Street, next to the Corner of Fifth. Here I had an Invitation, if I recollect, and being disposed to see if possible how People supported Grandeur, without apparently Friends, Money or Industry, I accordingly called. Mrs. Reynolds told me her Husband was in Gaol;

and on asking her for what, she said he had got a Man to administer to the Estate of a supposed deceased Soldier and give him a Power of Attorney to recover what was due to him by the Public. That he had accordingly recovered it, but that *incautiously* and *imprudently* having given the Heir-Apparent an indemnifying Bond, that when the Soldier came to Life, the Administration delivered the indemnifying Bond up to the real Heir, that then he was detected. That she said a Mr. Clingman, his Partner, was in the same Predicament. Before this Conversation was ended, in entered Mr. Clingman, to whom I was introduced. She referred to him for a more correct Narrative. But his Conversation seemed to me as if he wished to darken instead of throwing Light on this Information. He asked her what Luck she had in her Applications for Reynold's Liberation? She said she had called on the Governor, Mr. Mifflin, and that he felt for her: Referred her to Mr. Dallas and that he felt also. She said she called on Mr. Hamilton, and several other Gentlemen; and that they had all felt.

In a few Days after Reynolds was liberated, possibly in consequence of the Coincidence of Sympathy these Gentlemen had in Feeling. Here the Curtain dropt from my View, their Career, till perhaps a Year or two after Mrs. Reynolds wrote me a Letter to call on her at a very reputable and genteel Lodging House in Arch Street, No.   . In this note she apprized me of her Marriage with Mr. Clingman, which is annexed. Her Business she gave me to understand, was with me, to clear up her Character in East Nottingham, Cecil County, Maryland. That she lived there happily with Mr. Clingman, at the House of a Distant Relation of mine, till she had mentioned the knowing of our Family in Philadelphia; and that a Cousin of mine had given out that she must be the same Person who had left with her an infamous Character by the Name of Mrs. Reynolds. She wished me to clear it up. I expostulated on the Inconsistency of this, that as it was bad before she had certainly increased it, as her Husband, Reynolds, I understood was alive in N. York. She said she had a Divorce; and that only one Fault she had incurred in her Change,—that she got married to Clingman one half Hour before she obtained the divorce. Since I have heard Nothing from her; only that she wrote me a very pathetic Letter—begging, as she was to return, that I would clear up her Character. This I have mislaid—but it would move any one almost to serve her, that was not perfectly acquainted with her Character, confirmed by actual Observation.

I believe the Dates of these material Circumstances may be readily ascertained where necessary. I intended to digest the Confusion in which I throwed my former Observations that were mislaid. But you expressed Hurry. Had I a copy of that, this should be better arranged. The same Reason of Hurry induces me to submit that this may be sent to Colonel Hamilton as it is. Relying that he will Retrench and improve—allowing me to alter what may not be agreeable to myself. My Brother told me, when he was in N. York, a young Man of good Character before,—Clerk to Henry Manly of this City once) was hung in N. York for Forgery. That he saw his Dying Speech—that it said, he was deluded by Clingman and Reynolds to the Fact for which he was to suffer. Mr. Hamilton can ascertain this.

It is now two o'Clock on Sunday Morning. I am sleepy. I shall have Opportunity to do, with Mr. Jones's Approbation and my own, what Defect may be here, that Col. Hamilton with this may not entirely do.

RICH. FOLWELL.

That he had never got himself involved so before; though frequently he and his partner had done the same.

INDEX

Absent-mindedness, example of Hamilton's, 42.

Adams, John, 40, 278, 284, 422; election expenses of, 236; goes abroad, 284; sends Gerry, Marshall and Pinckney to France, 319; sends Vans Murray to France, 320.

Adams, Mrs. John, entertains, 314.

Adet, Pierre Augustus, French minister, 312, 314, 318; schemes of, 318.

Ambition of Hamilton, 52.

André, Major, trial of, 121.

Angerstien, financial relations with Aaron Burr, 387.

Annapolis Convention, 202.

Argument in Trespass Case, Hamilton's, 153.

Arnold, Benedict, 131; escape of, 118.

Ashburton, Lord, 160.

Aurora, The, 65, 68.

Autun, the Bishop of, 239.

Barclay, James, English Consul in New York, 289.

Bard, Dr. Samuel, 267; writes after death of Philip Hamilton, 345.

Bayard, James A., 389.

Bayard, William, 267, 404.

Beaumetz, 109.

Benson, Egbert, 269; appointed commissioner, 269.

Bentham, Jeremy, 299.

Bingham, William, banker in Philadelphia, 253, 314.

Bishop Moore administers last communion to Hamilton, 406.

Bollman, Dr., helps La Fayette to escape, 247.

Boudinot, Elias, 2, 21, 160, 267.

Boudinot, Elisha, 2, 160.

Bradford, Thomas, 312.

Brissot de Warville, J. P., 34.

Brown University confers degree upon Hamilton, 92.

Burgoyne, General, 136.

Burr, Aaron, 44, 154, 160, 161, 169, 171, 180, 185, 187, 192, 197, 212, 218, 240, 246, 375, 377, 378, 379, 380, 381, 382, 383, 385, 386, 389, 390, 391, 392, 396, 398, 399, 400, 404, 408, 422, 423, 425, 426, 427, 428, 429; accompanies Arnold to Quebec, 375; alleged use of bullet-proof silk garments, 400; becomes an atheist, 375; chooses Van Ness as second, 390, 392; death of, 429; describes his smoky chimney, 343; dishonest practices of, 379; elected vice-president, 377; enters Princeton College, 375; fascination of, 376; Hamilton and himself compared, 357; member of convention to revise constitution, 377; partisan of Jefferson, 376; takes sides with Lee against Washington, 375.

Cabot, George, 86.

Callender, William Thompson, 76, 431.

Carter, Mrs., 147.

Cazenove, Theophile, 32, 168.

Ceracci, Giuseppe, makes Hamilton's bust, 33, 34.

Charles X., overthrow of, 251.

Chastellux, Vicomte de, 123, 209, 239, 274.

Cheetham, 90, 431.

Church, Angelica, 96; writes to her brother regarding duel, 404.

Church, John Barker, 168, 277, 408, 409, 413, 414.

Church, "Peggy," 103.

Church, Philip, 408.

Church, Richard, 409.

Cincinnati, Society of, 389, 393.

Clarkson, Matthew, 267.

Clinton, George, Governor, 245, 292.

Clymer, George, 314.

Cobbett, William, 69.

Cochran, Mrs., 96, 108.

Colbert, Chevalier, asks Hamilton to press his suit, 228.

Colden, Cadwallader, Lieut. Governor, 185.

Coleman, William, editor of *New York Evening Post,* 71, 72, 350, 399, 400, 404, 406, 409, 412; duel with Captain Thompson, 72.

LETTERS